THE
BALLAD TREE

A STUDY OF BRITISH AND AMERICAN BALLADS,
THEIR FOLKLORE, VERSE, AND MUSIC

~~~~~

TOGETHER WITH SIXTY TRADITIONAL
BALLADS AND THEIR TUNES

By

EVELYN KENDRICK WELLS

ASSOCIATE PROFESSOR OF ENGLISH
WELLESLEY COLLEGE

THE RONALD PRESS COMPANY ⋅ NEW YORK

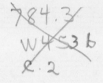

PRINTED IN THE UNITED STATES OF AMERICA

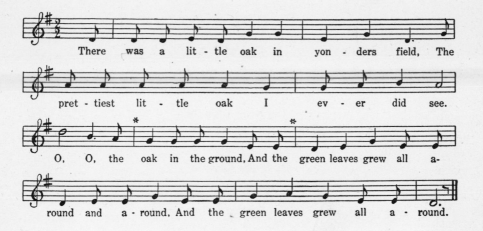

There was a lit - tle oak in yon - ders field, The
pret - tiest lit - tle oak I ev - er did see.
O, O, the oak in the ground, And the green leaves grew all a-
round and a - round, And the green leaves grew all a - round.

And on that oak there grew a branch . . .
And on that branch there grew a limb . . .
O, O, the * limb on the branch
And the branch on the oak
And the oak in the ground,
And the * green leaves grew all around.

ACKNOWLEDGMENTS

IN the preparation of this book I am obligated to many individuals and experiences. My long-standing associations with the Pine Mountain Settlement School in Kentucky, the English Folk Dance and Song Society, and its American branch, the Country Dance Society, have focused my attention on the collecting and teaching of traditional song, while a course given for a number of years at Wellesley College has served as proving ground for its presentation in more or less the form of this book. The reactions of many students, friends, and colleagues have wholesomely checked as well as encouraged me. In particular, Miss Maud Karpeles, Mrs. John C. Campbell, and Dr. Laura H. Loomis have given helpful comment on certain chapters; Miss Helen Joy Sleeper, Research Librarian in Music, Wellesley College, and Mr. Melville Smith, Director of the Longy School of Music in Cambridge, have prevented many amateur slips in preparing the musical texts. Grants from the Wellesley College Committee on Research Awards have been of practical help.

The courtesy of many publishers and individuals in permitting quotation from printed sources, or reproduction of unpublished matter, is gratefully noted here and specifically acknowledged where the selections appear.

EVELYN K. WELLS

Wellesley, Mass.
. January, 1950

NOTE

THE footnote references to works listed in the Bibliography cite author, work, and page only.

A number in parentheses following the name of a ballad indicates its position in *English and Scottish Popular Ballads*, by Francis J. Child. This is the standard reference collection for all ballad study, to which, in the one-volume edition of Sargent and Kittredge, the student may have ready access. In general, ballads are referred to by their title in Child's work, rather than the particular singer's title. Thus "The Wife of Usher's Well" (79) is mentioned as such, rather than as "Lady Gay."

Since many of the texts from Child's work, to which reference is frequently made, were found in ancient manuscripts or early print, or recovered from singers who spoke Lowland Scots, a brief explanation of some archaisms and dialect words is given here.

In the printed sources of the fourteenth and fifteenth centuries two characters, þ and ʒ, are most nearly matched in sound by *th* and *y*. The initial *f* is often doubled, and *v* and *u* are used interchangeably. Pronouns which look like *her* and *hem* may be *their* and *them*. *It* appears with its ancient aspirate as *hit* (*cf. haint—aint*). There are condensed forms such as *ychone* for *each one*, and old inflected forms like *shoon* for *shoes*. Words are formed by analogy: the verb *put* is conjugated *put—pat—pitten*. The dropping of final letters results in *gi* for *give*, *na* for *not*; and vowel changes give *wae* for *woe*, *ony* for *any*, etc. One soon builds up a small basic vocabulary of such words as *greet* (*weep*), *gar* (*make*), *spier* (*ask*), *bairn* (*child*), *dree* (*undergo, work out*), and *weird* (*fate*). Thus "Ye maun dree your weird" means "Man cannot escape his destiny." A word which looks familiar may mean something quite different: when *flatter* means *waggle*, "a young man's flattering tongue" takes on new significance. Two lovers *halsing* are embracing (from Teut. *hals—neck*): modern slang often has an interesting linguistic past. The homely vigor of many a phrase is felt only in the light of the glossary's information: the picture of the lady who "burnt like hoky-gren" is made considerably more realistic when we know that hoky-gren is "a fire that has been covered up with cinders, when all the fuel has become red."

Corruptions of words or phrases, caused by faulty memory or understanding, are sometimes intelligible, sometimes quite baffling. The nonsense syllables of the refrain are discussed on pages 95–96. Vagaries of spelling may be laid to scribes who were illiterate, or who lived before the days of uniformity in such matters.

CONTENTS

ILLUSTRATIONS

THE BALLAD TREE

INTRODUCTION

IN the long history of ballad criticism, a recurrent note voices the belief that the ballad is dead—that its best days are over, that its creative period is gone by, that nobody sings the old songs any more. In this nostalgic vein forty years ago Cecil Sharp wrote, "The English ballad is moribund; its account is well-nigh closed." But ten years later Sharp was to find in America a living tradition of folk song in the isolated parts of the Southern Appalachians, and his exhaustive researches were to add to Francis J. Child's definitive *English and Scottish Popular Ballads* the missing element of music, and the proof that people still sang ballads. And today Sharp would find that folk song not only lives in the remote and rural parts of America, but has returned in new vigor to the country as a whole. For better or for worse, a folk song renascence is upon us. Ballad singers have reached the professional stage, both literally and metaphorically. They sing in concert halls and night clubs and over the radio, and their albums of recorded songs are best-sellers. During the last few years the American "musical" has drawn on native song, both directly and by implication, and the inspiration for today's song hit may often be found in a folk song. One Theatre Guild production, *Sing Out, Sweet Land*, dramatizes the migration of song westward through America with the advancing frontier. The composer of today, like his Elizabethan forebear, finds in the folk song new sources of music for orchestras and choruses. Two popularly presented collections for home or group singing—*The Fireside Book of Folk Songs* and *Folk Song U.S.A.*—have had large sales to people often, no doubt, first interested by hearing a singer over the radio, or in the theater, or on a record. Ten years ago children knew little more in the way of folk songs than "The Wraggle-Taggle Gypsies" and "Oh No, John." Today they sing in school and camp the folk songs of America and England and the world. At regional and national festivals singers, dancers, and fiddlers foregather before large audiences and with full press notices. Shakers, Mormons, Indians, Negro choirs, European and Asiatic as well as American ethnic groups take part. The annual festival of the Southern Appalachian folk movement has sprouted regional festivals from the parent stem. In the belief that "every git-box should be a soap-box," certain labor and leftist political groups sing about Senator Bilbo, and veterans' housing, and the Centralia mine disaster, and racial discrimination, to ancient folk tunes. Along with much that is good, much that is inferior and unworthy of the name of folk song fills our ears from radio and juke-box. And not only our ears, but those of the world. A young White Russian emigré who had spent the last ten years in China and had recently arrived upon our shores said to me at a folk song gathering, "Oh yes, I've heard your ballads on the radio from America. We call them 'hill-billy songs' in China."

There are many reasons for this revival. Scholarly research has opened up the field. The development of state and national archives is a mark of growing recognition of their cultural responsibilities by government agencies. During the depression years there was much salvaging of folk songs under the Federal Writers' Project. The growing interest in "the American way" which developed during the last war has led to the collecting of folk items of all sorts—not only songs and ballads, but fiddle tunes, dance calls, singing games, nursery rhymes, folk tales and sayings, recipes, quilt patterns, traditional remedies— anything that may be depended upon to travel where people go, changing with new conditions but maintaining an essential sameness.

But the periodic revival, or indeed the continuous practice of some of our older songs cannot be fully accounted for by the efforts of scholars and teachers and librarians. The principal reason for the return of the folk song is the vitality that lies in the song itself. Because it was good, it has lived. And the ballad is one of the most prevalent types of folk song in today's revival.

The folk ballad is the only form of medieval vernacular poetry which has continuously survived. The traditional ballad, however, which possesses the germ of poetic life, has only recently been isolated; only in the twentieth century was the term restricted to orally transmitted narrative verse set to a tune. There have been attempts, unsuccessful in part, to derive the word *ballad* from *ballare* (Italian, *to dance*), but the connection between ballad and dance, while it has existed in many countries—for the ballad is known throughout Europe —is not everywhere established. Dance has probably contributed to the British ballad such rhythmic elements as the refrain, ballad and dance-song having met at some medieval crossroads; but there is little evidence that ballads were danced in Britain. The fourteenth century

ballade is an elaborately contrived art lyric, subjective and nonnarrative. In the sixteenth century the term is used as loosely as *sonnet*. In the seventeenth, it is "a common song sung up and down the streets," obviously the broadside of the day; in the eighteenth it is "a song with sentiment." From this time on the narrative factor receives more attention, but a ballad may still contain the literary, sentimental, or moral note of recognized literary authorship. Even *The New English Dictionary* fails to take into account the ballad's traditional qualities, defining it as "a simple sentimental song composed of several verses, sung to the same melody," or "a poem in short stanzas narrating a popular story."

As we understand it today, the traditional ballad is "a song that tells a story," in simple verse and to a simple tune. It is the product of no one time or person; its author, if ever known, has been lost in the obscurity of the past and in the processes of oral tradition. Its medium is word of mouth rather than print. It goes its way independent of literary influences, carrying for a while the accretions of this or that day and singer, but sloughing them off as it passes to the next. It has no one original text, being freshly created by each successive singer as he makes his own version. It has periodically risen to the surface from the underground stream of continuous tradition, and has been caught and fixed in print, but it differs greatly from its printed form because of its unconsciousness of literary conventions. Because of this independence from the printed page, there is little literature of traditional song, its very character and life depending upon freedom from the shackles of print. Therefore we know only by allusion, more and more infrequent as we work back through the record, that the habit of singing stories learned from one's elders is a very old one.

To expand a little on these generalities:

The ballad depends for its life on themes of universal appeal—stories of family tragedy, of love and its many resulting situations—presented with a certain intellectual and emotional simplicity sometimes missed by the sophisticated who do not respond at once to its elemental situations and artless style. Let it be said at once, however, that this simplicity is not to be confused with ignorance or crudeness. The rural illiterate (for most folk songs have been recovered from rusticity), although unlettered and hence dependent upon his inner resources for entertainment, has sometimes a compensating power of

memory which has stored his mind more fully than that of a better-read man, to say nothing of an enviable store of good sense and good taste. Nor are ballads the countryman's peculiar possession. Recent collectors have learned that they cannot afford to neglect the urban field.

A ballad's life depends not only on theme and attitude, but on tune. Melody and rhythm, acting as a background for the tale, control its simplicity, color its emotion, and aid the work of memory. But ballad music is of a simplicity that prevents its independent existence, some-times, indeed, being only a stereotyping of the pattern of tonal pro-duction. Its quality was not recognized by the first collectors, who ignored the tune and omitted it from the record. Hence the ballad became the province of the man of letters, living a one-lunged life until its well-nigh atrophied second lung was inflated in the recent folk music revival. Like poetry read to oneself, the music of the verse was lost without the tune, and with it the rhythm and color that are a large part of its effect.

A ballad depends upon oral transmission. A ballad in print is a ballad already dying; it is no more the living organism than is a sheet of music the sound of that music. Printing stops the creative process; the ballad you sing word for word and note for note from the page is someone else's version; the ballad you sing from your memory and from your heart is subtly changed as it passes your lips, and, paradox-ically, becomes your own as it leaves you.

The highly developed ballad texts of the fifteenth century, as re-covered from manuscripts, imply a long preceding period of evolution. But literature paid practically no attention to the ballad until the eighteenth century, since when, despite progressive deterioration in the ballad itself, there has been a growing understanding of its im-portance in literary and social history and a growing sense of its vitality even in dissolution. Indeed, perhaps, like the structural arches of a ruined church, the ballad's inherent soundness is the more apparent in its present fragmentary state. Our imaginations respond the more quickly to its artless and economical choice of the essential and the suggestive; we are down to the bare bones of the human story.

For the last 150 years, appraisals of the ballad have appeared with gathering volume and impetus, so that today we may be well informed —if we take time to read all the books on the subject—as to what has

gone into its making, how it has passed from rustic obscurity to literary recognition, what its influence has been on writers of narrative verse and makers of music, what changes have come about in the traditionary process, what the singers are like and what way of life has favored the ballad's survival. In America in the 1910's and 1920's there began to appear collections, more or less scholarly, from the South, which Cecil Sharp's *English Folk Songs from the Southern Appalachians* in 1917 substantially amplified. Since then Maine, Nova Scotia, Newfoundland, Pennsylvania, Vermont, Ohio, Indiana, Michigan, and the Ozarks—to mention only a few areas at random—have been scoured for folk songs, and the collections printed. The songs of the chantey-man, lumber-jack, cowboy, Negro levee-worker, railroader, canaller, coal miner, and frontier bad-man, as well as those of a more stable society, are all in print. These collections differ considerably in purpose and skill of handling, but the best of them are standard and authentic. A few general trends may be observed. The introductions reveal the collectors' attitudes towards the singers and their songs, and the judicious use of anecdote is illuminating. There is a growing sense of the importance of setting down information as Child did; his work is the ultimate model. Child ballads are usually given first. If space permits, all collected versions are printed. Reference is made to other printed sources. Names of singers, how they came by their songs, and how the collector found them are all recorded. Tunes are more frequently given, and although some of the music is still set down in a lamentably amateur fashion, musical accuracy is increasingly evident. In justice to the attempts to reproduce the music, it should be said that many of the notation problems are still unsolved, as is shown by the varied treatments of the tunes from printed collections given in the following pages. The whole subject needs careful scrutiny, as the facilities for studying the music improve. There is, all in all, a growing recognition that it is the work of the expert and not the amateur to set down folk songs.

Some regional collections, like the Helen Hartness Flanders Archive at Middlebury College, Vermont, are open for reference and are beginning to issue recordings and to transcribe for publication. Most important of all is the work of the Archive of American Folk Song in the Library of Congress, which since 1928 has amassed over 40,000 field recordings of songs, fiddle tunes and varied instrumental pieces, as

well as tales, conversations and interviews, and related material. The
Archive classifies and interprets this material, to which it is constantly
adding, and its publication of phonograph recordings, as well as other
equipment for teachers and students, marks a new day in folk song
education. From its 10,000-item *Check-List of Folk Songs* one may
order individual pressings, thus becoming conversant with the style of
the singer. In this day of much pseudo folk song and singing, the
acquaintance with first-hand rendition is a wholesome check on insin-
cerities and mannerisms. For the wholesale revival of folk song, with its
growing commercial tinge, is not without its cultural and artistic
dangers. Yet the *Check-List*, voluminous though it is, is merely a cross
section of America's song. The surface is barely scratched. The three
pages given up to "Barbara Allen" entries, for instance, by no means
list all the singers or all the variants of that ballad. But even this cross
section is an index of the vitality of the older ballads transplanted from
British soil, and the development from their patterns of much indigenous American song.

The reason for another book about ballads is the very multiplicity
of the information available: it is a somewhat confusing matter for
the casual reader, as well as for the student or critic, to apprehend the
Child ballad as it is in America today. The following chapters present
texts and tunes as sung traditionally in the last fifty years in England
and America, with comment which selects from the many separate
and special studies and weaves them together into one fabric. In the
light of this comment the true ballad, compound of racial memories,
mirror of folkways, tried and refined by a hundred singers, may be seen
and enjoyed for what it is.

The ballads were sung, as the ancient chronicler puts it, *iocunde et
memoriter*—with pleasure and by word of mouth. Today, however, we
no longer learn our ballads like Sidney from a blind fiddler or like
Goldsmith from a dairymaid, or from a sailor in port or a farmer at
his plough, or even, alas, from our nurses or mothers. Yet even though
we no longer sing *memoriter* and must resort to books, we sing *iocunde*,
for fortunately much of the pleasure abides. For the ballad is far from
moribund. Anthropologists and philologists may search it to fill the
gaps in their records, but everyone may find in it the strength and virtue of common things. Moreover, if it is an archaic survival, it still
contains the living seed out of which art grows. "The persistence of

literary creativeness in any people," says T. S. Eliot in *What Is a Classic*, "consists in the maintenance of an unconscious balance between tradition in the larger sense—the collective personality, so to speak, realized in the literature of the past—and the originality of the living generation." The traditional ballad has always maintained this balance, building on its past and changing with its present. The end is not yet. As long as men love a story and their senses respond to the rhythm of sound and movement, the ballad tree, rooted in the past, living today, will send forth its branches into tomorrow.

Chapter 1

ROBIN HOOD BALLADS

BACKGROUND

TODAY the greatest prize a ballad collector can secure is a Robin Hood ballad. Once a flourishing branch of the ballad tree, there are now very few examples to be found, particularly in America. Yet since the Robin Hood ballads offer, even in their limited numbers, an excellent approach to balladry, this group is chosen as our starting point.

Their stories are perennially attractive. Their hero we have always known and loved, if not in ballads as our ancestors did, then in the stories of Howard Pyle and the films of Douglas Fairbanks. We still agree with the ancient chronicler that "he was the most humane and prince of robbers." [1] He is an expression of generosity, sportsmanship, and resourcefulness which for the Englishman are "qualities, one hopes, forever English." [2] Reflecting the social conditions of a definite time and place in history, the Robin Hood ballads also hint at a further past, and the inheritance of ancient folk beliefs. The many surviving ancient texts are complete enough for the neophyte to understand, not vaguely elliptical, like many a better-remembered song; in the method of narrative we find some notable traits of ballad poetry, and a norm of style by which we may judge other ballads. The surviving traditional versions show at once that a ballad is a song, gaining incomparably by association with its tune. In short, the Robin Hood ballads bring us at once into the ballad world of fact and legend, of native character and universal human nature, of ideal and earthly, weaving into the easy verse and tune that are the best results of the traditionary process a theme that has found favor for centuries.

Of the forty-odd Robin Hood ballads in Child's collection [3] many deal with the hero's encounters with the law, the church, or the aristoc-

---

[1] Major, *History of Britain* (1521). Quoted by J. W. Walker, "Robin Hood Identified," *Yorkshire Archaeological Journal*, Pt. 141 (May, 1944), p. 5.

[2] Entwistle, *European Balladry*, p. 13.

[3] *English and Scottish Popular Ballads*. Reference to ballads in this collection will include in parentheses after the title the number given by Child.

11

racy—encounters which result in the discomfiture of the privileged and the restoration of rights to the oppressed. Others tell of his more plebeian dealings with butchers, pedlars, and tanners, showing his noble behavior when bested and his method of finding good men for his band. The idyllic nature of forest life, the loyalty of the band to its master, and the nobility of the hero's character are constantly evident. The texts are of varying excellence and range from those of manuscripts and early printed versions of 1450 to later printed broadsides, the last one written by Martin Parker in 1632. Beside these isolated pieces there is "A Gest of Robyn Hode" (117), a collection of tales comprising about 450 stanzas in all, divided into eight "fyttes" or incidents. This is a sort of saga of the hero, a collection of ballads, put together possibly before 1400. One early copy is from the press of Wynkyn de Worde, an apprentice of Caxton who set up shop for himself in 1509.

The identity of a hero of such continuous popularity has long baffled literary detectives. Was he a real person? If so, when did he live? Was he a mere yeoman who attained remarkable fame considering his station, or a disguised nobleman in exile? Was he "a mere creation of the ballad muse," [4] arising out of the conditions of the times, which called for a symbol of popular resistance to privileged oppression? Was he a folk expression of inherited belief—a medieval modernizing of some pagan woodland deity? Examination of his origin must be inconclusive, and is given here merely to introduce us to the sources of popular story and their treatment in tradition.

First, the record as a basis for any facts. From a score of references to Robin or Robert Hoods in various documents of the thirteenth and fourteenth centuries, we select two for special attention, since they both deal with an outlaw who is connected with Yorkshire, Lancashire, or Nottingham, places mentioned in the stories.[5]

In the Pipe Rolls of the reign of Henry III, in 1230, we read that "the sheriff of Yorkshire owes 32 shillings and sixpence in the matter of the chattels of Robin Hood, fugitive." Here is an outlaw involved with a sheriff, perhaps our man. The other Robin was born sixty years later, and we piece together his story from the Rolls of the Manor of Wakefield in Yorkshire. This Robert Hood, the son of Adam, for-

[4] Child, *op. cit.*, III, 42.
[5] For the facts in the following paragraphs see Walker, *op. cit.*, *passim.*

ester of the Lord of the Manor, was born sometime between 1285 and 1295. The years 1308–1315 carry several entries against him for breaking the forest laws. In 1316 his handmaid is before the court for taking firewood, and in the same year he builds a five-room house on land rented from the manor for two shillings. Later he pays twelvepence for more land. His wife, Mathilda, is mentioned by name. He is by this time at odds with authority, married, and a man of sufficient substance to build a house commodious by the standards of the times. In 1316 Edward II orders the Lord of the Manor, Earl Warenne, to muster men to fight the Scotch, and Robert Hood is fined for not reporting. Did he perchance want to stay with his new-wedded wife, in his new-built house? Was there lack of political sympathy with the Lord of the Manor? In 1317, another muster is called by a new Lord of the Manor, Thomas of Lancaster, who has received Wakefield in reparation for the kidnapping of his wife by Earl Warenne. This muster is to collect troops to march against Edward II. Since the name of Robert Hood is not listed among the absent, we may assume that he reported for duty. Lancaster and his men, "the contrariants," were defeated by the king at Boroughbridge, they fled across the sea or to the nearby forests, and their lands were confiscated. In 1322 a listing of these lands shows among the holdings of the Manor of Wakefield "a dwelling house of five chambers of new construction." This may well be Robin Hood's house, built six years before, and its seizure would confirm him as a contrariant. There is no further mention until 1335, when he is again summoned "for resisting the Lord of the Manor."

Evidence from the Royal Household Rolls helps to fill this gap. Late in 1323 the king visited his rebellious lands of Lancashire and Yorkshire, where no doubt he heard tales of the outlaws living in the Forest. From December to the following November, 1324, payments are made at regular intervals to Robin Hood and certain "grooms of the chamber," whose duties are not specified. This would seem to follow the story of the "Gest," which tells of the king's coming to the north, his hunting in Plompton Park, his meeting with Robin and pardon of him, with the stricture that the outlaw and his band attend him at court, and their sojourn there for eleven months.

These references in the rolls are the only ones made to Robin Hood in his lifetime. In the following years, the earliest allusion to him is found in Langland's *Piers Plowman* in 1380, when Sloth, the lazy priest, says that although he does not know his paternoster and other prayers, he "can rymes of Robin Hood and Randolf erle of Chester." [6] This Randolf was born before 1172 and succeeded to the title in 1181 as fourth earl. He took the Cross twice, was Sheriff of Lancashire for eight years, joint commander of the army and then chief commander in Normandy. There are hints that songs, now lost, were made about his exploits.[7] Langland's coupling of his name with that of Robin Hood may imply that since Randolf was a historic person, Robin Hood may also have been; yet it is odd that an obscure yeoman should be associated with a famous soldier-crusader. The connection of the two also suggests that they were contemporaries. If so, this is the earlier Robin. There is a minstrel strain in the early ballads and the "Gest," and minstrels sang about the deeds of authentic persons. John Fordun, writing in *Scottichronicon* before 1384, says, "Robin Hood delights above all others." Another passage reads, "About this time (1265) arose Robin Hood, Little John and their companions. . . ." Another, suspect, however, as an interpolation by Bower in 1447, says, "Robin Hood never entered a church to hear the service without staying to the end, no matter what the danger." Major, writing in 1521, conjectures that he lived in the time of Richard I (1189), and says that songs of his exploits are sung throughout Britain.[8]

The early ballads and the "Gest" fit the record in giving Robin yeoman status, in telling of the visit to court, and in alluding to places known only to the Wakefield countryside—Sayles, Plompton Park, and Barnesdale Forest. This was a tract some five miles square, north of Doncaster, lying between the River Went on the north, Askern on the east, and Badsworth on the west. The Great North Road, an early travel route laid down possibly in Roman times, passed through the forest, and there is considerable early mention of the danger to travelers from highwaymen. Leland in the time of Henry VIII associates Robin Hood with this retreat.[9] Association with Sherwood Forest and Nottingham may have come about from a life such as Robin's, which would doubtless have led him from one forest fastness to another; or from confusion with some other outlaw and his band in another forest, and another set of incidents. Record and ballad may be brought together, but the record itself is not in agreement, and the two Robins

---

[6] *Piers Plowman*, p. 89.
[7] Walker, *op. cit.*, p. 8.
[8] *Ibid.*, p. 5.
[9] Leland's *Itinerary*, ed. 1745, V, 95.

of 1230 and a century later cannot be reconciled into one. Robin Hood is not yet historically identified.

There remains also the question of the accretion of legend about the doings of a mere yeoman till they reach saga-like proportions and songs about them are sung all over Britain. The extraordinary development of the Robin Hood theme in the fourteenth and fifteenth centuries is to be accounted for partly by the social conditions of the times. Other literature of the period shows the same sense of unrest, discontent, and protest. *Piers Plowman* itself is the hopeless dream of social justice, the expression of the gospel of equality backed by the gospel of labor. The medieval resignation to a hard earthly lot because it would be rewarded by heavenly bliss was being called into question. John Ball, the mad priest of Kent, was going up and down the land preaching the rights of the poor. His rhymed "missives" had a trenchant folk quality that led to their instant memorizing.

> Whan Adam dalfe and Eve span,
> Who was than a gentleman?

This propaganda was fomenting the Peasant Revolt at the time of the appearance of *Piers Plowman*. Back of the revolt lay many causes. With the breaking up of the manorial system bondsmen were moving to the towns and laboring classes were emerging. The nobles must finance the Hundred Years' War, as well as their own luxurious tastes, and demanded from the peasants "malt silver" instead of the malt itself as in the past. The ravages of the Black Death depleted the supply of labor. The line was sharpening between rich and poor, aristocrat and peasant, lord and subject.

Read in the light of these conditions, the Robin Hood ballads become an eloquent voice of the people crying out against oppression, and the hero is the people's champion made to order. The law, the church (but not religion), and the nobles (but not the king) are forces to be resisted to the limit, and Robin Hood is the man for the deed every time. This leader of a band of outlaws living their lives safe in the greenwood becomes the hero of a hundred exploits. One story gives rise to another. Finally, a noble pedigree is found for him, in harmony with the romantic ideals of popular story. By the end of the sixteenth century, when Sidney, Spenser, and Shakespeare are telling

tales of nobility frolicking disguised in the greenwood, Robin Hood
has become Robert, Earl of Huntingdon, and as such he is shown in
two plays by Anthony Munday, *The Downfall of Robert, Earl of
Huntingdon,* and *The Death of Robert, Earl of Huntingdon.* Up to
the eighteenth century the grave of Robin Hood near Kirklees Abbey
was pointed out, with the inscription claiming that Robert, Earl of
Huntingdon, lay there. Grave and stone have since disappeared, but
there are rubbings of the inscription, and an account of the stone,
which show similarity to other fourteenth-century stones still in
existence. The grave, however, was probably a later fabrication. The
lettering points to the time of Henry VIII, the spelling is suspect and
there was no such date as that given for his death.[10] All attempts to
prove the outlaw a nobleman have been unsuccessful. On this basis,
however, the later ballads arose, and on it our modern versions of the
stories have developed. Later exiles from the law, betaking themselves
to the forest, assumed Robin's name or that of a follower. As late as
the seventeenth century there was an outlaw calling himself Friar
Tuck.

But still other elements may have gone into the evolution of Robin
Hood. His supernatural origin was seriously argued by folklorists of
a past generation, but the theory was completely discarded by Child,
who "could not admit that a shadow of a case had been made out by
those who would equate him with Odin or account for him in accord-
ance with the supposed principles of comparative mythology." [11] To
uphold a theory discounted by Child, who himself based so much
upon comparative mythology, is to dare greatly. But evidence since
his day strengthens the possibility that in the Robin Hood cycle there
may be something far more ancient than the local exploits of a
medieval yeoman.

By the time of *Piers Plowman,* the ballad was a well-defined channel
for heroic tales, and the minstrel who sang of an ideal hero was following the traditional pattern of the bards and the scalds. Narrative
poetry was already a folk habit. We may certainly consider the early
ballads as the end of a long development, both of style, the sung narrative, and of theme, the folk hero's deeds. A heroic ancestry may perhaps be established for Robin Hood.

[10] Walker, *op. cit.,* p. 42.
[11] Child, *op. cit.,* III, 48. See also Sargent and Kittredge ed., p. 255.

As we look at the ballads, certain facts stand out. The reason for Robin's life in the forest is never given. His mysterious existence in a secret abode, his well-nigh magical sorties to aid the needy, his very special choice of companions, his wonderful skill with weapons, and his almost supernatural ability to be in the right place at the right time, and to extricate himself from apparently insurmountable difficulties—these are the roots of the stories. Now while flight to the forest is a reasonable course for a man escaping from the law, and the practical difficulties of finding him might help explain such stories, they do not fully account for them. England, like every other country with a pre-Christian culture, is full of vestiges of an earlier religion, enough, when they are collected, to prove the ancient worship of woodland deities a commonplace. As men fled to the Christian altar of the church for protection, so they fled earlier to the altars of the gods, and the deities of the woodland offered peculiar sanctuary to their votaries. In Needwood Forest in Staffordshire an "Asylum Oak" is still pointed out. The remarkable Horn Dance of nearby Abbots Bromley, still annually performed,[12] contains more than a hint of forest rites. Study of the gathering store of folk customs throws new light every day on the survival of pagan elements not known or not recognized in Child's day. The late Middle Ages, when the Robin Hood stories were in their heyday, were four centuries nearer to that pagan past than we are today. In the manner of his life, then, Robin Hood may hark back to the beliefs of that past.

There is also the matter of his name. Although the realists point to its common occurrence in the English record—there are still plenty of Hoods, and plenty of Roberts among them—the number of their connections with supernatural creatures becomes significant.

Since the twelfth century in Yorkshire (Robin's territory) we find references to the hob-thrush, a benevolent naked creature who works with supernatural speed and power, and disappears offended if offered clothing. The word "thrush" is derived from *þrys* or *þurs*, meaning *giant*.[13] As in the case of fairies, once perhaps superhumanly large, these creatures have shrunk, as man lost his fear of them, from giants to elves.[14] Generic proper names are a folk habit: we read of "Jack-

[12] See page 127.
[13] Dickens, "Yorkshire Hobs," *Transactions of the Yorkshire Dialect Society*, XLIII, Vol. VII (1942), 9–22.
[14] See page 139, note.

priest," and we speak of "George the waiter." Superstitious people feel
easier if they can dub familiarly that which they still hold in awe, even
if that awe is diminishing; and supernatural creatures, who may work
weal or woe to mere human beings, are more comfortably dealt with
if they are given friendly, common names.[15] Hob, Dob, Rob and Robin
are all diminutives of Robert. Thus hob-thrush becomes the familiar
name for the once terrifying, now benevolent household demon.
Other forms of the name appear in folk parlance. A version of "The
Wife Wrapt in Wether's Skin" (277) is about Robin-a-Thrush,[16]
though this person is human enough in his actions. The superhuman
and the familiar come together in such a phrase as "raising hob" for
"raising the devil." A hundred years after the "Gest" was printed,
people were talking about another other-worldly Robin, Goodfellow,
not unlike Robin Hood in his enjoyment of pranks shot through with
kindness.

As to Robin's second name: Cecil Sharp notes that country singers
invariably call Robin Hood "Robin of the 'ood" (wood).[17] The first
enthusiasts claiming supernatural origin for the ballad hero derived his
name from that of an ancient Germanic woodland deity, Hode, or
Wode (possibly a form of Wodin). Child very successfully exposed
the weaknesses of their arguments,[18] and for many years the sylvan god
theory of Robin Hood's origin was discountenanced. But in his notes
on another ballad, "Earl Brand" (7), Child relates the demon Old
Carl Hood to Carl Blind, who was Blind the Bad, or the one-eyed
wanderer of Norse tales, Wodin.[19] Carl Blind, in turn, suggests Billy
Blind, the household demon in "Willie's Lady" (6). Thus Hood and
Blind are supernatural kin, and we must again, in spite of Child's
rejection of the theory, relate them to Hode, Wode, and Wodin.

As we shall see later, the ballad has a strong propensity to absorb
and preserve the supernatural,[20] and the more we discover of this
element in other ballads, the more probable it becomes that the Robin
Hood ballads have appropriated their share. The theory is at least
tenable that in the Robin Hood stories there may be some confused
folk memories rationalized into the adventures of a folk hero, and that
in this stalwart English yeoman, so human and yet so mysterious, we

---

[15] See page 131.
[16] Broadwood, *English County Songs*, p. 92.
[17] Sharp, *One Hundred English Folksongs*, p. xix.
[18] Child, *op. cit.*, III, 48.
[19] *Ibid.*, I, 95.
[20] See Chapter 5, *passim*.

may have a reincarnation of the helpful household demon, as well as the god of the magic forest, who, with his carefully chosen and secretly initiated devotees, emerged to help the needy when the summons came. In name as well as in nature Robin Hood may strike deep into the pagan past of the English singer.

The earlier ballads make no reference to the lady who has since become an integral part of the Robin Hood story. Maid Marian, if she appears at all in the ballads, comes only into those of later composition. Her entrance may be explained by some reference to the May Games.[21]

In Medieval England the many church festivals of the year served to gather the people for all sorts of gaiety after their religious duties had been observed, and the spring festivals in particular were celebrated on every village green. We think of this festivity as a reaction of the secular to the religious, but actually the games, dances, plays, choice of May King and Queen, and May ridings were a continuation of pagan religious practices. The church calendar was based on the observances of the pagan countries which had been converted, and Whitsun, falling fifty days after Easter, was the same period during which the pagan ancestors of British Christians had observed the spring solstice, with all the ritual celebration of renewed fertility in man and nature which accompanied the return of the sun to the earth. An important part of this ritual was an imitation of the processes of nature, performed in order to assist those processes, and this imitation took the form of a dramatization of the myth of returning life. This simple play became stereotyped into a death-and-resurrection story in which the suitor of a lady is killed, and then brought to life again by a miracle-working doctor. The dance of a group of swordsmen culminates in the act of killing, and is sometimes repeated in the act of bringing to life. This drama symbolized the meeting of male and female elements in the creation of new life, and the cycle in which life emerges from death. Long after belief in the efficacy of this imitative act had been forgotten, the play lived on, with farcical embellishments, as a popular entertainment. This is Hardy's mummer's play, in *The Return of the Native*. Village after village has yielded up, even in

[21] See Chambers, *Medieval Stage*, I, 174–78, for a discussion of the May Games and their incorporation of Robin Hood and Maid Marian. See also Raglan, *The Hero*, pp. 51–53.

recent years, its particular version. At the time of the coronation of George VI in 1935, the village of Eynsham in Oxfordshire revived its folk play as part of the local rejoicing. The folk play was traditionally performed at any time from Christmas to Whitsun, or, in the heathen calendar, from the winter to the spring solstice. The same characters appeared, but under different names, according to the hero or the villain of the day. Thus we find St. George, or King George, or King Arthur; the Turkish Knight or Napoleon. In the fifteenth century the ballad hero Robin Hood was appropriated by the folk play, and his merry men became the dancers. The play was fruitless, however, without the lady, for courtship was a necessary part of the dramatic restoration of life to the earth. When Robin became the hero, the lady became Marian, although there was no such person in the ballads. Now in thirteenth-century France the folk play had been cast by Adam de la Hâle into the form of a small song-and-dance drama called *Le Jeu de Robin et Marion*, which was widely popular, and which doubtless, in view of the contact between England and France, was known in England. The English folk play hero was already Robin, as was, for other reasons, the French one; it was natural that the lady of the English play should take her name from the French Marion.[22] The combination did not last long. Ballad, play, and dance soon went their separate ways. The later ballads acquired Marian from the play. The dancers, having developed a highly skilled and intricate dance, performed with swords in the north and sticks or handkerchiefs in the midlands, continued to perform without the play down to the present century every year in the traditional season, and the attendant characters, all that was left of the persons of the play, were for a long time called after the followers of Robin Hood. The man-woman, who traditionally accompanies the sword or morris dancers of today, is still known in some villages as "the maid-marian."

CHARACTERISTICS AND EXAMPLES

The earlier songs about this hero, be he vegetation deity, yeoman-outlaw-contrariant, or champion of the folk created out of the ballad

[22] It was not only the folk play that appropriated Robin Hood. Other plays were based on his deeds, some obvious ballad dramatizations like *George a Green, the Pinner of Wakefield*, by Robert Greene, some, like Munday's, romantic expansions of the Robin Hood theme. These all contributed to the merging streams of Elizabethan drama.

TOLLET'S PAINTED WINDOW (BETLEY, STAFFS.)
Showing the Robin Hood characters attendant upon the May Games
and the Morris Dance (1460)

mind, give us some of the best traits of ballad style as practiced in the ballad's fifteenth-century heyday. Some of these traits have been traditionally preserved, others have disappeared in oral transmission. The following comment on the early text of "Robin Hood and the Monk" (119) points out these traits, and explains some of the more archaic aspects which might otherwise hinder one's initial enjoyment.

The ballad stanza is almost uniformly rhythmical. Longer and shorter lines like "Litull John seid he had won five shillings" or "The son up feyre can shyne" were no doubt smoothed out in the singing. Only since the separation of poetry from music has such irregularity of verse been adversely criticized. The older alliterative verse, with its initial rather than end rhyme, is reflected in such a stanza as the following, which seems rougher to us than it did to a fifteenth-century listener:

> The sheref made to seke Notyngham,
> Both in *s*trete and *s*tye,
> And Robin was in mery Scherwode,
> As *l*ight as *l*ef on *l*ynde.

The theme is that of all Robin Hood ballads, the setting of the fair, free, honest forest life against that of the town, the law, and the church.

The ballad's ninety stanzas give us a duly introduced and skilfully motivated tale. Robin's troubles result from his piety; Little John's false story to the monk is based upon the supposed robbery they both have suffered; Little John accompanies him through the forest ostensibly to protect him from the dangerous outlaw, Robin Hood; in order to get the keys to the jail, Little John and Much make the sheriff drunk (on his own wine); Little John, arriving at the gates of the town, finds them barred and inquires the cause, known to us from an earlier stanza; the king, though righteously angry at the trick played upon him, forgives the sheriff because he too has been duped. Transitions, summaries, and new starts provide fresh breath for the narrator and fresh attention from the listener: "Thus John gate Robin Hod out of prison," or "Thus endys the talking of the munke." Although the real adventure ends with the feast in the forest, the epilogue serves as balance in the long story. There is a bit of unconscious art in the implied comparison of the king with his temporal crown to "God, that is ever a crowned king" in the final invocation. With the shift of scene from forest to town, from town to court and back, there is a competent handling of the groups of people. Robin, Little John, the sheriff, and the monk are highlighted against a background swarming with merry men and townsfolk. Even the monk stands for the whole company of lesser clergy against whom Robin's hand is raised. "Many was the moder son" rushing staff in hand to the scrimmage in the church; the search of "every street and stye" implies the swarming excited town, as does the order to bar all the gates. But confusion and brawl alternate with quieter scenes, varying the atmosphere and tempo. It is a lonely road where the monk and the little page are murdered, a quiet church where the alarm is given. The idyllic quality of the forest setting permeates the ballad. Thicket and greenwood tree, the sunshine of a Whitsun morning, bird song and the movement of the deer, provide an opening every Englishman loves. English song since "Sumer is icumen in" has liked the conventional beginning, "One morning in May." There is continuous allusion to the "tristil-tre," the "levys smale" or the forest paths known only to the band. From this countryside the town is never far: cockcrow and day-spring appear in the same stanza with the ringing of the alarm bell in the jail; another stanza juxtaposes the search of the town with Robin "in mery Scherwode." The verse picks up the tempo of the action. Thus with a sense of leisure we read:

> Litul John stode at a wyndow in the morning,
>   And lokid forth at a stage;
> He was war where the munke came riding,
>   And with hym a litul page.

Here the feminine endings help to lengthen and quieten the verse. We feel there is plenty of time for Little John and Much to descend and be found by the monk strolling along the road, time to indulge in amenities with him, "as curtes men and hende." But when the excitement increases, so do the speed and vigor of the verse. Townsmen, alarmed by the monk, swarm about the church. "In at the durres they throly thrast"; Robin attacks where they are thickest, kills twelve, his sword breaking on the head of the sheriff himself. No time here for leisurely description—hard breathing, a curse on the smith who forged the sword. No ceremony with the monk; he is pulled down "Be the golett of his hode" and falls on his crown. Ironic touches add intensity: the little page is summarily dispatched "ffor fere lest he wolde tell";

Robin, when he is rescued, is given a sword "His hed therwith for to kepe." Thus the slow-paced lyrical beginning is followed by furious action, which in turn is resolved to harmony and joy in the forest, and ends with the king's dismissal of the episode: "Speke [we] no more of this mater."

Character is both expressed and implied. A single cloud drifts across the sky of that May morning, Robin's low spirits and their cause:

> 'Ʒe, on thyng greves me,' seid Robyn,
> 'And does my hert mych woo;
> Þat I may not no solem day
> To mas nor matyns goo.'

This thought is father to his daring adventure; the whole story develops because his piety must be satisfied. As he approaches Nottingham he has a momentary qualm, and prays "to God and myld Mary / To bryng hym out saue again." Little John alludes to his master's life in terms of one continued act of devotion:

> 'He has seruyd Oure Lady many a day,
> And yet wil, securly.'

The story is shot through with the pious ejaculations of the age: "With the myght of mylde Mary," "By hym that died on tre." The pious Robin is, however, humanly rash and hot-tempered. It is a good hearty quarrel that parts him from Little John. Ruefully he sees his mistake when he is beset, and like many an Englishman in a tight place, resorts to ironic humor:

> 'Alas, alas!' seid Robyn Hode,
> 'Now mysse I Litull John.'

But his temper and rashness are matched with fine generosity, and the quarrel ends with a splendid gesture:

> 'I make þe maister,' seid Robyn Hode,
> 'Off alle my men and me.'

Little John is drawn with equal deftness. He is inherently buoyant as he cheers Robin's drooping spirits:

> 'This is a mery mornyng,' seid Litull John,
> 'Be hym þat dyed on tre;
> A more mery man þen I am one
> Lyves not in Cristiantë.'

'Pluk vp þi hert, my dere mayster,'
Litull John can sey,
'And thynk hit is a full fayre tyme
In a mornyng of May.'

His quick-flaring anger commits him to a hasty vow after the quarrel:

'Get þe a man wher þou wilt,
For þou getis me no more.'

The vow is forgotten, however, when news of Robin's plight reaches
the greenwood and he at once rouses the stricken band, heartens them
with promises of his own action, and gives his parting orders:

'Let be your rule,' seid Litull John
'Ffor his luf þat dyed on tre,
ȝe, hat shulde be duȝty men;
Het is gret shame to se.'

.   .   .   .   .   .

'And I shal be þe munkis gyde,
With þe myght of mylde Mary.'

.   .   .   .   .   .

'Loke þat ȝe kepe well owre tristil-tre,
Vnder þe levys smale.'

He has a lusty enjoyment of every moment. "Now will I be porter," he
cries as he bears the porter to the wall with his sword and seizes the
keys of the jail. His wit is quick when the sheriff asks what has become
of the monk:

'He [the king] is so fayn of hym,' seid Litul John,
'For soþe as I yow say,
He has made hym abot of Westmynster,
A lorde of þat abbay.'

After the rescue of Robin, suddenly remembering the quarrel and his
vow, he becomes self-conscious and stiff with dignity:

'I haue done þe a gode turne,' seid Litull John,
'For sothe as I yow say;
I haue brouȝt þe vnder grene-wode lyne;
Ffare wel, and haue gode day.'

But Robin's forthright thanks set all right between them.

The interplay of the two personalities contributes largely to our
pleasure. The frequent dialogue is always natural, be it the casual talk

of intimates, the suavity of Little John with the monk, or the quick tossing of high words in the quarrel.

ROBIN HOOD AND THE MONK (119)

1. In somer, when þe shawes be sheyne,
      And leves be large and long,
   Hit is full mery in feyre foreste
      To here þe foulys song:

2. To se þe dere draw to þe dale,
      And leve þe hilles hee,
   And shadow hem in þe levës grene,
      Vnder the grene-wode tre.

3. Hit befel on Whitsontide,
      Erly in a May mornyng,
   The son vp feyre can shyne,
      And the briddis mery can syng.

4. 'This is a mery mornyng,' seid Litull John,
      'Be hym þat dyed on tre;
   A more mery man þen I am one
      Lyves not in Cristiantë.

5. 'Pluk vp þi hert, my dere mayster,'
      Litull John can sey,
   'And thynk hit is a full fayre tyme
      In a mornyng of May.'

6. 'Ȝe, on thyng greves me,' seid Robyn,
      'And does my hert mych woo;
   Þat I may not no solem day
      To mas nor matyns goo.

7. 'Hit is a fourtnet and more,' seid he,
      'Syn I my sauyour see;
   Today wil I to Notyngham,' seid Robyn,
      'With þe myght of mylde Marye.'

8. Than spake Moche, þe mylner sun,
      Euer more wel hym betyde!
   'Take twelue of þi wyght ȝemen,
      Well weppynd, be þi side,
   Such on wolde þi selfe slon,
      Þat twelue dar not abyde.'

shawes—woods	wyght ȝemen—strong yeomen
foulys—fowls	slon—slay
sheyne—shining	

9. 'Of all my mery men,' seid Robyn,
      'Be my feith I wil non haue,
   But Litull John shall beyre my bow,
      Til þat me list to drawe.'

10. 'Þou shall beyre þin own,' seid Litull Jon,
       'Maister, and I wyl beyre myne,
    And we well shete a peny,' seid Litull Jon,
       'Vnder þe grene-wode lyne.'

11. 'I wil not shete a peny,' seyd Robyn Hode,
       'In feith, Litull John, with the,
    But euer for on as þou shetis,' seide Robyn,
       'In feith I hold þe thre.'

12. Thus shet þei forth, þese ȝemen too,
       Bothe at buske and brome,
    Til Litull John wan of his maister
       Fiue shillings to hose and shone.

13. A ferly strife fel þem betwene,
       As they went bi the wey;
    Litull John seid he had won fiue shillings,
       And Robyn Hode seid schortly nay.

14. With þat Robyn Hode lyed Litul Jon,
       And smote hym with his hande;
    Litul Jon waxed wroth þerwith,
       And pulled out his bright bronde.

15. 'Were þou not my maister,' seid Litull John,
       'Þou shuldis by hit ful sore;
    Get þe a man wher þou w[ilt],
       For þou getis me no more.'

16. Þen Robyn goes to Notyngham,
       Hym selfe mornyng allone,
    And Litull John to mery Scherwode,
       The pathes he knew ilkone.

17. Whan Robyn came to Notyngham,
       Sertenly withouten layn,
    He prayed to God and myld Mary
       To bryng hym out saue agayn.

shete a peny—shoot for penny stakes   ferly—strange
buske—(1) bush, (2) dress   ilkone—each one
brome—broom

18. He gos in to Seynt Mary chirch,
     And kneled down before the rode;
    Alle þat euer were þe church within
     Beheld wel Robyn Hode.

19. Beside hym stod a gret-hedid munke,
     I pray to God woo he be!
    Fful sone he knew gode Robyn,
     As sone as he hym se.

20. Out at þe durre he ran,
     Fful sone and anon;
    Alle þe ȝatis of Notyngham
     He made to be sparred euerychon.

21. 'Rise vp,' he seid, 'þou prowde schereff,
     Buske þe and make þe bowne;
    I haue spyed þe kynggis felon,
     Ffor sothe he is in þis town.

22. 'I haue spyed þe false felon,
     As he stondis at his masse;
    Hit is long of þe,' seide þe munke,
     'And euer he fro vs passe.

23. 'Þis traytur name is Robyn Hode,
     Vnder þe grene-wode lynde,
    He robbyt me onys of a hundred pound,
     Hit shalle neuer out of my mynde.'

24. Vp þen rose þis prowde shereff,
     And radly made hym ȝare;
    Many was þe moder son
     To þe kyrk with hym can fare.

25. In at þe durres þei throly thrast,
     With staves ful gode wone;
    'Alas, alas!' seid Robyn Hode,
     'Now mysse I Litull John.'

26. But Robyn toke out a too-hond sworde,
     Þat hangit down be his kne;
    Þer as þe schereff and his men stode thyckust,
     Theþurwarde wolde he.

ȝatis—gates
euerychon—everyone
bowne—ready

lynde—linden
radly—quickly
ȝare—ready

27. Thryes thorowout þem he ran þen,
        For soþe as I yow sey,
     And woundyt mony a moder son,
        And twelue he slew þat day.

28. His sworde vpon þe schireff hed
        Sertanly he brake in too;
     'Þe smyth þat þe made,' seid Robyn,
        'I pray to God wryke hym woo!

29. 'Ffor now am I weppynlesse,' seid Robyn,
        'Alasse! agayn my wylle;
     But if I may fle þese traytors fro,
        I wot þei wil me kyll.'

30. Robyn in to the churchë ran,
        Throout hem euerilkon,

        *   *   *   *   *

31. Sum fel in swonyng as þei were dede,
        And lay stil as any stone;
     Non of theym were in her mynde
        But only Litull Jon.

32. 'Let be your rule' seid Litull Jon,
        'Ffor his luf þat dyed on tre,
     Ȝe þat schulde be duȝty men;
        Het is gret shame to se.

33. 'Oure maister has bene hard bystode
        And ȝet scapyd away;
     Pluk vp your hertis, and leve þis mone,
        And harkyn what I shal say.

34. 'He has seruyd Oure Lady many a day,
        And ȝet wil, securly;
     Þerfor I trust in hir specialy
        No wyckud deth shal he dye.

35. 'Þerfor be glad,' seid Litul John,
        'And let þis mournyng be;
     And I shal be þe munkis gyde,
        With þe myght of mylde Mary.

36. .   .   .   .   .   .
        'We will go but we too;
     And I mete hym,' seid Litul John,
        .   .   .   .   .

rule—lament   duȝty—doughty

37. 'Loke þat ȝe kepe wel owre tristil-tre,
        Vnder þe levys smale,
    And spare non of this venyson,
        Þat gose in thys vale.'

38. Fforþe þen went these ȝemen too,
        Litul John and Moche on fere,
    And lokid on Moch emys hows,
        Þe hye way lay full nere.

39. Litul John stode at a wyndow in þe mornyng,
        And lokid forþ at a stage;
    He was war wher þe munke came rydyng,
        And with hym a litul page.

40. 'Be my feith,' seid Litul John to Moch,
        'I can þe tel tithyngus gode;
    I se wher þe munke cumys rydyng,
        I know hym be his wyde hode.'

41. They went in to the way, þese ȝemen boþe,
        As curtes men and hende;
    Þei spyrred tithyngus at þe munke,
        As they hade bene his frende.

42. 'Ffro whens come ȝe?' seid Litull Jon,
        'Tel vs tithyngus, I yow pray,
    Off a false owtlay, [callid Robyn Hode,]
        Was takyn ȝisterday.

43. 'He robbyt me and my felowes boþe
        Of twenti marke in serten;
    If þat false owtlay be takyn,
        Ffor soþe we wolde be fayn.'

44. 'So did he me,' seid þe munke,
        'Of a hundred pound and more;
    I layde furst hande hym apon,
        Ȝe may thonke me þerfore.'

45. 'I pray God thanke you,' seid Litull John,
        'And we wil when we may;
    We wil go with you, with your leve,
        And bryng yow on your way.

tristil-tre—trysting tree
stage—balcony

spyrred—asked
tithyngus—tidings

46. 'Ffor Robyn Hode hase many a wilde felow,
     I tell you in certen;
   If þei wist ʒe rode þis way,
     In feith ʒe shulde be slayn.'

47. As þei went talking be þe way,
     The munke and Litull John,
   John toke þe munkis horse be þe hede,
     Fful sone and anon.

48. Johne toke þe munkis horse be þe hed,
     Ffor soþe as I yow say;
   So did Much þe litull page,
     Ffor he shulde not scape away.

49. Be þe golett of þe hode
     John pulled þe munke down;
   John was nothyng of hym agast,
     He lete hym falle on his crown.

50. Litull John was so[re] agrevyd,
     And drew owt his swerde in hye;
   This munke saw he shulde be ded,
     Lowd mercy can he crye.

51. 'He was my maister,' seid Litull John,
     'Þat þou hase browʒt in bale;
   Shalle þou neuer cum at our kyng,
     Ffor to telle hym tale.'

52. John smote of þe munkis hed,
     No longer wolde he dwell;
   So did Moch þe litull page,
     Ffor ferd lest he wolde tell.

53. Þer þei beryed hem boþe,
     In nouþer mosse nor lyng,
   And Litull John and Much infere
     Bare þe letturs to our kyng.

54.   .   .   .   .   .   .
     He knelid down vpon his kne:
   'God ʒow saue, my lege lorde,
     Ihesus yow saue and se!

bale—harm   lyng—heath
in nouþer—beneath

55. 'God yow saue, my lege kyng!'
    To speke John was full bolde;
He gaf hym þe letturs in his hond,
    The kyng did hit vnfold.

56. Þe kyng red þe letturs anon,
    And seid, So mot I the,
Þer was neuer ȝoman in mery Inglond
    I longut so sore to se.

57. 'Wher is þe munke þat þese shuld haue·brouȝt?'
    Oure kyng can say:
'Be my trouth,' seid Litull John,
    'He dyed after þe way.'

58. Þe kyng gaf Moch and Litul Jon
    Twenti pound in sertan,
And made þeim ȝemen of þe crown,
    And bade þeim go agayn.

59. He gaf John þe seel in hand,
    The sheref for to bere,
To bryng Robyn hym to,
    And no man do hym dere.

60. John toke his leve at oure kyng,
    Þe sothe as I yow say;
Þe next way to Notyngham
    To take, he ȝede þe way.

61. Whan John came to Notyngham
    The ȝatis were sparred ychon;
John callid vp þe porter,
    He answerid sone anon.

62. 'What is þe cause,' seid Litul Jon,
    'Þou sparris þe ȝates so fast?'
'Because of Robyn Hode,' seid [þe] porter,
    'In depe prison is cast.

63. 'John and Moch and Wyll Scathlok,
    Ffor sothe as I yow say,
Þei slew oure men vpon our wallis,
    And sawten vs euery day.'

so mot I the—as I hope to thrive   ȝede—went
dere—injury   sawten—assault

64. Litull John spyrred after þe schereff,
    And sone he hym fonde;
    He oppyned þe kyngus priue seell,
    And gaf hym in his honde.

65. Whan þe scheref saw þe kyngus seell,
    He did of his hode anon:
    'Wher is þe munke þat bare þe letturs?'
    He seid to Litull John.

66. 'He is so fayn of hym,' seid Litul John,
    Ffor soþe as I yow say,
    He has made hym abot of Westmynster,
    A lorde of þat abbay.'

67. The scheref made John gode chere,
    And gaf hym wyne of the best;
    At nyȝt þei went to her bedde,
    And euery man to his rest.

68. When þe scheref was on slepe,
    Dronken of wyne and ale,
    Litul John and Moch for soþe
    Toke þe way vnto þe jale.

69. Litul John callid vp þe jayler,
    And bade hym rise anon;
    He seyd Robyn Hode had brokyn prison,
    And out of hit was gon.

70. The porter rose anon sertan,
    As sone as he herd John calle;
    Litul John was redy with a swerd,
    And bare hym to þe walle.

71. 'Now wil I be porter,' seid Litul John,
    'And take þe keyes in honde:'
    He toke þe way to Robyn Hode,
    And sone he hym vnbonde.

72. He gaf hym a gode swerd in his hond,
    His hed [ther] with to kepe,
    And ther as þe walle was lowyst
    Anon down can þei lepe.

73. Be þat þe cok began to crow,
    The day began to spryng;
  The scheref fond þe jaylier ded,
    The comyn bell made he ryng.

74. He made a crye thoroout al þe tow[n],
    Wheder he be ȝoman or knave,
  Þat cowþe bryng hym Robyn Hode,
    His warison he shuld haue.

75. 'Ffor I dar neuer,' said þe scheref,
    'Cum before oure kyng;
  'Ffor if I do, I wot serten
    Ffor soþe he wil me heng.'

76. The scheref made to seke Notyngham,
    Bothe be strete and stye,
  And Robyn was in mery Scherwode,
    As liȝt as lef on lynde.

77. Then bespake gode Litull John,
    To Robyn Hode can he say,
  I haue done þe a gode turne for an euyll,
    Quyte þe whan þou may.

78. 'I haue done þe a gode turne,' seid Litull John,
    Ffor sothe as I yow say;
  I haue brouȝt þe vnder grene-wode lyne;
    Ffare wel, and haue gode day.'

79. 'Nay, be my trouth,' seid Robyn Hode,
    'So shall hit neuer be;
  I make þe maister,' seid Robyn Hode,
    'Off alle my men and me.'

80. 'Nay, be my trouth,' seid Litull John,
    'So shalle hit neuer be;
  But lat me be a felow,' seid Litull John,
    'No noder kepe I be.'

81. Thus John gate Robyn Hod out of prison,
    Sertan withoutyn layn;
  Whan his men saw hym hol and sounde,
    Ffor sothe they were full fayne.

be þat—by the time that   warison—reward
comyn bell—town alarm   stye—alley
cowþe—could   no noder kepe I be—none other care I to be

82. They filled in wyne, and made hem glad,
      Vnder þe levys smale,
    And ȝete pastes of venyson,
      Þat gode was with ale.

83. Than worde came to oure kyng
      How Robyn Hode was gon,
    And how þe scheref of Notyngham
      Durst neuer loke hym vpon.

84. Then bespake oure cumly kyng,
      In an angur hye:
    Litull John hase begyled þe schereff,
      In faith so hase he me..

85. Litul John has begyled vs bothe,
      And þat full wel I se;
    Or ellis þe schereff of Notyngham
      Hye hongut shulde he be.

86. 'I made hem ȝemen of þe crowne,
      And gaf hem fee with my hond;
    I gaf hem grith,' seid oure kyng,
      'Thorowout all mery Inglond.

87. 'I gaf theym grith,' þen seid oure kyng;
      'I say, so mot I the,
    Ffor sothe soch a ȝeman as he is on
      In all Inglond ar not thre.

88. 'He is trew to his maister,' seid our kyng;
      'I sey, be swete Seynt John,
    He louys better Robyn Hode
      Then he dose vs ychon.

89. 'Robyn Hode is euer bond to hym,
      Bothe in strete and stalle;
    Speke no more of this mater,' seid oure kyng,
      'But John has begyled vs alle.'

90. Thus endys the talkyng of the munke
      And Robyn Hode i-wysse;
    God, þat is euer a crowned kyng,
      Bryng vs all to his blisse!

grith—guaranty of safety

ROBIN HOOD AND THE TANNER (126) [23]

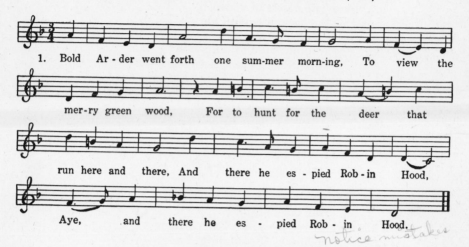

1. Bold Ar-der went forth one sum-mer morn-ing, To view the
mer-ry green wood, For to hunt for the deer that
run here and there, And there he es - pied Rob-in Hood,
Aye, and there he es - pied Rob - in Hood.

notice mistakes

1. Bold Arder went forth one summer morning,
   To view the merry green wood,
   For to hunt for the deer that run here and there,
   And there he espied Robin Hood,
   Aye, and there he espied Robin Hood.

2. What fellow art thou? quoth bold Robin Hood,
   And what is thy business here?
   For now to be brief, thou dost look like a thief,
   And come for to steal the king's deer.
   Aye, and *etc.*

3. No! I am the keeper of this parish;
   The king he hath put me in trust:
   And therefore I pray thee to go on thy way,
   Or else to upstand thee I must.
   Aye, or *etc.*

4. 'Tis thou must have more partakers in store,
   Before thou upstand me indeed;
   For I have a staff, he is made of ground graffe,
   And I warrant he'll do my deed,
   Aye, and *etc.*

[23] From Sharp, *One Hundred English Folksongs*, p. 8. Reprinted by permission of Theodore Presser, Philadelphia. Published and copyrighted by Oliver Ditson Co., Boston, 1916.

5. And I have another, quoth bold Robin Hood,
    He's made of an oaken tree;
He's eight foot and a half, and would knock down a calf,
    And why shouldn't he knock down thee?
      Aye, and *etc.*

6. Let us measure our staves, says bold Robin Hood,
    Before we begin and away;
If by half a foot mine should be longer than thine,
    Then that shall be counted foul play.
      Aye, and that *etc.*

7. Then at it they went, for bang, for bang,
    The space of two hours or more.
Every blow they swing they make the grove ring,
    And they played their game so sure.
      Aye, and *etc.*

8. Then bold Robin Hood drew his bugle horn,
    And blew it both loud and shrill;
And direct thereupon he espied Little John,
    Come running a-down the hill.
      Aye, come *etc.*

9. Oh what is the matter? then said Little John,
    You are not doing well, he cried.
O says bold Robin Hood, here's a tanner so good,
    And I warrant he's tanned my hide.
      Aye, and *etc.*

10. If he's such a tanner, then says Little John,
    A tanner that tans so true,
We'll make no doubt, but we'll have a fresh bout,
    And I warrant he'll tan my hide too.
      Aye, and *etc.*

11. That thing shall not be, says bold Robin Hood,
    For he is a hero so bold;
For he has best played, he is master of his trade,
    And by no man shall he be controlled.
      Aye, and by no man shall he be controlled.

ROBIN HOOD AND THE PEDLAR (132)[24]

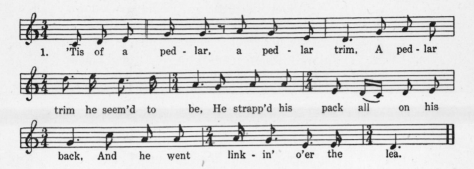

1. 'Tis of a ped-lar, a ped-lar trim, A ped-lar trim he seem'd to be, He strapp'd his pack all on his back, And he went link-in' o'er the lea.

1. 'Tis of a pedlar, a pedlar trim,
      A pedlar trim he seem'd to be,
   He strapp'd his pack all on his back,
      And he went linkin' o'er the lea.

2. He met two men, two troublesome men,
      Two troublesome men they seemed to be,
   And one of them was bold Robin Hood,
      And the other Little John so free.

3. What have you there, cried bold Robin Hood,
      What have you there, pray tell to me?
   I have six robes of the gay green silk,
      And silken bow-strings two or three.

4. If you have six robes of the gay green silk,
      And silken bow-strings two or three,
   Then by my faith, cried bold Robin Hood,
      The half of them belong to me!

5. The pedlar he took off his pack,
      And hung it down low by his knee,
   Saying, the man who beats one three feet from that,
      The pack and all, it shall go free.

6. Bold Robin Hood drew his nut-brown sword,
      The pedlar he drew out his brand,
   They fought until they both did sweat.
      O pedlar, pedlar, stay your hand!

[24] As sung by Mrs. Carrie Grover of Gorham, Maine, to E. K. Wells, May, 1944.

7. Oh fight him, master, cried Little John,
        Oh fight him, master, do not flee!
    Now by my faith, cried the pedlar trim,
        'Tis not to either he or me.

8. What is your name, cried bold Robin Hood,
        What is your name, pray tell to me?
    No, not one word, cried the pedlar trim,
        Till both your names you tell to me.

9. The one of us is bold Robin Hood,
        The other Little John so free.
    Oh now I have it at my good will
        Whether my name I'll tell to thee.

10. I am Gamble Gold of the gay green wood;
        Far far beyond the raging sea,
    I killed a man on my father's land,
        And was forced to leave my own countree.

11. If you're Gamble Gold of the gay green wood,
        Far far beyond the raging sea,
    Now you and I are sisters' sons;
        What nearer cousins can we be?

12. They sheathed their swords with friendly words,
        And so like brothers did agree,
    Then unto an alehouse in the town,
        Where they cracked bottles merrily.

In "Robin Hood and the Pedlar" (132) are traces of *The Tale of
Gamelyn,* a fourteenth century *lai* which was for a time erroneously
included in *The Canterbury Tales,* since Chaucer seems to have had
a copy of it among his papers; and which is one of the sources of
Shakespeare's *As You Like It,* by way of Lodge's *Rosalynde.* Gamelyn,
a fugitive from justice, takes refuge in the forest, and lives an outlaw's
life, involving fights, recognitions of near kin, and reconciliations. He
appears as Young Gamwell in "Robin Hood Newly Reviv'd" (128),
and Gamble Gold in this traditional version of the same ballad. One
is tempted also to identify him with Gandelyn in "Robin and Gandelyn" (115), a ballad which may be another version of the death of
Robin Hood, though Child denies this in his foreword. As a follower
of Robin Hood, Young Gamwell-Gamble Gold becomes Will Scath-
lock or Scarlet. For a review of these various connections, see Skeat,
The Tale of Gamelyn, Introduction, *passim.*

ROBIN HOOD AND THE BISHOP OF HEREFORD (144)[25]

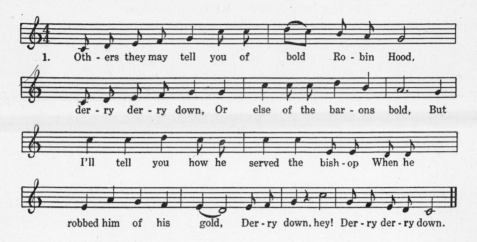

1. Oth - ers they may tell you of bold Ro - bin Hood,
der - ry der - ry down, Or else of the bar - ons bold, But
I'll tell you how he served the bish - op When he
robbed him of his gold, Der - ry down, hey! Der - ry der - ry down.

1. Others may tell you of bold Robin Hood,
Derry, derry down, or else of the barons bold,
But I'll tell you how he served the bishop
When he robbed him of his gold,
Derry down, hey! Derry derry down.

2. Robin Hood he dressed him in shepherd's attire,
Derry, derry down, and six of his men also,
And when the Bishop he did come by,
They around the fire did go.
Derry down, hey! Derry derry down.

3. "We are but poor shepherds," quoth bold Robin Hood,
Derry derry down, "And keep sheep all the year,
But we've resolved to taste today
Of the best of our king's deer."
Derry *etc.*

4. "Thou'rt a merry fellow," the old Bishop said,
Derry derry down, "The king of thy deeds shall know;
Therefore make haste come along with me,
For before the king shalt go."
Derry *etc.*

[25] From *Novello's School Songs* (1908), No. 1323. Reprinted by permission of Novello and Co. Ltd., London.

5. Robin Hood he set then his back to an oak,
Derry derry down, his foot against a thorn,
And underneath from his shepherd's cloak
Pulled out a bugle horn.
Derry *etc.*

6. Robin put the small end against his lips,
Derry derry down, and loudly a blast did blow,
Till full six score of his trusty men
Came a-running on a row.
Derry *etc.*

7. "What's the matter, Master?" says Little John,
Derry derry down, "You call us so hastily."
"Oh, here's the Bishop of Hereford,
For today he passes by."
Derry *etc.*

8. Robin Hood he took then the old Bishop's hand,
Derry derry down, and led him to gay Barnsdale,
And made him sup at his board that night,
Where they drank wine, beer and ale.
Derry *etc.*

9. "Call me in the reck'ning," the Bishop then said,
Derry derry down, "I'm sure it's growing high."
"Lend me your purse, Sir," said Little John,
"I'll tell you by and by."
Derry *etc.*

10. Little John he took then the old Bishop's cloak,
Derry derry down, and spread it upon the ground,
And from the Bishop his portmanteau
He told five hundred pound.
Derry *etc.*

11. Little John he took then the old Bishop's hand,
Derry derry down, and called for the pipes to play,
And made the Bishop to dance in his boots;
He went gladly so his way.
Derry down, hey! Derry derry down.

Chapter 2

HISTORICAL BALLADS

WE turn to this branch of the ballad tree with more definite information about our sources than in the case of Robin Hood ballads. For one thing, we have evidence since the early Middle Ages of the folk practice of turning actual events into some kind of narrative form for circulation. The twelfth-century chroniclers allude to popular songs about famous deeds, passed on by word of mouth. These early songs may not have been ballads as we know them, but by the time the minstrels began to capitalize upon popular taste, in the fourteenth century, they undoubtedly adopted some existing ballad form for their recounting of the glories of the past or the news of the day. They were professional newsmongers, as were the broadside ballad writers who followed them. From 1550 to 1700 the news ballad, printed and sold on the city streets, was the newspaper of the day. Subsequent reference to the peddling of news ballads is continuous. A later chapter will discuss this aspect of ballads in some detail.[1] Our present concern is with those ballads, which, based in the first instance upon actual occurrences of some public significance, and following an ancient pattern, have passed into tradition and are still to be found in the repertoires of traditional singers.

Some twenty-four ballads in Child's collection are clearly connected with events or persons of history.[2] These clearly historical ballads indicate a somewhat wider point of view than that of the singer of the Robin Hood tales, a consciousness of a nation rather than of groups within it. In "Gude Wallace" (157), "Flodden Field" (168), "King Henry V's Conquest of France" (164), and "The Hunting of the Cheviot" (162), for instance, there is patriotic pride in the valor of a national hero. As accurate accounts most of these ballads are quite untrustworthy: about the figure of William Wallace, for example, a great deal of apocryphal anecdote has accumulated which the ballads reflect; there is no foundation in fact for the ballad account of the

---

[1] See page 211 ff.   [2] *English and Scottish Popular Ballads*, Nos. 156–81.

death of Queen Jane Seymour. On the other hand, some ballads are truer to fact than the chronicle accounts. In "Johnny Armstrong" (169) the king's perfidy, glossed over in some of the prose accounts, is brought fully to light; many sixteenth- and seventeenth-century news ballads written immediately after the event caught up details lost in later accounts, and are therefore important contemporary documents. As told in "A newe ballade, declarying the daungerous shootyng of the Gunne at Courte," the story of the ill-fated Thomas Appletree is far more lively than Stow's account.[3]

Other ballads deal obliquely with the event, by allusion or selection of some aspect for highlighting. In their drift away from historical veracity human sympathy with the situation is the most potent traditional force. In some, folk emphasis has dwelt so strongly on the human aspect of the story that most if not all of the connection with the original incident has disappeared. Thus in "The Death of Queen Jane" (170) we have the pathos of a mother's death in childbirth, in "Mary Hamilton" (173) the eternally poignant appeal of a girl put to death far from home. "The Bonny House of Airlie" (199) and "The Bonny Earl of Murray" (181) have lost completely their historical or political significance, salvaging only bits of the older ballads which are now charged with emotion and treated with lyric allusiveness. Furthest of all from fact is such a ballad as "The Merry Golden Tree," a version of "The Golden Vanity" (286), in which not even a name remains to suggest its former connection with Sir Walter Raleigh. Only by comparing recent traditional versions with the earlier manuscripts or broadsides is it to be identified.

Since more historical than Robin Hood ballads have passed into tradition, we can observe in them the changes brought about, in the varying of structure, shortening as parts are forgotten or omitted because they are no longer understood, and blurring of outlines as time and place lose significance. The well-joined, fully motivated tale is less frequent. In general, interest centers upon gossip and old wives' tales rather than facts. The result, however, is always a good story.

While they do not belong strictly in this study, the many outcroppings of historical memory in folk song are added proof of the popular preservation of events. The theory that history is behind most of our nursery rhymes has been carried to fantastic if fascinating lengths,[4] but

[3] See below, page 219.   [4] See below, Chapter 6.

there is much to support the view that political cartoons have often
been incorporated into existing popular songs. Such a passage occurs
in the processional sung by the townspeople of Helston in Cornwall
as they dance through the town every seventh of May, a song that is a
hodge-podge of topical jokes, forgotten romance, folklore, and
rhythmic dance song. One stanza harks back to Henry V and the
Battle of Agincourt. "Being made by the folk, it naturally took no
heed of the prohibition attributed by Holinshed to King Henry: 'He
would not suffer any Ditties to be made of his glorious victorie.'" [5]

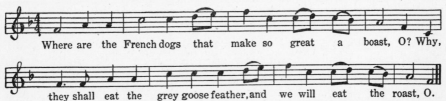

Where are the French dogs that make so great a boast, O? Why,
they shall eat the grey goose feather, and we will eat the roast, O.

KING HENRY V's CONQUEST OF FRANCE (164)[6]

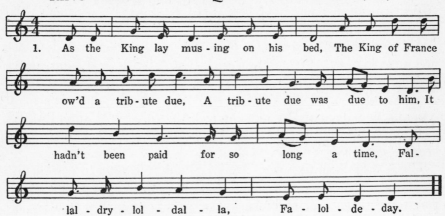

1. As the King lay mus-ing on his bed, The King of France
ow'd a trib-ute due, A trib-ute due was due to him, It
hadn't been paid for so long a time, Fal-
lal-dry-lol-dal-la, Fa-lol-de-day.

> 1. As the King lay musing on his bed,
>   The King of France ow'd a tribute due,
>   A tribute due was due to him,
>   It hadn't been paid for so long a time,
>   Fa-lal-dry-lol-dal-la,
>   Fa-lol-de-day.

[5] Greene, *The Early English Carols*, pp. ciii–civ. Tune from Sharp, *Morris Dance
Tunes*, IX, 18.

[6] From Henry, *Folk-Songs from the Southern Highlands* (1938), p. 106. Reprinted
by permission of J. J. Augustin, New York, Publisher.

2. He called for his lovely page,
His lovely page then called he;
Saying, "You must go to the King of France,
To the King of France, sir, ride speedily."
Fal-lal, *etc.*

3. O then went away this lovely page,
This lovely page then away went he,
And when he came to the King of France,
Low he fell down on his bending knee.
Fal-lal, *etc.*

4. "My master greets you, worthy sir,
Ten tons of gold that is due to he,
That you will send him his tribute home,
Or in French land you soon will him see."
Fal-lal, *etc.*

5. "Your master's young and of tender years,
Not fitten to come into my degree,
And I will send him three tennis balls,
That with them he may learn to play."
Fal-lal, *etc.*

6. Oh, then returned this lovely page,
This lovely page then returned he,
And when he came to our gracious king,
Low he fell down on his bending knee.
Fal-lal, *etc.*

7. "What news, what news, you brung to me?
What news you brung to me?"
"No news, no news," says he,
"For with its news you'll never agree.
Fal-lal, *etc.*

8. "He says you're young and of tender years,
Not fitten to come into his degree;
And he will send you three tennis balls,
That with them you may learn to play."
Fal-lal, *etc.*

9. "Not a married man,
Not a widow's son;
Nor a widow's curse shan't go with me."

. . . .

10. And then we marched into French land,
    With drums and trumps so merrily;
    And bespeaks the king of France:
    "Yonder comes proud King Henery."
        Fal-lal, *etc.*

11. The first shot that the Frenchmen gave,
    They killed our Englishmen so free;
    We killed ten thousand of the French,
    And the rest of them they ran away.
        Fal-lal-dry-lol-dal-la,
        Fa-lol-de-day.

Whilest in the Lent season the King laie at Killingworth, there came to him from Charles Dolphin of France certeine ambassadors, that brought with them a barrell of Paris balles, which from their maister they presented to him for a token that was taken in verie ill part, as sent in scorne, to signifie, that it was more meet for the king to passe the time with such childish exercise, than to attempt any worthie exploit. Wherefore the K. wrote to him, that yer ought long, he would tosse him some London balles that perchance should shake the walles of the best court in France.[7]

Holinshed in his *Chronicles* thus eternizes an incident that passed into much contemporary record. Child dates his version of the story from the early eighteenth century, but conjectures that it is based upon an earlier one. Our traditional version is very close to Child's except for the telescoping of the final stanzas about the battle of Agincourt. A naïve reasoning has applied literally the phrase "laie (at Killingworth)," the usual term for the court on progress, to the king "as he lay musing on his bed." It has also assumed the king's "young and tender years," although Henry was really eight years older than the Dauphin. In the historical account, therefore, the insult of the tennis balls was greater, implying in the king a childishness ill suited to his years. Ball-playing in ballads is so much a commonplace that a singer would find it natural to incorporate the reference here. We recall other tennis balls in popular literature, the one sent in scorn by Alexander to Darius, another offered in a different spirit by the shepherds at the manger, in *The Second Shepherds' Play*. The recent discovery of a tennis ball lodged in the rafters of Westminster Hall in London reminds us of the antiquity of the game. It is thought to be a matter

[7] Holinshed, *Chronicles* (Richard II, Henry IV, Henry V), III, 64.

of centuries since tennis was played there. Possibly some form of this ballad, as well as Holinshed's account, was running in Shakespeare's head when he gave his young King Henry the words:

> When we have match'd our rackets to these balls,
> We will in France, by God's grace, play a set
> Shall strike his father's crown into the hazard.[8]

The ballad seems to be an accidental rather than a popular survival, for the theme is not generally appealing. Accidental too was the finding of this version, which illustrates the unexpected turns in the path of a song collector. Mellinger Henry writes of the circumstances:

> In the summer of 1928, some traditional ballads had been recorded from the singing of members of the Harmon family of Cades Cove, Tennessee. Others were taken down by individuals of the family and forwarded by mail. . . . Meanwhile this entire family of Tennessee Mountaineers was compelled to sell their property holdings to the Great Smoky National Park Commission, and to remove to the mountains of Georgia. Though rather inaccessible and somewhat isolated, a visit to their new abode was contemplated by the writer during the summer of 1930 for the purpose of recording a promised version of "The Gypsie Laddie." Then the unexpected happened. On the writer's return from a camping trip to Thunderhead the entire family suddenly appeared at Cades Cove for a visit. "Uncle" Sam Harmon and his wife, "Aunt" Polly, spent the best part of two days singing at the mountain cabin of the writer.[9]

Some twenty-four ballads, many of them Child pieces, were taken down at this time. This was the first recording of "King Henry" in America. In the following year a version was found in Vermont.[10]

The ballad is included here as a rare piece, in spite of the fact that some features of the notation are unsatisfactory for singing. In the second measure, for instance, the text and melody do not scan together. A recording from the same singer was made ten years later than Mr. Henry's, by Herbert Halpert (Library of Congress record 2903 A2 and A3), but in the interval the old man's memory of both words and tune had failed, and the result is a fragment which is of little help. The Vermont version is likewise musically irregular.

[8] Shakespeare, *King Henry the Fifth*, I, ii.
[9] Henry, *op. cit.*, p. 106. For a discussion of collectors' luck, see page 266.
[10] See Flanders, *The New Green Mountain Songster*, p. 192.

THE DEATH OF QUEEN JANE (170)[11]

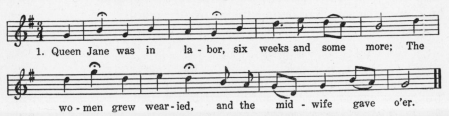

1. Queen Jane was in la-bor, six weeks and some more; The wo-men grew wear-ied, and the mid-wife gave o'er.

1. Queen Jane was in labor six weeks and some more;
   The women grew wearied, and the midwife gave o'er.

2. O women, kind women, I take you to be,
   Just pierce my right side open, and save my baby.

3. Oh no, said the women, that never could be;
   I'll send for King Henry, in the time of your need.

4. King Henry was sent for, on horseback and speed;
   King Henry he reached her, in the hour of her need.

5. King Henry he come and he bent o'er her bed:
   What's the matter with my flower, makes her eyes look so red?

6. Oh Henry, kind Henry, pray listen to me,
   And pierce my right side open and save my baby.

7. Oh no, said King Henry, That never could be,
   I would lose my sweet flower to save my baby.

8. Queen Jane she turned over, and fell in a swound,
   And her side was pierced open, and the baby was found.

9. The baby were christened all on the next day;
   But the mother's poor body lay cold as the clay.

10. So black was the mourning, so yellow was the bed,
    So costly was the white robe Queen Jane was wrapped in.

11. Six men wore their robes, four carrying her along;
    King Henry followed after, with his black mourning on.

12. King Henry he wept till his hands was wrung sore.
    The flower of England will flourish no more.

13. And the baby were christened all on the next day,
    And it's mother's poor body lying mouldering away.

[11] From Sharp, *English Folk Songs from the Southern Appalachians* (1932), I, 230.
Reprinted by permission of the Oxford University Press, London.

It is probable that the death of Queen Jane Seymour, the third wife of Henry VIII, twelve days after the birth of Edward VI, was due to overexertion demanded by the festive formalities marking the rejoicing at the arrival of the long-desired male heir to the throne. However, the story of the Caesarian operation arose very soon after her death. Here it is told with such affecting simplicity and realism that a certain amount of artistic, if not factual truth emerges. As the Appalachian singer of this ballad said to Cecil Sharp, "Hit must be true because hit's so purty." The human appeal of the situation is made the most of, and, contrary to the royal father's probable attitude at the time, the loss of the wife has become more important than the saving of the child. This mountain version suggests a singer who knows the perils of childbirth in faraway places, the gathering of "the good women," the hasty sending for the father, and the efforts of the primitive midwife. The "fine Flower of England" has become the mountain lover's tender epithet:

> What's the matter with my flower,
> Makes her eyes look so red?

The solemn royal burial cortege has its parallel in the homely train which winds up to the hillside graveyard from a mountain cabin. The tragedy of the mountains has long been death in childbirth, and this ballad is the threnody of a familiar sorrow.

MARY HAMILTON (173)[12]

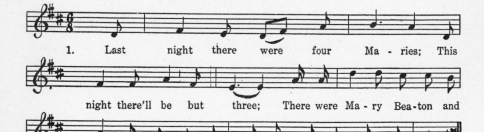

1. Last night there were four Maries; This night there'll be but three; There were Mary Beaton and Mary Seaton and Mary Carmichael and me.

1. Last night there were four Maries;
   This night there'll be but three;

[12] From Smith and Rufty, *An American Anthology of Old-World Ballads* (1937), p. 42. Reprinted by permission of J. Fischer, New York, Publishers.

  There were Mary Beaton and Mary Seaton
   And Mary Carmichael and me.

2. Oh, often have I dressed my Queen
   And put gold upon her hair,
  But now I've gotten for my reward
   The gallows to be my share.

3. Last night I dressed Queen Mary,
   And put on her braw silk gown,
  And all the thanks I've got this night
   Is to be hanged in Edinboro Town.

4. They'll tie a kerchief around my eyes,
   They'll no let me see to die;
  But they'll never tell my father and mother
   But that I'm away o'er the sea.

5. I charge ye all ye sailors,
   When ye sail o'er the foam,
  Let neither my father nor mother know
   But that I'm coming home.

6. Oh, little did my mother think,
   The day she cradled me,
  The lands I was to travel in,
   Or the death I was to die.

7. Last night there were four Maries,
   This night there'll be but three,
  There were Mary Beaton and Mary Seaton,
   And Mary Carmichael and me.

"The Queen's Maries" or "Mary Hamilton" (173) is included here because of its connection with the court of Mary Stuart. Its many variants—over forty counting Child's and those since discovered—prove its wide dispersion, and illustrate some of the more fascinating bypaths of ballad research.

If the story of Mary Hamilton arose from court scandal and gossip, there was every reason for its popular circulation as a ballad, for every bit of news in those days was balladed; [13] if the court was not its source, it was just the sort of story that would be attached in time to some prominent person. The disposal of an unwanted infant is always a sensational theme, and that it should crop up in this time and place is

[13] See page 211.

not surprising. Mary's court was a world of rumor and intrigue, romantic and political. Queen Elizabeth's agent wrote almost daily to London, including in his dispatches the idlest stories, the smallest details,
as straws showing the wind's direction. About Mary's person rumors
were especially rife. When she was ill of a cold at Loch Leven, was
that the true reason for her indisposition, or merely a cloak for the
fact that she had been delivered of a child? [14] What is the truth behind
the story told today by guides of Edinburgh Castle, that workmen
found, in the walls near Mary's apartments, an infant skeleton wrapped
in a fine cloth? What may be conjectured from the resemblance between pictures of the young James and the son of the Countess of
Mar, his foster-mother? [15] Any story remotely connected with an heir
to the throne of Scotland, and therefore England, would produce so
many offshoots and self-sowings that almost immediately a whole crop
of versions might be gathered. The story told in this ballad has every
element making for popular reproduction and distortion.

This ballad is called with equal freedom "The Queen's Maries" and
"Mary Hamilton." The puzzle has been to identify this particular
Mary. "The Queen's Maries" of history were her four ladies in waiting,
Mary Seaton, Mary Beaton, Mary Fleming and Mary Livingstone.
They were chosen as little girls to attend the young princess to France
when she was six, were her companions there, and returned with her
to Scotland in 1561. About their careers there is nothing of the nature
of the ballad story recorded, although John Knox, who continuously
hurled his Calvinist thunderbolts at Catholic Mary's court, writes that
"shame hasted the marriage betwix John Semple, called the Dancer,
and Mary Livingstone, surnamed the Lusty; what bruit the Maries and
the rest of the dancers of the court had, the ballads of the age did
witness." [16] But the Maries of the ballad are persistently Seaton,
Beaton, Carmichael, and Hamilton. Where did these last two come
from? A Mary Carmichael of the times married a John Hamilton of
Preston, and a "Mlle Hamilton, fille du gouverneur d'Ecosse," attended
Mary in France, but her name was not Mary, and neither she nor the
other Mary was involved in scandal.[17]

A hundred and fifty years after the time of Mary Stuart there was a

[14] Gorman, *The Scottish Queen*, p. 253, note.
[15] Largely discounted by Steeholm, *James I of England*, p. 41.
[16] John Knox, *History of the Reformation*, II, 415–16.
[17] Henderson, *The Ballad in Literature*, p. 103.

Miss Hamilton, whose story was that of the ballad. In 1719 this lady, who was attached to the court of Peter the Great of Russia, was executed for putting away her illegitimate child, whose father was a Russian officer of high rank.[18] For a long time ballad scholars, including Child at one time, believed that Mary Hamilton appeared in the ballad as a later grafting from the Russian affair onto the Scottish stock, since no version using the name of Hamilton could be found which antedated the Russian incident. Against this it was argued from literary evidence that by 1725 the ballad had a wide circulation in Scotland, and that six years was too short a time to have sent the story of the Russian Miss Hamilton to the four corners of the Scottish ballad world; furthermore, the style of "Mary Hamilton" was clearly earlier than that of the eighteenth century; so that all the "Hamilton" versions in circulation before 1725 must represent an earlier story.[19]

Now from the records of Mary Stuart's times we read: "The Queen's apothecary got one of her maidens, a French woman, with child. Thinking to cover his fault with medicine the child was slain." [20] A few days later the offenders were removed from their prison and publicly hanged, and the affair had a thorough airing. Child's conversion to belief in this incident as the source of the ballad came when he found in Sir Walter Scott's Abbotsford Papers a text with a stanza agreeing with the record:

> My love he was a pottinger (apothecary),
> Mony drink he gave to me,
> And a' to put back that bonnie babe,
> But alas, it wad na do.[21]

The singer of this version was an old lady in 1804, and since most singers learn their ballads when they are young, we may assume that the "pottinger" version was current at least by 1750, and had perhaps been in circulation for some time, developing independently of any faraway Russian story. The waiting-woman has become a lady-in-waiting in the ballad, just as "the highest Stuart" (Darnley) has evolved from "the highest steward" (the apothecary). It may incidentally be

---

[18] Maidment, *Scottish Ballads and Songs*, II, 19 ff.

[19] Lang, "The Mystery of the Queen's Marie," *Blackwood's Magazine*, CLVIII (September 1895), 381.

[20] Thomas Randolph, Queen Elizabeth's agent, writing to London. Quoted by Child, *English and Scottish Popular Ballads*, V, 298.

[21] Child, *op. cit.*, IV, 509, "Mary Hamilton" (173), U-version.

added that in other ballads "Mary" is a commonplace for an attendant. In "Brown Robin" (97) the heroine, Lady Mary, has "seven maries in her bower." Perhaps Mary Stuart had started a fashion of naming one's attendants for oneself. Or perhaps "Mary" may be a corruption for "Maiden" (Maid, May), which has been confused with Virgin Mary, who was a maid. Indeed, in some versions of our ballad the heroine is addressed as "Mary Mild," an epithet for the Virgin.[22]

The argument over the Russo-Scottish origin of this ballad is now a matter of literary history, and its interest for us at this point lies in the light it throws on the mingling in a traditional ballad of many elements. The fact would seem to be that a series of folk singers, picking up the gossip and rumor of Mary's court, combined into one story the authentic Maries, other ladies bearing famous Scottish names who might or might not be named Mary and about whom scandal was whispered though not recorded, and the Queen's French waiting-woman (confused with lady-in-waiting), whose tragic affair with the apothecary was a matter of fact and record.

The ballad, as it has been recently recovered in Scotland and America, has shrunk to four or five stanzas, the "four Maries" lines, and the lament of a girl dying in a foreign country for a crime she hopes her parents will never know about. A Scotchwoman who sang the song to me recently knew only these verses, and gave one reason for the loss of the rest: "My parents were so pauky,[23] they never told me the whole story." Certainly moral distaste would lead to censorship in singing to children. A better reason, however, is suggested by familiarity with folk practice. The remaining verses carry the strongest note of emotional appeal. It is in line with the traditional process to drop out those parts of a story which fix it too closely to definite place, time, and persons, and to save those parts which need no setting. The human and the pathetic are selected by tradition, and sympathy with the victim, no matter how guilty, is a popular response.

[22] Child, *op. cit.*, III, 396, N-version; Greig, *Last Leaves of Traditional Ballads and Ballad Airs*, p. 108.
[23] "*Pauky*—of a sly humor, wise, witty, cautious, discreet, and insinuating, all in one" (*New English Dictionary*). There is no English synonym.

THE MERRY GOLDEN TREE
(The Golden Vanity, 286)[24]

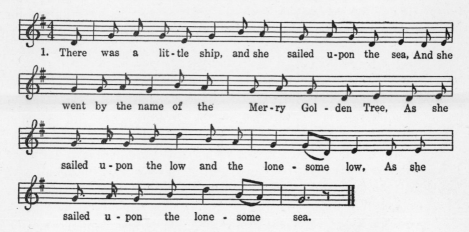

1. There was a lit-tle ship, and she sailed u-pon the sea, And she went by the name of the Mer-ry Gol - den Tree, As she sailed u-pon the low and the lone - some low, As she sailed u - pon the lone - some sea.

1. There was a little ship, and she sailed upon the sea,
   And she went by the name of the Merry Golden Tree.
   As she sailed upon the low and the lonesome low,
   As she sailed upon the lonesome sea.

2. There was another ship, and she sailed upon the sea,
   And she went by the name of the Turkish Robberie,
   As she sailed, *etc.*

3. There was a little sailor unto his captain said,
   Oh captain, Oh captain, what will you give to me,
   If I sink them in the low, *etc.*

4. Two hundred dollars I'll give unto you,
   And my oldest daughter I will wed unto you,
   If you sink them, *etc.*

5. He bowed upon his breast and away swam he,
   Till he came to the ship of the Turkish Robberie,
   As she sailed, *etc.*

6. Then out of his pocket an instrument he drew,
   And he bored nine holes for to let the water through,
   As she sailed, *etc.*

[24] As sung by children in the Pine Mountain Settlement School, Pine Mountain, Harlan County, Kentucky, to E. K. Wells, 1916.

7. Oh some had hats and some had caps,
  And they tried for to stop them awful water-gaps
  As she sailed, *etc.*

8. He bowed upon his back and away swam he,
  Till he came to the ship of the Merry Golden Tree,
  As she sailed, *etc.*

9. Oh captain, Oh captain, won't you take me on board,
  Oh captain, Oh captain, won't you be as good as your word,
  For I've sunk them, *etc.*

10. Oh no, I will neither take you on board,
  Oh no, I will neither be as good as my word,
  For I'm sailing, *etc.*

11. If it weren't for the love of your daughter and your men,
  I would do unto you as I done unto them,
  I would sink you, *etc.*

12. He bowed upon his breast and down sank he,
  Farewell, farewell to the Merry Golden Tree,
  For I'm sinking in the low and the lonesome low,
  For I'm sinking in the lonesome sea.

This ballad, recovered in many parts of America, has passed from the broadside version (Child, 286) into tradition, losing on the way all reference to the alleged incident connected with Sir Walter Raleigh, and acquiring a romantic note in the denouement.

Chapter 3

BORDER RAID BALLADS

THE center of the British ballad world has always been the Scottish
Border. Everything conjoins in its favor—its topography, its history, its
social economy, and its poetic tradition. Even the discovery of America's hoard, while adding greatly to our knowledge of the processes of
tradition, cannot detract from the importance of the Border as the
home of ballad makers, singers, and collectors. Indeed, our appreciation of our own ballads is in proportion to our familiarity with the
Border as a background for them. The romantic ballads, which throve
so heartily in the Yarrow and Ettrick region of the Border, have survived in great abundance in America and form indeed the core of our
older songs. While few of the Border Raid ballads have come to America, their type has doubtless inspired many of our indigenous songs.
Moreover, life in our own chief ballad country, the Southern Appalachians, bears many likenesses to that of the Border. A brief discussion
of the Border Country and its economy will then not be alien to this
study.

THE BORDER COUNTRY

"The Border" comprises on the English side the counties of Northumberland and Cumberland, on the Scottish side Berwick, Roxburgh,
Dumfries, Peebles, and Selkirkshire. This was a country cut off from
north and south, and it developed a strong sense of physical and cultural integrity. Symbolic of its isolation is the Roman Wall. One cannot follow its length from Newcastle to Carlisle, or drive the fifteen
miles from Hexham to Housesteads, without a sense of the significance
of that great barrier flung across the waist of Britain to keep the northern tribes from descent upon the part of the island which Rome had
won and civilized. While the mind is stirred by the thought of the
teeming life of the regiments once stationed along the Wall—its busy
trade, its baths, its temples and towns and garrisons, its complete

55

development of a transplanted foreign civilization—this very completeness emphasizes the fact that here civilization halted; here was the
jumping-off place. Our greater interest, however, is in the Wall as a
barrier that kept the north to itself, continuing its ancient life comparatively untouched by southern influences.

The moors on either side of the Wall form a sort of no-man's land
suspending us between two worlds; there is a neutrality in those wide
spaces which prepares the mind for new impacts. Washington Irving
writes of the "grey waving hills, monotonous in their aspect, and so
destitute of trees that one could see a stout fly walking along their
profile." [1] The entire country was wooded once, and Ettrick Forest,
now a sweep of bare upland with only stunted growth along the upper
water, was a royal chase in the sixteenth century.

> Etrick forest is a fair foreste,
>   In it grows manie a semelie trie;
> The hart, the hynd, the dae, the rae,
>   And of a' [wylde] beastis grete plentie. [2]

In Meggatdale King James V killed "aughteine score of deir" on his
periodic circuit to round up robbers and outlaws. Indeed, the king's
hunt was a ruse for assembling his best soldiers for the capture of
Johnny Armstrong (169). Even allowing for ballad exaggeration, the
hunt must have swept like an army across the country. In performing
his vow to kill "the fattiste hartes in all Cheviat," the audacious Percy
took with him

> fifteen hondrith archares bold off blood and bone;
> the wear chosen owt of shyars thre, [3]

But now those wooded hills are cleared and rounded, and look like
arrested waves, particularly in the spring when the land is softly green.
One is near the sky, too, as at sea. Later in the summer, green grass
becomes "the bent sae brown," and the heather turns purple, adding
richness and depth to the color. When one has traversed this wild
open moorland from the Wall to the top of Carter Bar, no-man's land
is left behind and the heart of the Border Country is spread out like a
map beneath one's eye. The high Cheviots form the vantage point

[1] Quoted by Gwynn, *Life of Sir Walter Scott*, p. 254.
[2] "The Outlaw Murray" (305).
[3] "The Hunting of the Cheviot" (162).

from which one looks north across hills decreasing in height to the valleys of Jed, Tweed, and Teviot. Barren grandeur at the headwaters gives way to grace and intimacy at the confluence of the streams, where trees and cultivated land afford a grateful variety. Of this country's charm no outlander can speak with the affection of a true Borderer like John Buchan:

> There is a graciousness there, a mellow habitable charm, unlike the harsh Gothic of most Scots landscape. . . . My chief passion in those years was the Border countryside, and my whole object was to reproduce its general charm, to catch the aroma of its gracious landscape and turbulent history and the idiom of its people. When I was absent from it I was homesick, my memory was full of it, my happiest days were associated with it, and some effluence from its ageless hills was laid like a spell on me, which has never been broken. I found in its people what I most admired in human nature. . . . I asked for nothing better than to spend my life by the Tweed.[4]

It was natural that this wanderer from his native Tweed, when he was ennobled by a grateful government, should assume the name of Tweedsmuir.

BORDER HISTORY

Even in those parts which are deserted today, this was a country of continuous habitation from prehistoric times, as the ancient hill forts and cave dwellings along the river courses bear witness. For several centuries even after the Romans evacuated Britain it was the home of the Cymric Celts, their last stronghold against the advancing hordes of Picts from the north and Angles from the east. Ancient names for physical characteristics of the country persist in abundance: a hill is a law, bank, dod, sware, house, fell, or rig; a wood is a shaw, dean, or field; a valley is a hope or dale. The Danish occupation has left its traces in the physical appearance of the race living there today, in many of the words they still use, and in the kinship of their culture with that of Scandinavia.

From the early Middle Ages the Border was "the soul of romance, but the bane of good government." [5] Trouble was never-ceasing;

[4] Buchan, *Pilgrim's Way*, pp. 25, 34. Copyright, 1940, by Lady Susan Caroline Tweedsmuir.

[5] Wingfield-Stratford, *History of British Civilization*, I, 407.

there was a permanent state of private warfare and looting. Because of its natural barriers and the ferocious independence of the Border dwellers, the difficulty of policing was great, the homes of the marauding families serving as beacon stations to spread the alarm if outsiders approached. With England to the south, and the wild Highland clans to the north as enemies, the borderers, though constantly at war with each other, made common cause against all foreigners. Thus there runs through all the history, literature, and oral tradition of the Border a continuous sombre note of treachery, murder, cruelty, barbarity—and romantic loyalty.

By the end of the thirteenth century a strong anti-English sentiment had centralized in the Tweed valley, bred of resentment against the English driven thither from Northumbria by the Normans pushing from the south of England. From 1298 to 1342, when the outbreak of the Hundred Years' War withdrew English attention from Scotland, there was continuous fighting. Edward I conquered the Scots, led by William Wallace; in seven years they rose again under Robert the Bruce. Edward II, troubled by his barons at home, could not maintain his strength in the north, and one by one the great Scottish strongholds were regained by Bruce. Later Edward III won back Berwick. A new period of hostilities broke out in 1513. Henry VIII was in France meeting the Emperor Charles at the Field of the Cloth of Gold; his consort Catherine of Aragon was left in command in England. James IV of Scotland, Henry's brother-in-law, hoping to take England unawares, seized the moment to march across the border, but was killed and his forces utterly routed by the English at Flodden Field, a victory celebrated in the ballad of that name. This gave the English the upper hand, and by the time of the Reformation Cromwell's men were continually harrying the Border and passing through with treasure seized in their raids on the rich abbeys of Tweed and Teviot. Another overwhelming defeat of the Scots came in 1542 at Solway Moss, and another in five years at Pinkie.

All this major activity was reflected in Border skirmishes which on a minor scale duplicated the war between Scotland and England. Family and intraborder feuds kept ancient loyalties and jealousies in a ferment. In the regency of the Earl of Murray, just before Mary Stuart returned to Scotland, the Border was reduced to comparative peace, but Mary's reign, with the Darnley and Bothwell marriages, stirred the local chieftains anew as feeling in all Scotland raged high, and as the claim of James VI to the English throne made the Border counties newly important to England. Upon his accession James made an attempt to subdue the fierceness of feeling, but little change occurred, for London was too distant, and Edinburgh, though nearer, was still distrustful of England. A beginning, however, had been made; the tide of mutual hatred began very slowly to abate. But the alien feeling founded on such different ancestries and cultures and fomented by such a long period of lawlessness and bloodshed was never completely outworn, and was occasionally fed anew, as in the Jacobite uprisings of the eighteenth century. For the Scot even today a major calamity is "as bad as Flodden," and he thinks of England as a foreign country. John Buchan is again the best exponent of this attitude, as he recalls with some humor his youthful feeling of shyness and distrust, and his unwilling acceptance of the fact that he was a Briton as well as a Scot:

> The history of Scotland, of which we alone had much knowledge, was to us not a legend but a living memory. . . . Brooding over Scottish history made us intense patriots of the narrowest school. Against our little land there had always stood England, vast, menacing, cruel. We resented the doings of Edward I, Henry VIII, and Elizabeth as personal wrongs. . . . Even as we grew older, and intolerance abated, England remained for us a foreign place, not too friendly, to be suspected and even dreaded. . . . I looked forward, therefore, to visiting this sinister and fascinating land with some forboding. The thing happened when I was seventeen, when, on a bicycle, I crossed the bridge of the Tweed at Coldstream and explored a strip of Northumberland. I entered England with the traveller's mingled sense of insecurity and distinction. To my surprise I found it very like my own countryside. The people spoke with almost my own accent. The bent and heather were like my own domestic hills. . . . The burns were in no way different.[6]

BORDER LIFE

The clan organization of the Border families in the sixteenth and seventeenth centuries, the time of the Border Raid ballads, centered around the chain of strongholds built along the river courses of Lid, Teviot, Yarrow, Ettrick, and Tweed, strongholds commanding a wide reach of territory and within beacon-hail of one another. The Border

[6] Buchan, op. cit., pp. 39, 40. Copyright, 1940, by Lady Susan Caroline Tweedsmuir.

peel [7] was usually built on the site of a more ancient dwelling. It was a strongly constructed stone tower of three stories, with a courtyard providing picketing for horses and cattle, and huts for retainers. The lowest story was a storeroom and stable, the second and third served as family apartments. The roof was used as a lookout station, a retreat, and a sort of rough terrace where the women of the household might take the air. Sometimes a rude hut was built there for the watchman. From the outer wall of a corner turret swung a huge iron basket in which coils of tarred rope were kept, ready to be touched into flame as a signal of danger. By means of this bale-fire, or need-fire,[8] the whole countryside could be aroused with almost telegraphic speed, the signal running from tower to tower at the warning of enemy approach. Thousands could be mobilized in the course of a night, and the intruder, when he arrived, met a thoroughly prepared resistance. In the Middle Ages the peel was the only dwelling, but by the sixteenth century many border lairds had built a more comfortable addition, not so heavily fortified, and retired to the peel only as a refuge. In general the English borderer lived in more comfort than his Scots neighbor; he was by nature and inheritance more dependent upon man-made protection from weather and enemy. The Scottish borderer, with his greater trust in natural barriers and hiding places, went on the theory that "it was better to hear the lark sing than the mouse cheep."

Although many Border peels·still stand, hardly a one is today in a condition to demonstrate the mode of life that went on within its walls. Branxholm Hall near Hawick, built in the typical fashion, is still the residence of the laird. Castle Doune, though north of Stirling and hardly a Border keep, has been somewhat restored to its sixteenth-century condition by the present owners, so that one may climb safely to the ramparts where Murray's mother looked out, hoping to see him "come sounding through the town." [9] The house of Mary Stuart at Jedburgh is much like a Border peel, being the "bastel hous" around which the town grew up. One climbs the stairs hewn out of the deep stone walls from the granary chamber and soldiers' quarters to the Queen's primitive apartments, ducking under the low doorways, peering out of the narrow slits of windows into the high-walled garden and

[7] Peel—(Cymric) moated fort.
[8] Bale—(AS) funeral pyre; need—(AS) nyd, force, friction.
[9] "The Bonny Earl of Murray" (181).

The Tay from Kinnoul Hill, Perthshire

A Border Peel—Borthwick Castle, Midlothian

BORDER SCENES

apple orchard overlooked by the ruins of Jedburgh Abbey. Here Mary nearly died of the fever resulting from exposure on a wild ride to visit the wounded Bothwell at Hermitage; here for days her nobles and priests were assembled waiting for the end, which seemed indeed to have come when "her majesty became deid and all her memberis cauld, her Eene closit, Mouth fast, and Feit and Armis stiff and cauld"; [10] here in the gardens by the Jed her long convalescence was a prelude to the next dramatic chapter of her life.

But aside from Branxholm, Doune, and Jedburgh, the Border peels are ruinous. Centuries of warfare, in which the owners themselves often followed a scorched-earth system, the marauders' constant use of fire to entrap their foes within the walls, and the eventual development of a more peaceful pastoral and agricultural life, when old feuds were finally quieted and the towers, converted to granaries and stables, fell slowly into ruins, have all set their mark on these once commanding and threatening strongholds. Today one finds an occasional ruin, still rudely dignified in its desolation, stark against the sky in a moorland waste, like Smailsholm near Kelso, or hidden by thickets that grow along a river road, like Goldielands. But even these melancholy suggestions can bring to mind the times when a whole countryside was constantly on the alert, when the bale-fires were within sight of each other, when walls were firm and gates strong.

Life in the Border was determined first of all by family organization, clan connection being a binding obligation and an unquestioned reason for fierce loyalty. The head of the family could command the instant service of all his kin, even the most distant, and the ramifications of this loyalty and its corollary enmity went sometimes beyond blood and dated from ancient debts still repeatedly claimed and paid. A traveler writes of arriving at an inn: "After I had diligently learned and enquired that there was none of any surname that had me in deadly fude, nor none that knew me, I sat downe." [11] The Earl of Surrey writes in 1532 to Henry VIII, "They are the boldest men, and the hotest, that ever I sawe in any nation." [12] Tempers were quick, customs brutal, retaliation a part of the code. Quarrels must be instantly taken

[10] John Leslie, Bishop of Ross, writing from Jedburgh at the time. Quoted by A. and J. Lang, *Highways and Byways in the Border*, p. 110.

[11] Sadler's *State Papers*, Edinburgh, 1809, II, 388. Quoted by Scott, *Minstrelsy of the Scottish Border*, p. 32, note.

[12] Scott, *op. cit.*, p. 72.

up and followed to fatal conclusions, till every drop of blood had been repaid in kind. Allegiance to the clan and all it might entail was symbolized by the baptismal rites of infancy, when the right hand of the male child was sometimes left unchristened, that it might be free to deal unhallowed blows. The child at nurse was not too young to take the oath of vengeance.

In the economy of the Border, wealth consisted of cattle and sheep. Other personal possessions were few. The Border keeps were bare and primitive refuges which might have to be abandoned at any moment. Clan organization was strengthened by a system whereby the rent of the feudal subordinate was paid in labor, corn, or base coin, which was called blackmail, as contrasted to *blanches mailles* or silver. This payment secured protection against the freebooter.

> Gae seek your succour where ye paid blackmail,
> For, man, ye never paid money to me.[13]

The modern sense of the word indicating extortion by means of libel or persecution has developed from the abuse of a system which offered the laird's protection to the small holder.

The boundaries of property were natural barriers rather than fences, and the straying of cattle led to quarrels and retaliating raids in which the clans were aroused. Cattle thieving was a legitimate form of support, dignified sometimes by a place on the family coat of arms. *Phoebe reparabit cornua,* the motto of the Scots of Harden, was the heraldic version of the Border saying, "We'll hae moonlight tonight again." Though he is no longer a cattle thief, today's borderer still says, "Tonight's the night, if the boys are the boys!" The mistress of the house had only to tell her menfolk that the last collop of beef was in the pot, to send them out on a replenishing raid. An amusing picture at Abbotsford shows "The Dish of Spurs" being uncovered at the table as a sign that the larder is bare and the sons of the house must ride again.

THE BORDER RAID BALLADS

Some sixty of Child's 305 ballads tell their tales against this background. They reflect the isolation of the wild moorlands, and the mazes of the back-country routes that baffle the intruder, the rude economy,

[13] "Jamie Telfer in the Fair Dodhead" (190).

the lawless individualism with its barbaric codes and stalwart virtue, the speed and tenseness of life, the internal dissension, and the hatred of England. Interest centers largely upon feats of prowess and valor rather than victory in and for itself, upon the loyalty of the clan rather than relations between individuals, and upon the vigor and zest with which the quarrels are pursued.

The frequent use of place names, while it may at times be quite inaccurate, lends realism: actual burns and waters rise to flood or dry to a trickle; from Mangerton House to Cholerford to Newcastle one may follow the exact route of Jock's deliverers;[14] Jamie Telfer's journey can be traced from point to point, although the knowing disagree about the length of time it would have taken him. Good mouth-filling words these place-names are, aiding not a little the lyric and emotional quality of the ballads as well as lending authenticity.

> On Philiphaugh a fray began,
> At Hairheadwood it ended.[15]

And in a different rhythm,

> Inverey cam doun Deeside, whistlin and playin,
> He was at brave Braikley's yett ere it was dawin.[16]

In "The Lads of Wamphray" (184) the singer takes time out to comment on local characteristics:

> It is the lads of Lethenha
> The greatest rogues among them a'.

> It is the lads of Leverhay
> That drove the Crichton's gier away.

> .   .   .   .

> It is the lads o' the Girthhead
> The diel's in them for pride and gred.

Time of action as well as place is exactly cited:

> The moon was up and the sun was down,
> 'Twas the gryming of a new-fa'n snaw;
> Jamie Telfer has run eight miles barefoot,
> Between Dodhead and Branxholm Ha.[17]

---

[14] "Jock of the Side" (187 B).   [16] "The Baron of Brackley" (203).
[15] "The Battle of Philiphaugh" (202).   [17] "Jamie Telfer" (190).

Action often begins "betwixt the daylight and the dawin." Many
stories belong to the late autumn:

> It was in October the woe began,
>   It lasts for now and aye.[18]

And here is no mere poetic convention, but the natural expression of
the countryman, whose clock is sun-time, and whose calendar is the
harvest:

> It fell about Martinmas
>   When steads were fed wi corn and hay,
> The Captain of Bewcastle said to his lads,
>   We'll into Tiviotdale and seek a prey.[19]

By Martinmas—November 11th—the work of harvest is over, the needs
of cattle and "gier" are met, the barns are full of fodder. Now men
may turn to the pleasure and excitement of life, and go raiding.

Although human relationships are those of the group rather than
the individual, and the stage is at times full of actors, there is plenty
of interplay of personality. A stanza or two will set forth a scene in all
its vividness, with just enough dialogue to enhance it; many a small
drama is played in the space of a few lines:

> 'Now halt, now halt, we needna try't;
>   The day is comd we a' maun die.'

> 'Poor faint-hearted theif!' quo the Laird's Jock,
>   'There'll nae man die but he that's fie.' [20]

With this philosophy the borderer meets every turn of fate. One dies
at the appointed time; the readiness is all. Here is the notorious Hobie
Noble (189), fast bound, being taken through the streets of Carlisle:

> They have tane him up the Ricker-gate;
>   The wives they cast their windows wide,
> And ilka wife to anither can say,
>   That's the man loosd Jock of the Side!

> 'Fy on ye, women, Why ca ye me man?
>   For it's nae man that I'm usd like;
> I'm but like a forfoughen hound,
>   Has been fighting in a dirty syke.'

---

[18] "The Fire of Frendraught" (196 C).   [20] "Jock of the Side" (187 B).
[19] "Jamie Telfer" (190).

Dickie and Jockie Hall set out to rescue their brother Archie from prison, in a tale of epic strength and boasting:

> He's taen the door aye with his foot,
>   And fast he followd it with his knee,
> Till a' the bolts the door hung on,
>   O' the prison-floor he made them flee.
>
> .   .   .   .
>
> Up bespake then Jocky Ha,
>   'Let some of th' prisoner lean on me';
> 'The diel o there,' quo Dicky than,
>   'He's no the wightdom of a flea.' [21]

Stories are told in detail, if not so completely as in the Robin Hood ballads. Here each ballad confines itself to one episode with increased selective power and emphasis, and there is no use of coincident. Plots depend upon wit and audacity, rather than on physical endurance, though that also is greatly admired. And although a man must "dree his weird" and meet his appointed fate, his own ingenuity plays an important role. Ruse and trickery are part of the game: horses are shod backward, disguise is often used. There is a sense of lusty enjoyment in every trick, such as Dick's clever outwitting of the powerful Armstrongs and his out-bargaining of the Laird's Jock and the Bailiff of Carlisle.[22] Dick, for all his reputation as a poor simpleton, comes off pretty well. He loses in the beginning three cows and three coverlets, and gains in the end three horses, two of which he sells for thirty pounds and a milch cow apiece; and then prudently withdraws to another part of the country for the rest of his life.

Circumstantial detail is important. The tree felled to scale the walls of Newcastle jail is "o'er three ells laigh" in meeting the specifications; we know that the Spanish irons that hold Jock of the Side prisoner weigh "full fifteen stane" or 210 pounds.[23] A bit of very natural carelessness puts the key to the Armstrong stables in Dick's hands: if you didn't come promptly when the dinner-bell rang, at that house, you went hungry till the next meal, so

> The lads, that hungry and aevery was,
>   Above the door-head they flang the key;

[21] "Archie o Cawfield" (188).
[22] "Dick of the Cow" (185).
[23] "Jock of the Side" (187 B).

> Dicky took good notice to that;
>   Says, There's a bootie younder for me.[24]

Jock, released from his irons, is bidden to show his agility after confinement in prison by jumping across the back of his horse. He shows it, indeed, by jumping across five horses at once.[25] Hobie Noble for reasons of prudence refuses an escort of more than five, and thus his great daring is implied in his setting out with a small force.[26] Such incidental touches scattered throughout the ballads promote the sense of joyful recklessness in adventure.

The Border code of revenge for wrongs is the usual theme. Retaliation is the excuse for indulging in a good fight, and this instinct cannot be instilled too early in life. Johnny Armstrong, foully betrayed by his king, leaves behind him a worthy offspring:

> O then bespoke his little son,
>   As he was set on his nurse's knee:
> 'If ever I live for to be a man,
>   My father's blood revenged shall be.' [27]

Revenge is limited by the code, however. Dick may not ride for redress without his laird's permission:

> 'To give thee leave, my fool,' he says,
>   'Thou speaks against mine honour and me;
> Unless thou give me thy trouth and thy right hand,
>   Thou'l steal frae nane but them that sta from thee.'

> 'There is my trouth and my right hand;
>   My head shall hing on Hairibie,
> I'le never cross Carlele sands again,
>   If I steal frae a man but them that sta frae me.' [28]

Woe to the clansman who ignores his laird's call:

> 'Fy, gar warn the water-side,
>   Gar warn it soon and hastily,
> Them that winna ride for Telfer's kye,
>   Let them never look i' the face o' me.' [29]

The district of Ettrick is still referred to as "the Water."

[24] "Dick of the Cow" (185).
[25] "Jock of the Side" (187 A).
[26] "Hobie Noble" (189).
[27] "Johnny Armstrong" (169 B).
[28] "Dick of the Cow" (185).
[29] "Jamie Telfer" (190).

In the midst of grimness and cruelty and at times utter barbarity, there is the occasional play of ironic lightness. The Lady of Rothiemay —one of the few women in this Border Ballad world of men—wishes she had wings "like yon turtle dove" that she might fly around the towers of Frendraught crying curses on her lord's murderers.[30] Since "the dow it is a gentle bird," her choice is less appropriate than Hotspur's:

> I'll have a starling shall be taught to speak
> Nothing but "Mortimer!" and give it him
> To keep his anger still in motion.[31]

"The Laird of Wariston" (194) begins like the most charming idyl:

> Down by yon garden green
> Sae merrily as she gaes;
> She has twa weel-made feet,
> And she trips on her taes.

But this lady, with "her middle jimp as any willow wand," assists in a particularly revolting murder and is burned at the stake. Dick takes leave of his victim with laconic irony:

> Now Dickie has feld Fair Johnë Armstrong,
>   The prettiest man in the south country;
> 'Gramercie,' then can Dickie say,
>   'I had twa horse, thou has made me three.'
>
> He has tane the laird's jack off his back,
>   The twa-handed sword that hang leiugh by his thigh;
> He has tane the steel cape off his head;
>   'Johnie, I'le tel my master I met with thee.' [32]

There is humor even in the tensest moments. Not pausing to strike Jock's irons from him, his rescuers mount him sidewise "like ony bride" and ride at once. The adventure ends, as all good ones should, in a spirit of conviviality. The prisoner is safe at "his ain fireside,/And there o's airns they make him free."

> They hae gard fill up ae punch-bowl,
>   And after it, they maun hae anither,

---

[30] "The Fire of Frendraught" (196).
[31] Shakespeare, *King Henry the Fourth*, Part I, I, iii.
[32] "Dick of the Cow" (185).

And thus the night they a' hae spent,
Just as they had been brither and brither.[33]

This forthright verse is never pedestrian. While, as is true of all ballad verse, there are few single lines that one remembers and quotes, the diction and the rhythm are truly poetic in their stimulus to the imagination and provision of that elusive quality, atmosphere. Smashing blows and falling timbers echo in such lines as "They banged wi trees and brake the doors," or "They gard it all in flinders flee." To a thundering gallop you are swept on with the horsemen: "And on they rode to the Waters of Tyne"; to a quickened canter—"And there by the help of the light of the moon"—you reach the goal with them. We have little information as to the tunes of the Border Ballads, for there are few traditional versions in circulation today. Leyden, the editor of the 1833 edition of Scott's *Minstrelsy of the Scottish Border*, prints a few airs which indicate their lively character. The recently collected fiddle tune for "Jock of the Side" (187) given below may be fitted to the verses of Child's B-version.

Practically no Border Raid ballads have stood transplanting to American soil, being too localized in time, place, and circumstance to maintain their hold elsewhere. Two versions of "Archie o' Cawfield" (188) are reported, one by Child from Plymouth, Massachusetts, in 1899, the other more recently from a Scottish-born singer in Michigan.[34] In the songs of the Southwest, however, there is a continuous reflection of the same lawlessness and violence, and the theme of the desperado and the outlaw has given rise to a frontier balladry which has adapted many later English and Irish highwayman songs to local incidents.[35]

[33] "Jock of the Side" (187 B).
[34] (a) Child, *English and Scottish Popular Ballads*, III, 494. Version F, sung by J. M. Watson as remembered from his father's singing. (b) Gardner, *Ballads and Songs from Southern Michigan*, p. 217. Sung by John Laidlaw, born in Aberdeen, ironically not recognized by the collectors as a singer until shortly before his death, too late to note down his other songs.
[35] See pages, 297 ff.

JOCK OF THE SIDE (187B)[36]

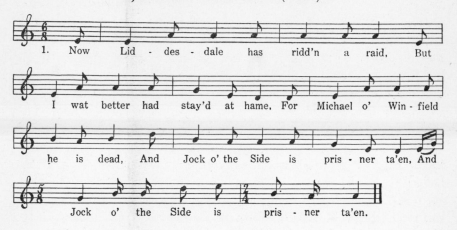

1. Now Liddesdale has ridd'n a raid,
   But I wat better had stayed at hame,
   For Michael o' Winfield he is dead,
       And Jock o' the Side is prisner ta'en.
       And Jock o' the Side is prisner ta'en.

2. For Mangerton House auld Downie is gane;
   Her coats she has kilted up to her knee,
   And down the water wi speed she rins
       While tears in spaits fa fast frae her eie.

3. Then up and bespake the lord Mangerton:
   'What news, what news, sister Downie, to me?'
   'Bad news, bad news, my lord Mangerton;
       Mitchel is killd and tane they hae my son Johnie.'

4. 'Neer fear, sister Downie,' quo Mangerton;
   'I hae yokes of oxen four and twentie,
   My barns, my byres, and my faulds, a' weel filld,
       And I'll part wi them a' ere Johnie shall die.

5. 'Three men I'll take to set him free,
   Weel harnessd a' wi best o steel;
   The English rogues may hear, and drie
       The weight o their braid swords to feel.

---

[36] Text from Child, *English and Scottish Popular Ballads*, III, 475. Tune from Anne G. Gilchrist, "Ten Songs from Scotland and the Scottish Border," *Journal of the English Folk Dance and Song Society*, III, 53.

6. 'The Laird's Jock ane, the Laird's Wat twa,
  Oh, Hobie Noble, thou ane maun be;
Thy coat is blue, thou has been true,
  Since England banishd thee, to me.'

7. Now Hobie was an English man
  In Bewcastle-dale was bred and born;
But his misdeeds they were sae great,
  They banishd him neer to return.

8. Lord Mangerton them orders gave,
  'Your horses the wrang way maun a' be shod;
Like gentlemen ye must not seem,
  But look like corn-caugers gawn ae road.

9. 'Your armour gude ye maunna shaw,
  Nor ance appear like men o weir;
As country lads be all arrayd,
  Wi branks and brecham on ilk mare.'

10. Sae now a' their horses are shod the wrang way,
  And Hobie has mounted his grey sae fine,
Jock his lively bay, Wat's on his white horse behind,
  And on they rode for the water o Tyne.

11. At Choler-ford they a' light down,
  And there, wi the help of the light o the moon,
A tree they cut, wi fifteen naggs upo ilk side,
  To climb up the wa o Newcastle town.

12. But when they cam to Newcastle town,
  And were alighted at the wa,
They fand their tree three ells over laigh,
  They fand their stick baith short and sma.

13. Then up and spake the Laird's ain Jock,
  'There's naething for 't, the gates we maun force';
But when they cam the gates unto,
  A proud porter withstood baith men and horse.

14. His neck in twa I wat they hae wrung,
  Wi hand or foot he neer playd paw;
His life and his keys at anes they hae tane,
  And cast his body ahind the wa.

corn-caugers—hucksters
branks—rope halter

brecham—straw pack-saddle
playd paw—stirred again

15. Now soon they reach Newcastle jail,
    And to the prisner thus they call:
'Sleips thou, wakes thou, Jock o the Side,
    Or is thou wearied o thy thrall?'

16. Jock answers thus, wi doleful tone:
    'Aft, aft I wake, I seldom sleip;
But wha's this kens my name sae weel,
    And thus to hear my waes does seik?'

17. Then up and spake the good Laird's Jock,
    'Neer fear ye now, my billie,' quo he;
'For here's the Laird's Jock, the Laird's Wat,
    And Hobie Noble, come to set thee free.'

18. 'O had thy tongue, and speak nae mair,
    And o thy tawk now let me be!
For if a' Liddisdale were here the night,
    The morn's the day that I maun die.

19. 'Full fifteen stane o Spanish iron
    They hae laid a' right sair on me;
Wi locks and keys I am fast bound
    Into this dungeon mirk and drearie.'

20. 'Fear ye no that,' quo the Laird's Jock;
    'A faint heart neer wan a fair ladie;
Work thou within, we'll work without,
    And I'll be bound we set thee free.'

21. The first strong dore that they came at,
    They loosed it without a key;
The next chaind dore that they cam at,
    They gard it a' in flinders flee.

22. The prisner now, upo his back,
    The Laird's Jock's gotten up fu hie;
And down the stair him, irons and a',
    Wi nae sma speed and joy brings he.

23. 'Now, Jock, I wat,' quo Hobie Noble,
    'Part o the weight ye may lay on me';
'I wat weel no,' quo the Laird's Jock,
    'I count him lighter than a flee.'

had—hold
flinders—splinters

24. Sae out at the gates they a' are gane,
  The prisner's set on horseback hie;
 And now wi speed they've tane the gate,
  While ilk ane jokes fu wantonlie.

25. 'O Jock, sae winsomely 's ye ride,
  Wi baith your feet upo ae side!
 Sae weel's ye're harnessed and sae trig,
  In troth ye sit like ony bride.'

26. The night, tho wat, they didna mind,
  But hied them on fu mirrilie,
 Until they cam to Cholerford brae,
  Where the water ran like mountains hie.

27. But when they came to Cholerford,
  There they met with an auld man;
 Says, Honest man, will the water ride?
  Tell us in haste, if that ye can.

28. 'I wat weel no,' quo the good auld man;
  'Here I hae livd this threty yeirs and three,
 And I neer yet saw the Tyne sae big,
  Nor rinning ance sae like a sea.'

29. Then up and spake the Laird's saft Wat,
  The greatest coward in the company;
 'Now halt, now halt, we needna try 't;
  The day is comd we a' maun die!'

30. 'Poor fainted-hearted thief!' quo the Laird's Jock,
  'There'll nae man die but he that's fie;
 I'll lead ye a' right safely through;
  Lift ye the prisner on ahint me.'

31. Sae now the water they a' hae tane,
  By anes and twas they a' swarm through;
 'Here are we a' safe,' says the Laird's Jock,
  'And, poor faint Wat, what think ye now?'

32. They scarce the ither side had won,
  When twenty men they saw pursue;
 Frae Newcastle town they had been sent,
  A' English lads, right good and true.

fie—destined to die

33. But when the land-sergeant the water saw,
    'It winna ride, my lads,' quo he;
Then out he cries, 'Ye the prisner may take,
    But leave the irons, I pray, to me.'

34. 'I wat weel no,' cryd the Laird's Jock,
    'I'll keep them a', shoon to my mare they'll be;
My good grey mare, for I am sure,
    She's bought them a' fu dear frae thee.'

35. Sae now they're away for Liddisdale,
    Een as fast as they could them hie;
The prisoner's brought to his ain fireside,
    And there o's airns they make him free.

36. 'Now, Jock, my billie,' quo a' the three,
    The day was comd thou was to die;
But thou's as weel at thy ain fire-side,
    Now, sitting, I think, tween thee and me.'

37. They hae gard fill up ae punch-bowl,
    And after it they maun hae anither,
And thus the night they a' hae spent,
    Just as they had been brither and brither.

THE POETIC TRADITION OF THE BORDER

A circuit of forty miles from Selkirk up Yarrow, across a hill and down Ettrick, takes one over soil thoroughly impregnated with ballad story and allusion. At Carterhaugh, the edge of fairyland where Janet broke the tabu and gained Tam Lin, we too enter another world. We pass by Philiphaugh where the fray began; Hangingshaw Tower, the scene of the Outlaw Murray's feats; the Dowie Dens of Yarrow, and Dryhope Tower where that Dickie lived who rescued Kinmont Willie. High on the moors above St. Mary's Loch is the ruin of Douglas Tower whence, it is claimed, Lady Mary of "The Douglas Tragedy" (7B) eloped with Lord William. Local legend attaches the reunion of the lovers in "The Gay Goshawk" (96) to St. Mary's churchyard, once on a traveled route from the south, reached now only by a sheep track through the fern. On Ettrick are reminders of Jamie Telfer, whose Fair Dodhead was a few miles up a tributary burn; and Mangerton House, Branxholm, and Liddesdale are nearby. The way is also associated with Scott and other ballad collectors. The stones of Newark

Castle, scene of *The Lay of the Last Minstrel*, which were once pulled down to build farmhouses, have been rebuilt into the semblance of a Border peel. In Yarrow churchyard Scott's great-grandfather is buried; the tiny cottage of Tibbie Shiel, hollyhocks to the eaves and gingham frills at the windows, was a rendezvous for Scott and Hogg; at the Gordon Arms, still the haunt of the canny fisherman, they had many meetings and here they parted for the last time.

The Border Raid ballads belong chiefly to Liddesdale and Eskdale; what we are to call the romantic ballads are more likely to be found along the waters of Ettrick and Yarrow. Here since early times the living branches of the ballad tree have put forth from the parent stock and drawn their life from its deep roots.

That a poetic and imaginative strain should have survived unbroken in a country so ridden by petty wars, so cruel and barbaric in its life, and apparently so unblessed by the arts of peace as the Scottish Border may be variously accounted for.

Stories, like thistledown before the wind, fly everywhere and attach themselves to any bush or twig; and no place more than the Scottish Border has had more winds of legend blow across it. Some of its stories have come down from its own prehistory, kept alive in some mysterious way. Some, taken by the retreating Celts to Armorica in the sixth century, were absorbed into Breton lore, and may later in the form of minstrel lays have found their way into the camps and courts of England, making new entry centuries later to their native Border when the English pushed further north. The Border is for example full of legends of Arthur: he is the champion of the Cymric Celts, fighting here his twelve battles, as the Scots prove by pointing to such place names as Ben Arthur in the Trossachs, Arthur's Seat near Edinburgh, or Bouden Hill (Mt. Badon) near Stirling. No romantic son of the Border forgets that Arthur sleeps beneath the Eildon Hills on Tweed, waiting like another Barbarossa for his country's summons. If Tristrem of Lyonesse was Drust of Lothian, a Pictish prince living about 780 A.D., Thomas Rymer, "consulted at Erceldoun touching the history of Tristrem," [37] needed only to refer to local history. Other tales were brought in from Scandinavia by the invading Norsemen. By importation as well as by unbroken rehearsal of indigenous stories a fund of lore and legend was built into traditional song.

[37] *Auchinleck MS*, quoted by Child, *English and Scottish Popular Ballads*, I, 317.

A nation beset by foes clings tenaciously to the stories of its own past; a sense of pride in all national inheritance is always a weapon of defense. An Arthurian revival supported the claims of the Tudor dynasty to the throne as England fought her way to eminence among the nations; the sedulous collecting of all folk tradition in Denmark, that tiny country encircled by greedy neighbors, reached a climax in the nineteenth century just after Germany had annexed Jutland; Nazi cultivation of Teutonic myth was a perverted form of this return to the past. National conciousness stirred by the dangers of war has no doubt entered into our own interest today in American folkways. So in Scotland a race steeped in its own tales and traditions made time in the midst of danger and turmoil to sing of its past, fighting with this weapon the intrusion of alien ways. Our very knowledge of the richness of Border poetry is due to an undying pride of race, for this was the stimulus that set Sir Walter Scott to gathering and publishing the traditional poetry and lore of his own countryside.[38]

Learning as well as folk culture found an early retreat in the valleys of Tweed, Teviot, and Tyne, whose monasteries became the homes of scholars and missionaries from the Celtic churches of the Hebrides and the Anglo-Saxon churches of Northumbria. Thus a Scottish school of learned poetry arose, which continued to yield verse in times when England was barren of poetic harvest. This was especially true in the fifteenth century. The interactions of learned and folk poetry are never long quiescent, and in Lowland Scotland the native and scholarly streams constantly replenished one another. The shepherds of *The Complaynt of Scotland* (1549) who have given us a list of contemporary dances, tales, and songs are not wholly rustic.[39] The Thomas Rymer of "True Thomas" (37) who figures largely in both legend and record toward the end of the twelfth century illustrates these mingled elements. Thomas was a courtly poet, but "Rymer," as Aubrey tells us, is the sobriquet of a popular singer.[40] Thomas' rhymed romance tells of his sojourn in Fairyland and his resulting power to foretell events. He was a sort of Scottish Merlin, retained at court to prophesy for the king. In and about his home, Erceldoune (now Earlston), legend is rife as to his magic powers. It was at the Eildon Tree on Huntley Bank near Erceldoune that he trysted with the Fairy Queen.

[38] See Chapter 11.
[39] *The Complaynt of Scotland*, pp. 65, 66.
[40] See page 213.

Scott liked to claim that Huntley Bank was on his property at Abbotsford. Thomas did not die a mortal death. Obedient to the summons of fairy fauns and does, he followed them one day into the forest and disappeared from men; and there, or under the Eildon Hills with Arthur, he still lives. An ancient stone reading

> Auld Rymers' race
> Lives in this place

has been built into the red brick walls of the plain little modern church of Earlston. With the cultivation of Border legend by its poets thus unbroken from early times, the ballad revival of the eighteenth century which in England was a new literary movement was in Scotland merely a continuation.[41]

True Thomas' traffic was with the otherworld, like that of many a ballad hero, and the borderer's dominating sense of another world and more than natural influences over his life has given us some of the finest ballads. Nature's influence on the imagination and temperament of a people, so consciously cultivated by the Romanticists, was an unconscious force in the poetic tradition of the borderers, who were always aware of the austerity and violence of the physical world. Wingfield-Stratford speaks of this "Gothic harshness" of the Scottish landscape:

> The gloomy skies, the sudden storms, the sombre moorland, created almost inevitably a belief in the eerie and the sinister presences. . . . Mr. Yeats has noted that the gentle fairy presences which haunt the imagination of his countrymen became formidable and evil as soon as they are transferred to Scottish soil.[42]

Thus instinctively selecting from inherited and imported legend, or making over into the folk pattern the events of their own times, the race of Border singers has never lapsed. Set apart by nature and history, fiercely loyal, recognized and favored in every age by their own literary world, they have worked over their ancient perennially adaptable stories. This is the climate of the ballads which are our main concern, the parent stock to which the American turns for instruction in his own ballad ways and ballad lore.

[41] See Chapters 10 and 11.
[42] Wingfield-Stratford, *History of British Civilization*, I, 410.

Chapter 4

ROMANTIC BALLADS

SINCE the life-span of a ballad is determined by the degree to which it can be adopted by singers anywhere and at any time, it is not strange that in England and Scotland today, and even more in those countries to which the British race has migrated, the ballads so far considered have survived only by chance and in few numbers. They are essentially topical in their themes. Robin Hood's romantic flavor today is due more to the work of the dramatists and later storytellers who took over the stories from popular singers than to the ballads which were their sources. Only by translating into more general terms of human experience have the historical ballads survived in tradition.

One can understand why their theme is outlived. It is harder to explain why tales so fully told, so full of detail, so powerful in description and at times so real in characterization should have been lost. In their best examples never tedious or redundant, their swift, clear stream of action flows along unmuddied by trivial matter. Why has not the manner of telling kept alive the matter of the tale itself?

The answer lies in the nature of those ballads which form the main trunk of the tree, songs of more ancient lineage and more telling simplicity than even the early Robin Hood Ballads. The year 1388, when Sloth was singing his rhymes of Robin Hood, is only yesterday for these ballads. Nobody has successfully named them: they are "simple" in that they have reduced certain universal stories to lowest terms of structure and style; "romantic" in their concern with the theme of love and adventure; and, because of these two aspects, "traditional," forming the largest group of ballads surviving today through oral transmission. For purposes of convenience if not adequacy, perhaps the term "romantic" will serve as well as any other, as we identify the traits of style and story in simple, romantic, traditional ballads.

The tendency to simplify we have already seen, in the gradual reduction in the bulk of the story, the growing concentration on one incident, the clearing of the stage for fewer actors, and at times the omission of introductory, local or contemporary detail. "Mary Hamilton" (173), "The Death of Queen Jane" (170), and "The Bonny Earl of Murray" (181), based on actual incidents, have lost their topical allusions and developed the note of common human appeal. In the romantic ballads this simplicity and concentration have grown to an ultimate fine perfection.

Since the romantic ballad deals with the stuff of life, as it would be understood in any age—not border raids, or national issues, or questions of social justice—it appeals today as it did five hundred years ago. Its simple and impersonal treatment of tragedy has some of the grandeur of Greek drama, and invites us to share its experiences in the same way. Like Oedipus, the ballad hero "drees his weird" as the story proceeds to its inescapable conclusion, exciting in us pity and fear.

But although most ballads are tragic, it should be said at once that some laughter breaks through the gloom. In the other ballads we have met plenty of laughter. The high-spirited borderers and Robin Hood's band jest continually. Ruse and trickery are heartily enjoyed in "Dick of the Cow" (185) and "Robin Hood and the Potter" (121). Jock's rescuers (187) mock him as he sits his horse sideways, "in troth like ony bride." The festive finale of reunion, reconciliation, or rescue takes place as bottles crack merrily, one punch bowl after another is filled, and the revelers drink together "like brither and brither." Robin's dramatic staging of his bargain counter under the sheriff's very windows collects all the women of Nottingham, giving him the publicity he wants, and us a fine comic scene.

In the romantic ballads laughter is often conventionalized. Sometimes it is the introduction to tragedy, as when Sir Patrick Spens (58) reads the first line of his letter with a loud laugh, the second with a blinding tear; or when Clerk Colvill's mermaid (42) laughs merrily at the fatal trick she has just played on him. The riddle ballads are built on the conventional jests of many ages.[1] There is a kind of humor in the disguise plot, which is resolved into the happy ending in such ballads as "The Kitchie Boy" (252), its ancestor, "Hind Horn" (17), and the much later "Lizie Lindsay" (226).

The comic ballad is at its best in satirizing human relationships. Stock characters, like the vain woman, the gullible husband, the shrew-

_____
[1] See pages 163–64.

ish wife, and the tongue-tied lover are sources of comedy for the ballads, as they were for the early plays, tales, and fabliaux. Some, like "The Friar in the Well" (276), concern themselves with outmoded sources of amusement. Others, although based upon bygone conditions, still entertain us, and have lived on in oral tradition because of their picture of the perpetual traits of human nature. In the medieval moralities the devil ran away with any unpopular character, so the fate of "The Farmer's Curst Wife" (278) was greeted with the delight of long acquaintance. "The Wife Wrapt in Wether's Skin" (277) is mentioned in *Laneham's Letter*, and the incident is used in *Taming of a Shrew*, Shakespeare's source.[2] Although as a whole, society has stopped beating its wife, and whipping posts and ducking stools and laws for the punishment of the scold are no longer part of our juridical equipment, we still relish these pictures of the vain and lazy woman, the scold, and the henpecked husband.

The satirical ballads have suffered many changes in their passage in and out of tradition. The broadside press found in social satire one of its best stocks in trade, and did all it could to vulgarize and cheapen the themes. In contrast, the traditional versions show a lack of coarseness, and restraint and irony rather than broad humor.

Simplicity and concentration are most obvious in the story pattern. Very few characters are involved, often only the triangle of lovers. In dialogue ballads like "Edward" (13) and "Lord Rendal" (12) there are only two characters, with allusion to a third. When other actors are brought in, they are grouped as one, like the pursuing brothers, the funeral cortege, or various attendants; or they are purely mechanical agents for forwarding the action, like the porter, the footpage, the waiting-woman, or the household fairy. The family circle is broken only by the lover. Gone is the clan, the nation, a society divided into classes. The situations concern the life of the family alone—the choice of a mate, tests of the new bride's chastity, faithfulness and unfaithfulness in love, the fatal or comic results of jealousy and misunderstanding.

Certain relationships are unfamiliar to us and hark back to a primitive social organization. The bridegroom's mother figures frequently, and her power and dignity suggest a society that is based on matriarchy. In "Gil Brenton" (5) she proves the new wife's chastity; in "Willie's

[2] *Robert Laneham's Letter*, ed. Furnivall, p. lxiv.

Lady" (6) she is "a vile rank witch" of a less benevolent nature; Lord
Rendal (12) goes to his mother with his untold tale of poisoning and
dies in her arms, and so does Sweet William in an Appalachian version
of "Earl Brand" (7). Edward (13) curses his mother as the bringer of
all his ill fortune; Child Waters' mother (63) is the first to hear the cry
of the new-born babe; Lord Thomas (73) asks his mother's advice in
the choice of a wife—and, alas, takes it. The mother's house receives
the young wife and the mother rules the household.

Matriarchy, which traces descent through the female line, may also
be recalled in "the sister's son." This stock figure is often a precocious
child endowed with second sight:

> Up then spak his sister's son,
>   Sat on his nurse's knee. . . .
>
> 'O yer hogs will die out in the field,
>   Yer kye ill die in the byre;
> An than, whan a' yer gear is gane,
>   A fusom fag by yer fire!
> But a' will thrive at is wi you,
>   An ye get yer heart's desire.' [3]
>
> O the first ystroke that they gae him,
>   They struck him off by the knee;
> Then up bespake his sister's son,
>   'O the next'll gar him die!' [4]

He may be less innocent as he grows up:

> ' 'Tis I forbid ye, Auld Ingram,
>   For to seek me to wed;
> For Lord Wayets, your sister's son,
>   Has been into my bed.' [5]

In more recent tradition he becomes the brother's son:

> She called to her little foot-page
>   That was her brother's son. . . .[6]

Or the phrase may become a ballad commonplace:

> O then we must be sisters' sons:
>   What nearer cousins can we be? [7]

---

[3] "Lord Thomas and Fair Annet" (73 I).   [7] See page 38.
[4] "Johnie Cock" (114).
[5] "Lord Ingram and Chiel Wyet" (66 C).
[6] "Lady Maisry," *Novello's School Songs*, No. 1263.

To the modern reader the frequent allusion to concubinage is startling. Read in the light of morality today, many a ballad, like many a medieval romance, is open to the criticism of a traditional singer who remarked as he began to sing, "There ain't nothing bad about this song, so fur ez I can see, 'ceptin' its criminality!" [8] The stories of the ballads and the romances, however, are built upon the social fabric of Western Europe of the early Middle Ages, and a system which we associate today with parts of the Orient or Africa was part of the European picture until a surprisingly recent date. The position of the unmarried wife was not only tolerated but legally recognized as late as the thirteenth century in Scotland; and even later in some Scandinavian countries illegitimate sons could succeed to property and title. The morganatic marriage of royalty is a remnant of this system. Marriage was an economic institution for the continuance of family property, but the love match whereby a man and woman could live together, parting at the will of either, provided for all human needs not recognized by legal marriage. Not until after the Renaissance was marriage romanticized. It was a common idea of the Middle Ages that jealousy was evil; the intelligent and superior woman recognized that her lord's position could include both his love for her, and the status of another woman as the married wife. This idea is echoed in "Fair Annie" (62):

> It's narrow, narrow, make your bed,
>   And learn to lie your lane;
> For I'm ga'n oer the sea, Fair Annie,
>   A braw bride to bring hame.
> Wi her I will get gowd and gear;
>   Wi you I neer got nane.

The fairy-tale dowry brought by Gil Brenton's wife (5) is merely emphasis on the economics of marriage, and the arranged weddings of Lord Thomas (73) and Young Beichan (53) do not discredit them as lovers, nor reflect on the characters of their true-loves. The ballads, moreover, do not judge; they simply narrate. The result of this absence of comment is to sharpen the outlines of the love story, the claims of the heart being all the more pitiful when they conflict with a marriage that excludes or at least does not expect love.

[8] *Songs from the Hills of Vermont*, collected by Edith B. Sturgis and arranged by Robert Hughes, p. vi. Copyright, 1919, by G. Schirmer, Inc. Copyright renewal assigned, 1946, to G. Schirmer, Inc. Printed by permission.

Change of setting does not radically change the story. Passing down the centuries, Edward's story is the same, whether the scene is laid in hall and bower, or more humbly; whether his bloodstain comes from his greyhound, symbol of a chivalric sport, or the old hound dog that hunts with him for 'coon and 'possum on an Appalachian moonlight night. The setting is never emphasized. A careful search may indeed produce references to castles and bowers, journeys by horseback with a little footpage running alongside, through a country marked by wells, crosses, dales, glens, and grassy banks. Infrequently towns are mentioned, more often churches. Vaguely one pictures that "wan water," the sea. But all such reference is shadowy, lacking in the specific realism, for instance, of Jamie Telfer's cross-country journey. Distances are measured by "a mile, a mile, a mile but barely three." Knights wander forth "strange countries for to see"; "There was a lady lived in a bower"; "There dwelt an old lord by the northern sea." There is no real interest in the whereabouts of the action; the story is the thing.

When things happen is of as little concern as where. "About Yule," "midday," "when bells were rung and mass was sung/ And all men bound to bed," "a twelve-month and a day being up," "in a year, or two, or three at most"—the ballad is rarely more explicit. The world moves at a timeless pace:

> Lord Thomas and Fair Annet
> Sate a' day on a hill;
> When night was cum, and sun was sett,
> They had not talkt their fill.[9]

A curious mixture of the aristocratic and the homely has come about. These lords and ladies living in bowers and castles are simply William and Henry and Thomas, Ellen or Annie. The familiar and the usual has helped in appropriating the stories. But names matter little, changing with the singer's taste. Occupations, too, are unimportant. Beggars, harpers, and outlaws are as dim in outline as lords and ladies. The trade of the mason Lamkin (93) does indeed precipitate the tragedy, for

> He built Lord Wearie's castle
> But payment he gat nane.

[9] "Lord Thomas and Fair Annet" (73).

Most concrete detail is likewise indistinct and conventional. The ballad, being concerned with the story, cannot cumber itself with individualizing each object, and resorts to a stock vocabulary which soon becomes familiar. Water is wan, hair is yellow, brands are bright or brown, gold is red, steeds are milk-white or iron-grey or coal-black, the lady's slender waist is "a middle sae jimp," horns blow both loud and shrill, the fatal instrument is the wee pen-knife (a curious corruption of *wea*pon-knife). Letters are read, the first line with a loud laugh, the second with blinding tears. Clothing is merely "the finest pa'," and beyond coats and shoes and sarks garments are not specified. Color, too, is used conventionally, as in "The Brown Girl":

> She dressed herself in a scarlet robe,
> Her waiting maid dressed in green.

Conventional, too, is the occasional extravagant and detailed description, as of Fair Annet preparing to meet her rival:

> 'My maides, gae to my dressing roome,
> And dress to me my hair;
> Wheree'er ye laid a plait before,
> See ye lay ten times mair.
>
> 'My maides, gae to my dressing room,
> And dress to me my smock;
> The one half of the holland fine,
> The other of needle-work.'
>
> The horse Fair Annet rode upon,
> He amblit like the wind;
> Wi siller he was shod before,
> Wi burning gowd behind.
>
> When she came to Marie's kirk
> She sat on Marie's stean;
> The cleading that Fair Annet had on,
> It skinkled in their een.
>
> And whan she cam into the kirk
> She shimerd like the sun;
> The belt that was about her waist
> Was all wi' pearles bedone.[10]

[10] "Lord Thomas and Fair Annet" (73).

There is a lavish richness in "Young Beichan" (53) which piles up lands, rents, cities as sources of income, meikle goud and white monie, white bread, Spanish wine, guineas for the porter's fee, and the lady's jewels, which are a double dowry, enough to buy an earldom.

This conventional description, known as the ballad commonplace, may belong to a primitive stage of narrative that preceded one of more detail; or it may represent evolution from detail in the direction toward which all ballad style progresses, that of simplifying to the utmost in order to intensify the action. Whatever its origin, the commonplace serves to free the attention of the singer and the listener for the business in hand, and to provide a chance for individual imagination to run its course. The stock adjective or action becomes surprisingly agreeable and adequate in the long run.

While concrete objects are comparatively unimportant in themselves, they play a definite role in ballad language. They stand for ideas in the folk idiom. I remember a guide who was taking me through a sixteenth-century manor house in the West of England, which had recently been stripped of its possessions after hundreds of years. "Ah," he said wistfully, "the furniture that once was here will never come together again." And I had a sense of all that furniture stood for in the way of family continuity, now broken forever. So the ballad singer phrases an idea in terms of things, unconsciously metaphorical. He approaches the abstract through the concrete in the "what-ails-you" formula:

> 'O moan ye for your meat,
>   Or moan ye for your fee,
> Or moan ye for the ither bounties
>   That ladies are wont to gie?'

> 'I moan na for my meat,
>   Nor yet for my fee,
> But I mourn for Christen land,
>   It's there that I fain would be.' [11]

Bribery for concealing a crime comes in the form of that most powerful bait for women, fine clothing:

> 'The silks that waur shappit for me at Yule
> At Pasch shall be sewed for thee.' [12]

[11] "The Queen of Elfan's Nourice" (40).
[12] "Young Hunting" (68 C).

Behind the reluctance of the Scots nobles to "weet their cork-hield schoone" lies the suggestion of seas beginning to wash the decks, but all we know of the drowning of that ship's company is "the hats that swam aboon" the waters that had closed over men and ship.[13] Many other instances come to mind. The visual image of "o' fifteen steps he made but three" is better than all the words it would take to describe haste and the motive behind it. "It cost me deep in purse" is eloquent of both gesture and idea, more effective even than its variant, "dear in purse." The fans and combs of the ladies who wait for the return of Sir Patrick Spens (58) stand not only for all their brave finery, but also for the state of expectation in which they put it on. Although to us these are suggestive and metaphorical, a recognized poetic device, to simple people whose lives are concerned with things and not with ideas they have a literal meaning and speak directly. One finds degrees of allusiveness, some more subtle than others. Thus one folk poet begins his ballad,

> I leaned my back up against some oak
> Thinking it was a trusty tree,
> But first it bent and then it broke,
> And so did my true love to me.[14]

And another sings more simply,

> She lean't her back against an oak,
> But first it bent and then it broke.

The next two lines,

> She lean't her back against a thorn,
> And it's there she had two fine babes born,[15]

give us to understand that this is a tragedy of the first water, a betrayal of love, and not merely an appearance of the familiar folk motif of forest birth.

The artistic economy of ballad language always makes a little serve for much. Some plots are entirely dependent upon the allusive method, in which one must guess the story from a few selected facts. In some versions of "Lord Rendal" (12) we are never told that he has been

[13] "Sir Patrick Spens" (58).
[14] "Waly waly," *Novello's School Songs*, No. 959.
[15] See page 150.

poisoned, but we guess it from the fact that he is sick, that he has eaten with his true-love who has fed him "eels" of a suspicious appearance. His symptoms are not described, but we infer his dire state from his iterated wish to go to bed. We gather from the making of the will that he is dying. In the final bequest of a rope to hang his sweetheart we learn for the first time that he knows her guilt. His matter-of-course statements to his mother are in ironic disproportion to the facts. If a nation's idiom is found in its folk songs, we might consider this an illustration of British understatement in the face of tragedy. Certainly the Italian version of this ballad is told with contrasting Latin expressiveness.[16] The allusive method puts the listener continually on his mettle, and sometimes baffles him if he lacks some bit of necessary information. Thus the knowledge that the unmarried girl in medieval Denmark wore a golden head-dress explains the force of the tabu with which "Tam Lin" (39), which seems to have come from Scandinavia, begins:

> O I forbid you, maidens a'
>   That wear gowd in your hair,
> To come or gae by Carterhaugh,
>   For young Tam Lin is there.

The allusive method is often ironic, using either the language or the situation for an indirect meaning or a hidden emphasis. Tragedy resulting from a trivial detail is ironic: Edward's fatal quarrel was about "a little bit of a bush that might have been a tree." Truth misunderstood is the irony of "Child Maurice" (83 D):

> 'I think I see the woman come
>   That I have loved lang.'

The irony of contrast is expressed in "Lamkin" (93):

> O sweetly sang the black-bird
>   That sat upon the tree;
> But sairer grat Lamkin
>   When he was condemnd to die.

> And bonny sang the mavis
>   Out o the thorny brake;
> But sairer grat the nourice
>   When she was tied to the stake.

---

[16] See Jewett, *Folk Ballads of Southern Europe*, p. 115.

The Clerk's Twa Sons o Owsenford (72), sent away to college, are hanged for a crime, and the report reaches their mother:

> 'It's I've putten them to a deeper lair
> And to a higher schule.'

Realistic touches, though they rarely occur, are unerring in their choice of the most suggestive detail and are thus a potent force in condensing the story.

> He took the holland sark off his back,
> He tore it frae breast to gare,
> He laid it to the bloody wound
> That still bled mair and mair.[17]

Here imagination seizes on the hint of urgency, the quick decisive movements, the futility of all effort; perhaps, too, the implication of the murderer's presence, in the wound that will not be staunched.[18]

Verbal economy is especially potent in the expression of the idea of "never." The fatalism that overcasts ballad skies deals constantly with the irrevocable. Lovers promise never to be faithless, are parted never to unite, leave for strange lands never to return; wives wait for husbands who never come back, mothers for children they will never see again, except perhaps as ghosts at Martinmas or "The hallow days of Yule." [19] The finality of death is vivid and concrete:

> O lang, lang may their ladies sit
> Wi thair fans into their hand,
> Or eir they se Sir Patrick Spence
> Cum sailing to the land.[20]

> And when will you come back, my love,
> O my love, tell me;
> When the sun sets yander in the sycamore tree,
> And that will never be.[21]

> The first stroke Little Musgrave stroke
> He hurt Lord Barnard sore,
> The next stroke that Lord Barnard stroke,
> Little Musgrave nere struck more.[22]

[17] "The Twa Brothers" (49 B).
[18] See page 129.
[19] See page 142.
[20] "Sir Patrick Spens" (58).
[21] See page 104.
[22] "Little Musgrave" (81).

His mither she has made his bed,
    His gentle ladie laid him down,
His brither he has unbent his bow,
    'Twas never bent by him again.[23]

Folk poetry is full of echoes of a marvelous "Never Never Land" like that of the nursery rhyme:

O sister, O sister, that may not bee
Till salt and oatmeale grow both of a tree.[24]

My boy was scarcely ten years auld
    When he went to an unco land
Where wind never blew, nor cocks ever crew,
    Ohon for my son, Leesome Brand! [25]

The same idiom is found in protestations of never-dying love:

If ever I prove false to you,
    Bright day may turn to night.

Bright day may turn to night, my love,
    The raging seas shall burn,
The fire shall freeze like snow and ice,
    The rocks shall melt and run.[26]

It has been said that a ballad's power lies not in what is told, but in what is left untold. Nowhere is this truer than in its use of the concrete for the abstract, its allusive statement.

The dramatic nature of the ballad, inherent in all these traits of style, becomes more and more apparent as we consider others.

The method of introduction to the situation is characteristic. All preliminaries to the final debacle are reduced, and sometimes swept entirely away. If a ballad begins,

There was twa sisters in a bower,
There came a knight to be their wooer.[27]

---

[23] "Clerk Colvill" (42).
[24] "The Twa Sisters" (10).
[25] "Leesome Brand" (15).
[26] "The Little Turtle Dove," sung to E. K. Wells by Mrs. Eliza Pace, Hyden, Ky., May 1929. It was a familiar ballad tag that Burns caught up into his rewritten folk song, "My luve is like a red, red rose":

And I will luve thee still, my dear,
    Till all the seas gang dry,
Till all the seas gang dry, my dear,
    And the rocks melt in the sun.

[27] "The Twa Sisters" (10 B).

one may guess that jealousy as a motive to tragedy is hardly more than
around the corner. There is very often the feeling that one has surprised a story already in action. "Fair Isabel sits in her bower sewing,"
and the curtain is drawn back on a scene already set. Sometimes one is
given the cardinal facts at once:

> 'It's narrow, narrow, make your bed,
>   And learn to lie your lane;
> For I'm ga'n oer the sea, Fair Annie,
>   A braw bride to bring hame.' [28]

Love for the mistress is at once pitted against the dowry of the wife:

> 'Wi her I will get gowd and gear,
>   Wi you I neer got nane.' [29]

Mary Hamilton's story bursts in a breath from the first lines:

> Word's gane to the kitchen,
>   And word's gane to the ha',
> That Mary Hamilton gangs wi bairn
>   To the hichest Stewart of them a'.[30]

Here is all the subtle suggestion of the speed with which rumor is
traveling through the castle, whispered by servants and nobles alike,
of the scandal involving Lord Darnley himself. "The ballad," said the
poet Gray, "begins in the fifth act of the play," thus phrasing for all
time this quality of thrusting into the midst of a tale. The remark
actually applied to Home's *Douglas: A Tragedy*, a play founded on the
ballad of "Child Maurice" (83) which was sweeping England at the
time.[31] The author, supplying the first four acts from his own imagination, used the ballad story for his fifth. One of the charms of ballads is
that they make a similar demand upon us: we are free like Home to
build up the beginnings for ourselves, just as we are free to draw our
own pictures from the conventional descriptions, or to make the nebu-
lous characters and settings into what we will.

If the ballad is the fifth act of the play, that fifth act is often divided
into scenes, which follow each other in quick succession and without
transition. Thus "Babylon" (14) is played in three similar scenes.
"Young Hunting" (68) is more elaborate. The lover stops at his lady's
door and is persuaded to alight and spend the night. The lady plies him

---

[28] "Fair Annie" (62).
[29] *Ibid.*
[30] "Mary Hamilton" (173).
[31] See page 227.

with drink and murders him, attempting to bribe an eavesdropping bird to keep her secret. She then submerges the body in the Clyde. The king sends for Young Hunting to ride to the chase with him. The lady falsely swears ignorance of his whereabouts. In the fear that he has been drowned, they drag for the body, but in vain. The bird discloses the position of the body and the lady's guilt. After trying to foist the guilt onto her waiting-woman, who survives the ordeal by fire, the lady herself is burned at the stake.

Like today's radio broadcast, the ballad achieves vividness in the use of the historical present tense:

> Janet has kilted her green kirtle
> A little aboon her knee,
> And she has snooded her yellow hair
> A little aboon her bree,
> And she's awa to Carterhaugh
> As fast as she can hie.[32]

Dialogue, often unassigned, is a dramatic device. It is used most effectively in "Edward" (13) and "Lord Rendal" (12), two powerful ballads consisting entirely of question and answer. These might be called ballads of situation, in which the story of previous action and its cause or result is told or implied by dialogue, with never a word to tell us who is speaking. We must identify the actors on the stage of our minds. The exciting quality of the conversation here lies in the repetition of the same question, or of a question that changes slightly in each repetition, and in the similar uniformity or slight variation of the answer. Thus the story is built up bit by bit, the listener's suspense increasing with every line. In "Edward" (13) a question twice repeated brings truth at last, and in the use of the same words each time the insistence of the questioner is felt rather than expressed. When this device is used in combination with a compact irony of phrase, we have a brief scene, charged with emotion, reduced to simplest terms, with more than a suggestion of major tragedy. Sometimes this repetition takes the form of balancing action with speech:

> 'Leave aff your ducking on the day
> And duck upon the night;
> Wherever that sakeless knight lys slain
> The candels will shine bright.'

[32] "Tam Lin" (39).

They left off their ducking o the day
   And ducked upon the night,
And where that sakeless knight lay slain,
   The candels shone full bright.[33]

This literal or practical iteration of a phrase or a line is called incremental repetition. Its effects are insidious. At first it seems a device of the nursery: this is the fairy-tale method we have all outgrown, and its use here seems cumbersome and naïve, slowing rather than quickening the pace. Then simple interest turns into absorption, taking the place of our nervous demand for variety of expression. The full effect of folk poetry and folk music is not to be derived from one hearing; it is felt only by repetition. One has only to try to write out all that is implied in this simple dialogue, to discover how much it contains. It is the simplicity of great art, as well as of great artlessness. Like the commonplace and the vague setting, incremental repetition is a means of freeing our imaginations. It is better understood in relation to the tune, and has perhaps evolved because of it.[34]

The ballad's dramatic insistence on the action of a single episode, its use of every means to reduce the formula of ballad making to simplest terms, and its avoidance of detailed description, fixed settings, or comment, result in a complete objectivity. It shows no evidence of authorship, and if an individual composer once existed, centuries of adaptation to the varying expressive needs and cultural backgrounds of singers and listeners have obliterated any trace of the original maker. If subsequent singers have fastened their marks to their versions, these have been sloughed off in the next generation. One ballad is much like another in method. Those indications by which we recognize the poet are lacking: there is no signature, no reference to himself, no personal comment or moralizing, no peculiarity of style that marks off one man's work from another's. There is no interest in the singer's point of view; he is merely the vehicle for the story, the medium for its transmission. The ballad is not the work of one hand or mind, but of a sort of composite authorship. In this sense, and in this sense only, is it true that "the throng composes." [35]

Various aspects of the ballad's prosody—its stanza and refrain—are also characteristic.

[33] "Young Hunting" (68).   [35] See page 193.
[34] See page 282.

The ballad stanza is normally a quatrain with alternating four- and three-stress lines of iambs. Many ballads are obviously cast in this form; many more, like "Edward" (13 B), when divested of their refrains, are seen to be inherently so. But a larger number than is generally supposed depart from the pattern. "Robin Hood and the Pedlar" has four stresses to the line, "The Laird of Wariston" (194) three. Sometimes a six-line stanza is found among the quatrains. "The trees they do grow high" has two long seven-stress lines followed by three short ones and a fourth still shorter.[36] "The Hangman" departs completely from stanzaic regularity. Further variation occurs in "The False Knight upon the Road" (3) and "Little Matthy Grove" ("Little Musgrave," 81), where an initial extra phrase or line introduces the story and disappears after the ballad has settled down into its narrative stride.

Metrical variety is likewise very great. Feminine endings are used throughout "Barbara Allen" (84) and "Georgie" (209). Trochees, anapests, and dactyls break in on the iambic pulse. "And there, wi the help of the light o the moon" Jock of the Side (187) is rescued. The essentially dactylic line from "Lord Rendal" (12), "Make my bed soon, for I'm sick to my heart," becomes spondaic when it is sung. As will be shown in a later chapter,[37] tune not only changes, but regularizes scansion in lines otherwise unforgivably rough.

Many quatrain ballads may be cast into a couplet form, when considered in connection with their melodies.[38] It is quite possible to consider "The Death of Queen Jane" (170) as made up of four-stress couplets. "Mary Hamilton" (173) and many others, may be divided into two long lines of seven stresses each. Indeed, this happens so frequently as to suggest that the four-line stanza is simply another more convenient way of writing out a couplet, by dividing the lines into shorter units. The long narrow pages of some of the old manuscripts suggest this arrangement. Child considered the couplet ballad older than the four-line ballad, because of its simpler structure as well as its more archaic matter.

Stanza and refrain cannot be considered apart. In Child's collection about a third of his 305 ballads appear with refrain—usually in couplet stanzas. Most of the quatrain ballads appear without refrain. The accepted opinion for many years, therefore, was that the refrain

---

[36] Sharp, *One Hundred English Folksongs* (1916), p. 58.
[37] See page 280.
[38] See page 282.

belonged chiefly to the couplet, or older, ballads. But now that more collectors' evidence is available, and we can examine a larger number of ballads as they are sung today, it is evident that many of those pieces which Child prints without refrain have kept it in tradition, and we may increase his third to at least half. Child's manuscript texts may have omitted the refrain through the sheer laziness of the copyists, his printed ones through the printer's wish to economize on space and paper. Both assume that the singer will know where the refrain should be inserted.

Our interest in the refrain is two-fold: we must account for its presence or absence more fully than by the obvious reasons just given, and we must observe its nature and function. The first question leads us back to the subject of ballad origin, and will be discussed later; [39] the second may be considered here.

The refrain occurs in various relationships to the stanza: it may be internal, interspersed with the lines of the stanza; external, sung after each stanza; or both internal and external, with an extra flourish at the end. Various illustrations of these arrangements are given here.

Internal Refrain. In addition to "Edward" (13), "The Cruel Mother" (20), "The Bonny Banks of Virgie O" ("Babylon" 14), and "Scarborough Fair" ("The Elfin Knight" 2), given elsewhere in this book, there are the following examples:

(1) Why dois your brand sae drap wi bluid,
       Edward, Edward,
    Why dois your brand sae drap wi bluid,
       And why sae sad gang yee O?
    O I hae killed my hauke sae guid,
       Mither, Mither,
    O I hae killed my hauke sae guid,
       And I had nae mair bot hee O.[40]

(2) There was three ladies playd at the ba,
       With a hey ho and lily gay,
    There came a knight and played oer them a',
       As the primrose spreads so sweetly.[41]

(3) It was a knight in Scotland borne,
       Follow, my love, come over the strand,

[39] See pages 195–202.   [41] "The Cruel Brother" (11).
[40] "Edward" (13 B).

Was taken prisoner and left forlorne,
    Even by the good Earle of Northumberland.[42]

(4) There is a feast in your father's house,
      The broom blooms bonnie and so is it fair,
    It becomes you and me to be very douce,
      And we'll never gang up to the broom nae mair.[43]

(5) There was twa sisters in a bowr,
      Edinburgh, Edinburgh,
    There was twa sisters in a bowr,
      Stirling for ay,
    There was twa sisters in a bowr,
    There came a knight to be their wooer,
    Bonny Saint Johnston stands on Tay.[44]

In all these examples the refrain is made up of actual words, which vary in relevance to the sense of the ballad, from a close connection, as in (1), to complete independence, as in (2). There may be a partial connection, as in (3), or a suggestion of the subject, as in (4). The refrain in (5) suggests a battle cry, and may well have been one, for the ballad sometimes contained political propaganda.[45]

External Refrain. Examples in this book are "The Two Magicians" (44) and "Robin Hood and the Tanner" (126). The form of the latter refrain is very common, being merely a repetition of the last line of the stanza. "The Two Magicians" (44) is much more elaborate. In these two instances, the refrain is closely connected with the story. Example (6) is obviously merely rhythmic:

(6) It was late in the night when the squire came home,
      Enquiring for his lady;
    The servant made a sure reply,
      She's off with the Gypsie Davy.
      Rattle-tuma-gypsum, gypsum,
      Rattle-tuma-gypsum, Davy.[46]

Internal and External Refrain. "The Two Sisters" (10), "Robin Hood and the Bishop of Hereford" (144), "The Gypsy Laddie" (200), and "The Three Ravens" (26) illustrate a refrain that is both within and without the stanza. We add one more:

[42] "The Fair Flower of Northumberland" (9).   [43] "Leesome Brand" (15 B).
[44] "The Twa Sisters" (10 B).   [45] See page 211.
[46] Sharp, *English Folk Songs from the Southern Appalachians,* I, 233.

(7) The maid she went to the well to washe,
    Lillumwham, lillumwham,
The maid she went to the well to washe,
    What then? What then?
The maid she went to the well to washe,
Dew fell off her lilly white fleshe,
      Grandam boy, grandam, boy, heye!
      Leg a derry, leg a merry, mett, mir, whoop, whirr,
      Drivance, larumben, grandam boy, heye! [47]

Here the refrain is more elaborate and more rhythmic. With the exception of (5) all these examples of internal and external refrain are made up of nonsense syllables.

"The Elfin Knight" (2) has a burden as well as a refrain, that is, a stanza at the beginning which is different in form and meter and which has no connection with the story. Although it is not repeated at the end, as it would be in a carol,[48] we may consider it choral rather than narrative.

(8) My plaid awa, my plaid awa,
    And ore the hill and far awa,
    And far awa to Norrowa,
    My plaid shall not be blown awa.

(*Stanza*)
    The elphin knight sits on yon hill,
      Ba ba ba lilli ba,
    He blaws his horn both loud and shrill,
      The wind hath blown my plaid awa.

Much pretentious scholarship has been expended upon the nonsense refrain, one of the more speculative theories being that those syllables which are more common, like the nonny-nonnies and the derry-downs, are corruptions of earlier British or Celtic words, derived indeed from Druid chants. "Hey nonny no" is "Hail to the moon," "Fal-lalla-la" is "the circle of the day," "Down, down, derry a down" is "dun, dun, daragon dun," meaning "To the hill, to the oak, to the hill." [49] Aside from conjecture, however, some statements about the nonsense refrain may be made with assurance. It is always fitted to the habits of the

[47] "The Maid and the Palmer" (21).
[48] See page 195.
[49] A fantastic theory, according to Sharp. See *English Folk-Song, Some Conclusions*, p. 95.

mother tongue. Cecil Sharp used to recall his difficulty in teaching
Yvette Guilbert, the French diseuse, to sing English folksongs, because
she could not master the nonsense syllables; similarly, the English
tongue boggles over French nonsense refrains. The ear picks them up
more quickly than the eye—another reason for their disappearance
from written or printed texts. Many of them are the result of corruption: "Parsley, sage, rosemary and thyme," possibly an old herb charm,
has become "Parsil, sedge, rose marry in time," and "Si-boney-O" was
once "Sae bonny O." Tradition repeats meaningless words which grow
increasingly corrupt, thus turning to nonsense, and the scholar sometimes tries to make sense out of a line which perhaps has never meant
anything. The strongly rhythmic nature of the refrain is evident, and
this is particularly true of the nonsense refrain. The implication of
dance in the variations in "The Two Sisters" may be evidence of a
one-time performance to rhythmic movements.[50]

In some cases refrains contribute directly to the atmosphere of the
ballad. In "The False Knight upon the Road" (3), as stanza after
stanza shows the temptations to which the child is put, the contest
between good and evil is sharper with every iteration of "He stood and
he stood, and its well because he stood." In other cases refrains may
be at complete variance with the mood of the story. A lyric and pastoral
quality which is ill suited to the stories themselves pervades many
ballads because of such choral lines as "Fine flowers of the valley" or
"Down by the greenwood sidey." Successive stanzas pile up the irony
of a terrible story unfolded against the smiling background of nature,
while "the broom blooms bonnie and so is it fair." In "The Cruel
Brother" (11) a dastardly murder is committed in a scene painted by
the lines "With a hey, ho and lily gay—And the primrose smells so

[50] See page 195. Sharp (*English Folk Songs from the Southern Appalachians,* I, No.
5) gives the following variants:

    (B)   The bough has been to me
    (C)   The boughs they bent to me
    (D)   The boughs were given to me
    (E)   The boys all bound for me
    (F)   The boys are bound for me
    (G)   Bow and balance to me
    (H)   Come bow to me
    (I)   Bow down to me
    (K)   The vows she made to me
    (L)   And thou has bent to me
    (N)   These vows were sent to me

sweetly." Thus the suitable refrain accents the mood of the listener, while the apparently unsuitable refrain, by ironic incongruity, throws the story into high relief.

The effect of the refrain on tempo and suspense is very great. Melodious, rhythmic, sometimes connotative, it helps to emphasize the story. One's interest is held by a singer who, with every other line, pauses for the refrain; the tale is dignified by the interruptions. Suspense mounts, and mounts rhythmically, with the regular recurrences of the refrain. The tempo of the tale is steadied, its stride evened. Incremental repetition produces the same effect, underlining rather than holding back the story. Particularly is this true of couplet ballads where the first line is given out, and then repeated twice. Some refrains are particularly euphonious and imaginative. The mind retains with pleasure such lines as "Follow, my love, come over the strand," "Come bend and bear away the bows of yew," and "For to bear the red rose company."

The refrain in general provides an emotional richness and a release of feeling which compensates for the restraint of the stanza itself. Its subjective quality sets off the ballad's objectivity. Its effect cannot be derived from a single singing: the ballad must be sung through, and many times. A good refrain, like a good tune—and indeed, it is a kind of tune—needs many repetitions before it is fully known. The illustrations quoted here should be tested out by the singing of the whole ballad.

In fine: The refrain is a regularly recurrent phrase or line, either alternating with the narrative lines, or at the end of the stanza, or in both places; in spirit either akin or alien to the narrative; made up of real words, which may or may not contribute to the sense of the ballad, or of nonsense syllables which are either corruptions of earlier sense words, or merely there to accentuate the rhythm. The syllables, whether sense or nonsense, are more easily caught by the ear than the eye, are familiar, because truly popular, and are always adapted to the racial twist of tongue. The refrain supplies feeling, melody, and rhythm, enhancing the narrative interest by emphasis or contrast. From its frequency in oral tradition, we may assume that the refrain was once more widely used than the printed collections indicate. It is characteristic of about half of the Child ballads, counting those traditional variants which have turned up since Child's day. It disappeared from many by the fortunes of print, which tries to save space and paper, or handwriting, which takes the easiest way. Both print and manuscript have assumed a familiarity with the ballad method, which would supply a refrain where it was not written in.[51]

The effect of oral tradition on the ballad characteristics discussed in this chapter is seen in American versions.

One notes at once that the singer has placed his story in a familiar setting, and place names are obvious evidence of his complete adoption of the ballad. The seven sleepers of "Earl Brand" (7) are done to death, not in Scandinavia, nor in Scotland near St. Mary's Loch on Yarrow where they still show you the spot, but in any mountain valley where the song is sung. Barbara Allen's coffin is shipped by freight from Dallas, Texas. A New Englander asks in "The Elfin Knight" (2) if you are bound for Lynn or Cape Ann. Proper names are also localized. In Virginia Lord Randal has become Jimmie Randolph. Concrete objects belong to the singer's economy. In Maine Lord Randal leaves his dog and gun to his brother, a petticoat to his mother, and to his sweetheart "a barrel of powder to blow her up high." The shrewish wife points to cold johnny-bread on the shelf, when her husband asks for his dinner. The two sisters go walking on the wharf, to "see their father's ships come in," an echo of the great days of New England seafaring. Babylon is "a rebel so vile." A garter is used by the Cruel Mother to bind the babes, and "a little check shirt" to stop the flow of blood in "The Two Brothers" (11). In Mississippi a swamp bird tells Barbara Allen of her lover's death. The southern mountaineer introduces a buzzard into "The Broomfield Hill" (43), and for him Edward's "reid-roan steed" has become "The old gray horse that ploughed the field." The South Carolina tidewater siren of "Young Hunting" (68) "sits out on her porch playing her piano." Lord Thomas leads his love to that most American of objects, and seats her "down in a rocking chair among the ladies all," and Lord Barnard is safely away, not at the wars or the chase, but "to see his fences." Local words and idioms are evident. In Maine, again, Lord Darnel "jobbed the pistol to her breast" and Lord Thomas "stove her head against the wall." "A fool debate" causes the quarrel in "Chevy Chase" (162), and the rose and the briar, growing out of the lovers' graves, "get contangled in a true-lovers' knot." Any Kentucky mountaineer would

[51] See below, Chapters 8 and 14, for further discussion.

recognize those "two little boys a-fishing just at the break of day" who discover Poor Omie's body.

In general, texts are shorter and more garbled, and ballad tags wander freely from ballad to ballad. Lovers' partings bring the inevitable question, "Who will shoe my foot (glove my hand, etc.)." Introductions are increasingly abrupt. "There were three gypsies came to my door," sings the Englishman, while the American is off on his story at once with "It was late in the night when the squire came home." Some fine poetic touches have disappeared, but some new ones have come into being, particularly in the shorter lyrics. The Ozarks version of "The Seeds of Love" has great charm,[52] as does the following stanza from another song:

> When your heart was mine, true love,
>   And your head lay on my breast,
> You could make me believe by the falling of your arm,
>   That the sun rose up in the west.[53]

Occasionally new light is thrown by an American text on some point of ballad derivation. Most American versions of "Sir Hugh" (155) retain the allusion to the little schoolboy, which is not generally found in the English texts. This may hint at a connection with the older source which Chaucer used in "The Prioresse's Tale." The name of Mary Hamilton in "The Queen's Maries" (173) was for some time believed to have come from the Russian incident. But in Illinois a pioneer family was found which, in spite of its rigid Presbyterian prejudice against secular songs, had clung to the "Four Maries" stanza (usually associated with the "Mary Hamilton" versions of the ballad) because of its pride in its descent from Hamiltons and Stuarts. Since the family had come to this country early in the eighteenth century, before the Russian incident story could have been widely circulated in Scotland, the theory of Russian origin for this ballad would seem to be further discredited by American evidence.[54] Barry points out the persistence of the phrase "King Henry's white hall" in some American texts of "Little Musgrave" (81), as placing these versions not later and not earlier than the reign of Henry VIII, for the King acquired White-

---

[52] See page 272.

[53] Sharp, *English Folk Songs from the Southern Appalachians*, II, 51.

[54] Moore, "The Influence of Transmission on the English Ballads," *Modern Language Review*, XI (1916), 390.

hall from Wolsey.[55] This is an indication, too, of early importation into this country. One may also find out something from the American texts about ballad migration. Trails of such a ballad as "Barbara Allen" (84) are laid down everywhere; and the relation between an Ohio and a Michigan version, or a Tennessee and an Ozarks one, may throw light on how a ballad travels, and indirectly may show certain pioneer routes westward.

Finally, what ballads does the American singer remember? There are few survivals among the historical ballads, such stories as that of Mellinger Henry's discovery of "King Henry V's Conquest of France" (164) being very rare. "The Death of Queen Jane" (170) was collected in two forms by Cecil Sharp. "Mary Hamilton" (173) exists often only as a lyric lament. Border ballads have not survived, and those cases in which "Archie o Cawfield" (188) was found are not typical. Robin Hood ballads are few, and news of a possible item has sent many a collector on a wild goose chase. An anecdote of the Battle of Lexington, quoted by Barry,[56] shows revolutionary Boston's acquaintance with a broadside version of "Chevy Chase" (162), but this ballad has not survived orally, in spite of its long popularity in England. The stock themes of comedy continue to be popular, as the many versions of "The Wife Wrapt in Wether's Skin" (277), "Our Goodman" (274), and "The Farmer's Curst Wife" (278) bear witness. But the sturdiest survivors among transplanted ballads are those which are independent of special setting and circumstance, which, in their dramatic form and interest, their special idiom, and their selection of themes of human experience treated in the most condensed manner and adjusted to the singer's experience, are the favorites of every folk singer.

[55] Barry, *British Ballads from Maine*, p. 184.
[56] *Op. cit.*, p. 248.

LORD RENDAL (12)[57]

1. Where have you been all the day, Ren - dal, my son? Where have you been all the day, my pret - ty one? I've been to my sweet - heart, Mo - ther; I've been to my sweet - heart, Mo - ther; Make my bed soon, for I'm sick to my heart, And I fain would lie down.

1. Where have you been all the day, Rendal, my son?
   Where have you been all the day, my pretty one?
   I've been to my sweetheart, Mother;
   I've been to my sweetheart, Mother;
   Make my bed soon, for I'm sick to my heart,
   And I fain would lie down.

2. What have you been eating, Rendal, my son?
   What have you been eating, my pretty one?
   Oh, eels and eel broth, Mother,
   Eels and eel broth, Mother;
   Make my bed soon, *etc.*

3. Where did she get them from, Rendal, my son?
   Where did she get them from, my pretty one?
   From hedges and ditches, Mother,
   From hedges and ditches, Mother;
   Make my bed soon, *etc.*

[57] From Sharp, *One Hundred English Folksongs* (1916), p. 44. Reprinted by permission of Theodore Presser, Philadelphia, published and copyrighted by Oliver Ditson Co., Boston.

4. What was the color of their skin, Rendal, my son?
   What was the color of their skin, my pretty one?
   Oh, spickit and sparkit, Mother,
   Spickit and sparkit, Mother;
       Make my bed soon, etc. *for I am sick to my heart
       and I fain would lie down.*

5. What will you leave your father, Rendal, my son?
   What will you leave your father, my pretty one?
   My lands and houses, Mother,
   My lands and houses, Mother;
       Make my bed soon, etc.

6. What will you leave your mother, Rendal, my son?
   What will you leave your mother, my pretty one?
   My gold and silver, Mother,
   My gold and silver, Mother;
       Make my bed soon, etc.

7. What will you leave your brother, Rendal, my son?
   What will you leave your brother, my pretty one?
   My cows and horses, Mother,
   My cows and horses, Mother;
       Make my bed soon, etc.

8. What will you leave your lover, Rendal, my son?
   What will you leave your lover, my pretty one?
   A rope to hang her, Mother,
   A rope to hang her, Mother;
       Make my bed soon, for I'm sick to my heart,
       And I fain would lie down.

Miss A. G. Gilchrist, in *The Journal of the Folk-Song Society* (III
[1908–1909], 44), suggests that the story of the poisoned lover, known
over Europe at least since the sixteenth century, was earlier in England
attached to Randolph, Earl of Chester. Because he divorced his wife
and remarried, he was forced to relinquish his honors to a nephew
"whose wife was famous for plotting to take away the life of her husband by poison." The "step-mother" versions (See "The Croodin'
Doo," p. 166) may allude to an attempt by the first wife on the life of
a son by the second marriage. Is this ballad perhaps one of the "Rymes
of [Robin Hood and] Randolph Erle of Chestre" mentions in *Piers
Plowman*? The story that King Henry I died "of a surfeit of lampreys"
may account for the "King Henry, my son" versions of this ballad.

EDWARD (13)[58]

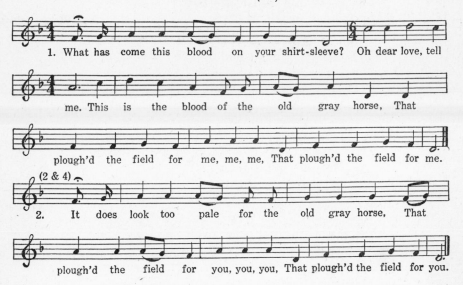

1. What has come this blood on your shirt-sleeve? Oh dear love, tell me. This is the blood of the old gray horse, That plough'd the field for me, me, me, That plough'd the field for me.

(2 & 4) 2. It does look too pale for the old gray horse, That plough'd the field for you, you, you, That plough'd the field for you.

1. What has come this blood on your shirt-sleeve?
   Oh dear love, tell me.
   This is the blood of the old gray horse,
   That plough'd the field for me, me, me,
   That plough'd the field for me.

2. It does look too pale for the old gray horse
   That plough'd the field for you, you, you,
   That plough'd the field for you.

3. What has come this blood on your shirt-sleeve?
   Oh dear love, tell me.
   This is the blood of the old gray hound
   That traced that fox for me, me, me,
   That traced that fox for me.

4. It does look too pale for the old gray hound
   That traced the fox for you, you, you,
   That traced the fox for you.

5. What has come this blood on your shirt-sleeve?
   Oh dear love, tell me.

[58] From Sharp, *English Folk Songs from the Southern Appalachians* (1932), I, 47–48. Reprinted by permission of the Oxford University Press, London, Publishers.

It is the blood of my brother-in-law
That went away with me, me, me,
That went away with me.

6. And it's what did you fall out about?
Oh dear love, tell me.
About a little bit of a bush
That soon would have made a tree, tree, tree,
That soon would have made a tree.

7. And it's what will you do now, my love?
Oh dear love, tell me.
I'll set my foot in yanders ship
And I'll sail across the sea, sea, sea,
And I'll sail across the sea.

8. And it's when will you come back, my love?
Oh dear love, tell me.
When the sun sets into yanders sycamore tree,
And that will never be, be, be,
And that will never be.

THE BONNY BANKS OF VIRGIE O
(Babylon, 14)[59]

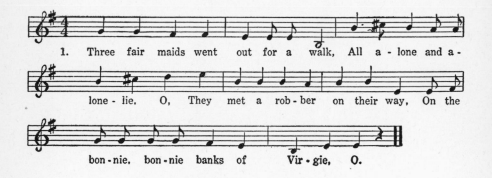

1. Three fair maids went out for a walk,
All alone and a-lonelie, O,
They met a robber on their way,
On the bonnie, bonnie banks of Virgie, O.

[59] From Karpeles, *Folk Songs from Newfoundland* (1934?) II, 79. Reprinted by permission of Miss Karpeles, and the Oxford University Press, London, Publishers.

2. He took the first one by the hand,
   And he whipped her around and he made her stand.

3. O will you be a robber's wife?
   Or will you die by my pen-knife?

4. I will not be a robber's wife;
   I would rather die by your pen-knife.

5. Oh, he took out his little pen-knife,
   And it's then he took her own sweet life.

6. He took the second one by the hand,
   And he whipped her around and he made her stand.

7. Oh, will you be a robber's wife?
   Or will you die by my pen-knife?

8. I will not be a robber's wife,
   I would rather die by your pen-knife.

9. Oh, he took out his little pen-knife,
   And it's then he took her own sweet life.

10. He took the third one by the hand,
    And he whipped her around and he made her stand.

11. Oh, will you be a robber's wife,
    Or will you die by my pen-knife?

12. I will not be a robber's wife,
    Nor will I die by your pen-knife.

13. Oh, if I had my brothers here,
    You would not have killed my sisters dear.

14. Oh, where are your brothers, pray now tell,
    Oh, one of them is a minister.

15. And where is the other, pray now tell?
    He's out a-robbing like yourself.

16. The Lord have mercy on my soul,
    For I have killed my sisters dear.

17. Then he took out his little pen-knife,
    And it's then he took his own sweet life.

THE BROWN GIRL
(Lord Thomas and Fair Annet, 73) [60]

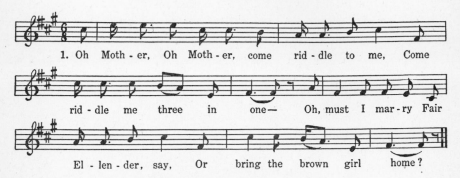

1. Oh Moth-er, Oh Moth-er, come rid-dle to me, Come rid-dle me three in one— Oh, must I mar-ry Fair El-len-der, say, Or bring the brown girl home?

1. Oh Mother, Oh Mother, come riddle to me,
   Come riddle me three in one—
Oh, must I marry fair Ellender, say,
   Or bring the brown girl home?

2. The brown girl, she has money and lands,
   Fair Ellender she has none,
My blessing on you, my own dear son,
   If you bring the brown girl home.

3. He rode till he came to Fair Ellender's gate,
   He tingled the bell on the ring,
No one so ready as Fair Ellender,
   To rise and bid him come in.

4. What news, what news, Lord Thomas, she cried;
   What news have you brought to me?
I've come to bid you to my wedding,
   For tomorrow it may be.

5. She dressed herself in a scarlet robe,
   Her waiting maid dressed in green,
And every town that she rode through,
   They took her to be some queen.

6. She rode till she came to Lord Thomas's gate,
   She pulled all up her rein,
No one so ready as Lord Thomas himself,
   To rise and bid her come in.

[60] As sung by children in the Pine Mountain Settlement School, Pine Mountain, Harlan County, Kentucky, to E. K. Wells, 1916.

7. He took her by the lily-white hand
    And led her through the hall,
And seated her down in a rocking-chair
    Among the ladies all.

8. Lord Thomas, Lord Thomas, is this your bride?
    I'm sure she's very brown;
You once could have had as fair a girl
    As ever the sun shone on.

9. The brown girl drew a knife from her belt,
    The blade being keen and sharp,
Between the long rib and the short
    Stabbed Fair Ellender to the heart.

10. Lord Thomas he drew his sword from his side,
    As he came in from the hall,
He cut off the head of his wilful bride
    And threw it against the wall.

11. Then placing the handle against the wall,
    And the blade against his heart,
Says, did you ever see three lovers meet,
    That had so soon to part?

12. Oh Mother, Oh Mother, go dig my grave,
    Go dig it long and deep,
And bury Fair Ellender in my arms,
    And the brown girl at my feet.

13. And by my side plant a willow tree,
    And on its branch a dove,
To testify to all the world
    That I have died for love.

LORD LOVEL (75)[61]

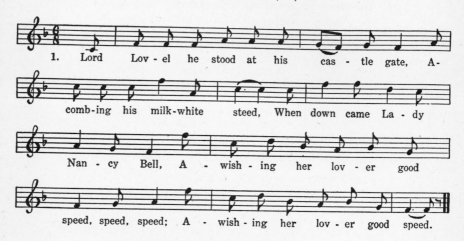

1. Lord Lov-el he stood at his cas-tle gate, A-comb-ing his milk-white steed, When down came La-dy Nan-cy Bell, A-wish-ing her lov-er good speed, speed, speed; A-wish-ing her lov-er good speed.

1. Lord Lovel he stood at his castle gate,
   A-combing his milk-white steed,
When down came Lady Nancy Bell,
   A-wishing her lover good speed, speed, speed;
   A-wishing her lover good speed.

2. Now where are you going, Lord Lovel, she said,
   Now where are you going, said she;
I'm going away, Lady Nancy Bell,
   Strange countries for to see, see, see.
   Strange countries for to see.

3. When will you be back, Lord Lovel? she said,
   When will you be back? said she.
In a year or two, or three at most,
   I'll return to my Lady Nancy, -cy, -cy,
   I'll return to my Lady Nancy.

4. Now he hadn't been gone a year and a day,
   Strange countries for to see,
When languishing thoughts came into his head,
   Lady Nancy Bell he would go see, *etc.*

[61] As sung in the family of E. K. Wells. This ballad was taken up by comic singers in America in the 1830's, and received a new impetus of an unfortunate character. My uncle used to break into sobbing over the words "sorrow-orrow-orrow!" to our exquisite amusement.

5. So he rode and he rode on his milk-white steed,
    Till he came to London Town,
And there he heard the high church-bells ring,
    And the people all walking around, *etc.*

6. Now who is dead, Lord Lovel he said,
    Now who is dead, said he.
A lady is dead, the people all said,
    And they called her the Lady Nancy, *etc.*

7. Then he caused the grave to be opened straight,
    And the shroud to be turned a-down,
And there he kissed her clay-cold cheek,
    While the tears came a-trickling down, *etc.*

8. Lady Nancy, she died it might be today,
    Lord Lovel, he died on the morrow.
Lady Nancy, she died of a broken heart,
    Lord Lovel, he died of pure sorrow, *etc.*

9. They buried them both in St. Clement's churchyard,
    They buried them under the spire,
And out of her bosom there grew a red rose,
    And out of his'n a briar, *etc.*

10. They grew, and they grew, till they reached the church top,
    When of course they couldn't grow any higher,
And there they entwined in a true-lovers' knot,
    All true lovers for to admire, -ire, -ire,
      All true lovers for to admire.

LITTLE MATTHY GROVE
(Little Musgrave and Lady Barnard, 81)[62]

1. Hol - i - day, hol - i - day, on the ve - ry first day of the
year, year, On the ve - ry first day of the year, Lit - tle
Ma - tthy Grove went to the church, The ho - ly word for to
hear, hear, The ho - ly word for to hear. 2.The first came in was
li - ly white, The next came in was a girl, The
next came in was Lord Dan - iel's wife, The fair - est one in the
world, world, The fair - est one in the world.

1. Holiday, holiday, on the very first day of the year, year,
   On the very first day of the year,
   Little Matthy Grove went to the church,
   The holy word for to hear, hear,
   The holy word for to hear.

2. The first came in was lily white,
   The next came in was a girl,
   The next came in was Lord Daniel's wife,
   The fairest one in the world, world,
   The fairest one in the world.

[62] As sung by Willie Nolan ("Singing Willie") of Incline, Ky., to E. K. Wells, 1920.

3. She placed her eye on Little Matthy Grove,
      And said, Go home with me this night;
   Go home with me, this night for to lie,
      Go home with me this night, night, *etc.*

4. I can't go home with you this night,
      For fear I do lose my life,
   For the rings that's on your fingers says
      You are Lord Daniel's wife, wife, *etc.*

5. But what if I am Lord Daniel's wife,
      Lord Daniel's gone from home;
   He has gone to the high king's house
      To see his fences, sir, sir, *etc.*

6. There stood that little foot-page,
      Hearing every word that they did say;
   He says, Lord Daniel shall hear of this
      Before the break of day, day, *etc.*

7. It was fourteen miles to the king's house,
      And seven of them he run;
   He run till he came to the broad river side,
      He bowed to his breast and swum, *etc.*

8. He swum till he came to the other side,
      He buckled up his shoes and run,
   He run till he came to the high king's gate,
      He rattled his bell and rung, *etc.*

9. The first came out was Lord Daniel,
      Said, What news have you to tell?
   Is my old scafel a-burning down,
      Or is my tavern won, *etc.*

10. Your old scafel is not burnt down,
       But neither is your tavern won,
    But your wife is at home, in the bed,
       With Little Matthy Grove alone, *etc.*

11. He had a trumpet and it would blow,
       And every time that it would sound,
    It seemed for to say, Rise up and go,
       It says, Rise up and go, *etc.*

12. She says, No, no, lie still with me,
       And keep me from the cold,
    It is nothing but them shepherd boys
       A-driving their sheep to the fold, *etc.*

13. They turned then to hugging and kissing,
      Till they returned to sleep,
    And when they wakened the next morning,
      Lord Daniel was at their bed-feet, *etc.*

14. Says, How do you like your blanket, Sir,
      And how do you like your sheet?
    Or how do you like this fair young miss
      That lies in your arms so sweet, *etc.*

15. Very well I do like my blanket, Sir,
      Very well I do like my sheet,
    Much better do I like this fair young miss
      That lies in my arms asleep, *etc.*

16. Get up, get up, put on your clothes,
      And fight me like a man,
    I can't have it said in the farest land,
      That I slew a naked man, *etc.*

17. How can I get up, put on my clothes,
      And fight you for my life,
    For I see you have two very bright swords,
      And me not as much as a knife, *etc.*

18. Sir, I have two very bright swords,
      That cost me deep in purse,
    And you can have the very best one,
      And I will take the worst, *etc.*

19. The very first lick Little Matthy stroke,
      He wounded him deep and sore,
    But the very first lick Lord Daniel stroke,
      Little Matthy couldn't fight no more, *etc.*

20. He took this lady by the hand,
      And placed her on his knee,
    Says, Which do you love the best,
      Little Matthy Grove or me? *etc.*

21. Very well I do like your red rosy cheeks,
      Much better do I like your chin,
    Much better do I like Little Matthy Grove
      Than you or any of your kin, *etc.*

22. He took this lady by the lily-white hand,
      He led her out in the lane,
    He drew his sword from his side,
      He split her head into twin, *etc.*

23. O don't you hear them larkins say,
    Don't you hear them sparrows cry,
    Today I have slain two the fairest ones,
    And tomorrow I will die, die,
    And tomorrow I will die.

BARBRY ELLEN (84)[63]

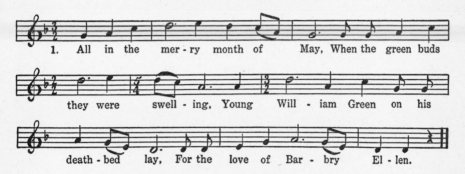

1. All in the mer-ry month of May, When the green buds
they were swell-ing, Young Will-iam Green on his
death-bed lay, For the love of Bar-bry El-len.

1. All in the merry month of May,
    When the green buds they were swelling,
    Young William Green on his death-bed lay,
    For the love of Barbry Ellen.

2. He sent his servant to the town,
    To the place where she was dwelling,
    Saying, my master bids you come,
    If your name is Barbry Ellen.

3. Then slowly, slowly she got up,
    And slowly came she nigh him,
    And when she pulled the curtains back,
    Young man, I think you're dying.

4. O yes, I'm sick, I'm very very sick,
    And I never will be any better,
    Until I have the love of one,
    The love of Barbry Ellen.

5. O don't you remember in yonder town,
    In the place where you were dwelling,
    You drank the health of the ladies all around,
    But you slighted Barbry Ellen.

[63] As sung by children in the Pine Mountain Settlement School, Pine Mountain, Harlan County, Kentucky, to E. K. Wells, 1916.

6. O yes, I remember in yonder town,
   In the place where I was dwelling,
   I drank the health of the ladies all around,
   But my love was to Barbry Ellen.

7. He turned his pale face to the wall,
   And death was in him dwelling.
   Adieu, adieu, my kind friends all,
   Be kind to Barbry Ellen.

8. As she was going through the field,
   She heard the death bells knelling,
   And every stroke they seemed to say,
   Hard-hearted Barbry Ellen.

9. She looked east, she looked west,
   And saw the pale corpse coming.
   Go bring him here and lay him down,
   And let me look upon him.

10. The more she looked, the more she grieved,
    Until she burst out crying.
    Go take him away, go take him away,
    For I am now a-dying.

11. O Mother, O Mother, come make my bed,
    Come make it soft and narrow;
    Sweet William died for me today,
    I'll die for him tomorrow.

12. O Father, O Father, come dig my grave,
    O dig it deep and narrow;
    Sweet William died for love of me,
    And I will die for sorrow.

13. They buried her in the old churchyard,
    And William's grave was nigh her,
    And out of his grave there grew a red rose,
    And out of hers a briar.

14. They grew and grew to the old church tower,
    And they could not grow any higher,
    They grew and grew till they tied love knots,
    And the rose wrapped round the briar.

THE HANGMAN
(The Maid Freed from the Gallows, 95) [64]

Hang - man, hang - man, slack up your rope; Slack it for a while, I look'd ov - er yon - der and I seen Paw com - in'. He's walked for ma - ny a long mile. Say, Paw, say, Paw, have you brung me an - y gold, An - y gold for to pay my fine? No, sir, No, sir, I've brung ye no gold, No gold for to pay your fine. For I've just come for to see you hanged, Hanged on the gal - lows line. You won't love and it's hard to be be - loved, And it's hard to make up your fine; You have broke the heart of ma - ny a true love, true love, and you can't break mine.

Hangman, Hangman, slack up your rope;
Slack it for a while,
I look'd over yonder and I seen Paw comin',
He's walked for many a long mile.

[64] As sung by children in the Pine Mountain Settlement School, Pine Mountain, Harlan County, Kentucky, to E. K. Wells, 1916.

Say, Paw, say, Paw, have you brung me any gold,
Any gold for to pay my fine?
No, sir, No, sir, I've brung ye no gold,
No gold for to pay your fine,
For I've just come for to see you hanged,
Hanged on the gallows line.
You won't love and it's hard to be beloved,
And it's hard to make up your fine;
You have broke the heart of many a true love,
True love, and you can't break mine.

Repeat, substituting "Maw," "Sisters," "Brothers," *etc. ad lib.* with the other necessary changes in wording. In the final stanza the true-love arrives:

Yes, sir, Yes Sir, I've brung ye some gold,
Some gold for to pay your fine,
For I've just come for to take you home
From out the gallows line.

(Omit the last three lines of music.)

THE GYPSY DAVY
(The Gypsy Laddie, 200) [65]

1. The squire came home late at night, En-quir-ing for his la-dy, The
ser-vant made him this re-ply, She's gone with the Gyp-sy Da-vy.
Tour-da-link-tum, tour-da-lie, Tour-da-link-tum ti-do: The
ser-vant made him this re-ply, She's gone with the Gyp-sy Da-vy.

1. The squire came home late at night,
Enquiring for his lady,
The servant made him this reply,
She's gone with the Gypsy Davy.

[65] As sung by Mrs. Carrie Grover, Gorham, Maine, to E. K. Wells, May, 1944.

(Tour-da-link-tum, tour-da-lie,
   Tour-da-link-tum ti-do;
The servant made him this reply,
   She's gone with the Gypsy Davy.

2. Go harness up my milk-white steed,
   The grey is not so speedy;
I'll ride all night and I'll ride all day,
   Till I overtake my lady.
     Tour-da-link-tum, *etc.*

3. He rode till he came to the river's side,
   It looked so dark and dreary,
There he espied his lady fair
   Along with the Gypsy Davy.
     Tour-da-link-tum, *etc.*

4. Would you forsake your house and home,
   Would you forsake your baby,
Would you forsake your own wed lord,
   'n go long with the Gypsy Davy? *etc.*

5. Yes, I'd forsake my house and home,
   Yes, I'd forsake my baby,
Yes, I'd forsake my own wed lord
   To go long with the Gypsy Davy, *etc.*

6. Last night I lay on a bed of down,
   My baby lay beside me,
Tonight I'll lay on the cold cold ground
   Along with the Gypsy Davy.
     Tour-da-link-tum, tour-da-lie,
     Tour-da-link-tum ti-do;
Tonight I'll lay on the cold cold ground
   Along with the Gypsy Davy.

GEORGIE
(Geordie, 209)[66]

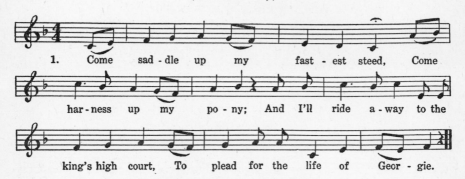

1. Come sad-dle up my fast-est steed, Come
har-ness up my po-ny; And I'll ride a-way to the
king's high court, To plead for the life of Geor-gie.

1. Come saddle up my fastest steed,
   Come harness up my pony;
   And I'll ride away to the king's high court,
   To plead for the life of Georgie.

2. The lady has great stores of gold,
   Of jewels she has many,
   All this she'd give to the royal king
   To save the life of Georgie.

3. As the King rode over London Bridge,
   So early in the morning,
   He met this lady on her way,
   Enquiring for her Georgie.

4. O where are you going, my fair pretty maid,
   So early in the morning?
   O she says, I'm going to the King's high court
   To plead for the life of Georgie.

5. The King looked over his left shoulder,
   So early in the morning,
   I'm afraid you're too late, my pretty fair maid,
   For he's condemned already.

6. O who has he murdered or what has he done,
   Or has he killed anybody?
   He has stole three pearls from the royal king
   And sold them in a hurry.

[66] As sung by Mrs. Carrie Grover, Gorham, Maine, to E. K. Wells, May, 1944. (The singer tends at times to sing A-flat, thus turning the tune into a modal minor.)

7. O he shall be hung with a chain of gold,
       Such chains they are not many,
    For he was born of the royal blood
       And was loved by a noble lady.

8. He shall be buried in marble stones,
       Such stones they are not many,
    And he shall be covered with the same,
       Saying, Here lies the body of Georgie.

THE LITTLE TURTLE DOVE [67]

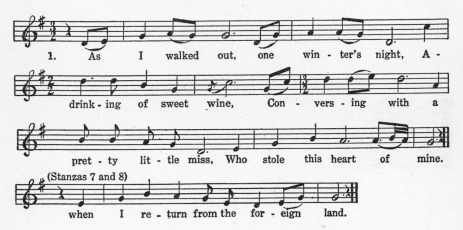

1. As I walked out, one winter's night,
       A-drinking of sweet wine,
    Conversing with a pretty little miss,
       Who stole this heart of mine.

2. Her cheeks were like some pink-a rose
       That bloomed in the month of June;
    Her voice was like some music or instrument,
       Just all put down in tune.

3. So don't you see yon little turtle-dove
       A-sitting in yonders pine,
    A-weeping for the loss of its own true love,
       Just as I weep for mine.

[67] As sung by Willie Nolan ("Singing Willie") of Incline, Ky., to E. K. Wells, 1920.
    A ballad made up largely of ballad tags. See "The Lass of Roch Royal" (76) for
stanzas 7 and 8; and Burns's "My luve is like a red red rose" for his indebtedness.

4. So fare you well, my own true love,
　　So fare you well for a while,
I'm going away, but I'll be back again
　　If I go ten thousand miles.

5. Ten thousand miles, my own true love,
　　Through England, France and Spain,
Supposing you were taken down sick,
　　And you so far from home?
(Repeat second half of tune)
O who would hear your loudly cries,
　　Or bear your pitiful moan?

6. O hush, my love, don't break my heart,
　　For I would hate to hear your cries,
For the best of friends do have to part,
　　And now it's you and I.

7. O, who will shoe my feet, my love,
　　And who will glove my hand,
And who will kiss my red rosy cheeks
　　When you are in the foreign land?

8. Your father will shoe your feet, my love,
　　Your mother will glove your hand,
And I will kiss your red rosy cheeks
　　When I return from the foreign land.

THE WIFE WRAPT IN WETHER'S SKIN (277)[68]

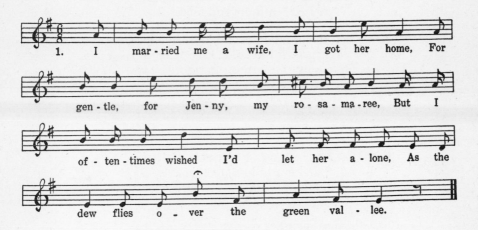

1. I married me a wife, I got her home,
        For gentle, for Jenny, my rosamaree,
    But I oftentimes wished I'd let her alone,
        As the dew flies over the green vallee.

2. Then I come in it's from my plough,
        For gentle, *etc.*
    O now, my kind wife, is my dinner ready now?
        As the dew, *etc.*

3. There's a piece of bread upon the shelf,
        If you want any more you can bake it yourself.

4. I gets me a knife and I went to the barn,
        And I cut me hickory just as long as my arm.

5. Then I come back it's to the house,
        I make my hickory go wickechy whack.

6. Then I come in it's from my plough,
        O now, my kind wife, is my dinner ready now?

7. She flew around, the board it was spread,
        And every word, it was Yes, Sir! and No, Sir!

[68] From Sharp, *English Folk Songs from the Southern Appalachians* (1932), I, 272. By permission of the Oxford University Press, Publishers, London.

THE DEVIL AND THE FARMER'S WIFE
(The Farmer's Curst Wife, 278) [69]

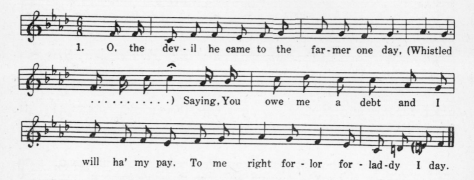

1. O, the dev-il he came to the far-mer one day, (Whistled
............) Saying, You owe me a debt and I
will ha' my pay. To me right for-lor for-lad-dy I day.

1. O, the devil he came to the farmer one day,
        (Whistled phrase, *etc.*)
    Saying, You owe me a debt and I will ha' my pay,
        To me right for-lor for-laddy I day.

2. It is not your children nor you that I crave,
        (Whistled phrase, *etc.*)
    But your old scolding wife and it's her I must have,
        To me right, *etc.*

3. O take her, O take her with all my heart,
    And I hope you and she will never part.

4. So the Devil he mounted her onto his back,
    And like a bold pedlar went carrying his pack.

5. Nine little devils were hanging in chains,
    She up with a poker and knocked out their brains.

6. She climbed up a stool for to make herself higher,
    She threw round her left leg and knocked nine in the fire.

7. The little blue devils peeped over the wall,
    O take her back, dad, or she'll kill us all.

8. So the devil he mounted her onto his back,
    And like a bold pedlar went carrying her back.

[69] As sung by Mrs. Carrie Grover of Gorham, Maine, to E. K. Wells, May, 1944.
(The singer varies between E-flat and E-natural in the last measure.)

AUNT SAL'S SONG [70]

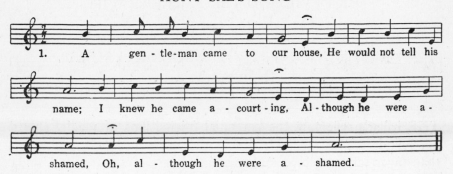

1. A gen-tle-man came to our house, He would not tell his
name; I knew he came a-court-ing, Al-though he were a-
shamed, Oh, al-though he were a-shamed.

1. A gentleman came to our house, he would not tell his name;
   I knew he came a-courting, although he were ashamed,
       Oh, although he were ashamed.

2. He moved his chair up to my side, his fancy pleased me well,
   I thought the spirit moved him some handsome tale to tell.
       Oh, some handsome tale to tell.

3. Oh, there he sat the livelong night and never a word did say,
   With many a sigh and bitter groan he ofttimes wished for day.
       Oh, he ofttimes wished for day.

4. The chickens they begun to crow, and daylight did appear,
   How d'ye do, good morning, Sir; I'm glad to see you here,
       Oh, I'm glad to see you here.

5. He was weary of the livelong night, he was weary of his life;
   If this is what you call courting, boys, I'll never take a wife,
       Oh, I'll never take a wife.

6. And when he goes in company, the girls all laugh for sport,
   Saying, Yonder goes that ding-dang fool, he don't know how
         to court,
       Oh, he don't know how to court!

[70] As sung by Mrs. Sallie Creech, Pine Mountain, Harlan County, Kentucky, to
E. K. Wells, 1916.

Chapter 5

REFLECTIONS OF THE SUPERNATURAL
IN BALLADS

THE ballads reflecting the perennial fascinations of magic, ghosts, fairies and their ways, send us deeper into ancient attitudes and beliefs than any so far considered, and demand a brief statement of the fundamental ideas involved. This discussion is obviously not exhaustive. It does not in any sense present a perfect system of primitive belief, complete and consistent with any one stage of folk thinking or reasoning, nor does it account for the many contradictions in ballad folklore. It does not explain the corporeal nature of the ghost and the spiritual nature of ships and bows and harps as part of the same system, nor the fact that fairies both dread and use cold iron, nor reconcile the uttering of a name with its proscription, nor justify the same method for invoking and exorcising a spirit. The same thing is now good, now bad, brings luck and ill-hap. Many contradictions mingle and jostle in the ballads, defying conformity. Here we attempt merely to point out and give perspective to some evidences of primitive thought and custom which have been swept into the stream of tradition and preserved in the ballads in a fragmentary, or vestigial, or only faintly reminiscent state.

"We think our civilization near its meridian, but we are yet only at the cock-crowing and morning star. In our barbarous society the influence of character is in its infancy," says Emerson in his *Essay on Politics*. The truth of this statement strikes home as we scan survivals of primitive thought around us. An everyday phrase may hark back to some hinterland of thought; a flippant "My stars!" may be descended from the ritual of swearing by the sun, the stars, the moon, turning oneself about thrice and repeating runes. Enlightened though we are, many of us feel slightly easier if we touch wood after boasting, as our ancestors did to propitiate the tree spirit, or cross our fingers to avert bad luck, as they did to confuse evil demons. The considerable number of people who still consult numerologists are resorting to a primitive belief in the magic properties of numbers literally almost as old as the hills. The college student who took her ballad examination with the aid of her mascot, a tiny toy dog, is the descendant of the animal worshiper faintly recalled in the ballads she studied. Superstition today is by no means confined to "the folk," as the avoidance of the number thirteen by the sophisticated shows. New forms of folklore appear. The last war produced the gremlin, at first an airplane pixy, but soon infesting all sorts of machinery. Animal superstitions abound—as that rats leave a sinking ship, and dogs howl at the approach of death. Cats, crows, black dogs, white horses, as every child knows, are the bringers of good and bad luck. The wisdom of birds is celebrated today by some of the wisest men alive. On the anniversary of the founding of Queen's College in Oxford, the dons in their gowns ascend to the roof of the college buildings to scan the heavens for the flight of wild duck, thus commemorating those early monks who as they floundered across the marshes vowed to found their college where the ducks settled.

Many superstitions have grown out of the idea that the abnormal or the unnatural was fraught with special virtue. Twins, albinos, hunchbacks, "sely folk" or naturals, still receive a certain amount of fascinated attention. But the sely or silly folk were once *selig* or blessed, and "I have a hunch" is said, perhaps with too much enthusiasm, to have evolved from the belief that good luck followed from touching a hunchback. The evil eye is black in northern countries, blue in the dark-eyed south. The fair hair of the "foreign devils" in China, being outside native experience, seemed supernatural; these white men must have come from a world of spirits.

It is a commonplace of information that Christianity has taken over bodily many of the practises of an earlier religion. Its rites of baptism, communion, marriage, and burial, its good and bad angels, its seasonal festivals like Christmas, Easter, and saints' days, derive from a heathen time. Other beliefs it has outlawed; animals once sacred, like the goat or the snake, it associates with Satan. Some it has converted to kinder uses: "Speak of the Devil" has become "Speaking of Angels." Those abnormal creatures, whistling girls and crowing hens, were once agents of magic; Christianity has completed the adage with a moral twist.[1]

[1] See page 176 ff., for discussion of the Christian use of pagan customs.

From his observation of nature, which he believed directed every act of his life, man evolved the primitive lore which was to give birth to modern sciences. Stargazers, reading man's fate in the heavens, became professional astrologers and then astronomers. The *abracadabra* of the alchemists is the forerunner of chemical formulae. The Indians of the Southwest assist the rain spirit by making a great noise; so our weathermen in the days of the oldfashioned Fourth of July celebrations knew that thunderstorms would follow the firecrackers. The well-digger uses a hazel divining rod; his forebears believed that the hazel tree had magic properties. Early principles of medicine are sometimes in surprising agreement with modern treatment. "The hair of the dog that bit you" is no longer the cure for dogbite, but a similar principle is involved in antirabies serum. You may be inoculated against an infection in one part of your body by antitoxin collected from another part. Thus "Like cures like," the homeopath's principle, would make sense to the pagan medicine man.

It was not until the last century that folklore emerged as a modern science. From the chroniclers down through Aubrey, Selden, and Pepys, amateur antiquarians had collected curious bits of folk belief and custom for centuries. In 1592 a Society of Antiquaries was founded in England, but it was suppressed in the reign of James I—somewhat illogically, for James himself was a serious student of the supernatural. In 1707 it was revived, if one can use the word for an organization so long dead, but the Age of Reason's treatment of the subject was ineffective and puerile. An attempt to classify and interpret this miscellany of superstitions began in Germany at the end of the Romantic Movement under the Brothers Grimm, editors of fairy tales in their lighter moments. Thanks to them, Folklore, as a branch of Anthropology today, is no longer a term to cover mere unrelated bits of credulity; it is a correlation of these bits, by which each gains significance when viewed in the light of its neighbor. This collecting and ordering of previously isolated details often sheds light on a whole culture hitherto unrecorded. Folklore searches and arranges all the miscellaneous traditional material of early record and current survival —the songs, dances, customs, sayings, ceremonies, and superstitions of not only the primitive and illiterate, but also of the sophisticated. To this material ballad poetry has made a substantial contribution. To understand this contribution better, we must go further than this brief mention of familiar superstitions, along less familiar paths, finding as we go that what is to us a metaphor of poetry is "not a mere figment devised to adorn a tale, but a real article of primitive faith." [2]

In the group of ballads dealing with the supernatural, one becomes at once aware of the relationship between man and animals. This is a vestige of totemism, the early belief that man's descent from animals gave him a kinship with them and involved their worship, with its sacrifice of the sacred animal and participation in a sacred meal. The blood of the sacrifice was holy; its entrails might be read for signs and omens; the wearing of a bit of its fur or skin gave one special powers. Any part of the animal, like the rabbit's foot, might bring its wearer good luck. Some feeling of special virtue attaches still to the possession of the fox brush, though today it is merely a sign that you were "in at the death." Shakespeare's foresters sing:

> What shall he have that killed the deer?
> His leather skin and horns to wear.
> Then sing him home.[3]

The Mexican Indian dancers who bind the horns of deer onto their heads today may seem a far cry from anything in our own heritage; yet this form of animal identification can be found in Abbots Bromley, a Staffordshire village not fifteen miles from Birmingham in the heart of industrial England, where the men dance annually in the streets and around the nearby farms, bearing the great reindeer horns which for the rest of the year hang in the village church. And it is bad luck if any onlooker fails to contribute his penny when the collection box comes around. In this way, as the folklorist explains it, everyone shares in the virtue of the horn dance.

> Take thou no scorn to wear the horn,
> It was a crest ere thou wast born;
> Thy father's father bore it,
> And thy father wore it.[4]

Totemistic belief accounts for the ability of animals to speak. They may be descended from man's ancestral animal, and being kindly disposed toward their kinsman, may wish to speak to him; they may once have been human, and now, as transmigrated souls, retain the power of communication; they may be under temporary transforma-

[2] Frazer, *The Golden Bough*, XI, 153.   [4] *Loc. cit.*
[3] Shakespeare, *As You Like It*, IV, ii.

tion by witches, or witches themselves in animal form. Children today show us something of primitive reasoning in attributing to animals powers similar to their own. They still live in a world where any bird or dog or horse may speak to them, and the presence of speaking animals in fairy tales finds them completely and uncritically receptive.

So, in the ballads, it is a bird in "Young Hunting" (68) who discloses the murder—a bird who is probably the translated hero himself. The Gay Goshawk (96) converses with the lovers, although he has been somewhat rationalized into a sort of carrier pigeon, with letters under his wing. Steed and hawk in "The Broomfield Hill" (43) do their best to awaken their master, and report their efforts later." A bird out of a bush" takes harp in hand and "harps them all asleep" in "Lady Isabel and the Elf-Knight" (4 B). And there are cases of transformation of men into animals, and occasional allusions to werewolf metamorphoses.

Animism is the belief in the presence of souls or spirits in various parts of the body, in personal possessions, and in objects which would be considered by us inanimate, or soulless. The spirit of man might choose special parts of the body for a dwelling place, or, released from the body by death, might choose a temporary or a permanent home in an animal, or a tree, or a plant, or flower, or body of water; or be lured to inhabit a specially prepared receptacle or fetish, such as a charm, talisman, or image. The spirit freed at death was evil and must be propitiated, so the homes of spirits were held in special reverence, and a system of nature worship developed, with its hierarchy of major and minor spirits.

Animism has left its traces in some of our practices. The child who looks out of the window chanting, "Rain, rain, go away," or who pettishly kicks the chair he has stumbled against, is animating the rain or the wood, as did his pagan ancestor. Folk tales of all kinds reflect this belief, the most familiar illustration being the end of the cumulative story of the Old Woman and her Pig:

> *Then,* The rope began to hang the butcher,
>   The butcher began to shake the stick,
>   The stick began to beat the dog,
>   The dog began to bite the pig,
>   Piggy jumped over the stile,
>   And so the old woman got home that night.

The story of Jonah contains the same idea. The ship, knowing that a guilty person is aboard, refuses to sail until he is cast into the sea. The ballad of "Bonnie Annie" (24) deals with a similar problem. Somebody on the ship is doomed to die; lots are cast by means of bullets, possibly animistically imbued, and as a result Bonnie Annie is thrown overboard. Then the ship is able to sail.

The spirit's dwelling place might also be in special parts of the body, particularly those which were removable, like the hair, teeth, nails, spittle, or blood. In Samson's loss of strength when his hair was cut, and in the long-haired "House of David" followers of today, we find a survival of this belief. The "hexing" of a person by means of a waxen image was made the more effective if the witch could incorporate in it the victim's nail cuttings, or some of his hair. Blood rituals were based on the belief that the blood was a favorite dwelling place for the spirit. Since loss of life and loss of blood went together, the life spirit must dwell in the blood. It may be said in passing that folk superstitions are often based on common sense: of course it is unlucky to break mirrors or walk under ladders, for the glass may cut you and the ladders may fall on you. The blood of enemies was mingled in a drink of blood brotherhood at reconciliation; a fatal wound bled anew at the approach of the killer:

> White, white waur his wounds washen,
> As white as ony lawn;
> But sune's the traitor stude afore,
> Then oot the red blude sprang.[5]

Since it contained the soul, the blood of the victim must be caught in some worthy vessel, silver and scoured clean for one of gentle birth:

> O scour the basin, nourice
> And make it fair and clean,
> For to keep this lady's heart's blood,
> For she's come o noble kin.[6]

From nursery days we have known about this custom:

> Who caught his blood?
> Who caught his blood?
> I, said the fish,
> With my little silver dish,
> It was I, Oh, it was I.

[5] "Young Hunting" (68 C).   [6] "Lamkin" (93).

The stains of blood were indelible, as Lady Macbeth's subconscious mind knew. Many a "wee pen knife" in a ballad will not be wiped clean.

> She washed her pen-knife in the brook;
> The more she washed, the redder its look.[7]

The spirit might dwell in something intangible, like light. Some connection of phosphorescence with decaying flesh may have assisted this belief. Today we have a relic of it in the emanation from a ghost, or more crudely, the light in the Hallowe'en jack-lantern. The body of Young Hunting (68) is located by passing candles over its resting place:

> Wherever that sakeless knight lys slain,
> The candels will shine bright.

The severed head of the lady in "Lamkin" (93 B) illuminates the room:

> Then he cut aff the head
> From her lily breast-bane,
> And he hung't up in the kitchen;
> It made a' the hall shine.

By extension, the resort of the spirit might be the personal possessions, such as clothing, a ring, or a sword. There are many stories like that of the ring in "Hind Horn" (17) which reflects the condition of its owner. A mermaid's sark—indeed just a piece of it—is the undoing of Clerk Colvill (42). The words of Johnie Cock (114) are not metaphorical apostrophe, but the echo of a literal belief:

> O bows of yew, if ye be true,
> In London, where ye were bought,
> Fingers five, get up belive,
> Manhuid shall fail me nought.

The harp made of the drowned girl's bones and hair, in "The Twa Sisters" (10), is perforce a messenger of her murder, having received her spirit so completely.

The belief that the most secret, remote, and inviolable home of the spirit was in a man's name has left many traces. A secret and personal name is given today to the young Indian when he is initiated

---

[7] Barry, *British Ballads from Maine*, p. 81.

into the tribe. Among the ancient Jews, the real and secret name of God was too sacred for utterance. A substitution for the ineffable was therefore composed of the consonants of Jahweh (God) and the vowels of Adonai (The Lord), resulting in the name Jehovah. The fairy-tale maiden set to an endless task buys her freedom by guessing the name of her tormentor, Rumpelstiltskin. *Lohengrin* is based on the same belief: Elsa must part from her knight once she has broken the taboo and asked his name. "My father Parzifal, and Lohengrin my name" is indeed the swan-knight's swan song. Good and bad spirits might be invoked or exorcised by speaking their names. Evil spirits might be placated by giving them pleasant names: the Irish fairies are "The Good Folk." Hamlet, speaking in a superstitious age, is risking his very soul in daring to address the ghost, which may be an evil spirit or goblin damned, by his father's name: "I'll call thee Hamlet . . ." [8] The devil went by many names, all spiced with danger. Today he is The Dickens and Mr. Scratch; in the ballads he is "Auld Clootie"—Old Cloven-Hoof,[9] or metamorphosed into the Knight upon the Road (3).

Here too we are not far from the nursery, for many a child lives a secret life, with a name he alone knows, and which belongs to a personality he puts on or takes off at will. Christian baptism is a development of a heathen rite which allied the name to life itself. To Christianize was to spiritualize, and the connection of formal naming with dedication to God became a symbol of spiritual rather than physical life. For many people today, the adoption of a saint's name at baptism is added blessing, and the child that dies unbaptized is doomed.

In "Earl Brand" (7) a vestige of this belief is found. It is only from the narrator that we know the hero as Lord William, or Sweet Willie. The lady herself never so addresses him until the critical moment, and this "dead-naming" is fatal to him. The form in which the story has come to us gives us the sequence of events, but not the reason for it. But in comparing our versions with the Scandinavian ones it comes clear. As if his life depended upon it, the lover strictly enjoins his lady from uttering his name. When she disobeys in fright, he receives his deathblow.

> And though my blood run red
> My name must not be said.

[8] Shakespeare, *Hamlet*, I, iv.   [9] "Riddles Wisely Expounded" (1 C).

Yea, though thou see me fall,
My name thou must not call.

Now first he struck down in mire and mould
Her seven brethren with hair of gold,

And next o'er threw in mould and mire
Her six bold kinsmen and her sire.

Ribold, Ribold, stay thy sword,
Stay it, O God and Christ the Lord!

E'en as she spake the fatal word
Wounded was he with many a sword.[10]

But the folklore of ballads is inconsistent. What is meat for one man
is poison for another, and the same thing may bring good or bad luck.
In the case of Tam Lin (39 E) it is the repeated utterance of his name
that redeems him. Janet is instructed to seize and hold him in spite
of all the shape-shifting that will take place. Finally,

They'll next shape him into your arms
Like the laidliest worm of Ind;
But hold him fast, let him not go,
And cry aye "Young Tamlin."

At this, the Queen of Faery admits her defeat and turns her horse
about, crying, "Adieu to thee, Tamlene."

The folklore of every race has its tree of life, whose roots touch
the bottom of the world and whose branches reach to heaven. Primitive man, who often built his home in a tree for security from beasts,
floods, enemies, or heat, was easily persuaded of the sacredness of all
trees. Greek myth associated with trees a whole family of woodland
deities, and Northern Europe had its share of sylvan gods, one of
whom was perhaps Robin Hood's progenitor. Norse mythology
argued that the red berries of the rowan tree were like fire; that fire,
associated with thunder and lightning, was the possession of the
thunder-god, Thor; that Thor must therefore have chosen the rowan
tree for a dwelling place; further, that since, as everyone knew, Thor
was a kindly god, the rowan berries must be good for men—as indeed
they were found to be. Corollary thinking invested trees with the
spirits of the dead. These spirits when they left their mortal bodies

---

[10] Olrik, *A Book of Danish Ballads*, "Ribold and Goldberg," pp. 248–49. See also
"The Griefs of Hillelille," p. 126.

were evil, and must be converted and propitiated. Thus funeral rites, sometimes very elaborate, evolved. The sacrifices and libations which took place at the burials of the dead made, as any farmer today would understand, especially fertile soil, and the bushes and trees which sprang up around such places became in the popular mind the resort of departed souls.

Belief in the tree-soul is a frequently repeated motif in the ballads, and it is usually expressed by the love knot which unites the trees growing from the graves of parted lovers. Metaphor for us, fact for our heathen ancestors. Read in the light of this belief, the animus of the Black Douglas towards the lovers in "The Douglas Tragedy" (7 B) becomes logical. Even in death he could not brook their union:

> Lord William was buried in St. Mary's Kirk,
>   Lady Margret in Mary's quire;
> Out o the lady's grave grew a bonny red rose,
>   And out o the knight's a briar.
>
> And they twa met, and they twa plat,
>   And fain they wad be near;
> And a' the world might ken right weel
>   They were twa lovers dear.
>
> But bye and rade the Black Douglas,
>   And wow but he was rough!
> For he pulld up the bonny brier
>   And flang't in St. Mary's Loch.

Intercourse with the spirits which so thoroughly populated the objects of this world was regulated by a system of laws, known to all and practiced by most people, which we call magic. Certain people, however, were better versed in the practice than others. These were witches.

Our idea of the witch as a malevolent old woman with a secret store of charms belongs to only one stage in her evolution. Woman's role in the primitive household gave her position and authority. She was, moreover, skilful in managing illness, producing foodstuffs, and caring for the children of her body. Every household act, since it concerned the handling of things conceived of as animated by spirits to be propitiated, was accompanied by a special ritual insuring their favor. Thus magic grew as a household science, and as the Just-So Story says, the woman was continually making a new magic. The older the woman, the greater her lore and experience, and the more powerful her magic. Since the abnormal in nature possessed special virtue, a woman past the age of childbearing, her normal function, was in particularly close league with spirits. Therefore all old women were especially qualified in magic; therefore all old women were witches. Here are all the ingredients of the brew which produced the traditional wicked witch, who was also sometimes the bad stepmother of the fairy tale. The wheel of reasoning came full circle in the corollary that all women, old or young, might be witches. The witch hunts of the eighteenth century, based on this stage of thinking, sent many an innocent young woman to the stake.

A witch therefore was not a supernatural being, but a member of ordinary society who was versed in special arts. Since her charms could overcome illness, make the butter come, help the cows to calve and in general assist the processes by which man lived, it must follow that she could also do harm, and she was held responsible for all strange maladies and misfortunes. Her skill with domestic animals, and her apparently secret understanding of her pets, led to a belief in an elaborate system of witch-familiars, or spirits transformed into cats or wolves or dogs to do her bidding. To pursue her business the witch sometimes transformed herself into the guise of her familiar, and the wounding of this animal produced similar wounds in the witch. The belief in man's kinship with animals, not yet outgrown, lies back of stories of self-transformation, such as *Beauty and the Beast*. Norse mythology refers to the berserkers, or warriors who because of their ferocity were supposed to be wolves. Among primitive peoples one still hears of werewolves, or individuals who at times change themselves into wolves. A group of Rumanian dancers at the London International Festival in 1935 claimed this distinction for one of their number.[11] The belief may possibly be reflected at times in the ballads, as in "Johnie Cock" (114) for instance:[12]

> The wildest wolf in aw this wood
> Wad not ha done so by me;
> She'd ha wet her foot ith wan water,
> And sprinkled it oer my brae,
> And if that wad not ha wakend me,
> She wad ha gone and let me be.

[11] For further description of this group, see pages 178–79.
[12] Wimberly, *Folklore in the English and Scottish Popular Ballads*, p. 59.

A derivation of the idea may be found in those satirical stories, like "The Wife Wrapt in Wether's Skin" (277), in which the husband absolves himself from the accusation of beating his wife by placing a sheepskin on her back: it is the sheep he has beaten, not his wife. In "The Twa Magicians" (44), "Tam Lin" (39), and "The Earl of Mar's Daughter" (270), self-transformations are used to aid courtship. Malevolent transformations by witches are also common. A trilogy of ballads deals with this theme: Kemp Owyne (34) is a ballad Perseus whose Andromeda has been turned to a monster; Allison Gross (35), her blandishments repulsed, has turned her lover into "an ugly worm"; the wicked stepmother is the agent of metamorphosis in "The Laily Worm" (36).

In these three ballads the monster is a sort of dragon. The prevalence of this creature in folk tales is conspicuous. Beowulf's deeds center about the destruction of the great "wurm." A giant turned dragon guards the Niebelung hoard. From somewhere east of Suez comes the story of St. George and the dragon. In China the dragon is sacred. Serpent worship was the cause of Hezekiah's wrath. The serpentine figures of ancient dances, such as survive today in the grand right-and-left of the country dance, were possibly once ritual imitations of snake-like movements by snake worshipers. The serpent traditionally possesses wisdom to the point of wile, and its association with therapy appears in the twisted snakes of the caduceus. The wide dispersion of these stories suggests very strongly that early man lived in awe of some terrible ophidian monster which must be propitiated through sacrifices and worship; and those ballads which contain allusions to "laily worms," "esks," or adders are therefore of especial interest. One looks for the appearance of the serpent in Eden in popular poetry, and finds him in a version of "Dives and Lazarus" (56) as Satan's familiar, and possessed of a curious anatomy:

> Rise up, rise up, brother Diverus,
>   And come along with me;
> For there is a place prepared in hell
>   For to sit upon a serpent's knee.[13]

Love and hate brews, incantations, passwords, sacred numbers, and hypnotism were all part of the witch's technique.

[13] Broadwood and Fuller-Maitland, *English County Songs*, "Lazarus," p. 102.

Take ye the blossom of the broom,
The blossom it smells so sweet,
And strew it at your true-love's head,
And likewise at his feet.[14]

Then out she has taen a silver wand
And she's turnd her three times roun and roun;
She's mutterd sich words till my strength it failed,
And I fell down senceless upon the groun.[15]

She stroked my head, and she kembed my hair,
And she set me down saftly on her knee.[16]

The occult and mystic numbers three and seven, however, have in most cases lost all reference to magic, and have become merely commonplaces.

A large part of witchcraft consisted of mimetic or imitative magic, the dramatic representation of a desired occurrence. The Indian leaps high in his dance to make the corn grow, and he builds smoke fire to simulate rain clouds and bring the rain. The Eskimo, to catch the rays of the sun and store them against winter's darkness, plays a game of cat's cradle to snare its beams in the meshes of his thread. There is a hint of imitative magic in some of our own acts. We tear up a letter that has hurt us, in an unconscious wish to hurt the sender: the letter is a projection of his spirit and personality, which we can reach in this way.[17] I once watched a very little girl trying to push a lawn mower. Finally she snatched up her father's hat and put it on, and tried again. A believer in animism would have followed her unconscious reasoning: she could partake of her father's nature if she wore his hat, for his possessions harbored his spirit. One of the most common uses of imitative magic was the making, naming, and pricking or melting of a waxen image in order to torture the victim. This practice was so prevalent, not fifty years ago, that a man living near Banbury in England supported himself by the sale of these little images.[18] The realism of the process made it universally appealing and credible, a popular "secret weapon." The investing of a doll with the spirit of a person or a god is not always baleful, however. A curious instance of this belief occurred recently when an artist, working on folk types on

[14] "The Broomfield Hill" (43).   [16] *Ibid.*
[15] "Allison Gross" (35).   [17] Harrison, *Themis,* p. 83.
[18] Wright, *Rustic Speech and Folklore,* pp. 231-32.

one of the islands west of Ireland, made portrait dolls of some of the natives. They were greatly interested, and most cooperative in posing and suggesting ways of reproducing accurately the costumes, accessories, and other realistic details. When, however, she wished to take the dolls home with her, the islanders were seriously disturbed, fearing what might happen to the models, once the reproductions were out of sight. The situation was saved by their own creation of a doll to accompany the portraits, as a sort of guardian spirit.

The ballad of "Willie's Lady" (6) is built upon this form of imitative magic:

> Ye'll doe ye to the market place
> And there ye buy a loaf o wax.

> Ye shape it bairn and bairnly like,
> And in twa glassen een ye pit;

> And bid her come to your boy's christening;
> Then notice weel what she shall do.

The mock christening which follows breaks the mimetic spell which has been cast on the lady to prevent the birth of her child. Every symbol of obstruction has been dramatically employed; her hair is tied in witch knots and tangled by combs, the twisted woodbine has been hung in her chamber, her left shoe string has been knotted. Once these symbols of pain and travail are removed, the curse is lifted, and the witch is hoist with her own petard.

These are some of the reflections of the supernatural as it appears in the natural world. Superstition, however, is in constant traffic with another world than that of mortals. This otherworld is not necessarily heaven, nor the land of the dead; nor is it specifically fairyland, although it is often so called.

> My boy was scarcely ten years auld
> When he went to an unco land,
> Where wind never blew, nor cocks ever crew,
> Ohon for my son, Leesome Brand! [19]

The unco' land is as vague in its topography as the mortal world. Some general laws, however, govern communication with it.

Passage thither is extremely difficult and perilous. Almost always the journey involves the crossing of water. Primitive associations with

[19] "Leesome Brand" (15).

water all help to explain its importance. Man early discovered that wells continued to spring when all other water went dry; that certain thermal and mineral waters were healing; that it cleansed and fertilized. Like the tree of life, there is a widely dispersed lore about the flood, the water of life, and the fountain of youth. Water was the boundary of the visible world, hence land on the other side, invisible to human eyes, constituted the otherworld. King Arthur disappeared in a mysterious ship to live forever beyond the sea; Norsemen sent forth their dead in their own ships, to reach the shores of the otherworld by the aid of unseen hands. In pagan times the sacred well was the home of the god, the source of fertility. Hence the mention of water, be it the sea, a river, a spring, or a well, may be significant. At the wall o Stream a well-fared may, washing her sark, turns out to be a mermaid, and Clerk Colvill's meeting with her leads to his death.[20] It is clear that Wearie's Well, where Lady Isabel meets the Elf-Knight, is the boundary of the otherworld.[21] When True Thomas went to Fairyland,

> For forty days and forty nights
> He wade thro red blude to the knee,
> And he saw neither sun nor moon,
> But heard the roaring of the sea.[22]

Trees, mountains, and caves were also entrances to the otherworld. Such natural disappearances as death by drowning were journeys by water to the otherworld; getting lost in the forest or in a cave was another sort of passage. King Arthur (according to another version of his death), Der Alte Barbarossa, Thomas of Erceldoune, and the Pied Piper with his horde of children vanished in this way. The many stories of strange journeys through the forest may have helped to form the conception of Robin Hood's domain, which could be reached only by the initiated.

Mortals disappeared into the otherworld sometimes forever, sometimes for a conventional period.

> Till seven years were past and gone
> True Thomas on earth was never seen.[23]

[20] "Clerk Colvill" (42).
[21] "Lady Isabel and the Elf Knight" (4).
[22] "Thomas Rymer" (37).
[23] Ibid.

Sometimes the most innocent act, like picking a flower or taking one's ease upon the grass, was one's undoing:

> True Thomas lay oer yond grassy bank,
>   And he beheld a lady gay,
> A lady that was brisk and bold,
>   Come riding oer the fernie brae.[24]

> Why pu's thou the rose, Janet,
>   And why breaks thou the wand?
> Or why comes thou to Carterhaugh
>   Withoutten my command? [25]

In both these cases, the creature who appears is a fairy. But unlike the tiny gossamer sprites which have invaded our latterday fairy tales, the ballad fairies were of human size, though often of superhuman strength and beauty.[26] Their wealth was prodigious, the trappings of their horses splendid and glittering, their green clothing likewise rich. We have glimpses of them riding, hunting, dancing, making love. Like the Lorelei they are discovered combing their hair with silver combs. Their approach is heralded by music, such as the ringing of bells on their bridles or the blowing of elfin horns. May Day and Hallowe'en bring them abroad, but they may also be summoned at other times by naming or trespassing on their preserves. The Elf Knight (4) reproaches Fair Isabel for her summons:

> 'It's a very strange matter, fair maiden,' said he,
> 'I canna blaw my horn but ye call on me.'

Fairy activities are usually nocturnal, but not necessarily so. True Thomas seems to have been reft away in broad daylight, but Janet grapples with the shape-shifting Tam Lin (39) "just at the mirk and midnight hour." Though fairies are sometimes domesticated like Billy Blin in "Willie's Lady" (6), they usually visit this world on a temporary errand—to court a mortal, as in "Tam Lin" (39) to secure a sacrifice to hell, as in "Thomas Rymer" (37), or to kidnap a mortal

---

[24] "Thomas Rymer" (37).

[25] "Tam Lin" (39).

[26] "The Wee Wee Man" (38) is a sort of monster, showing supernatural strength. A theory exists that the modern fairy represents a gradual shrinking in size from creatures once larger than men, and that in the state in which he is found in the ballads he is seen progressing from the gigantic to the minute. As man lost his terror of supernatural beings, they became less formidable physically. See Latham, *Elizabethan Fairies*, Ch. II *passim.*

nurse for a fairy child, as in "The Queen of Elfan's Nourice" (40).
They may be malicious, as in "Tam Lin" (39), or benevolent:

> But as it fell out on last Hallow-even,
>   When the seely court was ridin by,
> The queen lighted down on a gowany bank
>   Nae far frae the tree where I wont to lye.
>
> She took me up in her milk-white han,
>   And she stroakd me three times oer her knee;
> She chang'd me again to my ain proper shape,
>   And I nae mair maun toddle about the tree.[27]

Janet rescues Tam Lin at the eleventh hour, producing a fine fit of
jealousy in the Fairy Queen:

> Out then spak the Queen o Fairies,
>   And an angry woman was she;
> 'Shame betide her ill-far'd face
>   And an ill death may she die,
> For she's taen awa the boniest knight
>   In a' my companie.'

Child's version of "The Queen of Elfan's Nourice" (40), though not
clear as to situation, suggests a fairy kidnapping, and conveys the
poignant yearning of the mortal mother for her own child. The
strange lowing of the cow, one of the most lonesome sounds imagin-
able, is explained by a version reclaimed from a traditional singer a
few years ago.[28] This seems to come from an older form of the story,
in that the lowing of the cow is identified as an elf call, and the
obviously added verses about the roads to heaven and hell are omitted.
Yet in spite of its greater age, it was recorded a hundred years after
Child's. Child says of this ballad, "In the nature of the best popular
ballad, it forces you to chant it and will not be read." [29] The version
given here is even more suggestive of song, and a Hebridean tune
belonging to a song of similar theme and verse construction is borrowed here for a setting.

[27] "Allison Gross" (35).
[28] Beatty, "Some New Ballad Variants," *Journal of American Folklore*, XX (1907),
154.
[29] Child, *English and Scottish Popular Ballads*, I, 358.

THE QUEEN OF ELFAN'S NOURICE (40)[30]

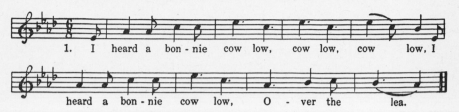

1. I heard a bon-nie cow low, cow low, cow low, I heard a bon-nie cow low, O-ver the lea.

1. I heard a bonnie cow low, cow low, cow low,
   I heard a bonnie cow low,
        Over the lea.

2. An' it was an elf call, elf call, elf call,
   An' it was an elf call
        Calling unto me.

3. An' the little elf man, elf man, elf man
   An' the little elf man
        Said unto me,

4. Come nurse an elf-child, elf-child, elf-child,
   Come nurse an elf-child
        Down 'neath the sea.

5. Then I fell a-moaning, moaning, moaning,
   Then I fell a-moaning
        Down where he could see.

6. What do you moan for, moan for, moan for,
   What do you moan for,
        Elf-king said to me.

7. Is it for your breakfast, breakfast, breakfast,
   Is it for your breakfast,
        Or for a fee?

8. 'Tis not for my breakfast, breakfast, breakfast,
   'Tis not for my breakfast,
        Nor an' for a fee.

9. 'Tis for my bonnie lad, bonnie lad, bonnie lad,
   'Tis for my bonnie lad
        That I never more shall see.

[30] Words from Beatty, *op. cit.* Tune from Moffat, *Minstrelsy of the Scottish Highlands* (n.d.), p. 24. Reprinted by permission of Bayley and Ferguson, London, Publishers.

The ballad ghost, like the ballad fairy, is corporeal and in general not to be distinguished from a living mortal. He is not an unsubstantial wraith, but a physical dead man, whose spirit may not seek its new home until his mortal affairs are in order. He returns usually to terminate relations unnaturally maintained after death—to chide those who grieve excessively for him and thus prevent his rest, to obey the summons of those unwilling to relinquish him, to satisfy the cravings of love, abduct the living, or break troth with a lover.[31] Sometimes he may bring warning of punishment for crime, as in "The Cruel Mother" (20):

> In seven years you'll hear a bell,
> In seven years you'll land in hell.[32]

The time of his return is often a feast day, Martinmas or Yule.

> Yer ain twa sons 'll no be here
> Till the hallow days of Yule.[33]

Although Horatio says that at Christmas "no spirit dare stir abroad," it was also believed that at this uncanny time spirits returned, and houses were therefore specially cleaned and prepared for them.[34] A Kentucky Mountain superstition is based on the visit of the Holy Family on the Eve of Old Christmas.[35]

The ghost's return is completely matter-of-fact. There is no evocation of horror or terror, no use of supernatural accessories, and no attempt to explain or prove. Unlike the modern ghost story, the ballad with its brevity and allusiveness, to say nothing of its assumption of complete belief on the part of the listener, tells its story with "simple, unastonished realism." [36] Often you must be told, with characteristic periphrasis, that this is a ghost:

> The carlin wife's three sons came home,
> And their hats were of the birk. . . .
> But at the gates o Paradise
> That birk grew fair eneugh.[37]

---

[31] Baring-Gould, *Songs of the West*, pp. 3, note, and 15.
[32] Sharp, *English Folk Songs from the Southern Appalachians*, I, 59.
[33] "The Clerk's Twa Sons o Owsenford" (72).
[34] Miles, *Christmas*, pp. 239–40.
[35] See page 289.
[36] Veitch, *History and Poetry of the Scottish Border*, II, 122.
[37] "The Wife of Usher's Well" (79).

> My mouth it is full cold, Margret,
>   It has the smell now of the ground;
> And if I kiss thy comely mouth,
>   Thy life-days will not be long.[38]

One learns little of the world of the dead; they return to the grave and can offer the living only a resting place beside them.

> The cock doth craw, the day doth daw,
>   The channerin worm doth chide,
> Gin we be missed out o our place,
>   A sair pain we maun bide.[39]

The after life, when it is suggested, is like that on earth:

> Lay my bible at my head, he says,
>   My chaunter at my feet,
> My bow and arrows by my side,
>   And soundly I will sleep.[40]

Lest the ghost walk, he is sometimes restrained. The Cruel Mother (20) binds the hands and feet of the babes with her yellow hair or a garter; Young Hunting (68) is buried in "the deepest pot of a',"

> A green turff upon his brest,
>   To hold that good lord down.

Sometimes heathen ideas of this world as "middle-earth" mingle with Christian conceptions:

> O Cocks are crowing a merry mid-larf,
>   A wat the wild foule boded day;
> The salms of Heaven will be sung
>   And ere now I'l be misst away.[41]

But allusions to heaven and hell may usually be identified as later and temporary moralizings.

One has only to turn to Child's "Suffolk Miracle" (272), a cheapened broadside treatment of a fine old ghost story, for contrast with folk style and treatment. Its pedestrian, explanatory manner, its anxiety to offer proof, and its moral adornment, are never found in

[38] "Sweet William's Ghost" (77 B).
[39] "The Wife of Usher's Well" (79).
[40] "The Twa Brothers" (49 B).
[41] "Sweet William's Ghost" (77 B).

the traditional ballad at its best. In "Sweet William's Ghost" (77A) the rational [42] and literary hand is reflected in such phrases as "with many a grievous groan" and "evanisht in a cloud of mist." At the same time, this is an honest ballad ghost. He makes his entrance not by passing through the solid substance of the door; like any living man he "tirls at the pin." He is not recognized as a psychic revenant, but is forced to declare that he is "no earthly man." But there is no such mixture of elements in a ballad like "The Wife of Usher's Well" (79). The ghost here, uncontaminated by literary touches, is a matter of course, not a subject for speculative wonder.

This elliptical and allusive, and at the same time unsensational treatment of the supernatural visitor is all the more effective in that it speaks to the heart and not to the mind. It selects the homely, telling detail to stand for heartbreak, loneliness, and the tragedy of separation. A whole story of repentance and reproach lies in the colloquy in "The Cruel Mother" (20):

> O babes, O babes, if you were mine,
> I would dress you up in silk so fine.
>
> O Mother, O Mother, when we were thine,
> You neither dressed us in the coarse silk nor fine.

Desolate lover and restless dead speak to each other in "The Unquiet Grave" (78):

> The twelvemonth and a day being up,
>   The dead began to speak;
> 'O who sits weeping on my grave
>   And will not let me sleep?'

A fire, a bed, and a well-spread board symbolize a mother's concern and love in "The Wife of Usher's Well," and its final stanza is briefly eloquent:

> Fare ye weel, my mother dear!
>   Fareweel to barn and byre!
> And fare ye weel, the bonny lass
>   That kindles my mother's fire!

Certain acts and things and places in the ballads are obviously connected with magic. One expects that a witch will tie witch knots,

[42] See page 311.

brew potions, utter incantations, and make waxen images of her vic-
tims, or that a monster may turn out to be a transformed mortal.
One recognizes the formula of turning thrice around, swearing by the
moon and the stars, and casting lots to discover guilt. But it is the
ordinary act, as well as the extraordinary, that evokes the supernatural.
For in the ballad world of prescription and proscription the simplest
act—pulling a flower, washing a garment, drinking from a well, eating
an apple, listening to a horn or a bell, kissing one's lover, combing
one's hair, asking a person's name, binding a handkerchief about an
aching head—may unloose strange and mysterious forces. A roadside
bank or a well may be dangerous, and the most everyday animal may
speak or act like a man. Boats move or stay without human guidance;
a man speaks to his bow or his fingers or the sheets of his bed, and
they can hear him and reply. There exists a continual state of fear of
unknown, and appeasement of known but unfriendly powers. Man's
existence thus depends upon obedience to taboo, explicit or implied.

The thou-shalt-nots of the ballad center about forbidden places and
acts. "I forbid you, maidens all . . . To come or go by Carterhaugh." [43] "For if I go to the Broomfield Hill. . . ." [44] Physical contact with fairies, monsters, or the dead involves one beyond hope of
rescue: "But if you touch me, tail or fin . . .," [45] "One touch of my
clay-cold lips. . . ." [46] Mortal food is taboo for the ghost. The widow's
sons may not eat with her.[47] Fairy loaf and claret wine once touched,
like Proserpina's pomegranate seeds, seal True Thomas to fairyland
for seven years, and to silence upon his return,

> For all the plagues that are in hell
> Light on the fruit of this countrie.[48]

Ghosts must return to their graves at cockcrow. Certain animals may
not be killed, being transformed or reincarnate mortals. "A man upon
the land, a silkie (seal) upon the sea" thus foretells doom for his
mortal love:

[43] "Tam Lin" (39).
[44] "The Broomfield Hill" (43).
[45] "Kemp Owyne" (34).
[46] "The Unquiet Grave" (78). The kiss is much more than a mere lover's caress, as
its use in the kissing of Christian relics, and of the Bible upon taking oath in English
courts of law suggest. Bembo's philosophy of the kiss, in his famous discourse in *The
Book of the Courtier* by Castiglione (p. 315), embodies in Renaissance Neoplatonism
ideas long familiar and very widespread.
[47] "The Wife of Usher's Well" (79).   [48] "Thomas Rymer" (37).

An it sall come to pass on a simmer's day
    When the sin shines het on evera stane,
That I will tak my little young son
    And teach him for to swim the faem.

An thu sall marry a proud gunner,
    And a proud gunner I'm sure he'll be,
An the very first schot that ere he schoots,
    He'll schoot baith my young son and me.[49]

Superstition is by no means confined to those ballads whose plots revolve about the supernatural and the marvelous. Incidental appearances of folk beliefs are frequent in many others. Omens constantly point to misadventure or worse:

They had not rode a mile but one,
    Till his horse fell owre a stone;
'It's a warning gude eneuch,' my Lord Dunwaters said,
    'Alive I'll neer come hame.' [50]

In another version the same lord suffers further ill luck:

The ring upon his finger burst
    And his nose began to bleed.[51]

Because it is the heel of her left shoe that Mary Hamilton (173) loses as she climbs the Tolbooth stair, we do not need to be told that she is condemned already. And no ship could survive a storm thus foretold:

Late late yestreen I saw the new moone,
    With the auld moone in hir arme.[52]

Traditional transmission of the ballads dealing with the supernatural tends to omit, or rationalize, or burlesque what it cannot explain. Gone is the explicit reference to dead-naming in "Earl Brand" (7), and to the harp of bones and hair in "The Twa Sisters" (10). A talking bird has become a parrot, the Elf-Knight a false priest; mermaids and sirens are only metaphorically glamorous. The three sons of the Wife of Usher's Well (79), no longer in pursuit of "gramaree"

---

[49] "The Great Silkie of Sule Skerry" (113).
[50] "Lord Derwentwater" (208 A).
[51] Ibid. (D).
[52] "Sir Patrick Spens" (58).

or magic, have become three little schoolboys sent away to learn "their grammars three." The gospelizing touch has been invoked to regularize the secular song for the good church member who cannot give up his old pleasures. Thus roads to heaven and hell appear in fairy ballads, and Jesus, not the cock, recalls the widow's sons at dawn. The comic sense turns the three ravens into the mock-macabre two crows, and they are well on their way to the Billie-Magee-Magaws of the college song book. On the other hand, tradition sometimes preserves in one version what has been lost from another, thus explaining the supernatural element only hinted at, as in the case of the elf-call to the mortal nurse. Tradition also restores to its folk simplicity a story debased by print, like "The Suffolk Miracle" (272).[53]

SWEET WILLIAM AND FAIR ELLEN
(Earl Brand, 7)[54]

1. Sweet William rode up to Fair El-len's gate, And he sound-ed on .... the ring; No one no read-i-er than she was to a-rise and let him come in.

   1. Sweet William rode up to Fair Ellen's gate,
      And he sounded on the ring;
   No one no readier than she was
      To arise and let him come in.

   2. He mounted her on a milk-white horse,
      And himself on an iron-gray,
   He swang his bugle about his neck
      And so went riding away.

[53] See page 217.
[54] As sung by Willie Nolan ("Singing Willie") of Incline, Kentucky, to E. K. Wells, 1920.

3. He rode till he came in three miles of town,
 He turned himself all around;
He looked and he saw some seven horsemen
 Come travelling over the ground.

4. Get you down, get you down, Fair Ellen, he said,
 And take my steed in hand,
Till I go back to yon little spring,
 And I will fight them seven horsemen.

5. She stood till she saw her six brothers fall,
 And her old father she loved so dear;
Slack your arm, slack your arm, Sweet William, she said,
 For your licks they are wonderful severe.

6. Are you offended at what I have done,
 Or at what's been said before?
I wish myself in Old England's land,
 And you was in the valley so low.

7. I am not offended at what you have done,
 Or at what's been said before;
I wish myself in Old England's land,
 And you was in the valley so low.

8. She drew her handkerchief from her side,
 And wiped Sweet William's wounds,
The blood kept rolling down his cheeks,
 As red as any wine.

9. He mounted her on her milk-white horse
 And himself on his iron-gray,
He swang his bugle around his neck
 And so went riding away.

10. He rode till he came to his mother's hall,
 And sounded on the ring.
Says, Sleeper, awake, dear Mother, he says,
 And arise and let me in.

11. As she were getting up, a-slipping on her clothes,
 To let Sweet William in,
Bind up my head, sweet sister, he said,
 For you never will bind it again.

THE TWO SISTERS (10)[55]

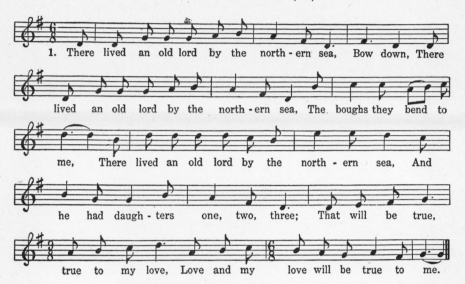

1. There lived an old lord by the north-ern sea, Bow down, There
lived an old lord by the north-ern sea, The boughs they bend to
me, There lived an old lord by the north-ern sea, And
he had daugh-ters one, two, three; That will be true,
true to my love, Love and my love will be true to me.

1. There lived an old lord by the northern sea,
    Bow down,
   There lived an old lord by the northern sea,
    The boughs they bend to me,
   There lived an old lord by the northern sea,
   And he had daughters one, two, three;
    That will be true, true to my love,
    Love and my love will be true to me.

2. A young man came a-courting there,
   And he took choice of the youngest there.

3. He gave this girl a beaver hat,
   The oldest she thought much of that.

4. He gave the youngest a gay gold ring,
   But never the oldest a single thing.

5. O sister, O sister, let us walk out
   To see the ships a-sailing about.

6. As they walked down by the salty brim,
   The oldest pushed the youngest in.

[55] From Sharp, *English Folk Songs of the Southern Appalachians* (1932), I, 28. Reprinted by permission of the Oxford University Press, London, Publishers.

7. O sister, O sister, lend me your hand,
   And I will give you my house and land.

8. I'll neither lend you my hand nor glove,
   But I will have your own true-love.

9. O down she sank and away she swam,
   Till into the miller's fish-pond she ran.

10. The miller came out with his fish-hook,
    And fished the fair maid out of the brook.

11. He robbed her of her gay gold ring,
    And into the brook he pushed her again.

12. The miller was hanged at his mill gate,
    The oldest sister was burned at the stake.

THE CRUEL MOTHER (20)[56]

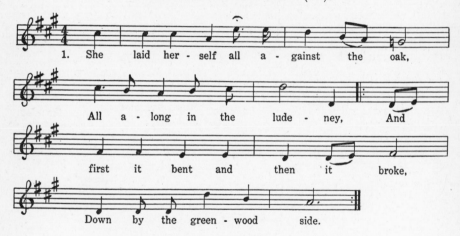

1. She laid herself all against the oak,
       All along in the ludeney,
   And first it bent and then it broke,
       Down by the greenwood side.

2. She leaned herself all against a thorn,
   And there she had two fine babes born,

3. She pulled out her snow-white breast,
   And she bid them a-suck, for that would be the last.

[56] From Sharp, *English Folk Songs from the Southern Appalachians* (1932), I, 56.
Reprinted by permission of the Oxford University Press, London, Publishers.

4. She pulled down her yellow hair,
   And she bound it around their little feet and hands.

5. She pulled out her little penknife,
   And she pierced all in their little tender hearts.

6. She was sitting in her father's hall,
   And she saw her babes a-playing with their ball.

7. O babes, O babes, if you were mine,
   I would dress you in the silk so fine.

8. O Mother, O Mother, when we were thine,
   You neither dressed us in the coarse silk nor fine.

THE TWO CROWS
(The Three Ravens, 26)[57]

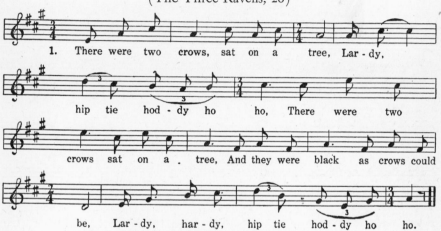

1. There were two crows sat on a tree,
       Lardy, hip tie hoddy ho ho,
   There were two crows sat on a tree,
   And they were black as crows could be,
       Lardy, hardy, hip tie hoddy ho ho.

2. One old crow said to his mate, Lar-dy, *etc.*
   What shall we have today to eat?

3. Yonder lies a horse in yonders lane, Lar-dy, *etc.*
   Whose body has not long been slain.

4. We'll press our feet on his breast-bone, Lar-dy, *etc.*
   And pick his eyes out one by one.

[57] Sharp, *English Folk Songs from the Southern Appalachians* (1932), I, 64. Reprinted by permission of the Oxford University Press, London, Publishers.

THE THREE RAVENS (26)⁵⁸

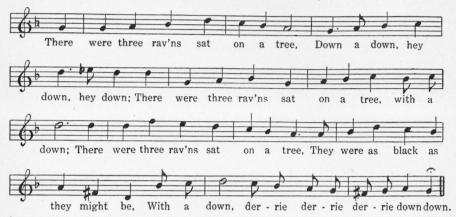

There were three rav'ns sat on a tree, Down a down, hey down, hey down; There were three rav'ns sat on a tree, with a down; There were three rav'ns sat on a tree, They were as black as they might be, With a down, der - rie der - rie der - rie down down.

There were three rav'ns sat on a tree,
Down a down, hey down, hey down;
There were three rav'ns sat on a tree, with a down;
There were three rav'ns sat on a tree,
They were as black as they might be,
With a down, derrie derrie derrie down down.

YOUNG HUNTING (68)⁵⁹

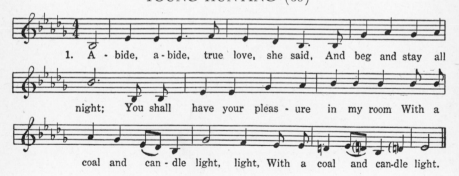

1. A - bide, a - bide, true love, she said, And beg and stay all night; You shall have your pleas - ure in my room With a coal and can - dle light, light, With a coal and can-dle light.

1. Abide, abide, true love, she said,
    And beg and stay all night;
    You shall have your pleasure in my room
    With a coal and candle light, light,
    With a coal and candle light.

⁵⁸ From Ravenscroft's *Melismata*, 1611, quoted by Chappell, *Old English Popular Music*, I, 75–76. This is the tune that fits the Child text.
⁵⁹ From Barry, Eckstorm, and Smyth, *British Ballads from Maine* (1929), p. 122. Reprinted by permission of the Yale University Press, Publishers.

2. I won't abide, faulse ladye,
      And beg and stay all night,
   For I have a far better love to enjoy,
   When I go home than you, you,
      When I go home than you.

3. As he stooped over saddle
      To kiss her lips so sweet,
   And with a penknife in her hand,
      She wounded him full deep.

4. Why woundest me, faulse ladye,
      Why woundest me so sore?
   There's not a doctor in all Scotland
      Can heal my mortal wound.

5. She awoke her maids in the morning,
      Just by the break of day,
   Saying, There is a dead man in my bed chamber,
      I wish he was away.

6. Some took him by the lily-white hands,
      And others by the feet,
   And they threw him into a very deep well,
      Full fifty fathoms deep.

7. Sleep there, sleep there, you faulse young love,
      Sleep there, sleep there along,
   And let the one that you love best
      Think you long a-coming home.

8. Then up spoke a pretty little bird,
      Sitting on a tree

          .   .   .   .   .   .

          .   .   .   .

9. Come down, come down, my pretty little bird,
      And sit upon my knee;
   For I have a golden cage at home
      I will bestow to thee.

10. I won't go down, faulse ladye,
      And sit upon your knee,
   For you have slain your own true love,
      And I'm sure you would slay me.

11. Oh, if I had my bow and arrow,
      Shuttle and my string,
   I would shoot you through the very heart,
      Among the leaves so green.

12. Oh, if you had your bow and arrow,
     Shuttle and your string,
   I would take my wings and away I would fly,
   And you never would see me again, again,
     And you never would see me again.

THE UNQUIET GRAVE (78)[60]

1. There been falling drops of dew, sweetheart,
     And heavy falls of rain;
   I've only had but one sweetheart,
     On the green fields he was slain.

2. I would do so much for my sweetheart
     As any young maid may;
   I'll sit and mourn upon his grave
     For a twelvemonth and a day.

3. When the twelvemonth and a day been up,
     This young man rose and spoke;
   What keeps you mourning upon my grave?
     You will not let me sleep.

4. Why do you weep, why do you mourn?
     What do you want of me?
   One kiss, one kiss from your lily-white lips
     That's all I want of thee.

5. My lily-white lips are cold as clay,
     And my breath smells vile and strong;
   If you takes one kiss from my lily-white lips,
     Your time it won't be long.

6. Down yonder meadow where the grass grows green,
     Where you and I used to walk,

[60] From Greenleaf and Mansfield, *Ballads and Songs of Newfoundland* (1933), p. 23.
Reprinted by permission of the Harvard University Press, Cambridge, Publishers.

The prettiest flowers that ever we had seen
It is withered unto the stalk.

7. It is withered unto the stalk, sweetheart,
    And the leaves will never return;
    But since I have lost my own sweetheart,
    What shall I do but mourn?

8. Mourn not for me, my own truelove,
    Mourn not for me, I pray,
    So I must leave you and all the whole world,
    And go into my grave.

LADY GAY

(The Wife of Usher's Well, 79)[61]

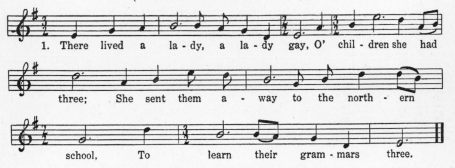

1. There lived a la-dy, a la-dy gay, O' chil-dren she had three; She sent them a-way to the north-ern school, To learn their gram-mars three.

1. There lived a lady, a lady gay,
    O' children she had three;
    She sent them away to the northern school,
    To learn their grammars three.

2. They hadn't been gone but a very short time
    Scarcely three weeks and a day,
    Till death, sweet death come hastening along
    And stole those babes away.

3. There is a king in heaven, cried she,
    A king of the third degree.
    Send back, send back my three little babes,
    This night send them back to me.

4. She made them a bed in the backward room,
    And on it put a neat white sheet,
    And over the top a golden spread,
    Much better that they might sleep.

[61] From Sharp, *English Folk Songs from the Southern Appalachians* (1932), I, 158. Reprinted by permission of the Oxford University Press, London, Publishers.

5. Take it off, take it off, cried the oldest one,
    Take it off, take it off, cried he,
   For what's to become of this wide wicked world
    Since sin has first begun.

6. She spread them a table of bread and wine,
    As neat as neat could be,
   Come eat, come drink, my three little babes,
    Come eat, come drink with me.

7. I cannot eat your bread, says one,
    Neither can I drink your wine,
   For my Saviour dear is standing near,
    To him we must resign.

8. Cold clay, cold clay hangs over my head,
    Green grass grows over my feet;
   And every tear that you shed for me
    Doth wet my winding sheet.

THE SEA CAPTAIN
or, The Maid on the Shore [62]

1. It's of a sea captain that ploughs the salt sea,
    The seas, they were fine, calm and clear, O,
   A beautiful damsel he chanced for to spy,—

[62] From Karpeles, *Folk Songs from Newfoundland* (1934[?]), I, 31. Reprinted by permission of Miss Karpeles and the Oxford University Press, London, Publishers.

A-walking alone on the shore, shore,
   A-walking alone on the shore.

2. O what will I give to my sailors so bold?
   Ten guineas I vow and declare O,
   If you'll fetch me that lady on board of my ship,
   That walks all alone on the shore.

3. The sailors did hoist out a very long boat,
   And straight for the shore they did steer, O,
   Saying: Ma'am, if you please, will you enter on board,
   And view a fine cargo of ware.

4. With long persuading they got her on board,
   The seas, they were fine, calm and clear, O,
   She sat herself down in the stern of the boat,
   And straight for the ship they did steer.

5. And when they arrived alongside of the ship,
   The captain he ordered a chair, O,
   Saying: First you shall lie in my arms all this night,
   And the next you shall marry me, dear.

6. She set herself down in the stern of the ship,
   The seas, they were fine, calm and clear, O,
   She sang so neat, so sweet and complete,
   She sang sailors and captain to sleep.

7. She robbed them of silver, she robbed them of gold,
   She robbed them of costly ware, O,
   The captain's broadsword she took for an oar,
   And she paddled away for the shore.

8. When the captain awoke and he found she was gone,
   He was like a man in despair, O,
   He called up his men and commanded a boat
   To row him away for the shore.

9. He lowered himself down in the stern of the boat,
   And away for the shore they did steer, O,
   She saluted the captain as well as the crew,
   Saying: I'm a maiden once more on the shore, shore,
     I'm a maiden once more on the shore.

Chapter 6

THE BALLAD AND THE NURSERY

OTHER salvage, loss, and change effected by tradition are strongly marked in nursery rhymes, many of which show their connections with ballads.

Mothers have from time immemorial adapted stories, songs, and customs to the children in their care, and children have always imitated their elders. This interchange between generations is a subject which lends itself to much pleasant speculation and personal recollection, as well as to extended study. Its possibilities are here merely suggested, as we gather up from the ballads additional evidence that the nursery is the great preserver of traditional matter.

In the child's world the beliefs of the racial past are constantly recalled. For him animals talk, things feel, a private name gives special virtue. His cat's cradle is imitative magic. "London Bridge," "Here We Go Round the Mulberry Bush," and "Farmer in the Dell," games he seems to know by instinct, are unconscious repetitions of a dramatized contest of the sexes, or of light and darkness, or commemorations of some sacred source of life like a well or a tree. In the counting-out game he is following a heathen method of selecting human sacrifice, his eenie-meenie syllables being possibly corruptions of Celtic numbering. "Go in and out the window," with its weaving figure, is descended from serpent worship; "Miss Jenny Jones" is ancient burial ritual. His patty-cake was once a *pater*-cake, or sacrificial wafer, marked with the runic character *Thyr* like our letter *T*, a symbol of sacrifice once highly venerated.[1]

The descent of the nursery rhyme from ritual is traced in a study of the Banbury Cross rhyme,[2] which explains it as a child's version of the May Ridings, well known in Medieval England. These in turn have been carried back by folklorists to fertility rites connected with

[1] L. Eckenstein, "Personal Amulets in Europe," *Transactions of the Third International Congress for History of Religions*, I (1908), 82.
[2] Potts, *Banbury Cross and the Rhyme*.

the Teutonic goddess Hertha. The fine lady is thus of divine stock, her white horse, bells, trappings, and attendant music all part of her worship. Banbury Cross, known to have been set up on an older heathen shrine, was the logical place for folk pilgrimages and continued to be a gathering place to which in later ages people came riding "cock-horse" (or two or three to a horse).

Not all rhymes and games stem from prehistory, of course. Sometimes a contemporary incident has given rise to a political cartoon, which has in due course passed into the nursery and lost its connection with the original event. There is, for instance, Little Jack Horner. This complacent youngster may have been one Sir John Horner, a Somerset gentleman of the time of Henry VIII. He was detailed by the Abbot of Glastonbury, who was anxious to ingratiate himself with the King and his henchman, Thomas Cromwell, to carry to court certain title deeds of the Abbey holdings. According to a custom of the times, the deeds were sent at Christmas, ceremonially wrapped up in the form of a great pasty. When Sir John returned from court he told the Abbot that as a reward for his services, the King had given him a deed to one of the Abbey lands. The satirical tone of the rhyme comments on the implications of the knight's story, and the Horners of Somerset still claim that they live on the property thus acquired.[3]

"The Frog's Courtship," known in many versions today as a nursery song, is first mentioned in 1549 in *The Complaynt of Scotland* as "The Frog he went to the Myl Dur."[4] In 1580 a song was licensed in the *Stationers' Register* entitled "A moste Strange Weddinge of the ffroge and the mouse,"[5] no doubt the same which we first find printed in Ravenscroft's *Melismata* in 1611 as "The Marriage of the Frogge and the Mouse." From then on, there is increasing printed evidence of the song's popularity, and today no folksong collection in England or America is without its traditional version. Animal rhymes and fables have been used in every age by satirists, and this particular song seems to have served as a lampoon in the reign of Elizabeth. The Queen's habit of giving her courtiers animal nicknames was well known, even state papers using them. Sir Walter Raleigh was her fish, Leicester her lapdog (or robin), Sir

[3] Thomas, *The Real Personages of Mother Goose*, chap. iii.
[4] *The Complaynt of Scotland*, pp. 64, 65.
[5] *Stationers' Register*, No. 21, 1580, II, 382.

Christopher Hatton her bell-wether, and Burleigh and Cecil were Old Leviathan and his Cub. At the time of her proposed marriage to the Duc d'Alençon, the French ambassador, Simier, was her ape, and the duke himself her frog.[6] An inventory of her jewels lists "Item, one little flower of gold, with a frog thereon and therein mounseer, his phisnomye, and a little pearl pendant," [7] possibly a gift of the duke. The idea of this foreign marriage was highly unpopular in England. Preachers inveighed against it, a pamphleteer who wrote about it had his right hand struck off in punishment, and Spenser's satire on the subject, *Mother Hubberd's Tale*, probably caused his exile to Ireland.[8] In 1580, just after the crisis of the French courtship, came the licensing of the song mentioned in the *Complaynt*, revised with topical import. If this is the version we find in *Melismata*, the stanzas about "Gib our Cat" and "Dick our Drake" may refer to Sir Humphrey Gilbert and Sir Francis Drake. After interest in this episode subsided, the song, newly familiar, returned to the nursery and gradually lost all connection with the special incident. In this way many old rhymes known to everyone from childhood have been periodically revived.

In all this nursery literature and lore the ballads play a part, adapted by either children or grownups. Mrs. Grover, the Nova Scotia singer, recalls that "playing grownup" meant to her singing grown-up songs.[9] "The Elfin Knight" (2) and "Proud Lady Margaret" (47) survive in the West of England as singing games.[10] "The False Knight upon the Road" (3) with its question-and-answer method suggests the parallel nursery rhyme:

> The man in the wilderness asked me
> How many strawberries grew in the sea.
> I answered him as I thought good:
> As many red herrings as grew in the wood.[11]

The identity of the False Knight is unmistakable: was the "man in the wilderness" also the devil, as has been suggested, or Wotan the

---

[6] Clark, *Elizabethan Fustian*, p. 95.

[7] Quoted by Strickland, *The Life of Queen Elizabeth*, p. 404, from Ellis, *Royal Letters*, Vol. II.

[8] Greenlaw, "Spenser and the Earl of Leicester," *Publications of the Modern Language Association*, XVIII (1910), 535–61.

[9] For an account of Mrs. Grover and her songs, see pages 305 ff.

[10] Baring-Gould, *Folk Songs of the West*, p. 14.

[11] Barry, *British Ballads from Maine*, p. 14.

Wanderer, who often appears unpredictably in folk tales and asks riddling questions? [12]

In other ballads the hand of the nurse or mother is evident. Some riddling ballads survive as lullabies, like "The Riddle Song." Just as Jack the Giant Killer, in the tales we tell today, has been reduced by the nursery from legendary hero to precocious little boy,[13] so ballad heroes have become children. Kittredge mentions in his note on "The Twa Brothers" (49) that "the age of the boys in the first two stanzas does not fit the story." [14] Were the two brothers, going to school and wrestling with each other on the way home, reduced thus to children by some mother singing to her child, knowing that a familiar touch at the beginning would lull him into an uncritical state in which he might drop asleep before she proceeded to thrill herself with the tale of horrible murder, unrequited love, and ghosts? So, perhaps, in "The Wife of Usher's Well" (79), as the sons become children, their "gramaree" or magic has become "grammars three," the three R's of a dame school. "The Croodin Doo" version of "Lord Rendal" (12), in which the dialogue between mother and son about his poisoning has been metamorphosed almost into a lullaby, is a clear instance of reduction of the ballad to nursery levels. "Thought and affliction, passion, hell itself" are turned to diminutive and endearment, and even the constant emphasis on going to bed, so sinister in the "adult" "Lord Rendal" texts, becomes the insistence of a sleepy little boy.

"The Twa Sisters" (10 A) seems to be an adaptation of that grim story to infant ears. The best versions carry the verses about the musical instrument made of the dead maiden's bones, which at the appropriate time plays and discloses the murder. The comic lines in this version about the use of her fingers, the bridge of her nose, her veins, and her shinbones dancing a macabre "Moll Sims" may have come from a child's demand for more detail, which has become fixed by conservative repetition. The song follows a common folk pattern, reminding us in particular of "The Red Herring," a sort of Baron Munchausen tale of marvelous accomplishment:

> What d'ye think I have made of my red herring's ribs?
> Why, forty new cradles and fifty new cribs.

[12] Chase, *The Jack Tales*, p. 193, note.
[13] *Ibid., passim.*
[14] Child, *English and Scottish Popular Ballads*, ed. Sargent and Kittredge, p. 91.

> Cradles, cribs and everything,
> And I think I've done well with my jolly herring.[15]

One could pursue with considerable fascination the theme of the marvelous creation of something out of nothing far into folk song, arriving with luck at the conclusion that this sort of magic comes of supernatural parentage. What sort of person, for instance, was Brian o' Lyn, whom the Kentucky Mountain lad sings about? Today he is clearly a joke; he puts shoe boxes on his feet and calls them shoes; he makes a hat of two straws and calls it a John B. Stetson. The song is a very old satire, mentioned in a pre-Elizabethan play, and in those days it began:

> Tom a lin and his wife and his wife's mother,
> They went over a bridge all three together.
> The bridge was broken and they fell in.
> "The Devil go with all," quoth Tom a lin.[16]

So Brian used to be Tom; and from Tom o Lin to Tam Lin is but a step. It is perhaps relevant to recall that the fairy ballad of "Tam Lin" (39), at least as old as our jingle, also deals with magic transformations. Thus the nursery is often the point of juncture between two types of popular song, children's rhymes and ballads.

In the Riddle Ballads one sees emerging a new point of view.[17] The fatalism reflected in ballads dealing with the supernatural, and also in those romantic ballads which show so tragically that love and physical prowess, however great, are not enough to avert man's doom, and that in general he must "dree his weird," unable to change the course of events or his relation to supernatural, unfriendly forces, is met in some ballads by a different attitude, when man discovers within himself a power to fend against his fate. There is a stronger force than strength itself. His mind and wit begin to work against powers previously felt to be insuperable, and this new weapon, with its keener thrust than the sword which was his stand-by, may be in hands apparently weak: a schoolboy outwits a knight, a maiden pre-

[15] "The Red Herring," *Novello's School Songs*, No. 990.
[16] Wager, *The Longer Thou Livest, the More Fool Thou Art*, fol. Aiii. This song became a political lampoon in the eighteenth century, when it was done over by rhymesters as "Bob o' Lyn," a caricature of Sir Robert Walpole, M.P. for Lynn, and his great campaign promises. See Graves, *The English Ballad*, p. 119.
[17] In commenting on riddle ballads I am indebted to Winifred Smith's "Elements of Comedy in the Riddle Ballads," *Vassar Medieval Studies*.

serves her chastity against all suitors, a mortal contends with a ghost, and a simple shepherd is cleverer than a king. There is a delight in pitting this new-found strength against what has once been strong; the tragedy has turned to comedy, and the ballad singer has a new trick in his trade, the "happy ending."

Child quotes an ancient Turkish tale in which one prince says to another, "Do not let us be killing and fighting, but let us guess riddles. If you guess all of mine, I will be your subject; if you fail, I will take all your having." [18] So the ballad finds an alternative to its tragic bloodshed and violence in the use of a series of riddles, the successful answering of which confounds the powers of evil, exorcises the fiend himself, or wins a lover otherwise lost.

The riddles used have long been common currency. They are found in many ancient tales, and in early collections like the *Gesta Romanorum*. They attach themselves to any kind of popular tale or custom, and travel on the winds of tradition to distant countries. A riddle found in Homer still circulates unsolved on the coast of Brittany: "What we caught we threw away, and what we could not catch we kept." The riddle of Samson—"Out of the eater came forth meat, and out of the strong came forth sweetness"—has a folk flavor, as does the metaphor with which he follows it up: "If ye had not ploughed with my heifer, ye had not guessed my riddle." Many of them, like "What is swifter than the wind?" are based on an analogy between nature and man, just beginning to be observed. Man's likeness to animals has inspired riddles like that of the Sphinx: "What animal goes upon four legs in the spring, two in the summer, and three in the winter?"

The use of riddles today as a part of Russian peasant wedding festivities suggests a more serious role than that of mere entertainment, an actual formula from the days of bride-stealing and later bride-selling, as does their presence in courtship ballads. Children's riddling forfeit games have evolved from primitive dramatizations of contests between the sexes, or between darkness and light, summer and winter, etc. Two riddle ballads, "The Elfin Knight" (2) and "Proud Lady Margaret" (47) are, as we have noted, still played by children. The prevalence of riddles in folk parlance is shown by such phrases as "Read me a riddle," or "Riddle me this," meaning no more than

[18] Child, *English and Scottish Popular Ballads*, I, 11.

"Answer me this one," or "Give me your advice." "The Brown Girl" ("Lord Thomas and Fair Annet," 73) begins:

> O mother, O mother, come riddle to me,
> Come riddle me three in one,
> O must I marry Fair Ellender, say,
> Or bring the Brown Girl home?

The riddling ballads arbitrarily include the most irrelevant questions, which we can accept as advancing the story only by remembering that certain stock questions and answers were in general usage as evidence of cleverness. Originality was not expected of the language of wit. The same riddles travel from ballad to ballad, being put by Captain Wedderburn, a fairy, or the devil. Riddle ballads have thriven in tradition, and Child's few very ancient specimens have been recovered in many delightful forms. There is a large number of "impossible task" songs in the formula of "The Elfin Knight" (2). Even the very rare "False Knight upon the Road" (3) has been found in a few variants. Surviving as a nursery lullaby are three stanzas from "Captain Wedderburn's Courtship" (46). It might be thought that the rather tedious and localized "King John and the Bishop" (45) would have disappeared, but a full and excellent version of it was sung at a folk festival in Middlebury, Vermont, a few years ago.

"The Two Magicians" (44) serves as a connecting link between ballads of the supernatural and riddle ballads proper. The successive self-transformations of the blacksmith and his love suggest the riddle method, action taking the place of question, and there is a possible interest for folklore in the fact that the suitor is a sort of mysterious Wayland Smith who inspires all the shape-shifting.[19]

[19] Early popular superstition attributed magic powers to the first workers in metal.

THE FROG'S WEDDING [20]

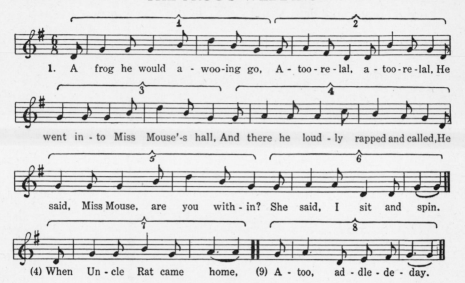

1. A frog he would a-woo-ing go, A-too-re-lal, a-too-re-lal, He went in-to Miss Mouse'-s hall, And there he loud-ly rapped and called, He said, Miss Mouse, are you with-in? She said, I sit and spin. (4) When Un-cle Rat came home, (9) A-too, ad-dle-de-day.

1. A frog he would a-wooing go,
   A-too-re-lal, a-too-re-lal,
   He went into Miss Mouse's hall,
   And there he loudly rapped and called,
   He said, Miss Mouse, are you within?
   She said, I sit and spin.

2. He took Miss Mouse upon his knee (1)
   And said, Miss Mouse, will you have me? (4)

3. She said, I cannot tell you, Sir (1)
   Till Uncle Rat comes home. (6)

4. When Uncle Rat came home, (7)
   He said, Who's been here since I've been gone? (1)
   A-too-re-lal, a too-re-lal, (2)

5. There's been a worthy gentleman (1)
   Who says he'll have me if he can. (4)

6. So Uncle Rat he went to town, (1)
   To buy Miss Mouse a wedding gown. (4)

[20] As sung by Mrs. J. Ford Kent of Troy, New York, to E. K. Wells, 1936. (The singer's irregular sequence of phrases which makes this variant unique is indicated by the numbers in parentheses, which correspond with those of the bracketed phrases of the tune.)

7. First came in it was a bee, (1)
   He carried a Bible on his knee. (4)

8. The second came in it was a snail, (1)
   He carried a fiddle on his tail. (4)

9. The frog came swimming across the lake (1)
   A-too-re-lal, A-too-re-lal, (2)
   And there got swallowed by a snake, (1)
   A-too, ad-dle-de-day. (8)

THE CROODIN' DOO
(Lord Randal, 12)[21]

1. Oh, where have you been this live-long day, My lit-tle wee croo-din' doo? I've been to see my step-mo-ther, Mar-mee, Oh, make my bed noo!

1. Oh, where have you been this live-long day,
   My little wee croodin' doo?
   I've been to see my stepmother,
   Marmee, Oh, make my bed noo!

2. And what did your stepmother give you to eat,
   My little wee croodin' doo?
   She gave me but a wee wee fish,
   All covered with green and blue.

3. And what did you do with the bones of the fish,
   My little wee croodin' doo?
   I gave them to my wee, wee dog.
   Marmee, Oh, make my bed noo.

4. And what did your dog when he'd ate up the fish,
   My little wee croodin' doo?
   He stretched his wee, wee limbs and died,
   Marmee, as I do noo,
   Marmee, as I do noo.

[21] From the *Journal of the Folk-Song Society*, V, No. 19 (1915), 117. Collected by Miss Anne G. Gilchrist, and reprinted here by her permission.

BRIAN O' LYN [22]

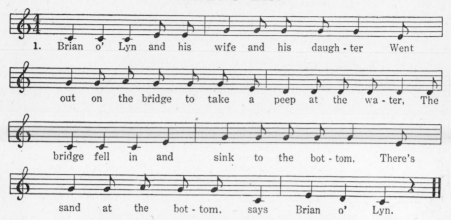

1. Brian o' Lyn and his wife and his daugh-ter Went
out on the bridge to take a peep at the wa-ter, The
bridge fell in and sink to the bot-tom. There's
sand at the bot-tom. says Brian o' Lyn.

1. Brian o' Lyn and his wife and his daughter
   Went out on the bridge to take a peep at the water,
   The bridge fell in and sink to the bottom,
   There's sand at the bottom, says Brian o' Lyn.

2. Brian o' Lyn had an old gray mare,
   Most of his back was wore off bare;
   One eye out and the other caved in,
   She's a walkin' old dodger, says Brian o' Lyn.

3. Brian o' Lyn he had no hat to wear,
   He's took two straws and he made him one;
   Turned one straw out and the other straw in,
   That's a John B. Stetson, says Brian o' Lyn.

4. Brian o' Lyn he had no coat to wear,
   He killed him a goat and he made him one,
   He put the horns right under his chin,
   That'll answer for a pistol, said Brian o' Lyn.

5. Brian o' Lyn he had no shoes to wear,
   He took him two boxes and he made him a pair;
   He took the lids off and put his feet in,
   That's a solid leather pair, says Brian o' Lyn.

6. Brian o' Lyn he had no watch to wear,
   He got him a turnip and he scraped it bare,
   Put him a cricket right under the skin,
   That 'll put it to tickin', says Brian o' Lyn.

[22] As learned from Henry Harris of Big Laurel by Elizabeth Miniard, who sang it to E. K. Wells at Pine Mountain, Harlan County, Kentucky, May, 1938.

THE TWO MAGICIANS (44)[23]

1. O she look'd out of the win-dow, as white as an-y milk, And
he look'd in-to the win-dow, as black as an-y silk. Hel-lo, hel-lo, hel-
lo, hel-lo, you coal-black smith, You have done me no harm. I
nev-er shall change my maid-en name that I have had so
long. I'd ra-ther die a maid, yes, but then she said, And be
bur-ied all in my grave, Than I'd have such a nas-ty, hus-ky, dus-ky,
mus-ky, fus-ky coal-black smith, A maid-en I will die. 2.Then
she be-came a duck, a duck all on the stream, And
he be-came a wa-ter dog, and fetch'd her back a-gain.

1. Oh, she looked out of the window, as white as any milk,
    And he looked into the window, as black as any silk.
        Hello, hello, hello, hello, you coal-black smith,
            You have done me no harm,
        I never shall change my maiden name
            That I have had so long.

[23] From Sharp, *One Hundred English Folksongs* (1916), p. 48. Reprinted by permission of Theodore Presser, Philadelphia. Published and copyrighted by Oliver Ditson, Boston.

I'd rather die a maid, yes, but then she said,
  And be buried all in my grave,
Than I'd have such a nasty, husky, dusky, musty, fusty
    coal-black smith,
  A maiden I will die.

2. Then she became a duck, a duck all on the stream,
   And he became a water dog, and fetch'd her back again.

3. Then she became a hare, a hare upon the plain,
   And he became a grey-hound dog and fetched her back again.

4. Then she became a fly, a fly all in the air;
   And he became a spider, and fetched her to his lair.

THE DEVIL'S QUESTIONS
(Riddles Wisely Expounded, 1)[24]

1. If you can't answer my questions nine, Sing
ninety nine and ninety; Oh, you're not God's, you're
one of mine, And you're not the weaver's bonny.

1. If you can't answer my questions nine,
     Sing ninety nine and ninety;
   Oh, you're not God's, you're one of mine,
     And you're not the weaver's bonny.

2. Oh what is higher than the tree?
     Sing ninety nine, *etc.*
   And what is deeper than the sea?
     And you're not, *etc.*

3. Oh heaven is higher than the tree, Sing, *etc.*
   And hell is deeper than the sea,
     And I am the weaver's bonny.

[24] From *Songs of All Time*, p. 11. Collected by Richard Chase.

4. Oh what is whiter than the milk? Sing, *etc.*
   And what is softer than the silk?
      And you're not, *etc.*

5. Oh snow is whiter than the milk, Sing, *etc.*
   And down is softer than the silk,
      And I am, *etc.*

6. Oh what is heavier than the lead? *Sing,* etc.
   And what is better than the bread?
      And you're not, *etc.*

7. Oh grief is heavier than the lead, Sing, *etc.*
   God's blessing's better than the bread,
      And I am, *etc.*

8. Oh what is louder than the horn? Sing, *etc.*
   And what is sharper than the thorn?
      And you're not, *etc.*

9. Oh thunder is louder than the horn, Sing, *etc.*
   And hunger's sharper than the thorn,
      And I am, *etc.*

10. Now you have answered my questions nine, Sing, *etc.*
    Oh you are God's, you're none of mine,
       And you are the weaver's bonny.

SCARBOROUGH FAIR
(The Elfin Knight, 2)[25]

1. To Scar-bor-ough Fair are you go-ing? Pars-ley, sage, rose-
ma-ry and thyme, Oh give my love to a
girl that lives there, For once she was a true
lov-er of mine. 2. Oh, tell her to make me a
cam-bric shirt, Pars-ley, sage, rose-ma-ry and thyme, Without an-y nee-dle or thread worked in it, And
she shall be a true lov-er of mine.

1. To Scarborough Fair are you going?
   Parsley, sage, rosemary and thyme,
   Oh give my love to a girl who lives there,
   For once she was a true lover of mine.

2. Oh, tell her to make me a cambric shirt,
   Parsley, sage, rosemary and thyme,
   Without any needle or thread worked in it,
   And she shall be a true lover of mine.

3. Tell her to wash it in yonder well
   Where never spring water nor rain ever fell.

4. Tell her to hang it on yonder thorn
   Which never bore blossom since Adam was born.

[25] From Carey, *Ten English Folk-Songs* (1915), p. 20. Reprinted by permission of the publishers, Curwen, London.

5. And when she has answered these questions three,
   If he can answer as many for me,
     Then he shall be a true lover of mine.

6. Tell him to find me an acre of land
   Betwixt the salt water all on the sea sand.

7. And tell him to plough it with a ram's horn
   And all over sow it with one peppercorn.

8. And tell him to cut it with a sickle of leather,
   And bind it all up in a peacock's feather.

9. And when he has done and finished his work,
   He can come unto me for his cambric shirt.

THE CAMBRIC SHIRT
(The Elfin Knight, 2)[26]

1. (He) I want you to make me a cambric shirt.
   Fum-a-lum-a-link, sou-pa-loo-my-nee. With
   nei-ther seam nor nee-dle work,
   Red-i-o, ted-i-o, tod-dle bod, bed-i-o,
   Fum-a-lum-a-link, sou-pa-loo-my-nee.

1. (*He*) I want you to make me a cambric shirt,
       Fum-a-lum-a-link, sou-pa-loo-my-nee,
   With neither seam nor needle work,
       Redio, tedio, toddle bod, bedio,
       Fum-a-lum-a-link, sou-pa-loo-my-nee.

[26] From Barry, Eckstorm and Smyth, *British Ballads from Maine* (1929), p. 3. Reprinted by permission of the Yale University Press, New Haven, Publishers.

2. (*She*) I want you to buy me an acre of land,
    Fum-a-lum, *etc.*
  Between salt water and the sea sand,
    Redio, *etc.*

3. Plow it o'er with an old buck's horn,
    Fum-a-lum, *etc.*
  Plant it o'er with one peppercorn,
    Redio, *etc.*

4. Reap it down with a peacock's feather,
    Fum-a-lum, *etc.*
  Bind it up with the sting of an adder,
    Redio, *etc.*

5. Thrash it out with a mouse's tail,
    Fum-a-lum, *etc.*
  Cart it in on the back of a snail.
    Redio, *etc.*

6. When you have completed your work,
    Fum-a-lum, *etc.*
  Come to me you shall have your shirt,
    Redio, *etc.*

THE FALSE KNIGHT UPON THE ROAD (3)[27]

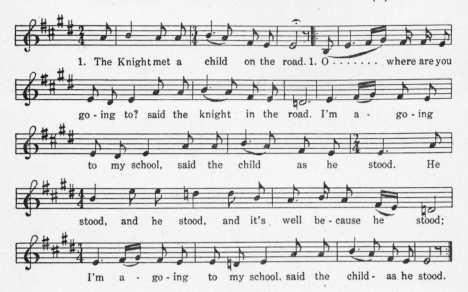

1. The Knight met a child on the road. 1. O . . . . where are you go - ing to? said the knight in the road. I'm a - go - ing to my school, said the child as he stood. He stood, and he stood, and it's well be - cause he stood; I'm a - go - ing to my school, said the child - as he stood.

1. The knight met a child on the road.
   O where are you going to? said the knight in the road.
   I'm a-going to my school, said the child as he stood.
   He stood, and he stood, and it's well because he stood.
   I'm a-going to my school, said the child as he stood.

2. O what are you going there for? said the knight in the road.
   For to learn the word of God, said the child as he stood.
   He stood and he stood, *etc.*
   For to learn the word of God, *etc.*

3. O what have you got there? said the knight in the road.
   I have got my bread and cheese, said the child as he stood.
   He stood and he stood, *etc.*

4. O won't you give me some? said the knight in the road.
   No, nary a bit nor crumb, said the child as he stood.
   He stood and he stood, *etc.*

5. O, I wish you were on the sands, said the knight in the road.
   Yes, and a good staff in my hands, said the child as he stood.
   He stood and he stood, *etc.*

[27] From Sharp, *English Folk Songs from the Southern Appalachians* (1932), I, 3.
Reprinted by permission of the Oxford University Press, London, Publishers.

6. O, I wish you were in the sea, said the knight in the road.
   Yes, and a good boat under me, said the child as he stood.
   He stood and he stood, *etc.*

7. O, I think I hear a bell, said the knight in the road.
   Yes, and it's ringing you to hell, said the child as he stood.
   He stood, and he stood, and it's well because he stood;
   Yes, and it's ringing you to hell, said the child as he stood.

THE RIDDLE SONG
(Captain Wedderburn's Courtship, 46)[28]

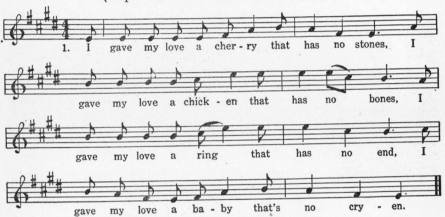

1. I gave my love a cherry that has no stones,
   I gave my love a chicken that has no bones,
   I gave my love a ring that has no end.
   I gave my love a baby that's no cryen.

2. How can there be a cherry that has no stones?
   How can there be a chicken that has no bones?
   How can there be a ring that has no end?
   How can there be a baby that's no cryen?

3. A cherry when it's blooming, it has no stones,
   A chicken when it's pipping, it has no bones,
   A ring when it's rolling, it has no end,
   A baby when it's sleeping, it's no cryen.

pipping—forming in the shell; breaking the shell.

[28] From Sharp, *English Folk Songs from the Southern Appalachians* (1932), II, 190.
Reprinted by permission of the Oxford University Press, London, Publishers.

Chapter 7

CHRISTIAN ELEMENTS IN THE BALLADS

IF there is a wealth of paganism in the ballads, there is a corresponding poverty of Christian elements. Ballad matter is largely secular, embodying themes not limited to Christian times or moral attitudes; and for many reasons traditional song has absorbed very little, either in theme or allusion, that may be attributed to Christian influences.

In the slow conversion of Northern Europe the rulers of the countries became Christian often only in name, and for political purposes, and the ensuing baptism of the people themselves was entirely superficial. Indeed, heathen practices continued throughout the Middle Ages; superstition was rampant in the sixteenth and seventeenth centuries; witch hunts in Western Europe, Britain, and New England were the disgrace of the eighteenth century; even today the remnants of pagan superstition are not confined to backwaters of ignorance. The making over of the minds and hearts of men professedly Christian, indeed, is still an unrealized dream.

In 601 Gregory the Great, almost as aware as the modern folklorist of what ages of entrenched belief and custom he had to meet, issued his instructions to his missionaries:

> Do not pull down the fanes. Destroy the idols; purify the buildings with holy water; set relics there; and let them become temples of the true God. So the people will have no need to change their places of concourse, and where of old they were wont to sacrifice cattle to demons, thither let them continue to resort on the day of the Saint to whom the church is dedicated, to slay their beasts no longer as a sacrifice but for a social meal in honor of Him whom they now worship.[1]

The missionaries, therefore, wisely converted to their purposes what they found. In Britain as well as Europe native divinities had given way to Roman gods, who now in turn were dispossessed by Christian

[1] Gregory the Great, writing to Ethelbert of Kent. Quoted from *Bede's Ecclesiastical History of the English People*, by Chambers, *Medieval Stage*, I, 95–96.

saints. One may often pick up the trail. Near Burford in Oxfordshire is a tiny stone church reached now only by field paths and opened for service once a year. Near the altar a bit of Roman pavement has been found, and a few rods away, through a grove of hawthorn trees, there runs a tiny stream. The presence of water and the circle of once sacred trees suggest the primitive ritual that once took place here, and the story of succeeding forms of worship is told by the pavement and the ancient building. Christian services were introduced not only at the same place, but on the same day. Thus many a heathen festival beside Christmas and Easter found its way into the church calendar. St. Stephen's Day, December 26th, had been sacred to the Scandinavian Frea, patroness of horses, and in Northern Europe horse-racing is still part of the celebration of "The Feast of Stephen." The sacrificial bone-fires of midsummer festivals became the holiday bonfires of St. John and St. Barnabas. The Christian significance of the day was merely superimposed on the older customs.

For a long time the literature of the new religion was familiar to a comparatively small group, and wherever a Christian story was told by the folk, it emanated from the monks, since they were the repository of sacred legends. Of the few that passed into oral tradition only a handful have reached us in ballad form. Doubtless many more existed at first, for we may assume the loss of many manuscripts. But while the monks may have started these stories on their way,[2] other elements of the Church fought against their dissemination in popular form. A continuing puritanism, which crops out in every age, has always frowned on the ballad,[3] discouraging particularly the association of a holy story with a secular form, and the liberties that form took with it. The selective taste of oral tradition also prevented any

[2] For a discussion of the monkish authorship of the ballads see Pound, *Poetic Origins and the Ballad*, pp. 183 ff.

[3] "I am informed that the Minds and Manners of many People about the Country are much corrupted by foolish Songs and Ballads, which the Hawkers and Pedlars carry into all parts of the Country. By way of antidote, I would procure poetical Composures full of Piety, and such as may have a Tendency to advance Truth and Goodness, to be published and scatterd into all Corners of the Land." Cotton Mather, "Diary," *Massachusetts Historical Society Collections*, 7th Series, VII, Pt. II, 242.

"That if they (the printers) sometimes print vicious or silly things not worth reading, it may not be because they approve such things themselves, but because the People are so viciously and corruptly educated that good things are not encouraged. I have known a very numerous Impression of Robin Hood Songs go off in this Province at 2 s/ per Book in less than a Twelvemonth; when a small quantity of David's Psalms have lain on my Hands above twice the time." *The Writings of Benjamin Franklin*, ed. Smyth, II, 175.

great spread of sacred ballads. Stories from the Bible and the apocryphal gospels, which were the source of many a good tale, were apt in
retelling to take on a moral tone which the ballad cannot successfully
manage—the singer does not like to be distracted from his main
interest, the story itself. The moralizing ballad, if it lived, was of an
inferior nature; and if it lost the moral it often lost as well all traces
of the religious story. At bottom, however, tradition has rejected
religious ballads because they deal with special experiences of special
people, rather than the experience of humanity as a whole. So, like
the Robin Hood, Border Raid, and historical ballads, they have suffered comparative oblivion.

In the passage of the secular ballad down the centuries, it has
picked up a few superficial imprints of Christian influences, or of the
Medieval Church as an institution. Robin Hood, for all his possible
pagan ancestry, goes to Mass at any cost to himself; a wicked monk
betrays him; he makes a bishop to "dance in his boots"; a prioress
bleeds him to death. The time of many a ballad action is "when bells
are rung and Mass is sung." We hear of Our Lady's draw-well and of
other saints' wells, but these were doubtless earlier pagan shrines. The
wish to equip oneself for a pagan afterlife is touched with Christian
piety:

> Put my Bible at my head,
> My busker (?) at my feet,
> My little Prayer book at my right side,
> The sounder will be my sleep.[4]

The Queen of Faery becomes the Queen of Heaven. Brown Robyn
(57), for his fair confession, is saved by the Virgin and her Son. The
entrance to Christian Paradise is marked by heathen birch trees.
Many other small details suggest the Christian influence, but they are
either superficial and temporary accretions, or conversions of older
ideas.

What the Church could not dispel, it tried to regularize. Thus the
collection taken up by the Abbots Bromley Horn Dancers, a survival
of the ritual of luck-sharing, is used for church repairs or put in the
parish poor box. The Rumanian Călușari dancers, a remarkable survival of ancient belief and practice, are annually excommunicated. For
six weeks every spring these men in women's costume, led by a masked

---

[4] "Sir Hugh" (155 N).

man and carrying flowering garlic, dance through the villages. Their dance has power to heal the sick and perform other miracles. Here are many recognizable elements: in the costume, the union of male and female necessary for fertility; in the mask the adoption of another personality and hence deification; in the name "Căluşari" or fairies, the assumption of divine power; in the flowering garlic the source of their magic; and in their miraculous cures the proof of their supernatural power. And during the period of their dance they may not go to Mass, and the leader, in whom the virtue of the dance chiefly resides, must take a vow of silence in further penance. Similarly, many an ancient ballad does penance for forbidden intercourse with spirits by taking on a semblance of piety. Roads to heaven and hell are pointed out in "Thomas Rymer" (37) and "The Queen of Elfan's Nourice" (40). Thomas "maun hold his tongue" about his sojourn in Fairyland. The good church member in parts of the Appalachians today, who has put away "devil's ditties" along with whiskey, tobacco, and coffee, may still indulge in his favorite songs if he moralizes them, so he introduces the Saviour into "The Wife of Usher's Well" (79), or a revivalist shout into the refrain of "The Two Sisters" (10):

> I will be true, true to my love,
> Yes, Lord! if my love will be true to me.[5]

Although purist and puritan in the Church have frowned upon the religious ballad, the popular evangelist has used the secular song for his purposes. So the Franciscans took over the secular carol,[6] and so the popular ballad, already endeared to the populace, has at times become the vehicle for the Gospel. The records of the Stationers' Company, which licensed all ballads for print in the sixteenth and seventeenth centuries, show the progress along this sawdust trail of "Rowe Well Ye Mariners," a secular ballad now lost except in the name of a country dance, which appears successively as "Rowe well ye maryners moralyzed with ye story of Jonas," "Rowe well Godes Marynours," and "Rowe ye well Christes Marynours." [7] This is a familiar story: in every religious revival there is a borrowing of secular tunes. The American white spiritual shows their strong influence on religious folk music, building up its shaped-note harmonies around such tunes as

[5] *Ozark Folksongs*, I, 53.
[6] See page 197.
[7] *Stationers' Register*, I, 355, 360, 362.

"Princess Royal" or "Captain Kidd." From "The Dear Companion," a love lyric, comes "The Wayfaring Stranger." [8]

Half a dozen Child ballads deal with subjects of Christian literature. One of these, the thirteenth century "Judas" (23), is our oldest ballad text. In this story, Judas is charmed to sleep by a sister, and then robbed of the thirty pieces of silver which Jesus has entrusted to him to buy food. The ballad has not come down in English tradition, although a Wendish ballad of the nineteenth century tells how Judas loses his money at play. A Coptic "Gospel of the Twelve Apostles" from the fifth century tells the story of Judas' wife, who is always tempting him.[9] There was a medieval concern to account for the sin of Judas, and the introduction into these ballads of the evil woman, a stock character in oriental tales, with her witch-like spells and hypnotic caresses, would serve to explain if not to exculpate him. Although Child's ballad is couched in language so archaic that it almost demands translation, the traditional style is here in all its force, using dialogue with dramatic freedom, passing without transition from scene to scene, building up the situation by incremental repetition, careless of the record in describing Pilate as a rich Jew with ten hundred knights, mounting with simple dignity to the final unforgettable rebuke:

> Still thou be, Peter, well I thee know,
> Thou wilt forsake me thrice ere the cock crow.

"St. Stephen and Herod" (22) is likewise from an early manuscript, and not found in oral tradition. Here, with the ballad's casual treatment of fact, Stephen the Martyr, who had no connection with Herod, takes the place of the Three Wise Men. Here, too, we have evidence that as early as 1400 the style of the ballad had developed certain formulae, such as the repeated "What-ails-thee" question and its reply. The ballad includes the familiar miracle of the roasted cock, a fine traditional version of which, "King Herod and the Cock," has come down to us. This appears also in the didactic dialogue of "The Carnal and the Crane" (55), hardly a ballad, but containing the makings of several fine ones in its group of stories from the life of Jesus, accepted

[8] For a discussion of white spirituals, see the studies of George Pullen Jackson (Bibliography).

[9] See Baum, "The English Ballad of Judas Iscariot," *Publications of the Modern Language Association,* XXXI (1916), 181–89.

or apochryphal. "Dives and Lazarus" (56), with its moral treatment of a popular theme, the contrast of rich and poor, has enough of the universally appealing to have given it life, and it too is found traditionally today. "The Maid and the Palmer" (21) shows how far secular treatment of a sacred story will carry it from its source. The picture of Christ's wanderings on earth, and his meeting with someone who seems to be a combination of Mary Magdalen and the Samaritan Woman, is hard to recognize, and the obvious association with some hearty and rhythmic dance tune which is indicated by the elaborate nonsense refrain reflects how thoroughly the folk has made over the popular theme of chastity, its part in the social code, and the punishment for its loss. It has not survived traditionally.

"The Cherry Tree Carol" (54)—misnamed, since it is ballad rather than carol—suggests another aspect of popularized religious story, the mystery play, which is briefly reviewed here in order to show the folk treatment of the sacred themes.

The fifteenth century was the heyday not only of the ballad but of the mystery play, a democratic and popular presentation of sacred stories heretofore the property of the clergy. It had begun in the tenth century, with the trope kernel of the liturgical drama, a brief rhymed dialogue in Latin between the priests at the altar. Thus, at Christmas there were verses about the Child in the Manger, and at Easter about the empty grave, with a suggestion of costume and one or two properties. Later the little play grew more elaborate, its production passed from the clergy to the laity, and the vernacular was substituted for the Latin. In this process it moved from the altar to the nave of the church, from the nave to the steps outside, and finally, scene by scene, onto moving platforms or pageants which were drawn through the town, stopping now and then for a performance. So you might sit in one spot, and view the drama of Isaac and Abraham, or Noah and the Flood, as it passed you scene by scene. More characters were introduced, at first from the Bible, and then fictitious ones like Noah's wife. Practically every story from the Creation to the Judgment was dramatized, and there was a play for every feast day in the year. Much popular material was included: favorite stock characters like the village scold or the braggart appeared; jokes and horseplay mingled with true piety; songs, aphorisms, and all the gnomic wisdom of the folk were interspersed throughout; and there was often comment on such current matters as labor conditions, fads in fashion, or differing ways of speech.

The immense vogue of the mystery play when it reached these proportions called for a business organization, and this was supplied by the *mysteres* or craft guilds. They furnished the capital to provide the properties, pay the writers, find and subsidize the actors and musicians. Certain plays were reserved to certain guilds, like the Noah and Jonah stories which the Fishmongers produced, and certain towns, like York and Townley and Chester, had their own special cycles of plays. Hundreds of people were involved in their production; thousands attended them. On feast days when the populace was making holiday, the whole countryside was alive with people traveling to the plays. Market places swarmed, inns were crowded. In Chester, a town famous for its plays, the famous Rows, a two-story arcade built along the fronts of the ancient houses of the principal street, may have been an architectural development to provide seats or covered standing room for spectators as the pageants went by.[10]

The same popular genius which produced the mystery plays stimulated the folk singers. In this democratizing of the stories of the Bible, singers and script writers borrowed from each other and many parallel passages can be found. Thus the verses of a German liturgy play, as sung by the priests, find their counterpart in a traditional carol:

Joseph, liever, never min,
Hilf mir wiegen daz kindelin.

Joseph dearest, Joseph mine,
Help me cradle the child divine,
God reward thee and all that's thine,
    In Paradise,
So prays the Mother Mary.

Gerne, liebe muome min,
Hilf ich dire wiegen kindelin.[11]

Gladly, dear one, lady mine,
Help I cradle this child of thine,
God's own light on us both shall shine
    In Paradise,
As prays the Mother Mary.[12]

"The Cherry Tree Carol" (54) corresponds to a passage in the Coventry Mysteries. The story of a tree which miraculously bows down

---

[10] There are other explanations. George Ormerod, in his *History of Cheshire* (1819), suggests that they were a defense against armed cavalry, or merely a device to escape the rain. (Quoted by editors of *Recording Britain*, III, 48.)

[11] Miles, *Christmas*, p. 108.

[12] *Oxford Book of Carols*, p. 165.

and yields its fruit for the refreshment of the Holy Family on various
journeys is found in many legends of the Infancy.

MARIA: A! my swete husbond! Wolde ye telle to me
            What tre is yon, standing upon yon hylle?

JOSEPH: Forsothe Mary it is clepyd a chery tre;
            In tyme of yere ye myght ffede you thereon your fylle.

MARIA: Turne ageyn, husbond, & beholde yon tre;
            How that it blomyght, now, so swetely.

JOSEPH: Cum on Mary, that we worn at yon cyte,
            Or ellys we may be blamyd, I telle yow lythly.

MARIA: Now my spowse, I pray yow to behold
            How the cheryes growyn upon yon tre;
            Ffor to have therof, ryght ffayne I wold,
            & it plesyd yow to labore so meche for me.

JOSEPH: Your desyre to ffulfylle I shall assay sekerly:—
            Ow! to plucke yow of these cheries it is a werk wylde!
            Ffor the tre is so hygh it wold not be [don] lyghtly,
            Therfore lete hym pluk yow cheries, begatt yow with childe.

MARIA: Now good lord, I pray the, graunt me this boun,
            To haue of these cheries, & it be yo' wylle;
            Now, I thonk the god, this tre bowyth to me down,
            I may now gadyr anowe, & etyn to my fylle.

Joseph then humbles himself, the miracle convincing him that he has
offended "god i' trinyte." [13]

As the sacred stories were taken over from the Church, the folk en-
livened them by means of a bold and realistic treatment, modernizing
and placing them in times and settings that the singers themselves
knew, yet without any loss of piety. Thus, in the *Second Shepherds'
Play*, the shepherds on the heath, gossiping and talking about their
problems, are the Yorkshiremen of the times; their pious joy as they
proceed to Bethlehem with their offerings is not the less because they
have just tossed Mak their mate in a blanket for his sly trick of disguising a stolen sheep as his own new-born child. The farcical offering
of gifts to the sheep-baby is followed by a devout presentation at the
manger, which is one of the most simply pious scenes in all literature.
In "The Cherry Tree Carol" (54) the stock characterization of Joseph

[13] "English Nativity Plays," ed. Hemingway, *Yale Studies in English*, XXXVIII, 102.

as the jealous husband, his rough and insulting words to his wife, and the ancient folk jest of disputed paternity, accentuate rather than detract from the impressiveness of the miracle, as the babe speaks from his mother's womb. The folk singer, unable to conceive of the persons of sacred story as different from himself, does not fear to preserve in men and women exalted by the Church to superhuman goodness, the faults and foibles of real people. Anything familiar to him, no matter how crude and everyday, helps him make the tale his own.

This is the spirit that informs much religious art of the past, contributing to it a realistic naïveté which can still touch us strangely. In almost every age there has been an attempt to reanimate stories which have been dulled by fearful reverence. Today *The Ageless Story* by Lauren Ford recounts in pictures the birth of the Virgin, her life, and the birth and childhood of Jesus, in the setting of a Connecticut village. The renewal of tenderness and piety that comes from looking at these pictures so full of contemporary detail—the Temple a white New England meeting house, the dwelling of the Holy Family furnished with four-posters and patchwork quilts, the flight into Egypt past silos and red barns—is a process the folk singer has always understood. The mind that thinks of a story in these terms is naïve, but not irreverent.

"The Bitter Withy" is conceived in this spirit. This is a ballad discovered since Child's day, which because of its traditional quality he would certainly have included had he known about it. The legend is found in one of those pseudo gospels of the second century containing tales of the birth and childhood of Jesus. The monasteries of Northern Africa, Greece, and other centers of the early Church specialized in these accounts, which represent a mixture of Eastern myth and Christian accretion. From the Orient came many stories of magic bridges made of the beams of the moon or the sun, and of fatal falls from them.[14] The legend of the Bitter Withy was a favorite, as the fresco on the outside of a church in Lucca long attested. Here, for all that Italian town to see daily, was the story of a naughty little boy and his punishment. An English clergyman traveling in Italy in 1846 describes it:

> The Virgin is represented as inflicting corporeal punishment upon the youthful Jesus. She holds a rod in her hand; with the other she holds the garments of the Child. She is in the act of inflicting pun-

[14] Phillips Barry in "The Bridge of Sunbeams," *Journal of American Folklore*, XXVII (1914), 79–89, carries aspects of the legend back to sun worshipers of the Nile.

ishment. The Child is in alarm and its eyes are eagerly directed to St. Anna, the mother of the Virgin, in the background, entreating her intercession to escape the cruel ordeal.[15]

Our ballad shows the incident against a background of village life as it might be anywhere, in Palestine or England, with its ball-playing mischievous children, their taunts and quarrels, and their complaining mothers. In the line, "Up Lincull and down Lincull" (Lincoln) there is an identification with the singer's own country, perhaps his own town, and a confusion of this story with another ballad about a little boy who played at ball, Sir Hugh of Lincoln. In another version, "The Holy Well," the beginning of a more conservative veneration for Jesus appears. Here Mary is the one who wants to retaliate, and Jesus refuses to yield to base motives:

> Sweet Jesus, go down to yonder town
> As far as the Holy Well,
> And take away those sinful souls
> And dip them deep in hell.

> Nay, nay, sweet Jesus said,
> Nay, nay, that may not be,
> For there are too many sinful souls
> Crying out for the help of me.[16]

Religious ballads and carols have survived in American song and are now receiving a good deal of interested attention, both for the naïveté of their texts and the beauty of their music. These white spirituals which were the stock in trade of the singing-school teachers as they worked their way west and south from Colonial New England may be picked up today in byways of the middle west and south. The curious Easter ballad called after its singer, a child in a mountain settlement school, "Edna's Song," has considerable dignity; and the parallel use of a vernacular and more learned expression for the same thing, "betrayed him"—"sold him"; "crucified him"—"nailed him to the cross," is suggestive of fourteenth-century practice, when the promotion of the mother tongue, and the need for explaining the foreign

---

[15] *Notes and Queries*, Third Series, III (1863), 334 ff. See also Gerould, "The Ballad of the Bitter Withy," *Publications of the Modern Language Association*, XXIII (1908), 141–67. Recent reports of the present existence of this picture, or others like it, are unreliable. My efforts to secure information on this point from the archivist of Lucca have so far met with no success.

[16] Sharp, *English Folk Carols*, pp. 59–61.

term, were introducing the English word in company with its Latin-derived synonym. Mary as the "niece" of Jesus was perhaps once his "nourice" or "nurse." Ancient usage is inexact in terms of kinship; the folk singer would not question this. In the German cradle song quoted above, Mary calls Joseph her *liever neve*, or dear nephew, since they were both of the Seed of David. "The Little Family" is of comparatively modern origin, and though rather tedious and circumstantial in style, it is included here as an example of the productivity of simple poets that filled many an old-fashioned hymnbook with ballads which have since passed into tradition. Another example from the same period, "In the Valley," absorbs into its solid and pulsating dignity a favorite folk refrain.

KING HEROD AND THE COCK
(From The Carnal and the Crane, 55) [17]

1. There was a star in Da-vid's land, In Da-vid's land ap-pear'd, And in King Her-od's cham-ber. So bright it did shine there.

1. There was a star in David's land,
    In David's land appear'd,
    And in King Herod's chamber,
    So bright it did shine there.

2. The Wise Men they soon spi-ed it,
    And told the King a-nigh
    That a Princely Babe was born that night,
    No king shall e'er destroy.

3. If this be the truth, King Herod said,
    That thou hast told to me,
    The roasted cock that lies in the dish
    Shall crow full senses three.

senses—(?) times

[17] From Sharp, *English Folk Carols* (1911), p. 2. Reprinted by permission of Novello and Co., London, Publishers.

4. O, the cock soon thrustened and feathered well,
   By the work of God's own hand,
   And he did crow full senses three
   In the dish where he did stand.

THE CHERRY TREE CAROL (54)[18]

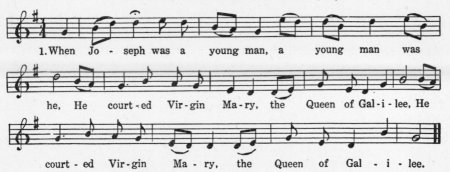

1. When Jo - seph was a   young man, a   young   man   was
   he, He   court-ed   Vir-gin   Ma-ry, the   Queen of Gal-i-lee, He
   court - ed   Vir-gin   Ma-ry,   the   Queen   of   Gal - i - lee.

1. When Joseph was a young man, a young man was he,
   He courted Virgin Mary, the Queen of Galilee,
   He courted Virgin Mary, the Queen of Galilee,

2. As Joseph and Mary were walking one day,
   Here is apples and cherries enough to behold.

3. Then Mary spoke to Joseph so neat and so mild:
   Joseph, gather me some cherries, for I am with child.

4. Then Joseph flew in angry, in angry he flew;
   Let the father of the baby gather cherries for you.

5. Lord Jesus spoke a few words all down unto them,
   Bow low down, low down, cherry tree, let my mother have some.

6. The cherry tree bowed low down, low down to the ground,
   And Mary gathered cherries while Joseph stood around.

7. Then Joseph took Mary all on his right knee,
   He cried, O Lord, have mercy for what have I done.

8. And Joseph took Mary all on his left knee,
   Pray tell me, little baby, when your birthday will be?

9. On the fifth day of January my birthday will be,
   When the stars and the elements doth tremble with fear.

neat—(?) meek   fifth day of January—Old Christmas Eve. See page 289.

[18] From Sharp, *English Folk Songs from the Southern Appalachians*, I, 92. Reprinted by permission of the Oxford University Press, London, Publishers.

THE BITTER WITHY [19]

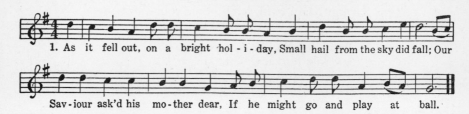

1. As it fell out, on a bright hol-i-day, Small hail from the sky did fall; Our Sav-iour ask'd his mo-ther dear, If he might go and play at ball.

1. As it fell out, on a bright holiday,
    Small hail from the sky did fall;
 Our Saviour ask'd his mother dear
    If he might go and play at ball.

2. At ball, at ball, my own dear son,
    It is time that you were gone;
 And don't let me hear of any doings
    At night when you come home.

3. So up Lincull and down Lincull
    Our sweetest Saviour ran,
 And there he met three rich young lords;
    Good morning to you all.

4. Good morn, Good morn, Good morn, said they:
    Good morning, then said he.
 O which of you three rich young lords
    Will play at ball with me?

5. We are all lords' and ladies' sons,
    Born in our bower and hall;
 And thou art nothing but a poor maid's child,
    Born in an ox's stall.

6. If you're all lords' and ladies' sons,
    Born in your bower and hall,
 I will make you believe in your latter end;
    I'm an angel above you all.

7. So he made him a bridge with the beams of the sun,
    And o'er the water crossed he.
 These rich young lords followed after him,
    And drowned they were all three.

[19] From Sharp, *English Folk Carols*, p. 5. Reprinted by permission of Miss Maud Karpeles.

8. Then up Lincull and down Lincull
   These young lords' mothers ran,
   Saying: Mary mild, fetch home your child,
   For ours he has drowned all.

9. So Mary mild fetched home her child
   And laid him across her knee;
   With a handful of green withy twigs
   She gave him slashes three.

10. O withy, O withy, O bitter withy,
    Thou hast caused me to smart;
    And the withy shall be the very first tree
    That shall perish at the heart!

EDNA'S SONG [20]

1. Christ was born in Bethlehem,
   Christ was born in Bethlehem.
   Christ was born in Bethlehem,
   And Mary was his niece.
       And Mary was his niece.
   Christ was born in Bethlehem,
   And Mary was his niece.

2. Judas, he betrayed him, *etc.*
   And sold him to the Jews.

3. The Jews, they crucified him, *etc.*
   And nailed him to the cross.

niece—(?) nurse, nourice

[20] As sung by Edna Feltner, Pine Mountain, Harlan County, Kentucky, to E. K. Wells, 1919.

4. Joseph begged his body, *etc.*
   And laid it in the tomb.

5. The tomb it would not hold him, *etc.*
   He burst the bands of death.

6. Four angels they came flying, *etc.*
   And rolled the stone away.

7. So early in the morning, *etc.*
   Mary came weeping.

8. O what's the matter, Mary? *etc.*
   They've stole my Lord away.

9. O go and tell my brethren, *etc.*
   That Jesus has arose.

THE LITTLE FAMILY [21]

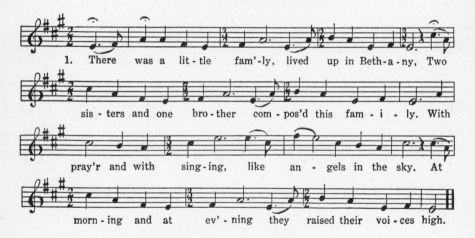

1. There was a lit-tle fam'-ly, lived up in Beth-a-ny, Two
sis-ters and one bro-ther com-pos'd this fam-i-ly. With
pray'r and with sing-ing, like an-gels in the sky. At
morn-ing and at ev'-ning they raised their voi-ces high.

1. There was a little fam'ly, lived up in Bethany,
   Two sisters and one brother compos'd this family.
   With pray'r and with singing, like angels in the sky.
   At morning and at ev'ning they raised their voices high.

2. They lived in peace and pleasure for many lonely years,
   And laid away their treasure beyond this vale of tears;
   Though poor and without money, their kindness made amends.
   Their house was ever open to Jesus and his friends.

[21] As sung by May Ritchie, Pine Mountain, Harlan County, Kentucky, to E. K. Wells, 1916.

3. Although they lived so happy, so kind, so pure and good,
Their brother was afflicted, and by it thrown in bed.
Poor Martha and her sister, they wept aloud and cried.
But still he grew no better; he lingered on and died.

4. The Jews came to the sisters, laid Lazarus in the tomb,
And tried for to comfort, and drive away their gloom.
When Jesus heard the tidings, far in a distant land,
So swiftly did he travel to see that lonely band.

5. And while he was a-coming, Martha met him on the way,
And told him that her brother had died and passed away.
He blessed and he cheered her, and told her not to weep,
For in him was the power to raise him from his sleep.

6. Yet while he was a-coming, Mary met him, lonely too,
Down at his feet a-weeping, rehearsed the tale of woe.
When Jesus saw her weeping, he fell a-weeping too,
And wept until they showed him where Lazarus was entombed.

7. He rolled away the cover, and looked upon the grave,
And prayed unto his father, his loving friend to save.
And Lazarus in full power, came from the gloomy mound,
And in full life and vigor he walked upon the ground.

8. So all you who love Jesus, and do his holy will,
Like Mary and like Martha, you'll always use him well.
He'll comfort and redeem you, and take you to the skies,
And bid you live forever, where pleasure never dies.

IN THE VALLEY [22]

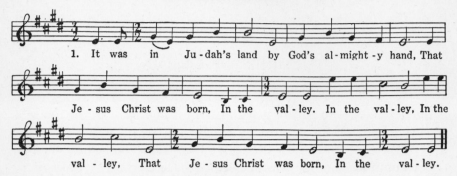

1. It was in Ju-dah's land by God's al-might-y hand, That
Je-sus Christ was born, In the val-ley. In the val-ley, In the
val-ley, That Je-sus Christ was born, In the val-ley.

1. It was in Judah's land
   By God's almighty hand
   That Jesus Christ was born
   In the valley.
       In the valley, in the valley,
       That Jesus Christ was born
       In the valley.

2. It was by his mother's hand
   That he was clothed in swaddling bands
   And in the manger laid him down
   In the valley.
       In the valley, *etc.*

3. It was on the gloom of night
   When Mary took her flight
   And in Egypt she did light
   In the valley.
       In the valley, *etc.*

4. Then news was spread abroad
   That he was the Son of God,
   And now he makes a start
   From the valley.
       From the valley, *etc.*

5. Now the scriptures are fulfilled,
   I've done my father's will,
   And I stand upon the hill
   .From the valley.
       From the valley, *etc.*

[22] As sung by Abner Boggs, of Big Laurel, Harlan County, Kentucky, to E. K. Wells, 1938.

Chapter 8

THEORIES OF ORIGIN

EARLY reference to ballads gives us no information as to the method of their composition: it proves only the existence, before 1300, the date of the "Judas" text, of the ballad form as we now know it. The vexed question of origin was launched in the eighteenth century by Percy's sweeping claim for minstrel authorship, and since then the matching of theories by scholars and collectors has drawn the literary world into increasingly fervid, if not heated debate. Stated oversimply, the varied sources of the ballad are held to be these:

(1) The dance, because of the rhythmic refrain, and because primitive races today make up songs as they dance. *Das Volk dichtet*—the "singing, dancing throng" is the poet. (2) Individual poets, also of the folk. (3) The courtly poets, often minstrels, since it is sometimes possible to trace the humble setting of today's ballad back to an aristocratic Medieval background. (4) The monks, because the ballad stanza shows a metrical similarity to the Latin hymn, thus bespeaking some learning and skill, and because the earliest text, "Judas" (23), is religious in subject.

All these theories have their fallacies. It is difficult to see how "the singing, dancing throng" can give itself simultaneously to two different stimuli, that of rhythmic bodily movement in the dance, and that of intense interest in the story. A try at dancing a ballad soon shows the difficulties, though the Norwegians say it is possible. It is dangerous to argue for communal authorship from the analogy of primitive custom: although the South Sea Islanders of today compose songs as they dance, the resulting songs are lyrical and nonnarrative, not ballads. And although a ballad of humble background may be traced back to a Medieval courtly singer, this does not preclude all lowly authorship. Poetic skill has come from a Jonson, a Marlowe, a Burns, even a Shakespeare. The fact that our earliest copy of a ballad is on a religious subject is not enough to prove monastic authorship of all ballads. If the monks wrote the ballads, why are religious ones so scarce, and secular ones so plentiful? As for minstrel authorship, ballads would seem to have been in the field long before the minstrels began to include them in their stock in trade.[1] The truth of ballad origin lies among the many theories. Verse so varied was born of varied strains— the clerical, with its Latin ancestry, the courtly, with its romance, the minstrel idiom, contact with the dance song and its refrain, and popular practice with its renewing pulse. The contributing elements were worked over by the sure canons of popular taste and polished in the process of tradition. Successive singers fused the many strains of ancestry, and obliterated all trace of individual composition. The ballad, if not communal in origin, was communal in development.

Some ballads, because of their simple structure, may indeed have evolved from the improvisation of the throng. "The Hangman," as sung in the Southern Appalachians, shows this possibility more clearly than its more formally organized British cousin, "The Maid Freed from the Gallows" (95). More complicated, but still within the scope of communal composition by a group familiar with the method, is "Babylon" (14), in which the story grows by spontaneous imitation of the first incident. The incremental repetition which underlies its structure may have been developed by the improvising throng. Communal authorship, however, is inconceivable in ballads of more intricate structure. A poet of no mean ability must have composed such a ballad as "The Wife of Usher's Well" (79). Many ballads dealing with aristocratic life, sung today by Scottish peasants or Southern Highlanders, were probably born in court circles, becoming democratized as they were appropriated by humble singers. Archer Taylor in his study of "Edward" (13)[2] traces this ballad back from its present lowly setting to a poet who knew courtly life: the old gray hound that traced the fox in Tennessee is descended from a pedigreed medieval grayhound. As for clerical authorship: the interplay of learned and secular elements in Medieval poetry and music has frequently been noted. If, as is claimed,[3] the meter of the Latin hymns influenced both Latin and Anglo-Saxon secular verse, it may well have helped to create the ballad stanza. There is evidence that some monasteries supported minstrels, and "Judas" (23) and its like may have been written by them for the monks, or by the monks under minstrel influence.[4] For

[1] See page 208.   [2] Edward and Sven I Rosengard.
[3] Discussed by Gerould, The Ballad of Tradition, pp. 218–23.
[4] Pound, Poetic Origins and the Ballad, p. 184.

the minstrels are indeed responsible for some of the ballads. Thus clerks and minstrels, as well as courtly and lowly poets, may all have taken a hand.

In the midst of all these commingled possibilities, it becomes necessary to reconcile the two elements of narrative content and rhythmic expression in the ballad, and to clarify the connection between ballad and dance. It will therefore be helpful, and not irrelevant, to turn at this point to another traditional survival, the carol, since its contribution to the ballad form as we know it is fairly well substantiated.

The carol, like the religious ballad and the miracle play, was another Medieval democratizing of religious themes for the common people. As we know it today, it is lyrical, subjective, full of a merry piety; and it deals chiefly with the Christmas story. But its scope was once greater, including New Year's, Easter, Whitsun, and Harvest songs, carols for any feast of the church year. Still older carols are secular, dealing with love, politics, hunting, or drinking. A refrain is inherent in the stanza; there may be also a burden, or stanza at the beginning which is repeated at the end, somewhat disconnected from the song itself, such as a call for the music to strike up, or an invitation to sing. Both burden and refrain are popular in substance, and con‑tribute to the mood rather than the content of the song. Their strong rhythm, and at times the indication of movement, like "Come let us join hands," or "Why stand we still? Why move we not?" indicate a connection with dance and point to the word *carole*, Old French for a circular dance often accompanied by song. This in turn suggests the still current circle dances of the Balkans, the *horo* and the *kolo* (from Greek *choros*). Thus the evidence gathers for an earlier link between the carol and the dance.[5]

The origin of social dance in folk forms, and of folk dance in ritual forms, is practically established by the study of primitive art and customs. The earliest forms of folk dance are the circle, the double line, and the hey, or serpentine processional. Maypole dances are the remnant of ancient religious celebrations around some object of worship, such as a well or a tree. The "Roger de Coverly" type of dance was

[5] *The Oxford Book of Carols* Preface gives a short history of the carol and quotes these derivations of the word. Sachs, in *A World History of the Dance* (p. 271), derives the word from *corolla*, Latin for "little crown." German *reigen* or ring-dances are also known as crown-dances. In 1943 a group of young Boston Greeks danced a horo at a folk festival in the Boston Garden.

earlier the primitive dramatization of the life principle symbolized by
the contest and wooing of the sexes, of opposite forces in nature, such
as light and darkness. The magic connotations of the hey, or serpentine dance (still seen in the grand right-and-left of the country dance)
are not well understood: some imitation of the movements of the serpent, often an object of fear and therefore veneration, may have been
intended. Of all these forms, the circle dance was the most widely
dispersed. As the carole, it became the social dance all over Europe,
having completely lost any serious significance. When, after the Black
Death, Europe was seized by a dance mania which was the expression
of a hysterical gaiety in the face of doom, its medium was the carole,
popular, hypnotic, and long familiarly practiced although people had
forgotten why. The abuse of the dance offended decent and orderly
folk, and Robert Mannyng in his homiletic poem, *Handlyng Synne*
(1303), includes it with wrestling, May Games, interludes and the
disorder inspired by the wanton pipe and tabor:

> Carolles, wrastlynges, or somour games,
> Whosoever haunteth any swyche shames
> In cherche other yn cherche3erd,
> Of sacrylage he may be aferd;
>
> .   .   .   .
>
> All swyche thyng forbodyn is
> While the prest stondeth at messe.[6]

By the fifteenth century there is graphic witness to the general performance of the carole. The peasant round in a Book of Hours is like
that of the lords and ladies dancing in a formal garden, and even
Botticelli conceived of his angels in heaven as dancing in a ring.

There are traces of the secular medieval carole in the ring-games of
the nursery and in play-party games of the South and Middle West.
Most of us have left behind us "The Farmer in the Dell," but in some
rural parts of our country grownups still sing and dance for hours at a
time similar games, like "Old Bald Eagle" and "Jubilee." Here is the
ancient ring dance, the lyric, local-allusion verse, the popular refrain,
and the hypnotic rhythm, which help us understand the great vogue
of the carole in the Middle Ages. From a comparison of early pictures
and texts with present performance of ring-games, it seems probable
that the leader of the carole not only directed the movement but sang

[6] Robert Mannyng of Brunne, *Handlyng Synne*, ll. 8987–94.

LA RONDE DES BERGERS
A peasant carole from a fifteenth century Book of Hours

A COURTLY CAROLE

From *Le Roman de la Rose*

THE NATIVITY—BY BOTTICELLI
Illustrating an angelic carole

the stanza, during which the dancers remained in position, swaying rhythmically; and that the whole group joined in the refrain as it moved around the circle. In "Captain Jinks" this distinction is made between movement in place during the stanza, and the "rig-a-jig-jig and away we go" of the refrain.

The transference of this strongly entrenched song-dance from the secular to the sacred is one more instance of the use by religious reformers of a folk custom on which to build a better life for the people. The Franciscan friars were the chief agents of this change. "What are the servants of God, if not his minstrels, who ought to stir and incite the hearts of men to spiritual joy?" [7] In their sermons they emphasized the humility and poverty of Christ, and dwelt upon his birth in a manger; and they are said to have given great impetus to the use of the Christmas crèche. The existing caroles, often lewd but always rhythmic and popular, they turned from worldly uses to those of innocent piety, by writing new words for the popular refrain so that people might instantly join in. Like Wesley at a later date, they asked themselves why the devil should have all the good tunes. In their industry and sincerity they set up new associations for old tunes wherever they preached. [8]

The dance element is still evident in such a carol as "My Dancing Day," [9] a worldly and amorous song turned into a description of the entire life, preaching, and death of Christ.

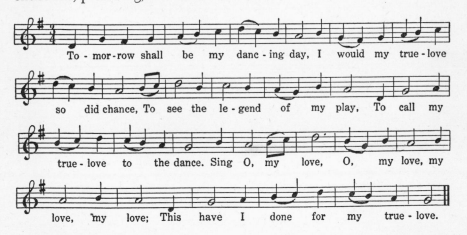

To - mor-row shall be my danc - ing day, I would my true - love so did chance, To see the le - gend of my play, To call my true - love to the dance. Sing O, my love, O, my love, my love, my love; This have I done for my true - love.

[7] Sabatier, *Life of St. Francis*, p. 307. Chambers, *Medieval Stage* I, 46, quotes the Latin from *Speculum Perfectionis*: "Quid enim sunt servi Dei nisi quidam ioculatores eius qui corda hominum eriger debent et movere ad laetitiam spiritualem."

[8] Greene, *Early English Carols*, cxxi ff. [9] *The Oxford Book of Carols*, No. 71.

The learned touch of the friars is seen in the use of Latin tags and lines from familiar hymns, like the refrain, "A solis ortus cardine," which everyone knew even if he did not understand, and which provided the necessary rhythm and euphony. In a macaronic carol like "In dulci jubilo" [10] the mingling of the Latin and vulgar tongues is sometimes more complete, and gives the same childlike pleasure as a schoolboy's hog-Latin:

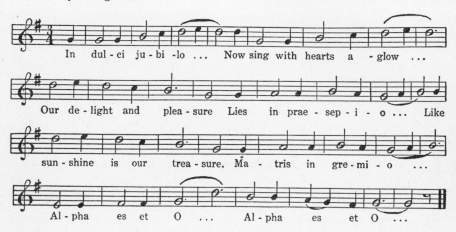

In dul-ci ju-bi-lo ... Now sing with hearts a - glow ...

Our de-light and plea-sure Lies in prae-sep-i-o ... Like

sun-shine is our trea-sure, Ma-tris in gre-mi-o ...

Al-pha es et O ... Al-pha es et O ...

The clerical hand often worked over a folk theme for religious uses. The ancient rivalry of the holly and the ivy, symbols of the male and female principles in nature, had long been celebrated, and primitive ritual had used the myth in fertility observances following the winter solstice. If some pious brother knew such a version as the one given below, it took little effort on his part to convert it to his holy purposes, and create the forbear of the carol we sing today.

> Nay, Iuy, hyt shal not be, iwys;
> Let Holy hafe the maystry, as the maner ys.

> 1. Holy stond in the hall, fayre to behold;
>   Iuy stond without the dore; she ys ful sore a-cold.

> 2. Holy and hys mery men, they dawnsyn and they syng,
>   Iuy and hur maydenis, they wepyn and they wring.

> 3. Iuy hath a kybe, she kaght yt with the cold;
>   So mot they all haf ae that with Iuy hold.

kybe—chillblain

[10] *Op. cit.*, No. 86.

4. Holy hat berys as rede as any rose;
   The foster, the hunters kepe hem fro the doo(s).

5. Iuy hath berys as blake as any slo;
   Ther come the oule and eye hym as she goo.

6. Holy hath byrdys, a ful fayre flok,
   The nyghtyngale, the poppynguy, the gayntyle lauyrok.

7. Gode Iuy, whatt byrdys ast thou?
   Non but the howlat, that kreye, 'How, How!' [11]

slo—sloe   lauyrok—lark

THE HOLLY AND THE IVY [12]

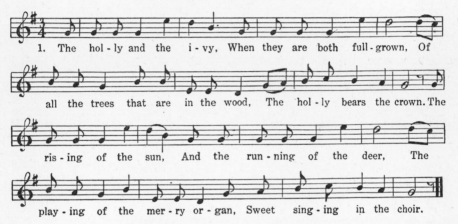

1. The holly and the ivy,
      When they are both full-grown,
   Of all the trees that are in the wood,
      The holly bears the crown.
         The rising of the sun,
         And the running of the deer,
         The playing of the merry organ,
         Sweet singing in the choir.

2. The holly bears a blossom,
      As white as the lily flower;
   And Mary bore sweet Jesus Christ
      To be our sweet Saviour.
         The rising, etc.

[11] Greene, *Early English Carols*, No. 136 A.

[12] From *Novello's School Songs* (1913), No. 1177. Reprinted by permission of Novello and Co., London, Publishers.

3. The holly bears a berry,
    As red as any blood;
    And Mary bore sweet Jesus Christ
      For to do us sinners good.
        The rising, *etc.*

4. The holly bears a prickle
    As sharp as any thorn,
    And Mary bore sweet Jesus Christ
      On Christmas Day in the morn.
        The rising, *etc.*

5. The holly bears a bark
    As bitter as any gall,
    And Mary bore sweet Jesus Christ
      For to redeem us all.
        The rising, *etc.*

6. The holly and the ivy,
    When they are both full grown,
    Of all the trees that are in the wood,
      The holly bears the crown.
        The rising, *etc.*

From a fifteenth century manuscript comes an early text of "The Carol of the Five Joys," which has never disappeared from popular currency. A Virginia version preserves it admirably, in a majestic tune accompanying verses which run the emotional gamut from naïve and tender motherly pride, to the splendor of salvation.

I may synge of a may
  Of joyis fyve and merthis most.

1. The ferste joye, as i you telle:
    With Mary met Seynt Gabrielle:
    'Heyl, Mary, I grete the welle,
      With Fader and Sone and Holy Gost.'

2. The secunde joye, in good fay,
    Was on Crystemesse Day;
    Born he was of a may,
      With Fader [and Sone and Holy Gost.]

3. The thredde joye, withoutyn stryft:
    That blysseful berthe was ful ryf
    Quan he ros fro ded to lyf,
      With Fader, *etc.*

4. The forte joye, in good fay,
   Was vpon Halewyn Thursday:
   He stey to heuene in ryche aray,
      With Fader, *etc.*

5. The fyfte joye, withoutyn dene:
   In heuene he crownyd his moder clene;
   That was wol in the eyr asene,
      With Fader, *etc.*[13]

THE JOYS OF MARY [14]

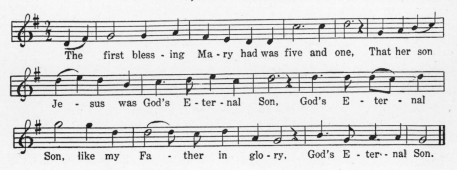

The first blessing Mary had was five and one,
That her son Jesus was God's Eternal Son,
God's Eternal Son, like my Father in glory,
   God's Eternal Son.

The second blessing Mary had was five and two,
That her son Jesus could read the Bible through,
Could read the Bible through, like my Father in glory,
   Could read the Bible through.

The third blessing Mary had was five and three,
That her son Jesus could make the blind to see, *etc.*

The fourth   —   five and four,
               make the rich man poor, *etc.*

The fifth   —   five and five,
               make the dead man rise, *etc.*

The sixth   —   five and six,
               relieve the sick, *etc.*

[13] Sloane MS 2593, British Museum, quoted by Greene, *op. cit.*, No. 231.
[14] From Jackson, *Down-East Spirituals* (1939), p. 62. Reprinted by permission of J. J. Augustin, Publisher, New York.

The seventh	—	five and seven carried the keys of heaven, *etc.*
The eight [*sic*]	—	five and eight, went through the pearly gate, *etc.*
The ninth	—	five and nine could turn the water to wine, *etc.*
The tenth	—	five and ten, bring the world to an end, *etc.*
The eleventh	—	five and eleven, turn the world to heaven, *etc.*
The twelfth	—	five and twelve, turn the sick to well, *etc.*

At a time when English lyric poetry was still colored by an earlier pessimism, and by medieval preoccupation with mortality and the sense of sin, the carol made its appearance. With its light-heartedness, its modern touch, its reflection of natural emotions and its pervading rhythm, its popularity is not surprising. Its later history is soon told. Until the time of the Commonwealth there must have been much honest guileless carol singing, but the Puritans suppressed it as a pagan practice, along with the Maypole and the Morris dance and Christmas. Recent collectors have found few really ancient carols, though there are some which in their moral tone show an effort to adapt their earlier gaiety to a graver pace, and thus pass muster with the Puritans. There are many allusions to the tomb, to falling from glory, to the pangs of death and hell, in carols meant originally to wish you joy at the New Year. An interpolation in the beautiful May Day carol from Bedford-shire, commemorating the ancient custom of bringing in the may, strains thus at an unnatural sobriety:

> Take a Bible in your hand
> And read a chapter through,
> And when the Day of Judgment comes,
> The Lord will think of you.[15]

The carol is another instance of song revived and strengthened by oral tradition, showing the endless revolutions of folk poetry and dance, from ancient ritual through the secular and back to the reli-

[15] Broadwood, *English Traditional Songs and Carols*, p. 85.

gious again. The Franciscans unwittingly caused a wheel to come full-circle when they restored to sacred uses the song of a once religious expression, the circle-dance.

As ancient as the ring-dance is the chanted story, told by the professional storyteller since earliest times. "In the infancy of society every author is necessarily a poet, because language itself is poetry," says Shelley,[16] and all simple people speak a language very close to poetry when, in repeating a story again and again, with a sense of its importance for narrator and listeners, they stereotype its phrases and rhythms more and more. The character of some ballad tunes recovered from tradition often points to a beginning in chanted speech.[17] The ballad without refrain may have evolved from the chanted tale. As the carole met this chanted story, it gave it a more marked rhythm and a refrain, and possibly took from it narrative elements which produced the danced ballad still practiced or recorded in some European countries. The point of contact between chanted story and dance song must have occurred before the twelfth century, if we are to count the evidence of the dancers of Kölbigk. Punished by the priest for interrupting his celebration of the mass, they were doomed to dance till they died. They wandered over Europe seeking release from the curse, and often resorted to the shrines of St. Vitus for penance, thus becoming known as the St. Vitus dancers. In the twelfth century one of them appeared at Wilton Abbey in England. His account gives a stanza of the song which accompanied the ill-fated dance:

> By þe leued wode rode Beuolyne,
> wyþ hym he ledde fayre Merswyne.
> Why stonde we? Why go we noght? [18]

The lines of the couplet indicate the matter of a ballad, a story about a knight and a lady in the forest, while the refrain, with its allusion to dance movement, is very much like that of an early carole. This is the earliest record of a ballad with a refrain, and we know from the narrative that this ballad was danced.

Gerould, in *The Ballad of Tradition*, working back from the earliest ballad texts of the thirteenth and fourteenth centuries to the written

[16] Shelley, A *Defense of Poetry* (*Works*, Vol. VII, ed. Forman; London, Reeves and Turner, 1880), p. 103.
[17] See page 280.
[18] Robert Mannyng of Brunne, *Handlyng Synne*, ll. 9049–51.

poetry of the eleventh and twelfth centuries, finds in them similar traits, and postulates the existence at that time of a traditional unwritten poetry which may have been the basis of the ballad form. He points to the appearance in Anglo-Saxon alliterative popular poetry of the rhymed couplet, the substitution of four-beat accentual for quantitative verse in hymns, and the appearance of vernacular hymns themselves, as suggesting that the ballad form is about to emerge.[19]

The carole's evidence of contributed refrain shows the influence of the dance. Social evidence as to the practice of song, in the carole and by minstrels of the lower orders, would account for the spread of the vogue. Three centuries, more or less, of indigenous cultivation would stabilize the form. Thus, by the fifteenth century, when we begin to find many ballad texts, the form has become fixed.

In Scandinavian countries, where almost all ballads have refrains, they are still danced. This is now a folk practice, but was formerly an occupation of the highborn. British observance of the custom, in comparison, does not seem to have been so widespread. British ballads are as often as not without refrain, and there is no indication of the danced ballad today, and little reference to it in the past. Early allusions are, moreover, not wholly clear. One, from Barbour's *Bruce* (1378), refers to the celebration of local events in song, but does not mention dance, unless we interpret "play" as "dance"—a somewhat fantastic claim.

> I will nocht reherss all the maner;
> For quha sa likis, thai may heir
> Young women quhen thai will play,
> Syng it emang thame ilke day.[20]

Another is from Fabyan's *Chronicles* (1516):

Than the Scottis enflamyd with pryde, in deryson of Englysshe men, made this ryme:

> Maydens of Englonde, sore may ye morne,
> For your lemmans ye haue loste at Bannockisborne,
> With heue a lowe.

[19] *The Ballad of Tradition*, chap. viii *passim*.
[20] Barbour, *The Bruce*, xvi, 11, p. 399, ll. 519–22. In some remote parts of America "play" as a euphemism for "dance" is used to obviate religious prejudice.

> What wenyth the Kynge of Englonde
> So soone to have woone Scotlande
> With rumbylowe.

> This songe was after many dayes syngyn in daunces, in carolis of the
> maydens and mynstrelles of Scotland, to the reproofe and disdayne
> of Englysshemen.[21]

Although the ballad couplet meter is here, we are uncertain as to the
content of the song. It may be a patriotic ballad, or a lyrical chant of
victory.

Some weight has been given to the listing as "dances" in *The Complaynt of Scotland* (1549) of three recognizable ballads, "yong tamlene," "Johny Ermistrangis daunce," and "Robene hude." [22]

It may be, however, that by this date ballad tunes, as we know from
abundant evidence was true later, had already been separated from
the songs and had been adapted to dancing. The ensuing centuries saw
a continual borrowing of ballad tunes for dances, and of dance tunes
for ballad settings. We assume that these later tunes were not sung as
people danced, partly because there is no record of the fact, and partly
because the tunes, in their dance versions, are not suited to singing.
Deloney's *Jack of Newburie* (1597) gives a version of "The Fair
Flower of Northumberland" (9). He is explicit as to the way of singing, but does not mention dance.

> The maidens in dulcet manner chanted this song, two of them sing-
> ing the Ditty and the rest bearing the burden (refrain, in this case).[23]

Thus dance and song, whether ballad or carol, seem to have parted
company in England before the sixteenth century. Whatever fragments of the custom of dancing to song are left today are found in the
singing games and the processional lyrics of some folk observances.
The term "ballad," as has been pointed out in the Introduction, has
been used through the ages for many forms of verse, both sophisticated
and simple. We cannot, therefore, prove dance origin or dance association of the ballad from the derivation of the word itself, even though
the word implies dance. We can at the most say that dance has been
a contributing, but not a dominant factor in the development of the
ballad form.

[21] Fabyan, *Chronicles*, p. 420.
[22] *The Complaynt of Scotland*, pp. 65, 66.
[23] Deloney, *Jack of Newburie*, p. 33.

Chapter 9

MINSTREL AND BROADSIDE BALLADS

HOWEVER the ballad began in the first instance—whether by communal, aristocratic, or popular individual composition—it has at times been subjected to the touches of the professional singer. Two groups, the minstrel and the broadside ballads, show signs of the professional doctoring of existing songs, and of composition of new ones in the idiom of the trade, designed to attract the attention of an audience, and to advertise the singer or writer and his wares. The long lineage of the professional singer is noted here because the professional ballad has been grafted onto the traditional ballad tree at many points.

Reference has been made to the early practice of chanting stories, which in repetition grew more stereotyped, and which, meeting the more rhythmic carole, may have produced something akin to the ballad as we know it. The professional storyteller—bard or scôp—took at first for his particular responsibility the narration of public events, and his songs of former heroes and present deeds were by the twelfth century recognized sources for the chroniclers. Thus Geoffrey of Monmouth writes in 1136:

> Nought could I find as concerning the kings that had dwelt in Britain before the incarnation of Christ, nor nought even as concerning Arthur and the many others that did succeed him after the Incarnation, albeit that their deeds be worthy of praise everlasting and be as pleasantly rehearsed from memory by word of mouth in the traditions of many peoples as though they had been written down.[1]

Another writer, a few years later, says:

> So far I have written concerning the king from verified sources; the following I have learned more from ballads (*cantilenis*) handed

[1] "Nichil de regibus qui ante incarnationem christi inhabitaverunt, nichil etiam de arturo ceterisque compluribus qui post incarnationem successerunt reperissem, cum et gesta earum digna aeternitate laudis constarent et a multis populis quasi inscripta iocunde et memoriter praedicarentur." Geoffrey of Monmouth, *Historia Regum Britanniae*, Epistle Dedicatory, p. 1.

down through generations than from books written for the enlight-
enment of posterity. . . . I have included them, not as necessarily
true, but in order to share all information with the reader.[2]

A twelfth century *cantilena* may not have been the ballad as we know
it; but it may have been one of its ancestors. Sung narratives "pleasantly rehearsed by word of mouth" and "popular through succeeding
times" sound very much like ballads, both in the method of transmission and the implication of lyric form. Perhaps the early professional
song composers laid down a pattern and established a habit of dealing
with public events for popular audiences, by which the minstrels of the
fifteenth century, and the broadside writers who followed them, largely
profited.

MINSTREL BALLADS

In 1765 Bishop Percy, impressed by the number of ballads bearing
minstrel touches, and catering perhaps to the pre-Romantic revival
of the Medieval, wrote an essay on the thesis of minstrel origin for all
ballads, a thesis current for some time, although it was at once brought
under the fire of such critics as Ritson.[3] The subsequent confusion and
acrimony in ballad criticism was probably due to the failure of Percy
and Ritson to discriminate between minstrels of upper and lower
degree.

The term *minstrelsy* covers the varieties of entertainment offered to
all classes of society, throughout the five centuries we term the Middle
Ages—harping, *contes*, *dits* or dialogues, *fabliaux*, *lais*, wrestling,
juggling, peddling, bearbaiting, japes, and jests—the gamut from lordly
entertainment in the castle to buffoonery in the market place. The
minstrel inherited from the Teutonic scôp his repertoire of tales and
legends, and his prestige as a narrator of great deeds; from the mime
of the Roman theater came his popular antics. His presence in hall and
bower, in battle camp and priory—for although the Church reserved its
approval of his secular wares it employed his talents for some religious

---

[2] "Et haec quidem fide integra de rege conscripsi; sequentia magis cantilenis per suc-
cessiones temporum detritis, quan libris ad instructiones posterum [sic] elucubratis, didi-
cerim. . . . Quae ideo apposui, non ut earum veritatem defendam, sed ne lectorum
scientiam defraudam." William of Malmesbury, *Gesta regum Anglorum*, Liber II, par.
138, pp. 221–22.
[3] See page 231.

song—and his constant mingling with the common people exposed him to a range of tastes and interests which he turned to his own considerable account. In time a difference in degree developed. While some minstrels kept to the road, certain others became attached to the great houses and to the court. It was to these that Percy accredited ballad authorship. For a long time they enjoyed a halcyon period of prosperity. They were given the title of "Leroy," they ranked with heralds, were richly rewarded with lands and gold, wore a distinctive dress, were organized into an elaborate hierarchy and better paid than most of the clergy. They accompanied kings to battle, were the registrars of pedigree, had preferred entrée everywhere, even to the enemy camp, and were generally protected and exempt from duties. From the galleries of hall and castle they dispensed nightly entertainment, harping and singing lays and romances; in the bowers of the ladies they offered relief from boredom when the knights were absent at war or the chase. But in time such privilege and preferment led to abuse and unwarranted license. Moreover, their prestige faded as their stock of songs and tales became dulled by repetition and their style increasingly stereotyped. As the trouvères, or court poets, became more refined and literary, the minstrels were unable to compete with them. Finally, with the decay of feudalism and the breaking up of the great manorial houses, they were ousted from their high and unique standing in the household, and forced to take to the road. Once the aristocrats of minstrelsy, they now found themselves competing with hoi polloi of their craft, gentry who had never lost touch with the popular audience. They overcame this disadvantage to some extent by offering new ballads, cast in the popular mode but dealing with their own past romantic repertoire. Thus, if they did not originate the ballad form, they undoubtedly adopted it for their tales of adventurous knights, ladies in distress, fabulous fairies, and monsters.

The many social changes taking place in the late Middle Ages made the minstrel's means of existence more and more tenuous. Roving became outright vagabondage, and the minstrel a synonym for wanton disorder and imposture. In Elizabeth's reign the minstrel was legislated out of existence. But not before he had put his stamp upon balladry. His traffic in ballads at what was perhaps their best period, the fifteenth century, helped to perpetuate their salient features, and the few texts which remain to us from those days have caught and fixed for the moment those traits. Undoubtedly, too, the minstrel spread certain ballads in his travels. If Robin Hood was indeed only an obscure Yorkshire yeoman, we can account for the sudden growth of his legend partly by minstrel broadcasting.

Aside from the Robin Hood ballads, some romantic themes from Arthurian story, and glorifications of ancient great houses like the Percies and the Howards, there are few minstrel texts.[4] And of these texts few have passed into tradition, being too special to an age and a class.

Minstrel style is recognizable through its appeal to the audience. Here is no unconscious singer telling his tale to himself, or sharing it with a domestic group who occasionally join in, being around, rather than before him, but the professional addressing the crowd: "Hearken, god yemen, comley, cortys and god," "Now list you, lithe gentlemen," "Lordings, listen and hold you still." Norman-French echoes come to us in such words as "magger" (*maugré*) and "verament"; and in the wrenched accents of "countré," "ladyé," or "courtesié." Alliteration prevails, as in "Bomen byckarte vppon the bent," and there are stock epithets—gentle knights, gay ladies, noble King Arthur, doughty Douglas. These are the conventional phrases of Medieval verse romance. The vocabulary, like the stories, belongs to the world of courtesy and chivalry. There is great interest in armor and jewels—"fyn myllan," "spear, bylle and brande," and in the techniques of the joust or the hunt. These are evident in "The Hunting of the Cheviot" (162 A):

> They blewe a mort vppone the bent,
>   the semblyde on sydis shear;
> To the quyrry then the Persë went
>   to se the bryttlinge off the deare.

Veracity is backed by detail: "This begane on a Monday at morn"; "the wear twenti-hondrith spear-men" (and this is true, "withoute any

---

[4] Some minstrel ballads in Child's collection are:

No. 29	The Boy and the Mantle	118	Robin Hood and Guy of Gisborne
30	King Arthur and King Cornwall	119	Robin Hood and the Monk
31	The Marriage of Sir Gawain	120	Robin Hood's Death
45	King John and the Bishop	121	Robin Hood and the Potter
48	Young Andrew	161	The Battle of Otterburn
60	King Estmere	162A	The Hunting of the Cheviot
61	Sir Cawline	167	Sir Andrew Barton
116	Adam Bell	176	Northumberland betrayed by Douglas
117	A Gest of Robyn Hode	177	The Earl of Westmoreland

feale"). Since the minstrel must compete with all the distractions of fair, feast, or miracle play—the side shows, hawking of wares, and milling of the crowd—he gathered in the fringes of his audience or revived flagging interest by such lines as "For soth as I yow saye," or "I tell you in this stounde." Thus, halfway through "The Hunting of the Cheviot" (162 A) he lures in, or reanimates his listeners by a familiar device:

> That day, that day, that dredfull day!
>   the first fit here I fynde;
> And youe wyll here any mor a the hountynge a the Chyviat,
>   yet ys ther mor behynde.

Five stanzas roll off the list of the noble dead. Percy's eulogy of the Douglas appeals not only to the romantic idealism of the high-born, but to the hero-worshiping populace:

> The Persë leandye on his brande
>   and saw the Duglas de;
> He tooke the dede mane by the hande
>   and sayd, Wo ys me for the!

> To haue savyde they lyffe, I would haue partyde with
>   my landes for years three,
> For a better man, of hart nare of hande,
>   was nat in all the north contre.[5]

The formal close, often a pious prayer, is typically minstrel:

> Ihesue Christ our balys bete
>   and to the blys vs brynge!
> Thus was the hountynge of the Chivyat;
>   God send vs alle good endyng!

Most of the traits of the minstrel's style are the result of economic pressure. He had to gain his livelihood, so his reputation was important. He therefore flattered his hearers, assured them of his veracity, advertised his large and unique stock of tales, and emphasized the high-class character of his repertoire. But his constant reference to his noble and worthy audience, and to himself as a true teller of tales inspires neither our interest nor our confidence, and his stock epithets and turns of phrase, unlike those of the traditional ballad which keep their freshness, soon wear thin.

[5] Shakespeare's "I could have better spared a better man" (*King Henry the Fourth,* Part I, V, iv) curiously echoes these lines as another victor eulogizes another Percy.

BROADSIDE BALLADS

The lineal descendants of the minstrel ballads are the broadsides, which flourished from 1550 to 1700. The professional composers of these were the tavern poets and rhymsters who began to produce just as the minstrels fell into their final decline. The broadside mill ground unceasingly, and all was grist to it. For broadsides were the newspapers of the sixteenth and seventeenth centuries. Politics, religion, sermons, satirical comment on society and human nature, comic and romantic stories of the past and present, sensations and monstrosities, public events, and the most trivial daily occurrences were all cast into rough ballad verse, printed in black-letter with a crude woodcut at the head and decorated borders, headlined with a bit of explanatory prose, directed to be sung to a familiar tune, and hawked in the streets or sold at the stalls in Paul's Churchyard and other gathering places. Like the minstrel, the broadside writer catered to popular taste and used what came to hand; like his ballad forebear also, he introduced new subject matter. He spread the news, both truth and rumor. He might report a shooting match in Yorkshire, or a murder in Wiltshire, or a sea serpent off Dungeness or a child born with three hands in Dorset, or an attempt to poison the boy king James VI in Scotland, or a "daungerous shootying of the gunne" at Elizabeth's court.[6] He might comment on the illicit loves of a famous courtier, thinly disguising his name, or on the compensations to be sought when married life was unsatisfactory. He satirized the types of the day—the pimp, the beggar, the courtesan. A tale which Shakespeare might be dramatizing in the next street he cast into ballad form. He inveighed against the Puritans, the Catholics, the Bishops, and the Rump Parliament. And nothing, no matter how trivial, escaped his attention: "Scarce a cat can look out of an alley, but out starts a halfpenny chronicler, and presently a proper new ballet of a strange sight is indited." [7]

[6] See below, this chapter. Rollins discusses this ballad in "William Elderton," *Studies in Philology*, XVII (1920), 243, as "a contemporary document of as real importance as are the sober and abbreviated passages dealing with the same event in Stow and Camden." Of another journalistic ballad by Elderton he says, "The psychology of the common people is far more trustworthily revealed in Elderton's ballad of 'The Rising of the North' than in the dull pages of these chronicles" (*Ibid.*).

[7] Martin Mar-Sixtus, 1592, quoted by Chappell, *Popular Music of Olden Times*, I, 106.

If real life did not supply enough sensation for his public, he rewrote some existing popular ballad about the love of Fair Rosamond, or the adventures of Robin Hood, or the affair of Little Musgrave and Lady Barnard, thus meeting the demand for romance. There were ballad serials about favorite comic-strip characters, like Jock the Scot, whose fans followed his misadventures with as much delight as Orphan Annie's today.

Social and literary criticism is vocal as to the influence of the broadside. It was the breeder of credulity: "The shepherd lighteth no sooner on a quagmire, but he thinketh this is the foretold earthquake whereof his boy hath the ballett." [8] It was the last word in poetic decadence:

> If I passe the unaccountable rabble of rhyming Ballet makers and compylers of senseless sonnets who be most busy, to stuff every stall full of gross devices and unlearned Pamphlets, I trust I shall be with the best sort held excused. For tho' many such can frame an Alehouse song of five or six score verses, hobbling upon some tune of a Northern Iygge, or Robin Hoode, or La Labber etc. and perhaps observe a just number of syllables eight in one line, six in another, and therewithal an A to make a iercke in the ende: yet if these might be accounted poets (as is said some of them make means to be promoted to ye Laurell) surely we shall shortly have whole swarms of Poets: and everyone that can frame a booke in ryme, though for want of matter, if he but speak in commendation of copper noses or Bottle Ale, wyll catch at the garlande due to Poets.[9]

The broadside was the disseminator of political opinion. Statesmen realized its power and collected political ballads containing dangerous sentiments; foreign ambassadors watched its output and sent copies home. It was a straw, but it showed the wind's direction.[10] The govern-

---

[8] Nashe, *Anatomie of Absurditie*, I, 23.

[9] Webbe, *Discourse of English Poetrie*, pp. 36–37. The "iercke" or additional a- or o-syllable, is seen in

> Where be those French Dogs
> That make so great a boast, O?
> Why, they shall eat the grey goose feathers
> And we will eat the roast, O!

[10] "Lilliburlero," an anti-Catholic, anti-Irish ballad set in 1687 to Purcell's contagious tune, so inflamed national resentment against James II that it helped to precipitate the Battle of the Boyne, James's defeat and dethronement, and was called "The tune that lost three kingdoms." British soldiers have marched to it ever since, singing most recently words by Eric Linklater:

> London's on fire, that's where we begin,
> How many miles from here to Berlin?

("Lilliburlero, the Victory Song," London, Paxton.)

The Lamentable and Tragicall History of Titus An-

dronicus, with the fall of his five and twenty sons in the wars of the Goaths
with the ravishment of his daughter Lavinia by the Empresse wo sons,
through the means of a bloody Moor, taken by the swor of Titus
in the war, with his revenge upon them for their cruell
an in humane act.
To the tune of Fortune my Foe.

YOu noble minds and famous martial wights
  That in defence of Native Country fights:
Give erre to me that ten years fought for Rome,
Yet reapt disgrace at my returning home.

In Rome I liv'd in fame full threescore years,
My name beloved was of all my Peers:
And five and twenty valiant sons I had,
Whose forward vertues made their father glad.

For when Romes foes their warlike forces felt,
Against them still my sons and I were sent:
Against the Goaths full ten years weary war
We spent, receiving many a bloody scar.

Just two and twenty of my sons were slain,
Before I did return to Rome again:
Of five and twenty so is I brought but three,
Alfoe the stately Towers of Rome to fee.

When wars were done, I conquest home did bring
And did present my prisoners to the King:
The queen of Goaths her sons and eke a Moore,
Who did such murders like was none before.

The Emperour did make the Queen his wife,
Which bred in Rome debate and deadly strife:
The Moor with her two sons did grow so proud,
That none like them in Rome was then allowd,

The Moor so pleas'd the new made Empress eye
That she consented with him secretly:
For to abufe her husbands marriage bed,
And fo in time a Blackamore she bred.

When she whose thoughts to murder was inclin'd
Consented with the Moor with bloody mind:
Against my self my kind and all my friends,
In cruel fort to bring them to their ends.

So when in age I thought to live in peace,
Both woe and grief began then to increase:
Amongst my Sons I had one daughter bright,
Which joy'd and pleased best my aged sight.

My Lavinia was betrothed then
To Cesars son, a young and noble man:
Who in a hunting by the Empereurs wife,
And her two sons bereaved was of life.

He being flain was cast in cruel wife,
Into a darksome den from light of skies,
The cruel Moor did come that way as then,
With my three sons, who fell into that den.

The Moor then fetcht the Emperour with speed,
For to accuse them of that murderous deed,
And then my sons in prison were put,
In wrongfull prison they were kept and bound.

A BLACK-LETTER BROADSIDE
(Courtesy of the Folger Shake

But now behold that wounded most my mind
The Empresse two sons of Tygers kind:
My daughter ravished without remorse,
And took away her honour quite perforce.

When they had tasted of so sweet a flower,
Fearing so sweet should quickly turn to sower:
They cut her tongue, whereby she could not tell,
How that dishonour unto her befell.

Then both her hands they basely cut off quite,
Whereby their wickness she could not write:
Nor with needle on her Sampler sow,
The bloody workers of her dismall woe.

My brother Marcus found her in the wood,
Staining the grassy ground with purple blood:
That trickled from her stumps & handless arms,
No tongue at all she had to tell her harms.

But when I saw her in that wofull case,
With tears of blood I wet my aged face:
For my Lavinia I lamented more,
Then for my two and twenty sons before.

When as I saw she could not writ nor speak,
With grief my aged heart began to break:
We spred a heap of sand upon the ground,
Whereby these bloody tyrants we out found.

For with a staffe without the help of hand,
She writ these words upon a plot of sand:
The lustfull sons of the proud Emperesse,
Are doers of this hatefull wicke onesse.

I tore the milkwhite hairs from off my head,
I curst the hour wherein I first was bred:
I wisht the hand that fought for Countries fame
In cradle reckt had first been strucken lame.

The Moor delighting still in villany,
Did say to set my sons from prison free:
I should unto the King my right hand give,
And then my three imprisoned sons should live.

The Moor I caus'd to strike it off with speed,
Whereat I grieved not to see it bleed:
But for my sons would willingly impart,
And for their ransome send my bleeding heart,

But as my life did linger then in vain,
They sent to me my bootlesse hand again:
And therewithall the heads of my three sons,
Which fild my dying heart with fresher groans.

Then past relief I up and down did go,
And with my tears writ in the dust my woe,
I shot my arrow towards heaven high,
And for revenge to hell did sometimes cry.

The Empresse thinking then that I was mad,
Like Furies she and both her sons were glad:
So nam'd revenge, and rape and murder they,
To undermine and know what I would say.

I fed their foolish veins a little space,
Untill my friends and I did find a space:
Where both her sons unto a post were bound,
Where just revenge in cruell sort was found.

I cut their throats my daughter held the pan
Betwixt her stumps, wherein the blood did ren:
And then I ground their bones to powder small,
And made a paste for Pies streight therewithall.

Then with their flesh I made two mighty Pies,
And at a banquet serv'd in stately wise:
Before the Empresse set this loathsome meat,
So of her sons own flesh she well did eat.

My self bereav'd my daughter then of life,
The Empresse then I slew with bloody knife:
And stab'd the Emperour immediatly,
And then my self, and so did Titus dye.

Then this revenge against the Moor was found,
Alive they set him half into the ground:
Whereas he stood untill such time he sterv'd.
And so God send all murderers may be serv'd.

Printed for F. Coles, T. Vere and VV. Gilbertson.

ROBIN HOOD's Rescuing WILL. STUTLY,

From the Sheriff and his Men, who had taken him Prisoner, and were going for to Hang him, &c.

To the Tune of, *Robin Hood* and *Queen Catherine*, &c.

Licensed and Entered according to Order.

WHen *Robin Hood* in the green wood stood,
   derry, derry, down,
Under the green wood tree,
Tydings there came to him with speed,
Tydings for certainty,
   hey down, derry, derry, down:
That *Will Stutly* surprized was,
And eke in prison lay;
Three Varlets that the King had hir'd,
Did likely him betray:

Ay, and to morrow hang'd must be,
To morrow as soon as 'tis day:
Before they could the victory get,
Two of them did *Stutly* slay.

When *Robin Hood* did hear this news,
Lord, it did grieve him sore;
Ay, and to his merry Men he said,
Who all together swore,

That *Will Stutly* should rescued be,
And be brought back again,
Or else should many a gallant Wight,
For his sake there be slain.

He cloathed himself in scarlet then,
His Men were all in green,
A finer show throughout the World,
in no place could be seen.

Good Lord, it was a gallant fight,
To see them all on a row,
With every Man a good broad sword,
And eke a good yew bow.

Forth of the green wood are they gone,
Yea, all couragiously,
Resolving to bring *Stutly* home,
Or every Man to dye.

And when they came to the castle near,
Whereas *Will Stutly* lay.
I hold it good, said *Robin Hood,*
We here in ambush stay;

And send one forth some news to hear,
To yonder Palmer fair,
That stands under the castle-wall,
Some news he may declare.

With that steps forth a brave young Man,
Which was of courage stout and bold,
Thus he did say to the old Man,
I pray thee, Palmer old,

Tell me if that thou rightly ken,
   derry, derry, down,
When must Will. Stutly die?
Who is one of bold Robin's Men,
And here doth Prisoner lye;
   hey down, derry, derry down.

Alas, alas, the Palmer said,
  derry, derry, down,
And for ever woe is me,
Will Scutly hang'd will be this day,
On yonder gallows tree;
  hey down, derry, derry down.

O had his noble Master known,
He would some Succour send;
A few of his bold Yeomandree,
Full soon would fetch him hence.

Ay, that is true, the young Man said,
Ay, that is true, said he;
Or if they were near to this place,
They soon would set him free.

But fare thou well, thou good old Man,
Farewel, and thanks to thee;
If Stutly hanged be this day,
Reveng'd his death will be.

He was no sooner from the Palmer gone,
But the gates was opened wide,
And out of the castle Will. Stutly came,
Guarded on every side.

When he was forth from the castle come,
And saw no Help was nigh,
Thus he did say unto the Sheriff,
Thus he said gallantly:-

Now seeing that I needs must die,
Grant me one boon, said he,
For my noble Master ne're had Man,
That yet was hang'd on tree:

Give me a sword all in my hand,
And let me be unbound;
And with thee and thy Men I'll fight,
Until I lie dead on the ground.

But this desire he would not grant,
His wishes were in vain,
For the Sheriff swore he hang'd should be,
And not by the sword be slain.

Do but unbind my hands, he says,
I will no weapons crave,
And if I hanged be this day,
Damnation let me have.

O no, no, the Sheriff he said,
Thou shalt on the gallows dye;
Ay, and so shall thy Master too,
If ever in me it lye.

O dastard Coward, Stutly crys,
Thou faint-hearted peasant Slave,
If ever my Master do thee meet,
Thou shalt thy payment have.

My noble Master thee doth scorn,
And all thy cowardly Crew,
Such silly Imps unable are
Bold Robin to subdue.

But when he was to the gallows come,
And ready to bid adieu,
Out of a bush steps Little John,
And steps Will. Stutly too;

I pray thee Will, before thou dye,
Of thy dear Friends take leave:
I needs must borrow him a while;
How say you Master Sheriff?

Now as I live, the Sheriff said,
That Varlet will I know;
Some sturdy Rebel is that same,
Therefore let him not go.

With that Little John so hastily,
Away cut Stutly's bands,
And from one of the Sheriff's Men
A sword twitcht from his hands:

Here Will, take thou this same,
Thou canst it better sway;
And here defend thyself a while,
For Aid will come straightway.

And there they turn'd them back to back,
In the middle of them that day,
Till Robin Hood approached near,
With many an Archer gay.

With that an arrow from them flew,
I wist from Robin Hood:
Make haste, make haste, the Sheriff he said,
Make haste, for it is not good.

The Sheriff is gone, his doubtless Men
Thought it no boot to stay,
But as their Master had them taught,
They run full fast away.

O stay, O stay, Will. Stutly said,
Take leave e're you depart;
You ne're will catch bold Robin Hood,
Unless you dare him meet.

O ill betide you, said Robin Hood
That you soon are gone;
My sword may in the scabbard rest,
For here our work is done.

I little thought, Will. Stutly said,
When I came here to this place,
For to have met with Little John,
Or to have seen my Master's face.

Thus Stutly he was at liberty set,
And safe brought from his Foe:
O thanks, O thanks to my Master,
Since here it was not so.

And once again, my Fellows dear,
  derry, derry down,
We shall in the green woods meet,
Where we will make our bow-strings twang,
Musick for us most sweet,
  hey down, derry, derry, down.

London: Printed by T. Norris, at the Looking-glass on London-bridge.

ment legislated against its appearance, but censorship was its breath of life, and the more it was persecuted, the more it flourished. License to print was required, but not always secured, and many a ballad was "bootlegged" into existence. The voluminous entries of the official licensers in *The Stationers' Register* are merely a cross section of all the ballads read, quoted, or sung in the streets.

Broadsides, though they were born in the town, traveled far afield. Peddlers took them all over the countryside. It was for the rural trade that Autolycus carried in his pack not only inkles, cadisses, cambrics and lawns, but also ballads about a usurer's wife, and a fish that was a woman, and two maids wooing a man.[11] The professional improviser, too, still had his following in the early part of the seventeenth century, if we may believe John Aubrey:

> Before the Civil Warres, in Staffordshire, and about Coventry, War-wickshire and those parts, there went along with the fidler Rymers. . . . that upon any subject given would versifie extempore halfe an hour together. . . . These Rymers were of great antiquity in England, as appears by many families called by that name.[12]

Flimsy and evanescent, most of the broadsides have disappeared, but enough have been salvaged by early collectors like Pepys and Selden to give us a picture of the broadside literature, and an occasional allusion tells us of how some were preserved.

> We in the country do not scorn
> Our walls with ballads to adorn
> Of Patient Grissel and the Lord of Lorn.[13]

Izaak Walton describes a fisherman's retreat, an inn where the sheets smell of lavender and twenty ballads are pasted on the walls.[14] As recently as the nineteenth century Jamieson collected a copy of "Young Beichan" (53) "off an old wall in Piccadilly." [15] But by 1700 modern type had ousted the heavy, illegible black-letter; printed matter was more prolific, news books began to take the place of news ballads, and the newspaper itself was not far distant. "White-letter" ballads persisted into the nineteenth century, however, and were sold on city street corners by the Silas Weggs of Dickens' day.

[11] Shakespeare, *The Winter's Tale*, IV, iii.
[12] Aubrey, *Anecdotes and Traditions*, p. 107.
[13] Quoted from Charles Cotton, *Osterley Park Ballads*, Introduction, p. x.
[14] Walton, *The Compleat Angler*, I, chap. ii, p. 63.
[15] Jamieson, *Popular Ballads*, II, p. 117.

Most of the later Robin Hood ballads in the Child collection are broadsides, and one of them, "A True Tale of Robin Hood" (154), is by the well-known Martin Parker. Child has included 31 ballads that appear in the *Stationers' Register*, and many others showing broadside contacts. He has used them either because of the traditional character of the story, or because they have at some time cropped up in tradition, although he characterizes broadsides as a whole as "veritable dunghills, in which, only after a great deal of sickening grubbing, one finds a very moderate jewel." [16] Indeed, recent criticism of the broadside is as unflattering as that of its own period.

Compared with the traditional ballad, the broadside is a moderate jewel indeed. Its verse is jog-trot, its narrative overfull, circumstantial, lacking in dramatic selection and suspense. Instead of inspired flashes which light up special scenes, a continuous cheap daylight exposes all the dusty corners. Here is no sense of mystery or hint of a loftier past. It reeks of the town and the printing press. Refrains are largely lacking, as well as incremental repetition and other lyric qualities. It has been consciously set to its tune, rather than growing up with it. There is a feeling of authorship and audience, with an eye to business and profit.

"The Suffolk Miracle" (272) brings out these qualities. Here is a fine folk tale, which has been found in many parts of Europe, ironed out by the broadside press. The verse jogs along, maintaining its rhythm often by distorted word order—"Which when her uncle understood," "She by no means could to him send." Fine phrases like "Her heart's espousèd friend" ring false. It is endlessly particular. Distances and times are exactly stated. All parts of the story receive the same emphasis, with the result that significant parts fade into the general blur. The high spot of the story, the evidence of the handkerchief and the opening of the grave, is thus trivially treated:

> A handkerchief she said she tyed
> About his head, and that they tryed;
> The sexton they did speak unto
> That he the grave would then undo.

The central interest is in the proof of the supernatural happening, rather than the happening itself. Cause and effect are singled out for

---

[16] Hustvedt, *Ballad Books and Ballad Men*, p. 254.

careful explanation, rather than woven into the fabric of the story. "How cam'st thou here?" is answered in detail. "For fear of grieving her full sore" the father holds back the truth and goes to the boy's father, "with this intent/ To tell him what his daughter said." We do not guess at the emotions; fright, love, and amazement are named for us. There is, finally, the moral note. "For her good" the maid is sent away. And with a solemn warning the poet concludes:

> Part not true love, you rich men, then,
> But if they be right honest men
> Your daughters love, give them their way,
> For force oft breeds their lives' decay.

In the Southern Appalachians true love is treated with a fatalistic respect, and there are many versions of this ballad surviving. The one given below, though still crude in verse and tainted with broadside morality, has begun to yield to corrective treatment. All particular reference to places and times and distances has gone; against a general and shadowy background each singer may imagine his own specific details. Unassigned dialogue sweeps us along. Fright is indicated by a bit of concrete description—"it made the hair stand on his head." Cause and effect do not concern this singer. Mystery and drama have been restored by understatement. A lyric increase in repetition, an emphasis on the power of love, a lack of analysis of the supernatural, and a loss of connecting detail all bring the story back into line with folk song.

In contrast with the minstrel "Chevy Chase" the broadside version (162 B) shows how certain portions have been worked over in a new idiom. The verse has been smoothed out, often to the point of dulness:

> Who sent Earle Percy present word
> he wold prevent his sport;
> The English Erle, not fearing that,
> did to the woods resort.

So fluent is the writer that many stanzas have open endings, which with their appeal to the eye rather than the ear are unknown in the traditional ballad. Chivalry, with its emphasis on the details of hunting and fighting, has disappeared. An occasional prosaic word dispels any lingering romance: "With such a vehement force and might" the fatal blow is given. Some lines, however, are highly effective:

Against Sir Hugh Mountgomerye
his shaft full right he sett;
The grey-goose-winge that was there-on
in his hart's bloode was wett.

Some of the poignancy of the women's lament has been lost. The minstrel sings:

So on the morrowe the mayde them byears
off birch and hasell so gray;
Many wedous, with wepyng tears
cam to fache ther makys away.

Tivydale may carpe off care,
Northombarlond may mayk great mon,
For towe such captayns as slayne wear thear
On the March-parti shall never be non.

This becomes in the broadside:

Next day did many widdowes come
their husbands to bewayle;
They washt their wounds in brinish teares,
but all wold not prevayle.

Theyr bodyes, bathed in purple blood,
the bore with them away;
They kist them dead a thousand times
ere the were cladd in clay.

And in place of the simple devoutness of the minstrel ending there is a somewhat canting patriotism:

God saue our king, and blesse this land
With plentye, ioy and peace,

And grant henceforth that foule debate
twixt noble men may ceaze!

Until a fairly recent date this ballad was sung through the north of England, and Kidson gives us its usual tune, "which used to be sung by ballad singers in the West Riding": [17]

[17] Kidson, *Traditional Tunes*, p. 19.

The "moderate jewel" is dwelt upon at this length because of its relation to the traditional ballad. The broadside gathered up and crystallized in print the fluid traditional matter of the day, showing us one of the stages through which ballads have passed, and making obvious by comparison the peculiar beauties of the traditional style. Many a broadside ballad, also, became traditional as it passed from the professional to the domestic medium. Aubrey tells us that

> Before woomen were Readers, ye history was handed downe from mother to daughter. . . . So my nurse had the history [of England] from the Conquest downe to the time of Carl. I in ballads.[18]

Some broadside ballads, become traditional, were changed to fine folk poetry in the process. Many an American ballad, like "The Nightingale," originated in the broadside press. The importance of the broadside in literary criticism of the ballad will be evident in the following chapters. It was Addison's discussion of the broadside "Chevy Chase" which first drew literary attention to ballads,[19] and it was a translation of a Romantic German elaboration of "The Suffolk Miracle" (272) which played a part in Scott's publishing of *Minstrelsy of the Scottish Border*.[20]

THE SUFFOLK MIRACLE [21]

1. Come you people old and young,
   Pray don't do as I have done;
   Pray let your children have their way,
   For fear that love breeds a decay.

[18] Aubrey, *Remains of Gentilisme and Judaisme*, p. 68.
[19] See pages 225–26.   [20] See pages 238 ff.
[21] From Sharp, *English Folk Songs from the Southern Appalachians* (1932), I; Tune p. 264, text p. 261. Reprinted by permission of the Oxford University Press, London, Publishers.

2. When her old father came this to know,
   That she did love young Villian so,
   He sent her off three hundred miles or more,
   And swore that back home she should come no more.

3. This young man wept, this young man cried,
   In about six months for love he died;
   Although he had not been twelve months dead
   Until he rode a milk-white steed.

4. He rode up to his uncle's home
   And for his true love he did call.

5. Here's your mother's coat and your father's steed;
   I've come for you in great speed.
   And her old uncle, as he understood,
   He hoped it might be for her good.

6. He jumped up, and her behind,
   And they rode faster than the wind;
   And when he got near her father's gate
   He did complain his head did ache.

7. A handkerchief she pulled out
   And around his head she tied it about,
   And kissed his lips and thus did say:
   My dear, you're colder than the clay.

8. Get down, get down, get down, says he,
   Till I go put this steed away.
   While she was knocking at the door
   The sight of him she saw no more.

9. Get up, get up, get up, says he,
   You're welcome home, dear child, says he,
   You're welcome home, dear child, says he;
   What trusty friend did come with thee?

10. Dear old father, do you know,
    The one that I once loved before.
    The old man knowing he had been twelve months dead,
    It made the hair rise on his head.

11. He summoned clerks and clergies too,
    The grave was open and him to view.
    Although he had been twelve months dead,
    The handkerchief was round his head.

12. Come all of ye, both young and old,
    Who love your children better than gold,
    And always let them have their way,
    For fear that love might breed a decay.

A NEWE BALLADE,

declarying the daungerous shootyng of the Gunne at Courte,
to the tune of "Siche and Siche." [22]

Weepe, weepe, still I weepe, and shall doe till I dye
To think upon the gunne was shot, at court so daungerouslie.

(Imprinted at London for Edward White, dwelling at the little North
Doore of Sainct Paules Churche, at the Signe of the Gunne.)

The seventeenth day of Julie laste, at Evening towards night,
Our noble Queene Elizabeth took barge for her delight,
And had the watermen to row, her pleasure she might take,
About the river too and fro, As much as they could make.

And of her counsell with her Grace were nobles two or three,
As fittest were to be in place, regardying their degree;
The French ambassadour likewise, to comon with her grace,
Of weightie causes satte with her, each one in comely place.

But when her Grace an hower or two had past to take the aire,
Returnying reading on a book, she said, Rowe soft and faire;
Whereby, as God the matter wrought, the slackness and the staie,
Softely she paste, and nothyng thought of gunshotte anywaie.

But all this while upon the Thames, in Schuller's boate unknowne,
A wretched felloe got a gun, that was none of his owne,
And shot a bullet two or three at random all about,
And gave no great regard to see what time the Queene went out.

But as her Grace came passing by, had given his peece a charge,
And there out let a bullet flie, that hitte one in the barge,

[22] Text from *Harleian Miscellany*, X, 272. Tune from *Dorothy Welde's Lute Book*,
as quoted by Chappell, *Old English Popular Music*, I, 73. As in the singing of most
broadsides to the tunes indicated, the singer here must take some liberties in fitting in the
syllables. It is possible that the first phrase was sung twice, then the second twice.

A waterman, through both his armes, as he began to rowe,
That he cried out about his harmes, whereat the Queene was woe.

Herself in sight and presence by, when that the bullet came,
She sawe him hurt, she sawe him fall, yet shrunck not at the same:
Neither made she any fearful show, to seem to be dismaied,
Nor seemed to the ambassadour of anything afraid.

But having such a mightie mind, as passeth tonge to tell,
She stept up to the wounded man, and bad hym take it well.
His gushing blood could not abash her noble courage then,
But she was readier to give help than all the nobel men.

But what her highness said and did in that so sodeine feare,
Hereafter in my sorie tale the substance you shall heare:
"Let boats go out and fetch him in, (she said) that this hath done,"
And quickly was the person brought, that so discharged the gun.

The noble councellors most abroad to whom these tidings came,
Made haste to court with trembling hearts, to think upon the same,
Applauding God, upon their knees, most humbly in their place,
With tears of joy, that bitter ball had so escaped her Grace.

His name was Thomas Appletree of court a serving man,
Which was no little greef to see to his good maister than,
He was committed to gaile, at counsellors grave regard,
That they might judge what vilest death were fit for his reward.

With blubring tears it is no boot to tell the weeping eyes
That were full woe of such a shot, where all our saftie lies,
The bullet came so nere her Grace, within six feet at least,
Was never such a cursed case, by such a wilful beast.

Wherefore it was decreed and judged, by all that counsell gave,
That hanging was too good a death for such a wretch to have.
A gibbet was set up in haste against the court full nye,
Where this unhappie Appletree was pointed for to die.

And on the tuesday following then, this wicked prisner came
Well garded with the marshall's men, to hang upon the same.
His master standing by the bank, to heare what he could say,
He humbly fell upon his knees and mercy did him praie.

Would God thou hadst never served me, (quote he with woful look)
But God (he said) forgive it thee, that cursed marke thou took.
And after prayer said and done, on the ladder as he stood,
He took his oath before them all, he was a subject good,

And never meant to hurt her grace, nor any in the barge,
Nor meant to hurt in any place, to shoot with any charge.

But wished he never had been born, for his good master's sake,
Whom he had made a woeful man, and no amendes could make.

For troth it was, and truth it is, the Queene and Counsel know
Not wittingly tho' willingly he let the bullet go,
Which matter hath been sifted so, it moveth more her Grace
To let the passion of it go the meeklier in his case.

The Queene that saw this sacrifice a ready wretch to die,
Whose pitie pleadeth pardon still, put forthe her princely eye,
And sent the captain of her gard, a counselor grave and wise,
To make the fact and favor known, as he could best devise.

Who gave a thundering peale of grace the prisner's fault to show,
And all the people in the place, what prince they had to knowe,
What courage in her noble grace in peril did appear,
Before the French ambassadour's face, in such a sodaine fear.

And told again, if that mishap had happened on her grace,
The stay of true religion, how perlous were the case:
Which might have turned to bloody wars, of strange and foreign foes,
Alas, how had we been accurst, our comfort so to lose!

Then of the mercy of her grace, her subjects lives to save,
By whom these twentie yeares in peace, such quiet lives we have.
The teares fell down on every side, and aloud the people cry,
The Almightie long preserve her grace to govern prosperouslie!

And last of all he said again, mark yet this piteous queene,
For all this vile unhappy fact, so loudly done and seen,
Returns to her inured course, of mercy to forgive,
That this accursed shall not die, but pardons him to live.

And then to hear the people shout, and see them clap their hands,
Who would have torn his flesh before, being in hangman's hands,
To see the goodness of her Grace, to such great pitie bent,
It made the stoniest heart of all, astonied to lament.

The counselor that the pardon brought, then kneeling on his knee,
And every subject, as they ought, kneeled as well as he,
And said a praier for her Grace, upon the doleful ground,
Whereof the peoples sighing sherles [sic] about the skies rebound.

All loving subjects, learn to know your duties to your Queene,
By land and water where ye go, that no such deed be seen;
But pray to God that rules the skies, her highness to defend,
To reign with him perpetually, when her Highness' life shall end.

  Weepe, weepe, and still I weepe, and shall doe till I dye,
    To thinke upon the gunne was shot, at court so daungerouslie.

THE NIGHTINGALE [23]

1. One morn-ing, one morn-ing, one morn-ing in May, I met a fair coup-le a-mak-ing their way, And one was a la-dy so neat and so fair, The oth-er a sold-ier, a brave vol-un-teer.

1. One morning, one morning, one morning in May,
   I met a fair couple a-making their way,
   And one was a lady so neat and so fair,
   The other a soldier, a brave volunteer.

2. Good morning, good morning, good morning to thee.
   O where are you going, my pretty lady?
   I'm going a-walking by the banks of the sea,
   To see the waters a-gliding, hear the nightingale sing.

3. They had not been standing but one hour or two,
   When out of his knapsack a fiddle he drew.
   The tune that he played made the valleys to ring;
   O harken, says the lady, how the nightingales sing.

4. Pretty lady, pretty lady, 'tis time to give o'er.
   O no, pretty soldier, please play one tune more;
   I'd rather hear your fiddle or the touch of one string,
   Than see the waters a-gliding, hear the nightingale sing.

5. Pretty soldier, pretty soldier, will you marry me?
   O no, pretty lady, that never can be;
   I have a wife in London and children twice three;
   Two wives in the army's too many for me.

6. I'll go back to London and stay there one year,
   And often I'll think of you, my little dear;
   If ever I return, it will be in the spring,
   To see the waters a-gliding, hear the nightingale sing.

[23] As sung by Mrs. Betty Creech at Pine Mountain, Harlan County, Kentucky, in 1916 to E. K. Wells.

Chapter 10

THE ENGLISH BALLAD REVIVAL IN THE EIGHTEENTH CENTURY AND BISHOP PERCY

MINSTREL and broadside ballads are brief crystallizings of the ballad in print, consciously composed on an ancient and vital form, which in themselves have died, while the form itself has lived on in the traditional ballad. Belonging first to the folk as a whole, when that term meant any homogeneous group, the traditional ballad was relegated, as society grew more complicated, to that part of the folk which kept to its inherited customs uninfluenced by outside currents of change. Handed on by oral tradition, never subjected to the narrowing influences of print, it was created again with every singer, and yet maintained its character—in fact, intensified it—by the manner of its handing on. Certain conservative influences kept it true to type, while certain others kept it free and fluid, constantly changing, constantly modern. It was always supremely indifferent to written literature, and, for a long while, literature was as supremely indifferent to it. The story of the literary recognition of this neglected and forgotten native song begins in the eighteenth century. Until this time there is only infrequent allusion to ballads and their singers. A few guides along this ill-lighted path we do, however, pick up.

The reference in *Piers Plowman* (1380) to the lazy priest who knew rhymes of Robin Hood shows that in the fourteenth century these ballads were already profuse and popular—already, too, perhaps, the subject of moral criticism. *The Complaynt of Scotland* (1549) lists some ballads which survived long afterwards and which Child includes in his collection: "The battel of the hayrlau" ("The Battle of Harlaw," 163), "Thom of lyn" ("Tam Lin," 39), "ihonne ermistrangis dance" (possibly "Johny Armstrong," 169), "The hunttis of cheuat" ("The Hunting of the Cheviot," 162), and "the perssee and the mongumrye met" ("The Battle of Otterburn," 161).[1] A pre-Shakespearean moral-

[1] *The Complaynt of Scotland*, pp. 64, 65.

ity, "The Longer Thou Livest, the More Fool Thou Art," suggests not only a ballad singer's repertoire, but his habits of song and his concern lest the old songs be forgotten:

> I have twentie new songes yet,
> A fond woman to my mother,
> As I were wont in her lappe to sit,
> She taught me these and mony other;
> I can sing a song of Robin Redbreast
> And my litle pretie nightingale,
> There dwelleth a jolly coster here by west,
> Also, I come to drink some of your Christmas ale.
> When I do walk by myself alone,
> It doth me good my songs to render,
> Such pretie things would soon be gone,
> If I should not sometime them remember.

But like Master Merrythought, whose every speech is interlarded with the tags of ballads, in *The Knight of the Burning Pestle* (1613), this innocent singer Moros is a symbol of wanton pleasure, "counterfeiting a vaine gesture and with a foolish countenance singing the foote of many songs, as fooles were wont." The virtues and vices contend for his soul, and Discipline, speaking for respectability, exhorts him: "Leave this childishness behind. Don't go up and down like a witless boy, singing and bellowing like a daw!" [2] But the Devil runs away with him at the last. Another singer and his susceptible listener emerge in Sir Philip Sidney's reminiscences: "Certainly I must confess mine own barbarousness; I never heard the old song of the Percy and the Douglas that I found not my heart moved more than with a trumpet, and yet it is sung but by some blind crowder, with no rougher voice than rude style." [3] And from 1600 on there is reference not only to the song, but to its singer and its effect upon the listener. Sir Thomas Overbury, early in the seventeenth century, describes the milkmaid, who "dares go alone to unfold her sheep at night, and fears no manner of ill, because she means none; yet to say truth, she is never alone, she is still accompanied by old songs, honest thoughts, and prayers, but short ones." [4] Aubrey's nurse used to sing not only his-

[2] Wager, *The Longer Thou Livest, the More Fool Thou Art*, fol. A iv.
[3] Sidney, *The Defence of Poesie*, p. 24.
[4] Overbury, *Miscellaneous Works in Prose and Verse*, "A Faire and happy Milke-mayde," p. 118.

torical rhymes [5] but also the ballad of Fair Rosamond.[6] Dorothy
Osborne writes in 1663 to Sir William Temple:

> The heat of the day is spent in reading and working, and about sixe
> or seven o Clock, I walke out into a Common that lyes hard by the
> house, where a great many young wenches keep Sheep or Cows, and
> sitt in the shade singing of Ballads; I goe to them and compare theire
> voyces and Beautyes to some of the Ancient Shepherdesses that I
> have read of, and finde a vaste difference there; but trust me I think
> these are as innocent as those could bee.[7]

Three years later Mrs. Knipp, the celebrated actress, sings for Pepys'
"perfect pleasure" "her little Scotch song of Barbary Allen," and the
two exchange notes signed "Barbara Allen" and "Dapper Dicky." [8]

In general these singers, wanton or innocent, are singing from
memory, in the traditional manner. Yet the ballad criticism of the
eighteenth century, when it began, was based upon the printed broadside and not the traditional song. Thus it stressed text rather than tune,
and a long time elapsed before the ballad was recognized in its dual
capacity, as a story told in song.

To appreciate the full effect of the first critical light directed towards popular song, one must recall the type of poetry which was most
admired in the early eighteenth century. It was characterized by wit
and urbanity, by elegance, by the selection of the most poetically effective diction, by artificial ornament, and by a moral and didactic tone.
It was dominated by the classic tradition. The polished and witty
school of Pope was assiduously cultivated not only by the socially elegant and the intellectually nimble, but by the middle classes now becoming an important factor in society as a whole. One of the most
potent agents in forming their taste and manners was *The Spectator*,
which touched on a thousand subjects and was read at the breakfast
tables of the business man and the beau, discussed at the coffee houses,
and carried by the ladies to their drawing rooms and boudoirs. During
the editorship of Joseph Addison the readers of *The Spectator* opened
their papers one morning to a letter on popular verse. "It is impossible," Addison wrote, "that anything should be universally tasted and
approved by the Multitude, tho' they are only the Rabble of a Nation,

[5] See above, page 217.
[6] Aubrey, *Remains of Gentilisme and Judaisme*, p. 70.
[7] Dorothy Osborne, *Letters* (Oxford, Clarendon Press, 1928), p. 51.
[8] Pepys, *Diary and Correspondence*, V, 261, 264–65.

which hath not in it some peculiar Aptness to please and gratify the Mind of Man." [9] This was in line with the theory that all men were equally endowed by Nature with reason and taste, and that since the reason and taste of simpler people were less overlaid with prejudice, they were more easily expressed and more transparent in their art. Thus making the contemporary appeal to the *consensus gentium*, Addison discussed two ballads, "Chevy Chase," a broadside version of "The Hunting of the Cheviot" (162), and "The Babes in the Wood," another broadside quite lacking in any traditional merits. (This was not the first serious treatment of "Chevy Chase," for in 1685 the Bishop of London, "who thought it no derogation to his episcopal character to avow a fondness for this excellent old ballad," [10] had commanded a translation into Latin, which Dryden had included in his *Miscellany Poems*.) Addison, patronizing though he is, sounds for a wider public the first faint note of praise for popular ballads, and in spite of his apologetic tone shows a lurking affection for them, justifying their artless charm by the surprising claim that they possess "those precepts of morality" which should underlie every work of inspiration, and that they unwittingly obey the classic rules for epic poetry.

Addison's essay was pounced upon by the wits and the critics, and there was heated discussion and considerable jeering at his espousal of the ballad cause. For folk poetry, in its natural simplicity, its lack of conscious artistry, its tragic emotions implied rather than expressed, its untamed roughness of verse, and especially its entire disregard of reason and unconsciousness of mission, was poles asunder from the accepted standards of the day. Yet like many another pioneer Addison won his ultimate victory by immediate defeat: his theory, although it was attacked and satirized, lived on by virtue of this very publicity. In 1713 Rowe, in the prologue to *Jane Shore*, wrote,

> Let no nice sir despise a hapless dame
> Because recording ballads chaunt her name.
> Those venerable ancient song-enditers
> Soared many a pitch above our modern writers.[11]

John Gay, in *The Shepherd's Week* (1714), a revival of pastoral verse, took the opportunity to list the popular songs of the time, as did

[9] *The Spectator*, Nos. 70, 74, 85.
[10] Percy, *Reliques of Ancient English Poetry*, I, 253, note.
[11] Rowe, *Jane Shore*, p. 116.

the writer of *The Complaynt of Scotland* nearly two hundred years
years before him. He mentions "The Children in the Wood," "Chevy
Chase," "Lord Bateman" (53), "Fair Rosamond," "Robin Hood,"
"Troy Town," and several later broadsides.[12] Mallet's "William and
Margaret" (1723) was one of the most popular poems of the day.[13]
A *Collection of Old Ballads* (1723–1725) brought together a large
number of ballads "corrected from the best and most ancient copies
extant." The editor, who is possibly Ambrose Phillips, is a little at a
loss as to the proper attitude to take toward these pieces of unproved
literary merit. His three volumes were apparently well received,
and it is interesting to trace in the prefaces of the successive volumes a growing seriousness and a corresponding loss of nervous and
facetious levity. The collection is the first considerable anthology of
popular poetry, and if better known, might almost challenge the pre-
eminence of Percy's *Reliques*. The songs themselves, with a few ex-
ceptions, are of the less inspired broadside character, but a half-dozen
or so were acceptable to Child, and included in his *English and Scottish Popular Ballads*. By the middle of the century thoughtful writers
like Hume and Burke were beginning to comment favorably on popular taste, and on the advantages of simplicity over sophistication as
shown in the ballads. While Gay's *Beggar's Opera* (1728) was prima-
rily satirical, its use of "Lilliburlero," "Constant Billy," and other ballad tunes was a refreshing influence because the simple, lively nature of
the music imposed itself upon the verses. Lillo's *George Barnwell*
(1731) used the plot of a broadside ballad. Home's *Douglas* (1756),
a dramatization of "Child Maurice" (83), swept England and was
played for many years. Indeed our own past generation was brought
up upon the elocutionary thrills of the hero's revelation of identity:

> My name is Norval; on the Grampian Hills
> My father kept his flocks. . . .[14]

It was in connection with *Douglas* that the poet Gray described for
all time the ballad's plunge into catastrophe:

> I have got the old Scotch ballad on which "Douglas" was founded. It
> is divine . . . Aristotle's best rules are observed in it in a manner

---

[12] Gay, *The Shepherd's Week*, "Saturday," p. 53.
[13] See page 311.
[14] Home, *Douglas, a Tragedy*, II, i, p. 35.

that shows that the author had never heard of Aristotle. . . . It begins in the fifth act of the play.[15]

Gray's own response to ballad style shows how this particular ability of the ballad to thrust *in medias res* captured his fancy; for so does *The Bard* begin. Shenstone's *Pastoral Ballad* (1755) has a new simplicity devoid of Vergilian touches. Gray's poem, and Collins' *Ode on Popular Superstitions of the Highlands of Scotland* (1749) were inspired by newly translated Celtic and Teutonic poetry, and stimulated interest in rude, barbaric verse.

For Goldsmith two ballads known familiarly in his boyhood remain a constant touchstone for sentiment and a wholesome contrast to more refined pleasures. In *The Vicar of Wakefield* Farmer Flamborough and the Blind Piper take turns entertaining Parson Primrose: "While one played, the other would sing some soothing ballad, Johnny Armstrong's Last Goodnight, or The Cruelty of Barbara Allen." [16] Elsewhere Goldsmith writes:

> If I go out to the Opera where Signora Colomba pours out all the mazes of melody, I sit and sigh for Lisboy fireside, and Johnny Armstrong's last Goodnight from Peggy Golden [17]

This is the music which has "sung him into tears." In contrast, Mateo's is dissonance to him.[18]

This response to the power of popular song was one of the many reflections of the interest in the primitive. It also contained other seeds of romanticism, for the ballad appealed to feeling rather than to reason, and increased the interest in the past, the remote, and the supernatural, which was to mount to such heights in Scott's time. A most potent stimulus to the growing interest was the appearance, in 1765, of Percy's *Reliques of Ancient English Poetry*.

This book was the result of a strange accident. Thomas Percy, a clergyman of northern family, while staying with friends at Shifnal in Shropshire, observed that the chambermaid was lighting his fire with leaves from an old manuscript which she kept under the dresser. He rescued the book and found that it was a collection, in the handwriting of a hundred years previous, of old songs and verses. Percy, like

[15] Gray, *Works*, II, 316.
[16] Goldsmith, *Works*, I, 85.   [17] *Letters*, p. 29.
[18] *Works*, II; *The Bee*, II, "Happiness dependent upon the Constitution."

THOMAS PERCY, DEAN OF CARLISLE—BY SIR JOSHUA REYNOLDS
(Courtesy of Librarie Floury, Paris)

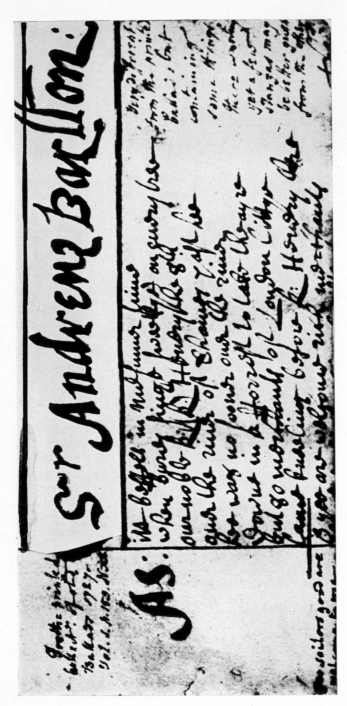

In the printed
Collectⁿ of old
Ballads 1727.
Vol. I. p. 159. N. xx

For (?) sailors good
are welcome to me.

Sʳ Andrew Bartton
AS: itt beffell in m[i]dsumer-time
when burds singe sweetly on euery tree
our noble K: (K.) Henery the 8th
ouer the riuer of Thames past hee
hee was no sooner ouer the riuer
downe in a fforrest to take the ayre
but 80 merchants of London Cittye
came kneeling before K: Henery there
O yee are welcome rich merchants

Very different
from the printed
ballad: but
containing
some things
there wanting
yet a few
stanzas may
be better given
from the other.

A FACSIMILE FROM THE PERCY FOLIO MANUSCRIPT

P. 490. Annotated by Percy.

many another clergyman of the time, was as much scholar as theologian. He was something of an antiquarian as well, and he was a student of other literatures, having made translations from the Norse and even from the Chinese. He was a friend of Goldsmith, Shenstone, and Dr. Johnson, and had followed the literary currents of the times, including, of course, the discussion of popular taste. He was, moreover, extremely anxious to stand well in the opinion of the Northumberland Percys, with whom he claimed a distant kinship. In the publication of this manuscript he saw the chance of realizing his hopes of noble patronage, as well as gratifying his real interest in popular literature and taking advantage of its current appeal.

He therefore set to work to edit the manuscript—and a glance at its facsimile gives us a wholesome respect for his ability. It was written in a cramped and antique hand; it was dog-eared and in fragments, and the work of a careless binder who prepared it for Johnson's inspection had encroached further upon the text. Percy chose from the Folio only a few ballads, and to chaperone them auspiciously into the world of polite letters combined them with selections from Shakespeare, Chaucer, and the romances, and an essay on minstrels. *The Reliques of Ancient English Poetry* appeared in 1765, dedicated to the Countess of Northumberland, in phrases which Percy says "owed their finest strokes to the superior pen of Dr. Johnson." [19]

This connection of Johnson with *The Reliques* is perhaps surprising in a man for whom written learning was the fixed luminary, tradition but a meteor. Johnson would have agreed with his contemporary, Warburton, who called ballads "specious funguses, compared to the oak." [20] Anyone, Johnson said, who had read "Johnny Armstrong" could imitate the abrupt beginning of a ballad.[21] Its "infantine style" he parodied in a now familiar quatrain:

> I put my hat upon my head
> And walked into the Strand,
> And there I met another man
> Whose hat was in his hand.

The ballad of "Chevy Chase" received his particular censure. It might please the vulgar, but it did not satisfy the learned; "it did not fill a

[19] Anderson, in *The Life of Johnson*, 3rd ed. (1815), p. 309. Quoted by Hazen, *Johnson's Prefaces and Dedications*, p. 162.
[20] Quoted in Preface, *Bishop Percy's Folio Manuscript*, II, xxix.
[21] Johnson, *Lives of the Poets*, III, 439.

mind capable of thinking strongly." [22] Its story "could not possibly be told in a manner that shall make less impression on the mind." [23] It was a masterpiece of "chill and lifeless imbecility." [24] Yet at times he quoted ballads like a ballad-lover. Boswell speaks of his muttering a line from "Johnny Armstrong" as he was being conducted through the apartments where Rizzio was stabbed at Holyrood: "And run him though the fair bodie." [25] Percy alludes in his preface to "the importunity of such judges as the author of the Rambler," [26] and more informally, in a letter, he says, "Mr. Johnson has seen my MS and has a desire to have it printed." [27] Johnson probably saw in the folio ballads a source of information about the manners and language of the past, which always delighted him. He would, then, have favored the publication of *The Reliques* as an antiquarian curio. But as examples of art or poetry he found the ballads worthless.

There was, then, much in favor of immediate popularity for *The Reliques*. Shenstone, Percy's chief adviser in the initial preparation, writes in 1761 of its forthcoming appearance, "The public has seen all that art can do, and they want the more striking effects of wild, original, enthusiastic genius." [28] Percy's own standing endorsed it in literary circles. It was welcomed both for its presentation of "wild, enthusiastic genius" and for its editor's art in making that genius conform to accepted literary standards. The budding elements of romantic taste were nourished by this fresh matter. And the occasional appearance of a parallel story helped to give the ballad good standing. Thus there was an obvious likeness between "The Ballad of Sir Gawaine's Marriage" and "The Wife of Bath's Tale," between "The Jew of Venice"

[22] Johnson, *op. cit.*, II, 148, note, quoted from *Windham's Diary*.
[23] *Op. cit.*, "Addison," II, 148.   [25] Boswell, *Tour of the Hebrides*, p. 186.
[24] *Loc. cit.*   [26] Percy, *Reliques*, I, 8.
[27] Hecht, *Thomas Percy und William Shenstone*, p. 5. There are other allusions to Johnson's collaboration in this volume of letters interchanged between the two men:
"If I regarded only my own private satisfaction, I should by no means be eager to render my Collection cheap by publication. It was the importunity of my friend, Mr. Johnson, that extorted from me a promise of the kind. Indeed, he made me very tempting offers, for he promised to assist me in selecting the most valuable pieces and in revising the Text of those he selected. Nay further, if I would leave a blank Page between every two that I transcribed, he would furnish it out with the proper notes" (p. 9).
"These promises he never executed, nor, except a few slight hints delivered *viva voce* did he furnish any contributions" (Note, p. 9).
A little later, Percy "has held a council of war with Mr. Johnson," and has concluded that he will scatter the popular pieces among the others, to show how one illustrates the other (p. 53).
[28] Hecht, *op. cit.*, pp. 53, 54.

and Shakespeare's *Merchant,* or between Titus Andronicus in ballad and in drama.

But the book was also received with criticism. That of the antiquary Joseph Ritson, with its open and heated expressions of disapproval, launched one of the bitterest of literary controversies. Percy's reluctance to show the folio to any but a few friends led to the suspicion, voiced by Ritson, that the manuscript did not exist. This, it may be said in passing, was in consonance with the times, when the authenticity of other products claiming to be the work of wild barbaric poets was being questioned. Chatterton's remarkable forgeries with their antique patina were soon to be exposed; MacPherson's *Ossian* had been proved to be largely MacPherson. Percy's somewhat naïve reply to the charge that the *Folio Manuscript* was another hoax was to have Reynolds paint his portrait with the book under his arm.[29] As one reads the story of this "Hunting of the Percy," [30] one wonders why all the doubts were not swept away by the simple offer of Percy to show his manuscript to Ritson and be done with it. But he never did, and for years Ritson continued to inveigh against Percy's ideas and methods. Percy did, however, modify some of his statements and change his texts as successive editions of the *Reliques* appeared, and this was due in part to Ritson's criticism. When Percy died, full of honors as Bishop of Dromore and complacent in the favor of the House of Northumberland, the manuscript found its way to the library of a son-in-law, but he and subsequent heirs consistently refused to have it studied, or even viewed. Only in 1868, after a hundred years in which the rumor of its nonexistence would not down, did the tact and efforts of Professor Child of Harvard, and a small group of English scholars, succeed in buying the manuscript. It was then edited in full and published, and the original now lies in the British Museum.

The publication of the *Folio Manuscript* revealed to a later generation not only the richness of Percy's store, from which he drew only a small part for the *Reliques,* but his methods as an editor. The tone

[29] A later observer points out the discrepancy between the portrait and the book: "It is not, gentle reader, as that dextrous artist Sir Joshua Reynolds hath represented it in his fine portrait of the Bishop, most picturesquely curling at the covers. . . . It is a narrow half-bound book with blue paper sides and brown leather back. It is 15 and ⅝ inches in length, by about 5 and 6/8 inches in width, and about an inch in thickness." (Dr. Dibdin in *Decameron,* quoted in the *Folio of Bishop Percy,* I, xvi.)

[30] Bronson, *Joseph Ritson, Scholar-at-Arms,* chap. viii.

of Percy's own introduction had already prepared the way for this revelation:

> In a polished age like the present, I am sensible that many of these reliques of antiquity will require great allowances to be made for them. Yet have they, for the most part, a pleasing simplicity, and many artless graces, which in the opinion of no mean critics have been thought to compensate for the want of higher beauties and, if they do not dazzle the imagination, are frequently found to interest the heart.
>
> To atone for the rudeness of the more obsolete poems, each volume concludes with a few modern attempts in the same kind of writing: and, to take off from the tediousness of the longer narratives, they are everywhere intermingled with little elegant pieces of the lyric kind.[31]

Literary ears and minds were not quite ready, in Percy's day, to accept popular poetry without some smoothing out of its crudeness, some dressing up for the parlor. The editor explains the need for correcting to "pale and wan" such careless copying as "wale and pan," and for the filling out of gaps caused by mutilation of the pages. He does not pretend that he has not made more significant alterations. He has refined the passages unsuited to the ears of the polite, the judicious, and the elegant, to quote three often used words. He has softened anything savoring of "the immoral and the indecent." But his power of conjecture, reinforced by his poetic ambition, has overworked itself in some of his readings, and his imagination has come too fully into play in dealing with the corruptions. The canons of the day have led him again and again to introduce neo-Classical refinements, original or borrowed. The simple pastoral beginning of "Sir Andrew Barton" in the *Folio*,

> As itt beffell in Midsumer time
> When birds singe sweetly on every tree [32]

becomes in the *Reliques* the rococo version he has found in *A Collection of Old Ballads*:

> When Flora with her fragrant flowers
> Bedeckt the earth so trim and gaye,
> And Neptune with his dainty showers
> Came to present the month of Maye [33]

---

[31] Percy, *Reliques*, I, 8–9.   [32] *Op. cit.*, II, 190.
[33] Phillips (?), *A Collection of Old Ballads*, I, 159.

His treatment of "Gil Morrice" shows most clearly the hand that itched to refine. He uses as his base a traditional ballad printed in 1755 from the memory of an old lady who had learned it "from the mouths of old women and nurses," in preference to a splendid sturdy version in the *Folio* which he considered too imperfect. He draws upon stanzas suggested by his friend Shenstone for the description of Gil [Child] Morrice, which goes beyond all bounds of folk reticence:

> His hair was like the threeds of gold
> Shot frae the burning sun [34]
> His lipps like roses drapping dew,
> His breath was a' perfume.
>
> His brow was like the mountain snae
> Gilt by the morning beam;
> His cheeks like living roses glow:
> His een like azure stream.
> The boy was clad in robes of grene
> Sweet as the infant spring;
> And like the mavis on the bush,
> He gart the vallies ring.[35]

The most substantial addition, however, is the moral discourse of four stanzas at the end :

> Obraid me not, my lord Barnard!
> Obraid me not for shame!
> Wi that saim speir O pierce my heart!
> And put me out o' pain.
> Since nothing bot Gill Morice head
> Thy jelous rage could quell,
> Let that saim hand now take hir life
> That neir to thee did ill.
>
> To me nae after days nor nichtes
> Will eir be saft or kind;
> I'll fill the air with heavy sighs,
> And greet till I am blind.
> Enouch of blood by me's bin spilt;
> Seek not your death frae mee;
> I rather lourd it had been mysel
> Than eather him or thee.

---

[34] This, upon consultation with Shenstone, he changes to "Drawn frae Minerva's loom." (Hecht, *Thomas Percy und William Shenstone*, p. 6.)

[35] Percy, *Reliques*, III, 97.

With waefo wae I hear your plaint;
    Sair, sair, I rew the deid,
That eir this cursed hand of mind
    Had gard his body bleid.
Dry up your tears, my winsome dame,
    Ye neir can heal the wound;
Ye see his head upon the speir,
    His heart's blude on the ground.

I curse the hand that did the deid,
    The heart that thocht the ill;
The feet that bore me wi' silk speid,
    The comely youth to kill.
I'll aye lament for Gill Morice,
    As gin he were mine ain;
I'll neir forget the dreiry day
    On which the youth was slain.[36]

This is entirely in the taste of the times—the wordiness, the improving thought, and the sentimentality so out of keeping with the grim story. The anticlimax does not improve matters. Ritson, who because of his love of genuine simplicity and admiration of neo-Classicism could not tolerate the mixture of the two, was roused by the cheap mawkishness of the poem to the extreme of calling Percy dishonest. But he was a voice in the wilderness, crying against a world that was charmed by Percy's "contaminated" ballads.[37]

In viewing the shortcomings of Percy as a ballad editor, we are inclined to judge him by modern standards. We must remember the positive value of his work. The important thing is that any scholar in the eighteenth century should give this material publicity, rather than that he should follow methods not acceptable today. *The Reliques* would not have attained its vogue, if Percy had not softened its antique roughnesses for the sensitive ears of his first listeners. Without this watered version of ballads as a first step toward our acceptance of true traditional material, ballad criticism might have taken a different, and perhaps a longer course.

[36] *Ibid.*, III, 99–100.
[37] Ritson's own editing of ballads was painstaking and thorough in its adherence to the copy as he received it. Neither Percy nor Ritson, however, had much interest in traditional song; both worked from manuscripts and broadsides. Ritson does allude to rumors that the songs are still sung; and Percy's letters hint at a plan for collecting from the memory of the people while yet there is time. See Ogburn, "Thomas Percy's Unfinished Collection, 'Ancient English and Scottish Poems,'" *English Literary History*, III, 183–89.

With the appearance of *The Reliques* the tone of criticism changes. In 1783 Cowper writes of the ballad, using the word, to be sure, in connection with a sentimental ballad imitation, and revealing some inaccuracies of knowledge which are characteristic of the times:

> The ballad is a species of poetry, I believe, peculiar to this country, equally adapted to the drollest and most tragical subjects. Simplicity and ease are its proper characteristics. Our forefathers excelled in it; but we moderns have lost the art. . . . We have many good ballads not inferior perhaps in true poetical merit to some of the very best odes that the Greek or Latin languages have to boast of. It is a sort of composition I was ever fond of, and if graver matters had not called me another way, I should have addicted myself to it more than to any other.[38]

At the end of the century Wordsworth points directly to the literary influence of *The Reliques*. "For our own country," he writes, "its poetry has been absolutely redeemed by it. I do not think that there is an able writer of verse today who would not be proud to acknowledge his obligation to 'The Reliques.' "[39] This debt was in a few years more to be paid again by Sir Walter Scott.[40]

The end of the century, then, sees a very different attitude toward popular poetry—a gradual loss of the patronizing tone and a growing respect for it in itself, rather than as a popular expression. Addison paved the way for *The Reliques*, and this book in turn led people further along the path of creation and criticism. From Addison to Percy the attempt had been to raise the ballad to literary levels; after Percy, there was an effort to simplify literary poetry, improving it so that it might be comparable to the ballad. From 1765 on, a stream of increasingly favorable criticism was released. The stimulus to collecting more and better texts sent people to the countryside rather than to old manuscripts, and the accumulation of traditional material gave critic and poet a stronger basis on which they might work toward a common end, the improvement of English poetry.

[38] Cowper, *Correspondence*, II, 91, 92.
[39] Wordsworth, *Poetical Works*, "Essay Supplementary to the Preface," V, 266.
[40] See page 248.

Chapter 11

THE SCOTTISH REVIVAL AND SIR WALTER SCOTT

IN England the stream of traditional poetry had suffered greatly from the influx of the printed ballad, which spread from the city presses and put its debasing stamp upon existing traditional song, even stopping it for a while. In Scotland traditional song suffered no such break. The Scots, Border-conscious for centuries after the union of the crowns, have never allowed the songs about their heroes to die, from Thomas of Erceldoune and William Wallace to Bonnie Prince Charlie; and Sir Walter Scott's *Minstrelsy of the Scottish Border* is the natural product of the Border's unbroken tradition of song, legend, and poetry.

David Herd, a contemporary of Percy and Ritson, had edited a volume of ballads and songs in 1769, collected from traditional singers and presented with the greatest respect for every fragment as he had found it. Like everyone who collected from singers themselves, he had been struck with the musical nature of the ballad. Percy had offered to "improve" Herd's fragments, but Herd had independently followed his own plan.

Literary attention in the eighteenth century turned also to popular poetry in Allan Ramsay's *Ever Green* and *Tea Table Miscellany*, which contained many ballads, some bowdlerized from tradition, some imitations, some fairly untainted by the pen, like "Johnie Armstrong," which was "copied from a gentleman's mouth of the same name, who is the sixth generation from this John." [1] *The Tea Table Miscellany* went through twelve editions between the years 1724 and 1763. This was the handbook for Scottish literary circles of the generation preceding Scott, and must be considered as one of his own literary influences.

The circumstances of Scott's youth drew him in many ways toward popular poetry. His pride in Border ancestry was a quickening force in

[1] *The Ever Green*, II, 190.

him from childhood, feeding his natural interest in local legends and developing his gifts as a storyteller. Childhood years spent in the country to gain strength after an illness brought him in contact with singers and storytellers, and he spent long days absorbing with an inactive child's compensatory eagerness the romance and poetry of the Border. When he was thirteen, a volume of the *Reliques* fell into his hands. Its impact upon his imagination is recalled in his *Memoirs:*

> But above all, I then first became acquainted with Bishop Percy's Reliques of Ancient Poetry. As I had been from infancy devoted to legendary lore of this nature, and only reluctantly withdrew my attention, from the scarcity of materials and the rudeness of those which I possessed, it may be imagined, but cannot be described, with what delight I saw pieces of the same kind which had amused my childhood, and still continued, in secret, the Delilahs of my imagination, considered as the subject of sober research, grave commentary, and apt illustration, by an editor who showed his poetical genius was capable of emulating the best qualities of what his pious labor preserved. I remember well the spot where I read these volumes for the first time. It was beneath a huge platanus tree, in the ruins of what had been intended for an old-fashioned arbour, in the garden I have mentioned. The summer day sped onward so fast, that notwithstanding the sharp appetite of thirteen, I forgot the hour of dinner, was sought with anxiety, and was still found entranced in my intellectual banquet. To read and to remember was in this instance the same thing, and henceforth I overwhelmed my schoolfellows, and all who would hearken to me, with tragical recitations from the ballads of Bishop Percy. The first time, too, I could scrape a few shillings together, which were not common occurrences with me, I bought unto myself a copy of these beloved volumes, nor do I believe I ever read a book half so frequently, or with half the enthusiasm.[2]

As a young man practicing law in Edinburgh, Scott was made sheriff of Selkirkshire, the heart of the Border country. His official tours of the countryside gave him a chance to add to his store of local legend and song, and his "raids into Liddesdale," as he called these expeditions, were perhaps more to collect than to correct. During these years the nucleus of *The Minstrelsy of the Scottish Border* was forming. At the Gordon Arms on Yarrow, or at Tibbie Shiel's cottage at the head of Loch St. Mary, there were many meetings with John Ley-

---

[2] *Memoirs of Sir Walter Scott*, ed. Lockhart, I, 52.

den or James Hogg, to listen to tales and songs from Tibbie, or William Laidlaw, or Hogg's mother. Many anecdotes reveal Scott's extraordinarily retentive memory for all he heard—as, for instance, his recitation of an eighty-eight stanza ballad which he had heard only once, three years before.[3] At this time, too, the future novelist was storing away in his memory such types of humanity as the Antiquary, who

> . . . had the scent of a slow-hound, sir, and the snap of a bull-dog. He would detect you an old black-letter ballad among the leaves of a law-paper . . . a rare broadside easily now worth the weight of the original penny in gold; [4]

or Edie Ochiltree, who

> . . . has been soldier, ballad-singer, travelling tinker, and is now a beggar. . . . An old Scotch mendicant who kept the rounds within a particular space, and was news-carrier, minstrel, and sometimes historian of the neighborhood. That rascal, now, knows more old ballads and traditions than any other man in this and the next four parishes.[5]

The precipitating cause of the publication of the *Minstrelsy* was Scott's introduction to the Romantic Movement in German poetry, which was fascinating his literary friends in Edinburgh. The *Reliques* had been enthusiastically received in Germany, where Goethe, Schiller, and Herder were already arousing interest in their own folk poetry. Herder's *Dissertation on the Songs of Rude Nations* had drawn the attention of Bürger to the English ballads published in *The Reliques*, and the influence of this collection is evident in much of his poetry. "Lenore," for instance, is a romantic treatment of the story we know as "The Suffolk Miracle" (272), but Bürger develops it directly from a German folk form of the story. Both poems are given here, the first showing the true simplicity of the folk ballad, with its suggestive condensation, its selection of significant detail, its unidentified speakers, its bare hint of the supernatural, and its incremental repetition; the second illustrating the length to which Bürger went in building up the atmosphere of horror, contributing circumstantial plot, and supplying a full background of medieval color and pageant.

[3] Hogg, *Domestic Manners and Private Life of Sir Walter Scott*, p. 67.
[4] Scott, *The Antiquary*, I, 32.
[5] *Op. cit.*, I, 48.

The stars are high in heaven,
The moon is shining bright.
The dead ride fast tonight.

Open thy window, dearest,
And let me in to thee;
Brief must my visit be.

The cock's already crowing,
He's singing in the day.
I cannot longer stay.

From far away I've ridden,
Two hundred miles away
I still must ride today.

O my heart's best beloved,
Come, mount upon my horse;
The road sets a straight course.

Far in the Hungarian country
I have a little house;
To that I take my spouse.

Upon a grassy meadow
There does my cottage bide
For me and for my bride.

O let me wait no longer!
Up, love, upon my horse!
Away upon our course!

The little stars will light us;
The moon is shining bright.
The dead ride fast tonight!

O whither wilt thou take me?
My God—what thinkest thou,
In the black night to go!

With thee I cannot travel;
Thy pallet is not wide,
The way too long to ride.

Now lay thee down, heart's dearest,
Sleep now, and never wake
Till Judgment Day shall break.[6]

[6] The German text of this ballad, given below, is from *Des Knaben Wunderhorn*, ed. Müller, p. 204. A note mentions that "Bürger heard this song at night in a neighboring room."

Es stehn die stern' am Himmel,
Es scheint der Mond so hell,
Die Toten reiten schnell:

Mach auf, mein Schatz, dein Fenster,
Lass mich zu dir hinein,
Kann nicht lang bei dir sein;

Der Hahn, der tät schon krähen,
Er singt uns an der Tag,
Nicht lang' mehr bleiben mag.

Weit bin ich hergeritten,
Zweihundert Meilen weit
Muss ich doch reiten heut';

Herzallerliebste meine!
Komm', setz dich auf mein Pferd,
Der Weg ist reitensvert:

Dort drin im Ungerlande
Hab ich ein kleines Haus.
Da geht mein Weg hinaus.

Auf einer grünen Heide
Da ist mein Haus gebaut
Für mich und meine Braut.

Lass mich nicht lang' mehr warten,
Komm, Schatz, zu mir herauf,
Weit fort geht unser Lauf.

Die Sternlein tun uns leuchten,
Es scheint der Mond so hell,
Die Toten reiten schnell.

Wo willst mich dann hinführen?
Ach Gott! was hast gedacht,
Wohl in der finstern Nacht?

Mit dir kann ich nicht reiten,
Dein Bettlein ist nicht breit,
Der Weg ist auch zu weit.

Allein leg' du dich nieder,
Herzallerliebste, schlaf!
Bis an der jüngsten Tag.

ELLENORE [7]

(Godfred-Augustus Bürger)

1. At break of day from frightful dreams
      Upstarted Ellenore:
   "My William, art thou slayn," she said,
      "Or dost thou love no more?"

2. He went abroade with Richard's host
      The paynim foes to quell;
   But he no word to her had writt,
      An he were sick or well.

3. With blore of trump and thump of drum
      His fellow-soldyers come,
   Their helms bedeckt with oaken boughs,
      They seeke their longed-for home.

4. And evry road and evry lane
      Was full of old and young
   To gaze at the rejoicyng band,
      To haile with gladsom toung.

5. "Thank God!" their wives and children sayde,
      "Welcome!" the brides did saye;
   But greet or kiss gave Ellenore
      To none upon that daye.

6. And when the soldyers all were by,
      She tore her raven hair,
   And cast herself upon the ground
      In furious despair.

7. Her mother ran and lyfte her up,
      And clasped her in her arm,
   "My child, my child, what dost thou ail?
      God shield thy life from harm!"

8. "O mother, mother, William's gone
      What's all besyde to me?
   There is no mercie, sure, above!
      All, all were spared but he!"

[7] A *Historic Survey of German Poetry*, ed. W. Taylor, II, 40–51. The editor notes that the poem is already (1830) in many translations, the earliest having been made in 1790. He associates the incident with a German scene, but changes it to the return of William from the crusade of Richard Lion Heart, thus moving the scene to England. He adds the "splash, splash, splash" lines, and admits borrowing "that tirled at the pin" from Percy. He compares the story with that of "The Suffolk Miracle" (272).

9. "Kneele downe, thy paternoster saye,
      'Twill calm thy troubled spright:
  The Lord is wise, the Lord is good;
      What He hath done is right."

10. "O mother, mother, saye not so;
      Most cruel is my fate:
  I prayde, and prayde, but watte avaylde?
      'Tis now, alas! too late."

11. "Our Heavenly Father, if we praye,
      Will help a suffring child:
  Go take the holy sacrament;
      So shal thy grief grow mild."

12. "O mother, what I feele within,
      No sacrament can staye;
  No sacrament can teche the dead
      To bear the sight of daye."

13. "Maybe, among the heathen folk
      Thy William false doth prove,
  And put away his faith and troth,
      To take another love.

14. "Then wherefore sorrowe for his loss?
      Thy moans are all in vain:
  But when his soul and body parte,
      His falsehode brings him pain."

15. "O mother, mother! gone is gone:
      My hope is all forlorn:
  The grave my only safeguard is—
      Oh, had I ne'er been born!

16. "Go out, go out, my lamp of life;
      In grizely darkness die:
  There is no mercie, sure, above!
      Forever let me lie."

17. "Almighty God! O do not judge
      My poor unhappy child;
  She knows not what her lips pronounce,
      Her anguish makes her wild.

18. "My girl, forget thine earthly woe,
      And think on God and bliss;
  For so, at least, shal not thy soul
      Its heavenly bridegroom miss."

19. "O mother, mother, what is bliss,
        And what the fiendis cell?
    With him 'tis heaven anywhere,
        Without my William, hell.

20. "Go out, go out, my lamp of life,
        In endless darkness die:
    Without him I must loathe the earth,
        Without him scorne the sky."

21. And so despair did rave and rage
        Athwarte her boiling veins;
    Against the Providence of God
        She hurlde her impious strains.

22. She bet her breast, and wrung her hands,
        And rollde her tearless eye,
    From rise of morn, till the pale stars
        Again orespred the skye.

23. When harke! abroade she herde the tramp
        Of nimble-hoofed steed;
    She herde a knight with clank alighte
        And climbe the stair in speed.

24. And soon she herde a tinkling hand,
        That twirled at the pin;
    And thro her door, that opend not,
        These words were breathed in.

25. "What ho! What ho! Thy door undo;
        Art watching or asleepe?
    My love, dost thou remember me?
        And dost thou laugh or weepe?"

26. "Ah! William here so late at night!
        Oh, I have wachte and waked:
    Whense art thou come? For thy return
        My heart has sorely ak'd."

27. "At midnight only we may ride;
        I come ore land and see;
    I mounted late, but soon I go;
        Aryse, and come with mee."

28. "O William, enter first my bowre,
        And give me one embrace:
    The blasts athwarte the hawthorn hiss;
        Awayte a little space."

29. "Tho' blasts athwarte the hawthorn hiss,
　　　　I may not harbour here;
　　My spurs are sett, my courser pawes,
　　　　My hour of flight is nere.

30. "All as thou lyest upon thy couch,
　　　　Aryse, and mount behinde;
　　Tonight we'le ride a thousand miles,
　　　　The bridal bed to finde."

31. "How, ride tonight a thousand miles?
　　　　My love, thou dost bemock;
　　Eleven is the stroke that still
　　　　Rings on within the clock."

32. "Looke up: the moon is bright, and we
　　　　Outstride the earthly men;
　　I'l take thee to the bridal bed,
　　　　And night shal end but then."

33. "And where is then thy house, and home,
　　　　And bridal bed so meet?
　　'Tis narrow, silent, chilly, low,
　　　　Six planks, one shrouding sheet."

34. "And is there any room for me,
　　　　Wherein that I may creepe?"
　　"There's room enough for thee and me,
　　　　Wherein that we may sleepe.

35. "All as thou lyest upon thy couch,
　　　　Aryse, no longer stop;
　　The wedding guests thy coming wayte,
　　　　The chamber door is ope."

36. All in her sarke, as there she lay,
　　　　Upon his horse she sprung;
　　And with her lily hands so pale
　　　　About her William clung.

37. And hurry-skurry off they go
　　　　Unheeding wet or dry;
　　And horse and rider snort and blow,
　　　　And sparkling pebbles fly.

38. How swift the flood, the mead, the wood,
　　　　Aright, aleft, are gone!
　　The bridges thunder as they pass,
　　　　But earthly sowne is none.

39. Tramp, tramp, across the land they speed;
     Splash, splash, across the sea;
"Hurrah, the dead can ride apace;
     Dost feare to ride with mee?

40. "The moon is bright, and blue the night;
     Dost quake the blast to stem?
Dost shudder, mayd, to seeke the dead?"
     "No, no, but what of them?"

41. How glumly sownes yon dirgy song!
     Night-ravens flappe the wing.
What knell doth slowly tolle ding-dong?
     The psalms of death who sing?

42. Forth creepes a swarthy funeral train,
     A corse is on the biere;
Like croke of todes from lonely moores,
     The chauntings meet the eere.

43. "Go bear her corse when midnight's past,
     With song, and tear, and wail;
I've gott my wife, I take her home,
     My hour of wedlock hail!

44. "Leade forth, o clark, the chaunting quire,
     To swelle our spousal-song;
Come, preest, and reade the blessing soone,
     For our dark bed we long."

45. The bier is gone, the dirges hush;
     His bidding all obaye,
And headlong rush through briar and bush,
     Beside his speedy waye.

46. Halloo! halloo! how swift they go,
     Unheeding wet or dry;
And horse and rider snort and blow,
     And sparkling pebbles fly.

47. How swift the hill, how swift the dale,
     Aright, aleft, are gone!
By hedge and tree, by thorp and town,
     They gallop, gallop on.

48. Tramp, tramp, across the land they speede,
     Splash, splash across the see;
"Hurrah! the dead can ride apace,
     Dost feare to ride with mee?

SIR WALTER SCOTT—BY SIR HENRY RAEBURN, R.A.
(Courtesy of the National Gallery of Scotland)

TIBBIE SHIEL AND HER COTTAGE

49. "Look up, look up, an airy crew
        In roundel daunces reele;
    The moon is bright, and blue the night,
        Mayst dimly see them wheele.

50. "Come to, come to, ye ghostly crew,
        Come to and follow me,
    And daunce for us the wedding daunce,
        When we in bed shal be."

51. And brush, brush, brush, the ghostly crew
        Came wheeling ore their heads,
    All rustling like the witherd leaves
        That wide the whirlwind spreads.

52. Halloo! halloo! away they go,
        Unheeding wet or dry;
    And horse and rider snort and blow,
        And sparkling pebbles fly.

53. And all that in the moonshyne lay
        Behind them fled afar;
    And backward scudded overhead
        The skie and every star.

54. Tramp, tramp, across the land they speede;
        Splash, splash across the see;
    "Hurrah! the dead can ride apace;
        Dost feare to ride with mee?

55. "I weene the cock prepares to crowe;
        The sand will soone be run;
    I snuffe the early morning air;
        Downe, downe! Our work is done!

56. "The dead, the dead can ride apace;
        Our wed-bed here is fit;
    Our race is ridde, our journey ore,
        Our endless union knit."

57. And lo! an yron-grated gate
        Soon biggens to their view;
    He crackde his whippe; the locks, the bolts
        Cling, clang! assunder flew.

58. They pass, and 'twas on graves they trodde;
        " 'Tis hither we are bound":
    And many a tombstone ghastly white
        Lay in the moonshyne round.

59. And when he from his steed alytte,
     His armure, black as cinder,
Did moulder, moulder all awaye,
     As it were made of tinder.

60. His head became a naked skull;
     Nor hair nor eyne had he,
His body grew a skeleton,
     Whilome so blithe of ble.

61. And at his dry and boney heel
     No spur was left to be;
And in his witherd hand you might
     The scythe and hour-glass see.

62. And lo! his steed did thin to smoke,
     And charnel fires outbreathe,
And pal'd and bleachde, then vanishde quite
     The mayd from underneathe.

63. And hollow howlings hung in air,
     And shrekes from vaults arose,
Then knewe the mayde she might no more
     Her living eyes unclose.

64. But onward to the judgment seat
     Through mist and moonlight dreare
The ghostly crew their flight pursewe,
     And hollowe in her eare:

65. "Be patient: tho thyne herte should breke,
     Arrayne not Heaven's decree;
Thou nowe art thy bodie reft,
     Thy soul forgiven bee!"

Scott details at some length the part this poem played in his literary development. A friend's chance account of its recitation, by a visiting English lady at an evening party where the company were "electrified by the tale," so aroused Scott's deep curiosity and interest, even though the friend could only imperfectly quote a few lines, that he set to work to secure a copy of Bürger's works in German. This was difficult enough even in London, almost impossible in Edinburgh, but he was finally successful. He went to work at once, sitting down after supper and arising from his desk at dawn, with his own translation of "Lenore" completed.[8] His friend, upon receiving it, commented, "Upon my word, Walter Scott is going to turn out a poet—something of a cross, I think, between Burns and Gray." [9]

> The same day he [Scott] read it also to his friend Sir Alexander Wood, who retains a vivid recollection of the high strain of enthusiasm into which he had been exalted by dwelling on the wild unearthly imagery of the German bard. "He read it over to me," says Sir Alexander, "in a very slow and solemn tone, and after we had said a few words about its merits, continued to look at the fire silent and musing for some minutes, until at length he burst out with 'I wish to Heaven I could get a skull and two cross bones!' " [10]

Wood took Scott at once to call on the celebrated surgeon John Bell, who smiled at his request, opened a cupboard and

---

[8] "Essay on the Imitations of the Ancient Ballad," *Minstrelsy*, p. 554. Many of Scott's lines (See *Poetical Works*, III, 97 ff.) show a youthful enthusiasm as yet undisciplined by literary taste and skill. The following examples may be compared with Taylor's stanzas, to which the numbers in parentheses refer.

iv
(3)
	Our gallant host was homeward bound
	    With many a song of joy,
	Green waved the laurel in each plume,
	    The badge of victory.

xviii (16)	O break, my heart! O break at once, Be thou my God, Despair!
xxvii (26)	Much have I borne since dawn of morn

xxxvi
(36)
	Strong love prevail'd, she busks, she bounes,
	    She mounts the barb behind,
	And round her darling William's waist
	    Her lily arms she twined.

lix
(57)
	Reluctant on its rusty hinge
	    Revolved the iron door,
	And by the pale moon's setting beams
	    Were seen a church and tower.

lxiv
(62)
	The furious barb snorts fire and foam,
	    And with a fearful bound,
	Dissolves at once in empty air
	    And leaves her on the ground.

lxv (64)	And howl the funeral song.

[9] Lockhart, *Memoirs of the Life of Sir Walter Scott*, I, 324.
[10] *Loc. cit.*

bade Walter enter and choose. From a well furnished museum of mortality he selected forthwith what seemed to him the handsomest skull and a pair of crossbones it contained, and wrapping them in his handkerchief carried the formidable bundle home to George's Square.[11]

Here, and later at Abbotsford, he kept them in an important and prominent position.

Under such naïve circumstances began Scott's translation of German poetry, which was to be reflected later in his own work. Here he found the ballad theme and verse to furnish forth the chivalric past, the sense of wonder and mystery, passion, a picture of nature in her wilder moods, and suggestions of the supernatural that every Scot well comprehends. Moreover, with Leyden translating from the German and Southey from the Spanish, it was inevitable that Scott in his enthusiasm should be reminded of his own store of ballads, and be moved to publish them. His *Minstrelsy of the Scottish Border* (1802) is in two senses a child of *The Reliques*; for his boyish taste, stimulated by the book's early charm, led him to collect for himself, and as a young man it was his response to the Percy-inspired Germans that turned him back to the songs he had gathered.

Scott the collector and translator now became Scott the editor. He was a friend of Ritson, and recognized the justice of his criticism of Percy, but he was also an admirer of Percy, and Percy's pervading spirit was his guide. This does not mean that he approved of Percy's decorations, some of which he terms "the quintessence of affectation." [12] After his initial experimentation on Bürger and others, he settled down to the poetic use of his own folk idiom. His songs were taken in large measure from living tradition, but for this very reason they were frequently fragmentary and corrupted, and he was too much the artist and poet to be satisfied to present them in this condition. If, therefore, he had several versions of the same ballad, he collated them into a standard text, and if this was not sufficiently complete, he filled in with a stanza or two of his own inventing, frankly and with no intention to deceive. He was not above refining or interpreting his text; he saw the defects of oral transmission as well as its virtues, and remedied them with a craftsmanship which, it must be said, was gen-

[11] *Ibid.*, pp. 324-25.
[12] *Minstrelsy of the Scottish Border*, p. 563.

erally in the vein of the folk. The Antiquary's slow-hound scent and bulldog snap is needed to catch some of Scott's patching. Only sometimes is the self-conscious literary touch evident. Child, for instance, comments on his "Kinmont Willie" (186), which was, according to Scott, "too much mangled by reciters, and some conjectural emendations were absolutely necessary to render it intelligible." [13]

The Minstrelsy is for Scott matter for patriotic and poetic expression. He is neither philosophic nor scholarly, though he has plenty of learning. He is not concerned with ballad origin, using the term "minstrel" loosely to denote almost any kind of individual author, and conceiving of the ballad as a corruption and popularization of romance. As in the case of Percy, we must forgive in Scott what seems to us editorial laxity. But he is one step nearer our ideal, in that he uses traditional texts rather than manuscripts. His methods as editor have been revealed, as were Percy's, by Child's access to his originals. As Child fought to secure the Percy Folio, so he insisted on investigating the Abbotsford Papers. Yet the final judgment on the value of Scott's material is Child's own acid test, his admittance to his own collection of more than half of Scott's.

The Minstrelsy's influence on Scott himself as a poet was considerable. It led him directly to the writing of romantic poetry, and it gave him a discipline which he applied in such ballad-inspired poems as Marmion and The Lady of the Lake. The Minstrelsy's effect on the times was to inspire greater activity than ever in the matter of collecting. Current opinion placed the book beside The Reliques, maintaining that it did for Scotland what Percy had done for England, "gently leading her back to the old simplicities." [14] One of his singers, however, made other pronouncement. James Hogg's mother has innocently made a searching criticism of Scott's improved texts. On being shown the printed versions of the songs she herself had sung him, she exclaimed, "There was never ane o' ma sangs prentit till ye prentit them yoursel' and ye hae spoilt them a' thegither. They were made for singing and no for reading, but ye hae broken the charm now and they'll never be sung mair. And the warst thing o' a', they're nouther right spell'd, nor right setten down." [15] Possibly modern criticism can do no better than to go to the folk for the final word.

[13] See page 256. [14] Buchan, Sir Walter Scott, pp. 372–73.
[15] Hogg, Domestic Manners and Private Life of Sir Walter Scott, p. 61.

Chapter 12

FRANCIS JAMES CHILD

THE years between Scott and Child bore fruit in ballad theory, the accumulation of texts, and anecdote concerning singers and their ways. "The Clan of Scott," as Hustvedt calls the men influenced by Scott to collect and theorize, includes such names as that of John Finlay, with his reliable theory of French influence on English and European minstrelsy; Robert Chambers, who compares the extreme age of the romantic ballad with the comparative youth of the historical; Robert Jamieson, who points out interesting Anglo-Norse connections, and traces the rise of some romances from earlier ballads; [1] and the highly discriminating and judicious George Kinloch. Peter Buchan, with his rather dubious blind harper, was first discredited as a collector, but later, by the researches of Gavin Greig in Buchan's own county, Aberdeenshire, in 1906, restored to good repute. William Motherwell's *Minstrelsy* is the result of the most careful recording, and in addition to his energy and scholarship he is humanly alive to the relation between singer and song, and between singer and collector. His notebooks, even his expense accounts, are touched with the selfless amateur's delight in treasure found, or depression over time lost—as when he writes of one day's expenses, "So much for a hobby horse, in the riding of which there is neither fame nor thanks." [2] His successors have given him both fame and thanks in good measure. Charles Kirkpatrick Sharpe fills in social background for the ballads in his pictures of the watch mender, or the tailor, or the tinker, traveling over the countryside and staying a week or so with the county families every year, passing on his store of gossip and folklore and tales and songs as he did his chores. Andrew Lang, known to every child for his many books of fairy tales, and to every ballad scholar as essayist, author, editor, and folklorist, links us with later nineteenth-century scholarship.

[1] Walter Nelles, in "The Ballad of Hind Horn," *Journal of American Folklore*, XXII (1909), 42, shows this ballad to have been evolved from a romance which in turn is derived from an earlier ballad.

[2] Notebooks of William Motherwell, in Harvard College Library.

His Scottish inheritance places him close to Scott; but his correspondence with Child shows his perspective on the ballad revival, and the benefit he has derived from the organization of the science of Folk-Lore by the Brothers Grimm and other Germans.

The forming of ballad societies is a comment on the steadily increasing volume of ballad texts and scholarship. The Roxburghe Club (1812), the Percy Society (1840), and the Ballad Society (1868–1898) drew together, in the light of increasing work in Old and Middle English, as well as the new science of folklore, much relevant matter which otherwise would have been lost sight of. In the "horseshoe nail theory" of collecting, nothing was too small or too insignificant to be discarded, and at the risk of making some ridiculous mistakes, like that of the lady who bought a churn at an antique sale and put it in her parlor, a good deal of worthless matter was given undue emphasis. The ballad was, indeed, so much in the foreground of literary consciousness that the inevitable reaction, burlesque and satire, set in. In one of the satirical romances of Thomas Love Peacock we find the ballad bore, Mr. Derrydown, at a house party. Called upon to defend his claim that "Chevy Chase" is a finer poem than "Paradise Lost," he says with dignity, "I do not know what you mean by a finer poem; but I will maintain that it gives a much deeper insight into the truth of things!" [3] Mr. Derrydown's conversations indicate the need of administering a corrective to the overappreciation of ballads and folk material.

The ballad had worked its arduous way from the patronage of Percy through the enthusiasm of the Romanticists to a new age. If it was looked upon in the eighteenth century as a foundling on the doorstep, it became in the early nineteenth century a spoiled child, taking up far more room than was comfortable or suitable in the literary family circle. The later part of the century was to psychoanalyze the ballad-child, helping it make its social and literary adjustments. With manuscripts now available, and traditional singers still to be found in abundance, the time was ripe for the assembling of a standard *corpus* of traditional ballad literature and for definitive comment upon it; the way was open for the greatest ballad scholar of all, Francis James Child.

Child was a New England sail-maker's son. He graduated from Harvard on scholarship at the head of his class in 1846; tutored for three

[3] *Melincourt* (London, Dent, 1893), I, 88.

years in subjects as remote from his later work in English as mathematics, history, and political economy; spent four years of study in Germany, then the Mecca of all American scholars; and returned to Harvard as Boylston Professor of rhetoric, oratory, and elocution, changing in 1876 to a professorship in English, a position which he held until his death in 1896. His more than forty years of teaching at Harvard brought many college generations to his study and classroom, and his supervision of the editing of a large collection of British poets, his five-volume *Spenser*, and his many Chaucerian studies show his distinguished scholarship.

It might be suggested that some groundwork for his interest in folk literature had been laid in his undergraduate days, which helped to set his steps later in the paths of popular poetry. If Child was one of Longfellow's students—and as far as dates go it would have been possible [4]—he would have been peculiarly receptive to the unique quality of this man, who was bringing into the Harvard classroom the life and matter of the native traditions as he had met them in his years in Europe. To a Cambridge still unprepared to admit the virtues of "degenerate modern tongues," Longfellow spoke a new and enchanting language. Van Wyck Brooks paints for us the Longfellow of this period:

> Beside the round mahogany table in University Hall, he sat among his pupils, discoursing with a silvery courtesy, in a style that was far too flowery, the older professors thought, but with a feeling for the romance of letters. . . . This lecturer was a painter and a poet. . . . His task was to provide the general outlines, to give the aroma, the bouquet; and in what corner of the house of song was there a chamber where he had not lived? . . . His mind was like a music-box, charged with all the poetry of the world. Ballads that rippled with the River Neckar. Ballads of summer mornings and golden corn, blossoms red and blue, leafy lanes and hedgerows. Spanish, Swedish, Danish ballads. Epics and fragments of epics. Sagas of ships and sea-craft and laughing Saxons dashing their beards

[4] As a sophomore and junior Child studied German, during the period when Longfellow, as Smith Professor of Modern Languages and Belles-Lettres, visited all sections of modern language courses and taught one. The class books of the instructors are no longer in existence, but Longfellow's annual reports to the Board of Overseers show his contacts with all the modern language departments. In any case, Child must have known him when he returned from Germany as instructor and tutor. He became Boylston Professor three years before the retirement of Longfellow (See various records, Harvard College Archives).

with wine. Songs of Norwegian chieftains, proud of their flowing locks; night-songs, songs of childhood, Christmas carols, stately Italian sonnets. The music-box unrolled its coloured stream; but the lecturer was not an antiquary; he was a poet and a teacher of poets who spoke with mildly apostolic fervour.[5]

Child's years in Germany brought him into contact with the researches of the Brothers Grimm, furnishing a technical approach to the problems of comparative literature and revealing its possibilities. He found in Germany also a Medieval revival and the Romantic treatment of popular poetry in full flower—all in all, enough to lead him to devote his time, leisure and otherwise, to the study of ballads upon his return to America.

Child's first collection of popular poetry was part of the *British Poets* series. It appeared in 1857–1859 in nine volumes, entitled *English and Scottish Ballads.* It included much nonpopular material, romances and shorter poems; the popular matter was chosen without the benefit of evidence from the *Percy Folio Manuscript*, which was still sequestered, or the *Abbotsford Papers*, which he had not then seen. He speaks of this work as published in overhaste, but the bare two years devoted to it are a logical step toward the more than twenty years of work on his later definitive collection, the great *English and Scottish Popular Ballads*, ten volumes bound in five, which appeared over the years from 1882 to 1898. The practical one-volume edition of selections published by George W. Kittredge and Helen Child Sargent in 1904 is a not insignificant candle reflecting the full brilliance of the complete work.

The publication of *Bishop Percy's Folio Manuscript* in 1867 had been largely due to Child's insistence that British scholars unearth this buried treasure, and to his help in collecting funds for its purchase. Its evidence, and that of the *Abbotsford Papers*, to which Child also finally secured access, showed to everyone the wide divergence between a *Folio* version of a ballad and its mate in *The Reliques*, or a song collected by Scott from a singer, and its edited form in the *Minstrelsy*, and made explicit for Child his first rule for ballad editing—to take no editor's word for his treatment, and to get behind all printed texts to their sources. His second rule—to omit all nonpopular and include all

[5] Van Wyck Brooks, *The Flowering of New England* (New York, Dutton, 1936; copyright 1936 by Van Wyck Brooks), pp. 150, 153.

available popular material—called for the exercise of a sixth sense in detecting the spurious touch. His editorial blue pencil, like a surgeon's knife, cut away all literary accretions, with a combination of training and taste and common sense. The proof of popular origin often lay in the evidence from other literatures, and thus a third rule, involving perhaps the most exhaustive work of all, came into practice—the sifting of the popular literature of other lands for all possible parallels. The diffusion and transmission of folk tales through the world and through the ages, when submitted to methodical study, brought the ballad material into sharper focus. Thus the discovery of the story of "The Suffolk Miracle" (272) in the tales of Greece, other Balkan countries, Austria, Germany, Holland, Denmark, Iceland, and Brittany decided him to include in his ballad corpus the version from the English broadside press, debased though it was. Finally, he printed every version, fragment, or derived form of every ballad with absolute fidelity to his source, without emendation or interpretation in the case of a corrupted text. The notes accompanying each ballad supplied every bit of information that could be culled, as to sources and analogues, as well as a comparison of the variants and a summary of their elements. Since such a collection can never be final, the addenda accumulated between the publication of the first volume in 1882, and the last in 1898, were included at the end, as well as fifty-four tunes. *English and Scottish Popular Ballads* gives us a standard collection which has ever since its appearance served as a touchstone for popular poetry, and a model for editing. "Child pieces" form the point of departure for all subsequent collectors, and practically no new ballads of genuine folk character have been uncovered since Child's day. "I never expect to hear a new ballad," said Cecil Sharp; "If I find a new variant of an old one, I am happy." [6] One of the few claims to eligibility from later discovery is "The Bitter Withy," found by Sharp and Sidgwick.

This monumental piece of work is the product of Child's leisure hours. Outside of his classroom he pursued his relentless task, which involved, as Hustvedt reminds us,[7] the careful study of rare books and periodicals, the collation of hundreds of variants, detailed comment on previous editorial methods, and knowledge of everything pertinent. A

[6] A remark made to the writer.
[7] *Ballad Books and Ballad Men*, p. 221.

vast correspondence with scholars known and unknown to him piled up. The matter so painstakingly accumulated began to present formidable problems of organization. In this stage the friendship and advice of Svend Grundtvig, the Danish ballad scholar, was of great value. Grundtvig, knowing of Child's earlier collection, wrote offering to help on the contemplated second work, and although the two never met, a friendship grew out of their eleven years' correspondence which is one of the most interesting in literary history. In Denmark scholarly interest in native ballads had never lapsed since 1591, when by royal command Vedel had published a full collection, with a defense of the ballad and a critical record of its history. Thus Denmark began in the sixteenth century with a body of texts, and developed its criticism from them, while England started with criticism in the eighteenth century, and found her ballads later. While Child must bridge gaps and interpret silences in the history of the British ballad, Grundtvig, who had the advantage of continuous record and had long been aware of kinship between Scandinavian and British ballads, was able to supply many of the missing pieces in Child's puzzle.

Other difficulties beset Child. The pioneer character of his work was not understood, and he had to educate people as to what he wanted. Ballad collecting was still largely a matter of recourse to printed, easily available sources. He did most of his work, of necessity, in this country, thus involving himself in a mass of letter writing over a period of twenty-five years. The faithful William MacMath, working for Child in Scotland, copied thousands of lines for him, and the pages of spidery handwriting now in the Child Memorial Library at Harvard bear witness to the loving labor of this scribe. But often owners of manuscripts to whom he applied were indifferent, dilatory, suspicious, or sometimes grasping. After sending out an inquiry for ballads to a list of Scottish schoolmasters, Child writes to Grundtvig:

A very large and wearisome part of my "preparation" has been the endeavor to stir up Scotsmen to an interest sufficient to induce them to exert themselves to save the things that may still be left. It is in vain. The Scot loves his ballads but is incurious about them.[8]

These adverse conditions, moreover, must be met under the burden of increasing years and failing health, and other exacting professional work, all of which delayed and discouraged him.

[8] Hustvedt, *Ballad Books and Ballad Men*, p. 283.

Such a task might well seem to us likely to produce a mass of unrelieved dulness. Child's collection, however, is saved from this partly by the liveliness of the traditional ballad itself, and partly by the humanity and sympathy which constantly appear in the editor's notes. Touches of wit and humor frequently enliven his interpretations. He comments on the "conjectural emendations" admitted by Scott to have been made in "Kinmont Willie" (186): "Probably a great deal more 'emendation' was done than this observation would indicate. One would like, for instance, to see stanzas 10 to 12 in their 'mangled condition.' " [9] He introduces us with kindly irony to Hobie Noble, who "though banished from Bewcastle for his irregularities, will always command the hearty liking of those who live too late to suffer from them," [10] and to Peter Buchan the collector, "who may be relied upon to produce a longer ballad than anybody else." [11] He mentions the "intelligent behavior" of the ship in "Young Allan" (245):

> "Spring up, spring up, my bonny ship,
>   And goud sall be yer fee!"
> And fan the bonny ship hard of that,
>   Goud was to be her fee,
> She sprang as fast fra the sat water
>   As life dos fra the tree.

Then in the briefest compass there follows a comprehensive discussion of other intelligent ships in other stories, and a whole field of animistic magic is laid before us. Of the fate of Dick of the Cow, whose enemies, the Armstrongs, are said to have plunged him into a pot of

---

[9] O is my basnet a widow's curch?
  Or is my lance a wand of the willow tree?
Or my arm a ladye's lilye hand,
  That an English lord should lightly me.

And have they taen him Kinmont Willie,
  Against the truce of Border tide,
And forgotten that the bauld Bacleuch
  Is keeper here on the Scottish side?

And have they een taen him Kinmont Willie
  Withouten either dread or fear,
And forgotten that the bauld Bacleuch
  Can back a steed, or shake a spear?

John Buchan, in his biography of Scott, agrees that these stanzas are undoubtedly from the pen of the editor. (*Sir Walter Scott*, p. 66.)
[10] Child, *English and Scottish Popular Ballads*, IV, 1.
[11] *Op. cit.*, II, 342.

boiling water, he says, "No well-wisher of Dick has the least occasion to be troubled by these puerile supplements of our singers." [12] Telling adjectives characterize the verses: "The Suffolk Miracle" (272) is "blurred, disfigured and enfeebled," "Young Waters" (94) is "a counterfeit of the lowest description." These and many other examples of the light touch that accompanied his scholarship, coupled as they are with his theory that no detail is too small for notice, no effort too great, give us not only Child's learning but his character and personality. For integrity and modesty were part of his thoroughness. The objective mind was always in full play. "Criticize my proceedings *like an enemy*," he writes to Grundtvig.[13] Unlike Percy, Ritson, or Scott, he had no ulterior motive, no axe to grind, "unless it were the edged tool of the honest workman. . . . His governing motive seems to have been that of doing a work that he liked in a fashion that competent judges might be expected to approve." [14]

Like many great books, the introduction was left till the last, and Child did not live to write it. In this, it is surmised, he would have made his final statement on the nature of ballads. One can, however, glean from comment along the way what that statement would have included. W. M. Hart, in an article summing up this comment, helps the picture to emerge:

> [Professor Child] regarded [the ballad] as a distinct species of poetry, which precedes the poetry of art, as the product of a homogeneous people, the expression of our common human nature, of the mind and heart of the people, never of the personality of an individual man, devoid, therefore, of all subjectivity and self-consciousness. Hence the author counts for nothing; hence, too, the ballad is difficult to imitate and most attempts in this way are ridiculous failures. In transmission the ballad regularly departs from the original form, least in the mouths of unlearned people, more in the hands of professional singers or editors. It is at its best when it has come down by a purely domestic tradition, yet even so it is sometimes influenced by printed literature; and much depends on the experience and selection of the reciters, and on their varying memory, which is, however, ordinarily remarkable for its tenacity. Less fortunate is the ballad when it passes through low mouths or hands, suffering corruption of various kinds,—in the style of the attorney's clerk, or the housemaid or the serving man or ostler, or blind beggar. In the hands of the

---

[12] Child, *op. cit.*, III, 462 note.
[13] Hustvedt, *op. cit.*, p. 255.   [14] *Ibid.*, p. 207.

Bänkelsänger or the minstrel, the ballad departs still further from its original form. Or, rewritten and marred, it may retain some original features, and there are thus degrees of departure from the original matter and manner. The broadside may, in turn, become tradition. It is, so far as it appears in Professor Child's collection, always founded on tradition, and this tradition lives after the composition of the broadside, and may influence the later versions of the printed form. Last comes the modern editor, and by him the ballad is sometimes lengthened,—by combination of different versions, or by interpolation of new stanzas, always more or less unlike the popular style; or it is sometimes "improved" or retouched, or emended, or altered,—changed to something in glaring contrast to the groundwork. Some results of the vicissitudes of transmission are, the changes of the hero's nationality, of his name, of his role; change of the scene of action; corruption of diction resulting in perversion of sense or in nonsense; introduction of learned words. The ballad thus suffers in transmission, and it is at its best when it is early caught and fixed in print. It is sometimes counterfeited or imitated, and counterfeits are included in the later collection for contrast, for much the same reason that thieves are photographed, or because they may contain relics of something genuine or better.

Of the subject-matter of the ballad, the sources may be, and in the best instances are, purely popular, consisting of material which appears only in popular literature. Professor Child mentions no instance where a prose tale is the source of a ballad, but the ballad, he says, may sometimes be resolved into a prose tale. Popular origin is attested by foreign parallels in folk-literature. Of such literature certain features or themes are characteristic, such as the quibbling oath, the miraculous harvest, the childbirth in the wood, the testament, the riddle, heroic sentiment, etc. The source may, again, be an actual occurrence, in which case the ballad, while not deliberate fiction, is yet not loyal to the fact. Or the source may be a romance, or the source of a romance, in which case oral tradition may be older than written, the ballad older than the romance. Or the source may be earlier ballads, mechanically and deliberately put together in later ones, made over and assimilated, as in A *Gest of Robyn Hode*. In the course of transmission certain features appear which are not characteristic of popular literature; the subject matter of the true ballad does not deal in extravagance, or exaggeration, or platitude; it is not prosaic, over-refined, cynical, sophisticated, sentimental, unnatural, trite, or moral, though the "pungent buckishness" of the broadside, and the gay cynicism of the minstrel, are foreign to it.

So far as technique is concerned, the ballad must have plot. The story may not be completely told; conclusion, transitions, and preliminaries may be omitted; but the result is not nonsense, the ballad is not incoherent. At its best it is, however, brief. It is careless of geography, and, except in some—and some of the best—of the Robin Hood ballads, it touches setting lightly. In dealing with the supernatural it does not attempt to explain the action or to describe supernatural figures; ghosts, however, do not walk without reason.

In style the ballad is artless and homely, and in it the conceit, and literary or learned words and phrases, are out of place. Yet it has certain conventions of its own, such as the "commonplace," the repetition of a message by a messenger, the verbally similar treatment of similar incidents as they occur in different ballads. Emotionally, the ghost ballad is impressive and affecting; and in general, the ballad may be infectious, or spirited and lifelike, or pathetic, or tender, or humorous, or vigorous and not lacking in color and flavor. It is essentially lyrical, and its lyrical quality is not less essential than plot. Often it absolutely requires the support of a melody and the comment of a burden. This burden sometimes foreshadows the calamity, sometimes enhances by contrast the gloom of the conclusion. It is usually less than the stanza with which it was sung; and, unlike the refrain, it was sung, not after the stanza, but with it. It is sometimes of different metre, sometimes not. The absence of the burden is in no case proof that it never existed.[15]

Although Child has laid down, probably for some time to come, the pattern for scholarly ballad study, it is not the only one followed by ballad editors today. In *The Oxford Book of Ballads,* Sir Arthur Quiller-Couch, for instance, follows Scott's method of collating a standard text from many versions. We are more aware than we used to be of diversities of editorial aim.Child's work has given us guides in study, safeguards for the integrity of folk poetry, and a collection stripped of all literary affectations, as the touchstone for every ballad student. His animating credo is perhaps found best in his own words:

Popular poetry cannot lose its value. Being founded on what is permanent and universal in the heart of man, and now by printing put beyond the danger of perishing, it will survive the fluctuations of taste, and may from time to time serve, as it notoriously did in England and Germany a hundred years ago, to recall a literature from false and artificial courses to nature and truth.[16]

[15] W. M. Hart, "Professor Child and the Ballad," *Publications of the Modern Language Association,* XXI (1906), 804–7.
[16] Child, "The Ballad," *Universal Cyclopedia,* I, 464.

Chapter 13

CECIL SHARP

IF, in his Cambridge study, Child could bring to life the quality of the British ballad in England and Scotland, what would he have done with American balladry, so much more prolific and lively in its traditional form, if he had turned his talents in this direction? He is singularly silent on the ballad in America. "A little girl in New York" has a version of "Sir Hugh" (155); a rare Border Raid ballad, "Archie o Cawfield" (188), is found in Plymouth, Massachusetts; from Stockbridge comes a "Gypsy Laddie" (200), and another from the singing of a lady in Huntington, Long Island, who may have learned it from a Revolutionary soldier; a "Fair Margaret and Sweet William" (74) from Massachusetts is dated about 1820. Emma Backus of Polk County, North Carolina, contributes "The Wife of Usher's Well" (79), "Lamkin" (93), and "The Maid Freed from the Gallows" (95). Not more than a handful in all, and Child's general conclusion is, as he writes to Grundtvig, that "the sources of British ballads are dried up forever." [1]

Ballad criticism in any age tends to regard the ballad as a thing of the past. The pre-Shakespearean clown sings his mother's songs lest they be forgotten. Of the survival of traditional song everyone from Ritson to Sharp is skeptical. "The editor has frequently heard of traditional songs, but has had very little success in his endeavors to hear the songs themselves." [2] "We know the ballad only in its last uncertain stages, and even that is now at an end." [3] "Sir Hugh" (155) and "The Maid Freed from the Gallows" (95), found in America in 1914, are "highly exceptional in occurring so recently." [4] Cecil Sharp, thirty-five years after Child, writes, "The English ballad is moribund; its account is well-nigh closed." [5]

[1] Hustvedt, *Ballad Books and Ballad Men*, p. 248.
[2] Ritson, *Ancient Songs*, p. ci.
[3] Gummere, *The Popular Ballads*, p. 286.
[4] Baldwin, *An Introduction to English Medieval Literature*, 235.
[5] Sharp, *English Folk-Song, Some Conclusions*, p. 102.

Child's own students were to disprove these statements, at first through chance discovery of the very ballads he had claimed were extinct, and then through deliberate search for them. Imbued by their master with a love for the ballad and with true standards for judging it, as they scattered over the country to teach, they were well prepared to recognize it in its American form, and began to turn up a harvest that Child himself never imagined.

The story of Josiah Combs may be told as showing how the multitudinous streams of folk song began to trickle down to the Bluegrass from faraway mountain coves and hollows of the Southern Appalachians. As a boy at the Hindman Settlement School, in Knott County, Kentucky, Josiah had comforted himself as he hoed corn or pulled weeds or hauled wood and coal, by singing long ballads he had learned from his father and mother, about Lord Thomas, or Barbry Ellen; and Katherine Pettit, one of the "fotched-on women" who conducted the school, although she knew little about the literary history of ballads, was struck with the remarkable repertoire of a little boy from back of beyond, who could sing about London Town and lords and ladies of high degree. She wrote his songs down and sent them to Professor George L. Kittredge, Child's successor at Harvard, and they appeared under the joint editing of Mr. Kittredge and Miss Pettit in *The Journal of American Folklore* in 1907.[6] Josiah eventually went on to college in the Bluegrass, where, in 1911, he worked on ballads with a student of Child, Professor H. G. Shearin, producing with him a *Syllabus of Kentucky Folk-Songs* which includes twenty Child pieces. His thesis at the Sorbonne, where he took a degree in Romance Languages in 1925, is on *Folk-Songs du Midi des Etats-Unis*. His subsequent career, which has taken him into university professorial ranks in this country, is more spectacular than that of most mountain boys and girls who went to college in the 1910's; but there were scores coming down to the lowlands at this time who knew as many songs as Josiah, and who contributed thus to the swelling stream of ballads now being collected. These were an indication to scholars of the vaster riches still held mountain-fast. Thus some substantial collections were in progress. Interest still centered, however, on the texts. The account of musical study must begin again with the amateur collector from firsthand mountain sources.

[6] *Journal of American Folklore*, XX (1907), 251–77.

Mrs. Olive Dame Campbell, whose husband, John C. Campbell, was director of the Southern Highland Division of the Russell Sage Foundation, often accompanied him on his trips of inspection to mountain schools. On one such visit, at the Hindman School, she heard one of the girls sing "Barbara Allen" (84). "That was what started me off . . . I was bewitched by the melody, so completely different from my childhood ones, and from that went on learning wherever I could find any singer." [7] Although she saw such collections of words as Josiah's, noted down by Miss Pettit, it was the music rather than the words that drove her on. By 1909 she had collected about seventy tunes, enough to persuade her that in the Southern Mountains was a valuable source of folk music which ought to have expert treatment, and she submitted her manuscript to the Sage Foundation for advice. Professor Kittredge and Professor L. R. Lewis of Tufts College both urged the Sage Foundation to proceed with publishing material which they recognized as not only unique, but indicative of greater riches in the area. Meanwhile Mrs. Campbell had found others in the mountains who had small amateur collections, and was anxious to bring them all together under scientific editorship. But since the right authority could not be found, many of the collectors preferred to keep their hands on what they had gathered, and the matter hung fire for some years—a period which must have been discouraging to those most unselfishly concerned with the work of salvage. But the delay was perhaps providential, for at this time Cecil Sharp arrived in America.

Sharp's approach to folk song had been that of a musician. He was a composer, an organist, a conductor, and a teacher. As a master of music in an English boys' school in the early nineties he had found nothing suitable for boys to sing; so he started to make his own collection of lively popular songs from printed works, occasionally inserting a traditional folk song. He seems to have been the first to use the folk song in schools. He became increasingly aware of the differences between songs collected from tradition and folk songs submitted to editing or imitation; and impressed by such pioneer work as that of Lucy Broadwood in collecting from the singers themselves, he set out to find his own songs, using as a base the house of a Somerset friend. He was almost instantly rewarded, for the first song he noted down was

[7] Letter to the writer.

from his friend's gardener, "The Seeds of Love," one of the finest in his whole collection.[8]

Cecil Sharp was over forty when he heard his first folk song. When he died at the age of sixty-three, he had collected from traditional singers in England and America some five thousand variants of songs and ballads. His notebooks, or photostat copies of them, are deposited at Clare College in Cambridge, at Harvard, and in the New York Public Library. As his notebooks filled up, he began at once to edit and publish. In the scrupulous care with which he studied every text and collated it with its kin, in his search for parallel treatments in other forms of literature, and in his critical discrimination, he ranks with Child. His study of the music of the songs, moreover, makes him so far indisputably the "Child" of the ballad tune.

It was logical that in the half-century following Child's work on texts, the musical parallels should be assembled. The men whom Child had trained were finding evidence of the life of his ballads as songs, and someone must inevitably have come to the fore to demonstrate the value of music in ballad study. That the man who actually did this was an Englishman seems to be the payment of a poetic debt. It was Child who had organized the mass of British ballad texts; it was Sharp who showed America her ballad tunes.

But it was Mrs. Campbell who showed the way to Mr. Sharp, introducing him, through her small amateur collection, to what might be retrieved in the Southern Appalachians by a trained musician. Sharp had no idea, when he was forced by the first World War to give up his work in England and come to America to lecture, that he was to find here a new field for collecting—that it was to be a turning point in

---

[8] It was "The Seeds of Love" that Hardy's Master Poorgrass sang at the sheep-shearing supper. Encouraged by the applause for his first song, "he rashly plunged into a second in the same breath, and after a few false starts:

'I sowe-ed the . . .
I sow'd th . . .
I sowed the-e seeds of love,
I-it was all i-in the-e spring,
I-in A-pril, Maay a-and sun-ny June,
When sma-all bi-irds they do sing.'

'Well put out of hand,' said Goggan, at the end of the first verse. ' "They do sing" was a very taking paragraph.'

'Ay! and there was a pretty place at "seeds of love," and 'twas well heaved out. Though "love" is a nasty high corner when a man's voice is crazed. Next verse, Master Poorgrass . . . 'Tis a very taking ballet.' "

(*Far from the Madding Crowd*, London, Macmillan, 1927, p. 178)

his work with English song and dance. At first he was hard to convince that we too had folk songs, and Mrs. Campbell, seeing in Cecil Sharp the possible answer to her search for the qualified editor of mountain music, found at the end of her special trip from the south to show him her tunes, a man who was reserved and skeptical about their merits. Warily he received her, critically he examined the tunes so unscientifically and yet so accurately noted down. And then,

> When he finally laid the pile of manuscripts on the table and turned to me, it was with a keen but relaxed and almost lenient look. All the charm of his most winning mood was shed on me as he explained how many people had brought "ballads" to him before, but that this was the first time he had come on any really original and valuable material.[9]

Mrs. Campbell had found her editor. And Mr. Sharp had found an invaluable collaborator. From that moment he forsook his lecture platform and followed the lure of the Appalachians. For a matter of three years, with a total of fifty weeks in the mountains, he traveled and collected, accompanied by Maud Karpeles, who worked with him here as she had for many years in England. Their headquarters was the Campbell home in Asheville, and the volume which appeared in 1917, *English Folk Songs from the Southern Appalachians*, bore Mrs. Campbell's name as well as Mr. Sharp's, and included thirty-nine of her tunes. In 1932 this book was amplified by Miss Karpeles to a two-volume edition including Sharp's later findings—in all 273 songs and ballads, and 968 tunes.

Sharp's work in this country might be construed by the jealous as an encroachment on others' preserves. It is to be noted that with unfailing courtesy and appreciation of what had already been done, he always consulted collectors before entering their field. Thus to Professor Alphonso Smith: "I should not wish to do this without your approval, or unless I felt assured of your cooperation." [10]

The difficulties of collecting, both in England where he had worked for years, and now in America, were enormous. "First catch your singer." This principle demanded absolute flexibility of plans: a letter in the morning mail would send him off at once to the most remote places, one scent leading to another. Although in England many of his singers belonged to a class attached to the land and therefore likely

[9] Fox Strangways, *Cecil Sharp*, p. 130.   [10] *Op. cit.*, p. 160.

to be found at home, he might upon arrival find that the quarry was sick abed, or had died, or that the visiting grandad had departed, or that the Gypsy encampment had pulled up stakes in the night and disappeared. Once the search for sword plays led him to the village of Ampleforth in Yorkshire, only to find that the leader of the players, now an old man, had gone to live with a married daughter in a large industrial town, and "I did use to have his address, but I've lost it." His informant being apparently helpless to find it, Sharp, with a flash of inspiration, looked through the contents of the china teapot on the mantelpiece—in a cottage household always the repository for valuables—and came upon a scrap of paper with the address he wanted. He set out at once, found the daughter, and her father in bed "with a poultice to keep him comfortable." The old man put his memory to work and dictated one of the fullest sword play texts ever recovered. Sharp took a second dictation a few weeks later to verify his notes, and none too soon, for the old man shortly died.[11] He followed the trail of "The Lark in the Morn" to an out-of-the-way village, to the cottage of the one person who knew it, from the cottage to the field where he found the singer, an old woman, at work. There in the cold wind, holding the lapels of his coat and closing her eyes, she sang it forthwith, Sharp doing his best to note it down. "When the song was finished, she gazed into his eyes with a sort of ecstacy, and in perfect detachment from herself, exclaimed, 'Isn't it lovely!' " [12]

Many of Sharp's songs are the result of being directed to a certain singer of a certain song; many, however, are pure lucky finds. The old man who sang Sharp a single stanza of "John Barleycorn," all he could remember of that remarkable ballad which is the life-and-death cycle of the folk play in lyric form, had heard it in his youth from a stranger passing through his village. Once in Kentucky Sharp and Miss Karpeles found themselves in a dismal and unpromising mining town. Miss Karpeles, however, said, "I'm not going to leave this town without a good song"; and knocking at the door of one of the dingiest of the little houses, she asked the woman who opened it if she knew any "song-ballets." "The Cuckoo," certainly as lovely as "The Lark in the Morn," was her prize. Folk songs are indeed thistledown, blown by the wind and caught on any bush; and when so much of the collector's work is actual drudgery, spending hours perhaps listening to inferior

[11] *Op. cit.*, p. 102.   [12] *Ibid.*, pp. 39–40.

songs in the hope that a real gem will be extracted from the singer's memory, the accidental finding of such treasure is so exciting as to repay all exertions.[13] Sharp collected most of his English folk songs from a dying generation, old people living in almshouses or with married children. What wonder that in the Southern Mountains, where everybody in the family knew the song, and it was often a youngster who prompted an older failing memory, he found a collector's paradise?

Collecting, however, was attended by great physical hardships. Journeys to remote spots must be undertaken, places of entertainment were strange, requirements for personal comfort must be ignored. Sharp was always frail, suffering increasingly from asthma, exacting as to diet, and with the Englishman's dependence upon tea at a regular hour. His achievements were very considerable in his orderly and familiar England, and in the Appalachians his difficulties were doubled. It was a rough, vast, strange country through which he traveled. The hotels in the little mountain towns were often execrable, and putting up for the night out in the country was an experience with hospitality rather than comfort. Heat and thunderstorms and strange insects and snake peril (all American phenomena) accompanied his walks to distant singers—for being no horseman he went everywhere on foot. But there was never a question of quitting. Barely recovered from a desperate bout with asthma brought on by early morning mists, he would set out on a seven-mile walk to visit a singer. Once Miss Karpeles, leaving him in bed to find a doctor, returned to discover him sitting up and noting down a song from a visitor. No journey was difficult, no hardship or illness noticeable if a song was at stake.

Physical difficulties are obvious, psychological ones less so. But it was never a serious problem for Sharp to establish proper contact with the singer, though there are many incidents recorded by other collectors, of singers who are suspicious, or surly, or capricious, or who refuse to sing because they have joined the church and no longer hold with "devil's ditties." Or worse still, their husbands or wives have "got religion" and will make trouble if they revert to godless songs. These prejudices must of course be respected. Sharp combined "the pachydermatous spirit and insidious bedside manner needed in order to

[13] See above, page 46, note on "King Henry V's Conquest of France," for collector's luck.

induce old folks to sing, with the skill to write down quickly queer modal tunes in queerer rhythms, set sometimes to highly embarrassing words." [14] But it was his natural interest in people rather than a deliberately cultivated manner that gave him his entrée. His approach was always without any tinge of patronage, with a respect for the dignity of the singer and with an evident love of the song. In the Appalachians, where suspicion of the stranger is oddly mingled with a warm hospitality, he was everywhere welcomed. "We like you," people said, "you're so common and homely." His singers often became life-long friends, with whom he kept up a correspondence and an exchange of gifts.

Sharp's absorption in the tunes made every contact with him an unforgettable experience. Thus when he came to the Pine Mountain School in Kentucky, finding there a group of people who were musical amateurs but convinced that the songs of the children were culturally valuable, to be sung early and often and as nearly as possible without change by "fotched-on" teachers, he made explicit values hitherto only vaguely felt; and from then on, casual though enthusiastic performance took on greater meaning. Elsewhere in the mountains, where there was no recognition as yet of the value and beauty of native songs, he was able to stir a spark that never died out. Today, all over the Southern Appalachians, the folk movement embraces a recreation program which emphasizes its local riches, largely because for three years a man traveled through the mountains with a divining rod which tapped the wellsprings of native music.

The history of ballad criticism would seem to illustrate the fact that nobody possesses this divining rod who does not have an insight into the intrinsic fineness of human nature. Addison assumed that "God must have loved the plain people, because he made so many of them," when he said that folk poetry must be good because the "rabble" were "the multitude of the nation." Scott's large humanity endears him still to the Border, where people even today allude to him as "Sir Walter"—as if he might come riding down the road at any minute. There are many anecdotes of Child's interest in people for themselves, of his special gift for friendship, of his charity and warmheartedness. This is reflected in what he says about the ballad: "Being founded on

[14] *The Musical Times*, XLVII (1906), p. 43. Report of a lecture by Cecil Sharp before the Tonic Sol-Fa Association.

what is permanent and universal in the heart of man . . . it will survive the fluctuations of taste," standing for "nature and truth." So for Cecil Sharp, it was the person as the creator of the folk song that accounted for song itself; it was the humanity beneath the product. His credo was the Romanticist's: "Folksongs, so far as they are the natural spontaneous products of uncultivated minds, must of necessity be beautiful, in the same way, and for the same reason, that all elemental things, the trees, clouds, hills and rivers, are beautiful." [15] Where poverty and ignorance and squalor would have turned away another man, Sharp penetrated beneath their surface to the human element, and thence to the artless art that is the folk song.

In estimating Sharp's work, one must recall that ballad criticism was at first marked by an almost complete indifference to the tunes. Percy, Scott, and Child, being men of letters, not musicians, left bequests which are literary in content, although Percy had some idea of a book which should include traditional songs, and Child prints fifty-four tunes in an appendix.[16] Scott made no secret of his inability to tell one tune from another. But for Sharp the tune was as important as the text, and not a line of verse appears in his notebooks without it. And since tunes are more easily remembered than words, his tunes are often complete where the verses are fragmentary. Sharp's demonstration of the ballad's dependence upon tune, and his evidence of the current practice of singing ballads, have resulted today in the inclusion as far as possible, in all serious collections, of tunes as well as words. In those collections where ballad texts must perforce appear without music, editors today emphasize that the ballad is "a story told in *song*." [17] Gerould, in *The Ballad of Tradition*, devotes a chapter to the subject of ballad music, and he elsewhere summarizes its function:

[15] Brockington, "Cecil Sharp," *The London Mercury*, XVII, 668.

[16] Leyden, in the advertisement to the 1833 edition of Scott's *Minstrelsy*, says: "The airs of some of these old ballads are for the first time appended to the present edition. The selection includes those which Sir Walter Scott himself liked best, and they are transcribed, without variation, from the manuscripts in his library." Henderson, however, who quotes this passage in his edition of the *Minstrelsy* (p. xxxviii), does not include the airs, as he doubts their genuine antiquity.

The amateur quality in the notation of some of the Child tunes may be gathered from his statement that "being then but a novice in music, he (Professor Scott, who collected from the singing of Mrs. Brown of Falkland) added in the copy such musical notes as he supposed might give some notion of the air, or rather lilts, to which they were sung." (*English and Scottish Popular Ballads*, V, 405.)

[17] *English and Scottish Popular Ballads*, ed. Sargent and Kittredge, Introduction, p. xi.

Since ballads are songs as well as stories, it is quite certain that their exquisite and subtle rhythms have resulted from the adaptation of words to music. . . . It is impossible to account for these beauties of rhythmic effect except by supposing that ballad singers (makers) have heard in their ears and felt in their blood the beat of the music.[18]

But other reasons than exclusively literary interest in the ballads have prevented the intelligent transcription of their tunes. Tunes, as we have said, were often omitted from the printed ballad, and this practice set the first literary editors in the way of looking only for texts. When people did become aware of the importance of the melody, and begin to write down traditional tunes, their inexperience or their musical prejudices stood in their way, and they wrote down what they thought they heard, or what they expected to hear, or what they considered the singer ought to be singing, rather than what the singer really sang. Thus they often missed the unique traits of folk music, and many a good tune lost, in amateur or conventionally musical recording, its essential quality, becoming so uninteresting as to discourage further attention.

A large part of the value of Sharp's collection lies in the fact that his songs have been carefully recorded from traditional singing, and are as untouched by the influence of print as it is possible to find songs. It has been frequently pointed out in these pages that tradition, with its sung or spoken rhythms, is what keeps the quality and strength of the song alive. Words and tune grow up together, not as separate things. Margaret Laidlaw reminded Scott that ballads "were meant for singin' and no' for writin' doon." Sharp's task was to save as much as possible of this unique quality of traditional song, and to do this he had to lay aside his conventional training, which other musicians had been unable to do. Self-schooled, self-scanned in a new technique, he deliberately forgot for the time being all his musical literacy, and taught himself to record exactly what he heard. This process called not only for intellectual and artistic honesty, but for singleminded concentration on the matter in hand. In his own words, "the listener must put off the habit of critic, divest himself of preconceived notions, seek not to analyze what he hears or compare it with art music of the concert

[18] *English Readings* (ed. Gerould, Jones, and Bernbaum, New York, The Ronald Press Co., 1939), I, 345.

hall, but prepare to receive impressions at once simple, direct, and elemental." [19]

A folk singer has a peculiar quality of voice that makes the music itself sound different: one is not sure of the intervals, or even the notes, and is puzzled by the frequent breaks of rhythm. Since the singer does not recognize his tune as existing apart from the story of his song—asked to hum the tune, or to recite the words, he is often at a loss—and since he considers the tune merely as a medium and not an end in itself, a background to enhance the beauty of the speech, his natural delivery sometimes does not sound like a tune at all. His curious tonal production often defies musical scoring, and his half-chant is more like speech than melody. And if he is old, toothless, and crack-voiced, the problem is increased. These are some of the reasons why the inexpert writing down of a folk song is so often the means of killing it. Its essential quality goes out of it unless all the fine distinctions can be caught. The nuances of tone and rhythm, inaudible or baffling to the amateur, become the concern of the expert.

It will be suggested that mechanical recording is the answer to the problem of accuracy. And so it is, today. But Sharp's work was done before technical facilities were satisfactory, though he did sometimes use a hand-power dictaphone. He tells of diverting the anger of a pious and domineering husband who returned from work to find his wife singing frivolous songs to a stranger: "See; I've got your wife's voice in a box." [20] But he felt in general hampered by mechanical inadequacy, and also by the self-consciousness of the singer. Since his day mechanical recording has made great progress and is very generally used. But even today rural electrification does not go everywhere, the most sensitive instruments break down, and the collector who cannot resort to pencil and paper is handicapped. Recording, too, is only half the battle. The problems of transcription from record to paper are still extremely complicated and by no means solved.

Thus writing down only what he heard, Sharp amassed a quantity of material which he was then able to submit to musical analysis; and he found that his queer tunes, with queerer rhythms, instead of defying musical canons, were actually regular according to the standards of

[19] *The Musical Times*, XLIX (1908), p. 371. Program Notes for a performance of folk songs in the Stationers' Hall for the Worshipful Company of Musicians.

[20] W. Shuldham-Shaw, *Cecil Sharp and English Folk Dances*, "Some Collecting Stories."

an earlier day. These tunes were made from the ancient modal scales of preharmonic music, the ancestors of the modern major and minor. Just as the dialect words of the countryman were often older, and sometimes better, than those of the townsman, so his tunes harked back to the discarded excellence of a forgotten age of melody. The modal quality especially evident in the American tunes implies their antiquity. The tune, more clearly remembered than the verse, has kept its integrity as the corruption inevitable in oral tradition has crept in on the words. If, then, accompanying the more fragmentary texts of American ballads we find excellent tunes of antique pattern, we can presuppose for those tunes an earlier, finer text. The high percentage of modal tunes found by Sharp, especially in America, proved their continuance today; and their peculiar suitability to folk song has been a matter of enthusiastic study ever since, not only for their musical evidence, but for some of the light they throw on ballad verse. Sharp's careful preservation of them affords a storehouse for the composer as well, in saving for England and America a treasure which was on the point of disappearing.

THE SEEDS OF LOVE [21]

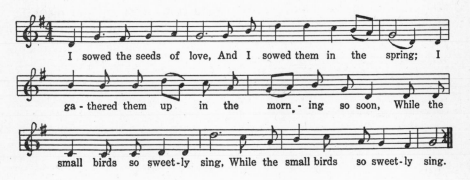

I sowed the seeds of love, And I sowed them in the spring; I ga-thered them up in the morn-ing so soon, While the small birds so sweet-ly sing, While the small birds so sweet-ly sing.

1. I sowed the seeds of love,
    And I sowed them in the spring;
  I gathered them up in the morning so soon,
    While the small birds so sweetly sing,
    While the small birds so sweetly sing.

[21] From Sharp, *One Hundred English Folksongs* (1916), p. 76. Reprinted by permission of Theodore Presser, Philadelphia. Published and copyrighted by Oliver Ditson Co., Boston.

2. My garden was planted well,
   With flowers everywhere,
   But I had not the liberty to choose for myself
   Of the flowers that I loved so dear.

3. The gard'ner was standing by,
   And I asked him to choose for me;
   He chose for me the violet, the lily and the pink,
   But those I refused all three.

4. The violet I did not like,
   Because it bloomed so soon;
   The lily and the pink I really overthink,
   So I vowed that I would wait till June.

5. In June there was a red rose-bud,
   And that is the flower for me.
   I oftentimes have plucked that red rose-bud,
   Till I gained the willow tree.

6. The willow tree will twist,
   And the willow tree will twine;
   I oftentimes have wished I were in that young man's arms
   That once had the heart of mine.

7. Come all you false young men,
   Do not leave me here to complain,
   For the grass that has oftentimes been trampled under foot,
   Give it time, it will rise up again.
   Give it time, it will rise up again.

KEEP YOUR GARDEN CLEAN [22]

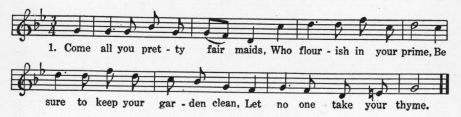

1. Come all you pret-ty   fair maids, Who flour-ish in   your prime, Be
sure to keep your   gar-den clean, Let   no one   take   your thyme.

1. Come all you pretty fair maids,
   Who flourish in your prime,
   Be sure to keep your garden clean,
   Let no one take your thyme.

[22] An American version of "The Seeds of Love," included for comparison. From Randolph, *Ozark Folksongs* (1946), I, 357. Reprinted by permission of the Missouri State Historical Society, Columbia, Missouri, Publishers.

2. My thyme it is all gone away,
   I cannot plant anew,
   And in the place where my thyme stood
   It's all growed up in rue.

3. Stand up, stand up, you pretty ʌope,
   Stand up, and do not die,
   And if your lover comes to you,
   Pick up your wings and fly.

4. The pink it is a pretty flower,
   But it will bud too soon,
   I'll have a posy of my own,
   I'm sure 'twill wait till June.

5. In June comes in the primrose flower,
   But it is not for me,
   I will pull up my primrose flower
   And plant a willow tree.

6. Green willow, green willow,
   With sorrow mixed among,
   To tell to all the wide world
   I loved a false young man.

THE LARK IN THE MORN [23]

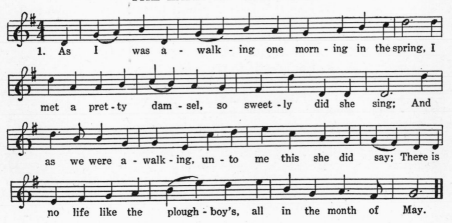

1. As I was a-walking one morning in the spring, I met a pretty dam-sel, so sweet-ly did she sing; And as we were a-walk-ing, un-to me this she did say; There is no life like the plough-boy's, all in the month of May.

1. As I was walking one morning in the spring,
   I met a pretty damsel, so sweetly did she sing;
   And as we were a-walking, unto me this she did say;
   There is no life like the ploughboy's, all in the month of May.

[23] From *Novello's School Songs* (1913), No. 996. Reprinted by permission of Novello and Co., London, Publishers.

2. The lark in the morn, she will rise up from her nest,
And mount up in the air with the dew all on her breast,
And like the pretty ploughboy, she will whistle and will sing,
And at night she will return to her own nest back again.

THE CUCKOO [24]

(Ref.) The cuck-oo is a pret-ty bird, She sucks flow'rs so sweet, She

brings us sweet mus-ic, In the spring of the year. 1. She

flies the moun-tains o-ver, She flies the world a-round, She

flies back to the moun-tains, and mourns for her love.

(*Refrain*)
    The cuckoo is a pretty bird,
    She sucks flow'rs so sweet,
    She brings us sweet music
    In the spring of the year.

1. (*Ref.* The cuckoo, *etc.*)
    She flies the mountains over,
    She flies the world around,
    She flies back to the mountains,
    And mourns for her love.
    (*Or*, And sits there and cries.)

2. (*Ref.* The cuckoo, *etc.*)
    They'll walk with you, they'll talk with you,
    They'll call you their own,
    While perhaps they have a true love
    Sits weeping at home.

3. (*Ref.* The cuckoo, *etc.*)
    Go away from me, Willie,
    And leave me alone,
    For I am a poor girl
    And a long ways from home.

[24] From Sharp, *English Folk Songs from the Southern Appalachians* (1932), II, 180.
Reprinted by permission of the Oxford University Press, London, Publishers.

Chapter 14

SOME CHARACTERISTICS OF FOLK TUNES

THE important role of the ballad tune, so far only implicit in this discussion, should now be made explicit, and some attention paid to qualities one notices as one comes to know ballads. There is a pervasive minor sadness about many of them. Some are of a free and chant-like simplicity, others more melodic and formally constructed. Although they take unexpected turns, certain note sequences, strange at first, become familiar as one's repertoire increases. Usually satisfying and sometimes inadequate, they vary in the degree of pleasure they give.

Like the ballad stories, the tunes have gathered up everything that came in their path—chanted recitative, dance rhythms and melodies, popular tunes circulated by the broadside writers, composed tunes from the theaters, and some which have drifted in from other countries. From all these sources and probably many others come the tunes in this book. But whatever their provenience, their treatment by oral tradition over a sufficient period of time has established certain traits which give them their peculiar flavor and that soundness which has led to their long life.

Most folk tunes are based on the ancient modal scales, which the amateur may learn by playing on the white keys of the piano from C to C, or from D to D, and so on. The characteristic quality of the scale is given by the position of the half-step. The C-to-C scale is Ionian, D-to-D is Dorian, G-to-G is Mixolydian, and A-to-A Aeolian—to mention the modes most frequently found in Anglo-American folk song.[1] Of these, the Ionian and Aeolian are the more common. The Ionian scale is practically the major; the Mixolydian differs from it in that it has a lowered 7th degree. The Aeolian is like the descending melodic minor, and the Dorian differs from it in having a raised 6th degree. In the following table of modal scales, the modes are shown first as they

[1] The names of these modes, together with those less familiar—Phrygian, Lydian, and Locrian (theoretical only)—were taken over into musical terminology from the church modes.

would be played on the white keys of the piano, and on the line below as reduced to the same dominant.

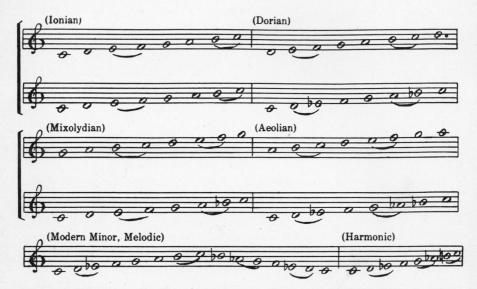

Reference to actual tunes is helpful in learning the modes.[2] "The Two Sisters" is in the Ionian mode; "The Sea Captain, or, The Maid on the Shore" is Mixolydian; "King Herod and the Cock" is Aeolian, and "Babylon" ("The Bonny Banks of Virgie O") is Dorian. The C-sharp in the latter tune is the characteristic note of the mode; in "The Sea-Captain" it is C-natural. A musician not grounded in theory, or surprised by the unusual note and not alert for accuracy, might miss the modal character of the tune, and early collectors and composers frequently sinned in this respect.[3] Modern musicians such as Vaughan Williams sedulously observe the modal character of a tune when setting it, and in today's concerts one often hears modal music of recent composition.

The modal tunes of earlier times disappeared from art music after the seventeenth century, being unsuited to the new harmonic requirements, but they were preserved in the countryside among singers and musicians as yet untouched by the change in musical styles, and they are still the folk musician's choice. Very often a new tune which he

[2] Unless otherwise indicated, the musical examples in this chapter are taken from tunes appearing elsewhere in this book.

[3] Sharp, *English Folk-Song, Some Conclusions*, pp. 48 ff.

hears does not suit him, and he changes it to his favorite mode by altering a note or two. Thus the cheap and banal "It ain't goin' to rain no more" becomes Mixolydian under a Kentucky Mountain fiddler's bow, picking up fresh character.

IT AIN'T GOIN' TO RAIN NO MORE

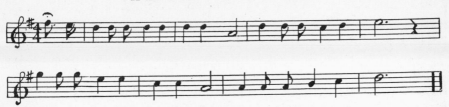

Usually, however, the history of a tune shows the reverse process, the modal tune becoming changed to a modern scale. The seventeenth-century "Oak and the Ash" [4] in the harmonic minor is derived from the sixteenth-century Aeolian dance tune, "Goddesses." [5]

THE OAK AND THE ASH

GODDESSES

[4] Chappell, *Popular Music of the Olden Time*, II, 457.
[5] Playford, *The English Dancing Master* (1650), p. 52.

The ancient gapped scales are often found in the Appalachians, where five- and six-note tunes are common. Sharp postulates that the gapped scale is the antecedent of the diatonic, the primitive chant from which the more elaborate tune evolved.[6] As more notes were added, they were weak, auxiliary rather than structural. "The Wife Wrapt in Wether's Skin" is hexatonic Dorian, lacking a 3rd. "Edward" is pentatonic, its scale lacking a 2nd and a 6th: if the 6th is B-natural, the tune is Dorian; if B-flat is preferred, the tune is Aeolian. In cases where the mode is doubtful because of missing notes, the singer may determine it by introducing these notes as he slides over the gap in the scale, to see which seem to him most in keeping with the tune.

Though limited by the gaps in the scales, the folk tune is melodically rich in its many modes, and makes much of its resources. A first hearing of "The Souling Song," [7] for instance, gives no sense of limitation, yet only four notes are used.

THE SOULING SONG

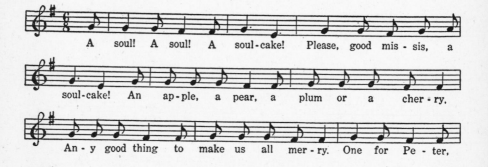

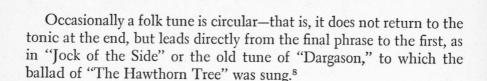

Occasionally a folk tune is circular—that is, it does not return to the tonic at the end, but leads directly from the final phrase to the first, as in "Jock of the Side" or the old tune of "Dargason," to which the ballad of "The Hawthorn Tree" was sung.[8]

---

[6] *English Folk Songs from the Southern Appalachians*, I, xxxi.
[7] Broadwood, *English County Songs*, p. 30.
[8] Words from Ritson, *Ancient English Songs*, II, 44. Tune from Playford, *op. cit.*, p. 71.

DARGASON

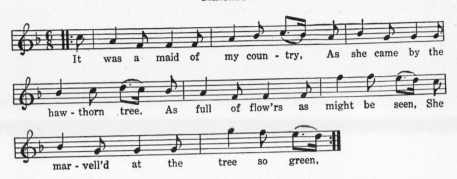

It was a maid of my coun-try, As she came by the haw-thorn tree. As full of flow'rs as might be seen, She mar-vell'd at the tree so green,

The melodic figures are as formal and typical as the rhetorical figures of the verse. There are characteristic openings and cadences, favorite groupings and sequences of notes, which soon become as familiar as "One morning in May" or "Out of her bosom there grew a red rose." The favorite musical idioms of English singers form a basic language of folksong.[9] The leap of an octave is common, as in "The Cruel Mother." The gapped scales perhaps account for some unusual intervals, like the jump of a 6th in "Sir Patrick Spens." [10]

SIR PATRICK SPENS

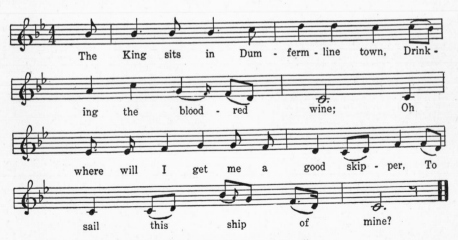

The King sits in Dum-ferm-line town, Drink-ing the blood-red wine; Oh where will I get me a good skip-per, To sail this ship of mine?

[9] Sharp, *English Folk-Song, Some Conclusions*, chap. vii.
[10] Greig, *Last Leaves of Traditional Ballads and Ballad Airs Collected in Aberdeenshire*, p. 47.

The beat of the tune is usually fundamentally regular, absorbing into its rhythm any irregularities of the verse, and giving to the ballad a feeling of fluidity akin to plainsong:

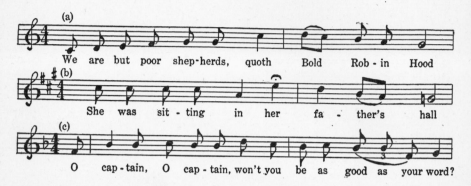

Superimposed upon the basic regular pulse, however, are minor and surface irregularities. The more closely allied to speech, the more frequent are these irregularities; and many ballads are half-spoken, half-sung, in a sort of *parlando*. Many ballad tunes seem to have evolved from a stereotyping of rhythmic speech, which has gradually taken on more and more melodic shape. Here only the careful and sensitive ear of the collector who is alive to the vagaries and subtleties of the folk tune will catch and painstakingly note the quality of rhythmic freedom which enlivens it. The conventional or amateur musician will reduce it to a more ordinary pattern.[11] "The False Knight upon the Road" and "The Hangman" show this speech quality allied with varying rhythms. "Barbara Allen," while more melodic, still departs from regularity, as the constant changes in time indicate.

The close association of tune and speech is seen very often in the tunes where the note-for-syllable relationship exists. If one begins to recite the "Hangman" ballad, one soon finds that he is singing the tune; the speech outline becomes fixed in melodic line. There is practically no slurring; for every syllable there is just one note. Such words as "walked" acquire a sort of Scotch snap, with a strong accent on the first note. This is what happens to the voice: often a word begun on

---

[11] On the other hand, too much musical machinery confuses the layman, and detracts from the essential simplicity of the tune and its integral relationship with the words. The variety of treatment of the tunes from printed sources in this book reflects some of the present uncertainty in folk song notation.

a higher pitch drops at once to a lower note. "The False Knight upon the Road" shows the sort of tune that would evolve from more emphatic and dramatic recitation. In such words as "child," "O—," with its decorated curve, and "knight," the tune reflects the natural change of pitch of the voice. Tunes like these would seem to be the direct result of repeated recitation. Barry, indeed, claims that the form of the "Hangman" ballad given in this text belongs to a folk tale treatment older than Child's more melodic and metrical "Maid freed from the Gallows" (95),[12] a form which has also, in such songs as "The Briery Bush," come down in tradition today.[13] Folk song, Gilbert and Sullivan patter, and jazz are all essentially singable because of this quality: the melody is a development of what the voice normally does, of the curve it takes, in the chant that is but one remove from speech.

Since it is the story which must be projected, the folk singer pays great attention to his words. Even the more melodic tunes show a submission to the requirements of diction. "Lord Rendal," for instance, carries us a stage beyond the speech-like "Hangman" or "The False Knight." The tune, beautiful in its own right, still obeys the dictates of syllabication. A glance at the other tunes in these pages will further show how true it is that the note-for-syllable arrangement is prevalent in folk song. A third stage of melodic development is found in many ballads where the first line is repeated twice, sometimes with internal refrain, like "The Two Sisters" or "The Three Ravens." These tunes are more independent in themselves, but they still enhance the words and they never divert attention from them.

The continuous rhythmic check on the adaptation of words and music has no doubt helped to form and maintain that poetic enigma, the ballad stanza. Most ballad tunes are essentially two long phrases, which may be broken up half-way into four short ones. Similarly the ballad quatrain may often be cast into the form of the seven-stress couplet, matching the long phrases of the tune, while its median break matches the four short musical phrases.[14]

[12] Barry, *British Ballads from Maine*, p. 212.
[13] See *Novello's School Songs*, No. 1080, and other collections.
[14] See Gerould, *The Ballad of Tradition*, pp. 125 ff., and Hendren, A *Study of Ballad Rhythm*, pp. 11 ff.

We can arrange "Mary Hamilton" in this way:

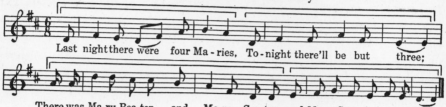

Last night there were four Ma-ries, To-night there'll be but three;
There was Ma-ry Bea-ton, and Ma-ry Sea-ton, and Ma-ry Car-mi-chael and me.

Thus there is a consonance of musical phrase and metric unit. The completeness of musical statement, also, matches the self-contained stanza, with its completeness of idea. This close agreement would indicate that ballad tune and verse have evolved together. The tune, however, has another function—to keep the story continuous and flowing. When one recalls not only the ballad's stanzaic unity, but its tendency to move without explanation from scene to scene, this continuity of tune becomes more important. Modal tunes succeed particularly well in providing this transition, and prevent any break in the listener's interest. The Dorian and Aeolian tunes, in particular, lead almost inevitably from the end of the final phrase back to the beginning. The occasional circular tune, since it is not a complete musical statement, is especially effective in providing this continuity.

The iteration of the ballad tune has perhaps influenced some of the rhetorical devices of ballad verse. It is quite possible that that most characteristic trait of all, incremental repetition, may have developed through association of verse and tune, the pattern of the melody suggesting the pattern of the narrative. When, for example, the second sister is approached by Baby Lon, the tune which has accompanied the telling of the first episode suggests similar wording for the second, which therefore quite naturally begins, "He took the second one by the hand," and, line for line, follows the earlier model.

An aspect of the ballad tune quite as important as these structural relations of verse and melody is its contribution to mood and feeling. While there is a similar bareness and restraint in both verse and tune, melody and rhythm do supply an element of satisfaction to both singer and listener, compensating for the unadornment and reticence of the text. The tune, moreover, possesses a certain chameleon quality. As the story develops, it is capable of receiving from the text, as well as contributing to it. Thus, without any dramatization or exploiting by the singer, it grows more emphatic, as in "Edward," or more stately and solemn, as in "King Herod and the Cock," or more pathetic, as in "Mary Hamilton." This may be due partly to the singer's feeling that "he's the feller it's happening to." But with these mysterious changes of emotional color, it still remains in the background. The test of a good tune is its ability to serve the narrator in this way, never obtruding itself; and the test of much good folk singing is this manner of treatment.

The emotional contribution of the tune is made through the variety of modes and the variety of rhythm. While we no longer believe, like the ancient Greeks, that each mode evoked a corresponding mood,[15] or like the Church Fathers that the Ionian *modus lascivus,"* being associated with secular song, awoke carnal desires and should not be used for sacred purposes, we still react to the forthright, direct statement of an Ionian or Mixolydian tune, and to Aeolian sentiment and reflection. Pace and rhythm accent the spirit of each ballad. There is the light and exciting but unhurried movement of "Jock of the Side" and "The Gypsy Davy," the martial tread of "Sir Patrick Spens," the liquid flow of "Lord Lovel," the regular pulse of "Robin Hood and the Tanner." The religious themes of "King Herod and the Cock" and "The Joys of Mary" are matched by tunes of great nobility and dignity. In many of the narratives, like "The Wife of Usher's Well" and "The Little Turtle Dove," a sense of unlimited leisure on the part of singer and listener alike is imparted by the frequent use of the five-beat measure, drawing out by an extra beat the linked sweetness of what might be, if noted without care, merely another regular 4/4 tune. In the feminine endings of "Barbara Allen" or in such dwellings on unaccented syllables as we find in "The Cruel Mother" or "The Nightingale," the solitary singer further invokes atmosphere. This individual treatment inevitably disappears in choral singing. A folk song is by nature a "lonesome tune," a solo. But the abiding impression left with you, after listening to such singing, is one of essentially steady forward movement, without haste and without rest, which is helped rather than hindered by these minor rhythmic irregularities.

[15] Such phrases as "the Dorian mood / Of flutes and soft recorders" and "Lap me in soft Lydian airs," from Milton, and Dryden's "Softly sweet, in Lydian measure" derive from the Greek idea of the ethical influence of the different modes.

Incremental repetition within the stanza attains its full effect only when assisted by the tune. The mounting interest of the musical phrases provides emphasis and thus emotional excitement for the repeated line. This is the beauty of such songs as "The Two Sisters," "The Three Ravens," and "Edna's Song." The tunes of the dialogue ballads show their versatility of mood, and one finds no two alike. Consider, for example, the diverse degrees of curiosity and apprehension expressed in these similar questions, as brought out by the tunes:

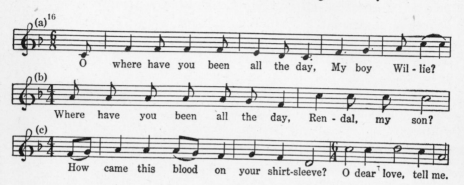

O where have you been all the day, My boy Wil - lie?

Where have you been all the day, Ren - dal, my son?

How came this blood on your shirt-sleeve? O dear love, tell me.

For most ballads there is an inherent resemblance in the tune variants, as there is in the texts. Most "Barbara Allen" tunes are generically similar, as are those for "Geordie." For some ballads, like "Mary Hamilton," there seem to be two families of tunes. Different tunes for the same song serve different purposes and provide different effects. Compare, for instance, the two versions in this book for "The Elfin Knight" (2), the chipper and sprightly "Cambric Shirt" and the pleasantly sentimental "Scarborough Fair."

It is from a full response to the mood of these modal tunes that one derives complete pleasure in ballads—a pleasure never gained from reading, or from the singing of a single verse, or from a single singing of a ballad through. A good tune is known only through many repetitions.

[16] Sharp, *One Hundred English Folksongs,* p. 132.

Chapter 15

AMERICAN FOLK SONGS AND SINGERS

BECAUSE of its very nature, the folk song depends for its existence on a certain kind of social and economic framework, and the student of folk song thus finds himself becoming a student of folkways. We have said that ever since people began to notice the songs of the countryside, they have spoken of them as almost extinct. And today, as we look for a source of traditional song, we realize that the passing of the "blind crowder," the ballad-hawker, and the milk-maid singer, together with their occupations, has removed many possibilities for gathering songs that former generations possessed. Has anyone taken their place today?

It is apparently true that those countries which have developed industrially have not preserved folk customs to the extent that those parts of the world have done where people still lead a pastoral or an agricultural life. But folk customs have a surprising amount of endurance, and have sometimes lived on in an underground way in the most industrially developed districts. In the midst of Arnold Bennett's Five Towns country in Staffordshire, with its potteries and smoking chimneys, the ancient ritual Horn Dance is still annually performed in the village of Abbots Bromley. In this country in recent years the Saturday night square dance has been brought to the city by city people from their skiing week ends. Dance is a group pursuit, demanding special conditions for survival, but song, which can be kept alive by one person, has an even greater chance for life

Although recent discoveries have shown us that we must not exclude towns and cities from our search for folk song, it is still true that the country is our richest field. Cecil Sharp's English collections come from rural settings, or from gypsies wandering always on the fringes of organized society, or from an occasional ancient pensioner in an almshouse, or from an old salt, whose days before the mast belong to a type of life that will never return. Sharp thought that they were the last fragments of a dying tradition until his American journeys in 1917 put him in touch with a paradise for the song collector, where people still removed from commercial and literate influences, still living close to the realities of existence, depended upon their own resources for entertainment.

The excitement of finding at our very door the conditions that keep alive the folk song, even though that discovery took place some thirty years ago, is still fresh in the minds of American folklorists. Child's work, impressive and definitive though it was, was yet "armchair study" gathered largely by correspondence and from libraries. After his students began to turn in samples of the living ballad, another day dawned for the ballad collector. From now on, it was to be the traveler along country roads to the door of the singer, who was to give the last word on the nature of the folk song. Today it is studied against a background of Nova Scotia fishing village, Newfoundland farm, Kentucky mountain cornfield, or Michigan lumber camp.

THE SOUTHERN APPALACHIANS

Reference throughout these chapters to the survival of ancient ballads in America has pointed frequently to the Southern Appalachians, and many of our ballad examples have been chosen from what has been gathered there. We know of the country as remote and romantically isolated, to the great advantage of folk song continuity. But what is that country really like? What exactly is it that has kept these riches fairly intact for us? How do these folk singers live and think? Can we find today the ideal conditions that gave Sharp and the others their opportunity?

The Southern Appalachian region may be defined as extending from Maryland to Georgia, following roughly the line of seacoast but about two hundred miles inland, a section shut off from the rest of the world by parallel mountain chains, into whose corresponding valleys migration has slowly filtered. The region includes today all types of life from the urban to the super-rural, but the difficulties of road building and travel have kept the rural parts much to themselves, so that the people, having once penetrated them, have remained for generations practically ignorant of the world beyond their own valleys. From Revolutionary times on for about a century people of English origin were working their way from the tidewater country of Virginia and North Carolina westward across the mountains in search of the promised rich farm lands; and the Scotch-Irish settlers from Maryland and Western Pennsylvania were pressing south, following the rivers and valleys, into the same wilderness, in search of good hunting, solitude and independence. English and Scotch-Irish stock predominate today, though some family names bear witness to German and Huguenot blood. Uncle Calvin Nolan's story of how his family came into the mountains is typical of many others.

His "great-grandpap, when he was only a chunk of a boy," was playing on the deck of a ship in Dublin harbor, and was carried out to sea before he knew it. The sailing master would not turn back, and the lad was forced to work his passage to America, "as was the way for one in his fix." He landed in Maryland and was bound out seven years to learn the potter's trade. One day while he was molding saucers, Miss Mary Wadkins came along and showed such interest in his occupation that he dropped a hot saucer into the apron she daringly held outstretched. The saucer burned a hole through the apron, and broke as it fell to the floor. "This action," said Uncle Calvin, "led to talk, which *pro*duced an inti*ma*cy, so to courtin' and weddin'."

The tale has it that he became one of the first gentlemen of Maryland and one of Washington's bodyguard. When the Revolutionary War was over, he settled in Mecklinburg County, Virginia, where Uncle Calvin's grandfather was born. Then you have the picture of the pioneer going deeper into the wilds, as far as the Clinch River in Virginia. "Come along the War of 1812," he volunteered at Tazewell, fighting under General Gaines at Fort Erie. Later, being "the game-follerin' kind," he led his family along the Wilderness Road, through Cumberland Gap, and into Kentucky County, Virginia, as Kentucky was then called. Where Middlesboro now is, he found a "wild and unappropriated land," which he and his son surveyed and which properly would belong to the Nolans, had they remained there instead of continuing to follow the game up the Pine Mountain valley. "Grandpap's twelve children populated the wilderness a right-smart in those days."

"Well," Uncle Calvin continues, "I've seed a sight of changes in my day. Them war the days of Injuns behind trees and pant'ers a-yellin' of a night. I've seen the woods full of wild turkey and deer, and I've seed 'em go west that man wouldn't *mo*lest 'em. My pappy used to throw rocks out of the path and say they'd be a road through here some day, and now there is,—and another one a-comin' across the top of the mountain." [1]

[1] *Notes from the Pine Mountain Settlement School*, November, 1921.

In the westward progress of the pioneers many were left behind in the mountains, some because they liked the independence of life there, others because they lacked the persistence to finish the hard journey to the Bluegrass or the Prairies. They settled the rich bottomlands at the mouths of the rivers, and their sons, looking for game or fresh land, followed the smaller watercourses to their heads, building their log houses, hunting and planting corn, using up the resources of the land and "populating the wilderness a right-smart." This process repeated itself, until today, when the descendants of the early settlers have reached the very heads of the hollows, the game is gone, their living must be wrested from the steep and barren mountainsides which after back-breaking toil are cleared of forest and forced to grow the corn that is the family's mainstay. They are now at an impasse: if they went further they would cross the mountain ridge and meet settlers coming up the other side. The mountains have closed in behind them; a green and rocky wall shuts out the rest of America. The section thus enclosed has been likened to an island in the heart of America, about as large as the Thirteen Colonies, with a similar population and ways. Until the turn of the century "our contemporary ancestors" pursued their pioneer manner of life and speech, with little influence from outside. Ancient farm methods, primitive medicine, household arts of spinning and weaving, and the tales or songs of their forebears generally prevailed. Generations of toil in combating the physical hardships of the country, instead of developing ingenuity and new methods, turned people back on inherited ways and bred a fatalism that kept them from self-improvement. Even the children of literate parents did not always learn to read and write. People used to level country did not adapt themselves to mountain farming. There was no money in circulation and economy depended upon barter. And the population continued to increase.

Uncle Calvin's farm was, however, near the "public road," and he watched the progress of the new road over the mountain. Like many another mountaineer whose memory went back to days of the trackless forest, he had seen the change come. After 1900 new roads began to penetrate the country, and a railroad was built here and there to take out timber, and later, coal. Since that day industry and the tourist trade have changed the face of the Appalachians, and mines, railroads, factories, and towns mushrooming up around them have drawn people from the lonely mountain farms, while motor roads have brought the head of the hollow within hours, instead of days, of the town. It should be borne in mind, therefore, that the following reconstruction of mountain life belongs to a period which has recently closed, and that only occasionally one may find today the ways of life described here, which saved the ballad for us.

———

Uncle Bill Forrester, asked where he lives, will give you not a post office for his address, but "Grassy Branch of Baker's Fork of Wolf of Coon of Cutshin," visualizing thus for you the journey to his remote dwelling. One may follow a wagon road along Cutshin to within a dozen miles of his house, though as "wagon road" it would hardly be recognized, so often does it disappear in the creek bed. Cutshin, they say, is named from the many crossings of the creek, and the consequent damage to the horses' shins on an icy morning. Up Wolf Creek to Coon, named from creatures once found there, the way becoming constantly narrower and steeper. One may still sit a nag, however. But the path up Grassy Branch must be traveled on foot, through woods and thickets of rhododendron by a tumbling watercourse and over rocks where rare ferns grow, to the grass patch that surrounds Uncle Bill's log house. The ridges gather around, rising steeply. The winter sun has set at three o'clock; it rose at ten. The cornfield, set on the precipitous mountain slope, is the central fact of existence. The children know the seasons as "plantin' time," "hoein' time," and "fodder-pullin'." Christmas? Yes, on the sixth day of January. So it was in England until 1751. Down on Wolf they celebrate New Christmas, December 25th, and Uncle Bill calls it "the shootin'est, drinkin'est, killin'est, chair-flingin'est day of the whole year." Back at his house they still keep Old Christmas, a day of sober and quiet family reunion. While he would not go so far as to say that on Old Christmas Eve the cattle really do kneel down and the elder bushes bloom out as the Holy Family passes by, he would never deny that this miracle, so long believed in by his foreparents, might not come to pass.

Uncle Bill's nearest neighbors live five miles away and are not very friendly, because three generations ago a dispute broke out between them concerning the location of a surveying line, one man holding that it should have been thrown the other side of a certain holly bush, the second as stoutly holding that the bush was his.

And it's what did you fall out about,
  O, my love, tell me?
About a little bit of a bush
  That soon would have been a tree.

Neighborly relations, therefore, are still strained. In fact, Uncle Bill takes his revolver with him when he goes down the branch.

This is a trip, however, that he makes very infrequently, for almost all his needs are supplied at home. In the open weather he goes to the mill which once a week grinds meal for people within a radius of twenty miles. At such times he calls at the store and brings back salt and coffee, enough to last for some time. At home there is plenty to do. The first frost has come, and a hog is to be killed: lard, sausage and "fat-meat" will fill the smokehouse, while for a few days there is a feast of fresh meat, with spareribs at every meal. The plenty associated with such a time has provided the mountaineer with an adjective signifying fantastic abundance. "Gee-oh, haint this the hog-killin'est place for books that ever I did see!" said a boy from the mountains when he first entered the Berea College library. The hide of the critter killed last month is now well tanned. Uncle Bill will be able to work on the children's shoes before the fire tonight, but he must whittle some wooden pegs for them first. Fodder is gathered and stacked, even the younger children helping their mother shuck corn. Popcorn around the fire tonight. Bins of corn for the animals, shocks left in the fields for winter feeding. Perhaps, up in the woods, a moonshine still which transforms a large part of the crop into condensed form so it can be "boodgetted up in packs" and taken across the mountain to town. The family cow has wandered up onto the mountain, and Ellender, age eight, is sent to hunt her. She goes off saying little, but with a prayer in her heart that it may not be a long search. If Pappy's fences have broken down and let the cow loose, she may be miles away. Pappy was away three weeks in the spring, making the rounds of his fields and mending fences after the winter storms. She remembers her mother's old song-ballet about Little Matthy Grove:

O what if I am Lord Dannel's wife?
  Lord Dannel's gone from home . . .
Lord Dannel's gone to see his fences,
  To see his fences, sir.

The sheep are cropping around the house, their new coats thick after the summer's shearing. The spinning wheel whirs on the porch, Fair-Annie walking rhythmically back and forth as the yarn grows in her fingers. Inside, Mammy is making the most of the daylight hours at the loom. It is threaded up with a piece of linsey. The children can wear their cotton jeans that she wove in the winter for a while longer; the linsey-woolsey will soon be ready to make into winter clothes, and one set apiece will see them through, eked out with last year's outgrown clothes for underwear. Maybe when this work is done she can indulge herself and make a coverlet. She meditates: the blue-pot is standing milkwarm by the fireside, ready for dyeing. There is plenty of sedge grass and hickory bark for yellows and greens. She has some extra-soft yarn saved up specially—not a "belly-hank" in the lot. A blue and white kiver, now. She might copy her granny's pattern of "Sixteen White Snowballs," but she kindly favors trying out a new one. She has figured it out in her head—she might call it "Cat-track and Snail-trail."

Dinner time. Cabbage, boiled potatoes, shucky beans with "meat" (a piece of salt pork). Cornbread, of course. Sweet butter, buttermilk, sweet milk. A jar of peaches salvaged from the many she put up that spoiled. Sterilizing jars, when you have to bring the water from the creek and build a fire under the outdoor kettle to heat it, is a task often unwisely shortened.

The children play in the yard. In the midst of her work she calls out to remind them that yesterday Pappy killed a rattler in them bushes; they'd better watch out less'n hits mate comes today to search for hit. The baby has "the thrash," hits pore little mouth is so sore! The twins, Vergil and Homer, will soon be back with medicine: there was a stranger stayed the other night with the Hensleys on Coon, a "man that never seed his pappy." He had offered to send the time-honored remedy for thrush, a little water poured by anyone born posthumously, from his shoe into a bottle for the baby to drink.

School? Yes, but you have to go clear to the Mouth of Wolf, five miles. The children hardly get there before it's time to turn back. Yes, hit's a good school. Fourteen children and a good teacher: he keeps good order; he whups 'em good. Fair-Annie went a whole term— from July to January—stayed with some kinfolks on Wolf. She learned to read a little, and can write her name. But Grandpap's books on the dark shelf by the chimney haven't been opened for years. *Pilgrim's Progress*, the Bible (King James Version), and a book in a strange language. That was where they found the names for the twins. There was another book that got lost—Grandpap used to read it to them, a story about that feller in the Bible, Samson, but it was in poetry.

The days pass much alike. Plenty of work, some of it grimly back-breaking, as when a new clearing is to be made; some of it pleasant routine. Responsibility for everyone in the family. At corn-hoeing time they all go to the field for the day. The baby is left under a shade tree, the next-least-un staying by to watch out for snakes. The others work up and down the long rows in the broiling July sun. Around the house there is always cooking, splitting wood, fetching water. The fine points of housekeeping, such as daily sweeping and weekly washing, are kept to a minimum in the face of more compelling demands.

An occasional break in the routine comes with illness. Sometimes Aunt Nancy Browning, the midwife, comes to stay. With biblical simplicity and directness Mammy meets her time. The birth-stool is brought from the loft. Pappy and the older girls stand by. The baby is wrapped in a piece of old linsey for the time being, until somebody can borrow a needle from a neighbor and make a dress. Mammy is able to work some in a few days, and Aunt Nancy goes on to her next appointment down Cutshin way.

The children all remember when Grandpaw died. It was the only time the women from down on Coon had ever come to spend the night. While the men built the black-walnut coffin in the yard, the women were busy in the house making the shroud (the coffin lining, not a corpse-garment). Every final detail was carried out by the family or neighbors. Burial was immediate, and another grave-house, or shelter to keep the ground from washing away from the grave, was added to the cluster on the hill, with its encircling fence, and the gate inscribed "God rest them sleeps here." But although Grandpaw died three years ago, his funeral has not yet been preached, for Preacher Blair has been busy with other funerals every October since. October is the best month for a funeral-occasion, for then the roads are dry and the crop is harvested and people can travel. Word has been norated about that Grandpap's funeral will be this year. There will be people riding in from miles around, and staying for the

CLOVER FORK, HARLAN COUNTY, KENTUCKY
(Courtesy of Arthur W. Dodd)

great dinner that will be cooked. Even Mammy's sister, married to a furriner who lives on the Middle Fork ten miles away, is coming back for the first time since her wedding. There will be even more to eat at the funeral, the children are told, than for the infare when Cindy-Ellen was married. They remember those nights beforehand, when they were hurried off to bed in the four-poster at an early hour because the young couple who were "talkin'" needed the privacy of the hearthside.

> He moved his chair up to my side,
> His fancy pleased me well,
> I thought the spirit moved him
> Some handsome tale to tell!

Cindy-Ellen and her young man just went off to the county seat and were married by the judge, but when they came back, all the neighborhood collected for the feasting and jollity of the infare and the chivaree.[2]

Once a stranger found his way up Grassy Branch and spent the night. He was fotched-on for sure, didn't have any kinfolk in this country. He was friendly and pleasant, "common and homely," they told him—and they had a fine time with him. He could sing song-ballets mighty-nigh as good as Pappy's. They swapped stories, too, about Jack in the bean tree, and Old Sol Shell who shot a peach-pit into the woods one winter's day and next year in that very same place saw a buck with a peach tree growing right out of hits head, and hit a-bloomin'. But the song-ballets were the best. The stranger could write, and put down every one of Pappy's songs in his little book. The children sang too, sometimes remembering verses the others had forgotten. Around the hearth that night, while apples roasted and corn popped, the singing went on and on, one child after another dropping off to sleep and being put down on one of the beds. Two of them awoke the next morning in different beds; they had been moved in the night to make way for the stranger. But song-ballets at night were no novelty; that was the way most evenings were spent. What was less usual was that the next morning, instead of going to work, Pappy continued to sing songs for the stranger. Even the daily chores were

[2] The infare is the wedding feast; the chivaree is the rough and noisy "welcome" given to the young couple at midnight in their new home.

neglected, in the face of such an unheard-of combination of a visiting stranger and an opportunity to sing songs to each other.

———

In the old-fashioned mountain home of thirty years ago one finds the ideal conditions for the preserving of folk song. It provided complete isolation from the outside world, and was almost cut off from the nearby haunts of men. It was economically self-sufficient, the family laboring for what they needed, and resting when that was secured. When necessities come hard, people are satisfied to stop work when they have enough; and when their food is the result of their own toil, they can trust nature to provide for them again at the right time. As for money, there was practically no use for it. Even the country store accepted payment in kind. There was leisure then, and a man is not afraid of leisure when he possesses inner resources for using it well. The literate man is limited, for he can read only when he has books, and enjoy music only when there is an instrument and somebody, usually professionally trained, to play on it. Old Mrs. Howard railed at her daughter, fresh from her settlement school training and so determined to clean house that they none of them had a chance to sit on the porch and look at the mountain, "and hit all October-colored." A generation ago, the mountaineer knew that enough was enough; and when that was secured, he could stop work and enjoy life. And his children absorbed this attitude toward the need of leisure. He said what he meant when he sang,

> As I was a-walking for pleasure one day,
> In sweet recreation I careless did stray.

The resources for leisure time were at hand—tales and songs, airs played on a homemade fiddle or banjo or dulcimer, passed on traditionally to each generation. The wealth of inheritance was a part of everyone's endowment, though naturally some people were better performers than others. Mrs. Jane Gentry sang for Cecil Sharp sixty-four songs, seventeen of them Child ballads.[3] Any one of the thirteen

[3] Mrs. Gentry knew the following Child ballads: "The False Knight upon the Road" (3), "The Two Sisters" (10), "Edward" (13), "Lord Thomas and Fair Annet" (73), "The Cherry Tree Carol" (54), "Young Hunting" (68), "The Wife of Usher's Well" (79), "Little Musgrave" (81), "Lamkin" (93), "Johnie Scot" (99), "Geordie" (209), "The Daemon Lover" (243), "The Grey Cock" (248), "Our Goodman" (274), and "The Golden Vanity" (286).

children of Balus and Abbie Ritchie might be relied upon to sing a ballad or lead a play-party game, and several of them are using today their family songs either vocationally or avocationally—truly "a singin' and a dancin' generation." [4] "Singing Willie" Nolan, so called to distinguish him from other Willie Nolans in the neighborhood, came rightly by his sobriquet, having learned his songs from a mother who could sing all night and not repeat herself. Many a fine song, however, has been recovered from smaller repertoires. Aunt Sal knew only one, but it is a fine example of mountain humor.[5] Little Henry Harris' only song was a nonsense jingle, but it proved to have pre-Shakespearian forebears.[6] Mrs. Maud Long, Mrs. Gentry's daughter, picked up the baby before she began to sing, saying that she always felt more like it when she was holding a young 'un. In this way many a child grew up familiar with tales of the most approved classic fiction, though he did not get them from books. His imaginative world was one of lords and ladies and castles, of unrequited love and tragic misunderstanding, of foreign lands, ships a-sailing, the wars of Germanee, strange birds like the nightingale and the cuckoo. His everyday world might give way at any time to the claims of romance. He sang as he was riding down the creek to mill, hoeing corn, milking the cows, sitting before the fire at night, or putting the baby to sleep.

It was moreover natural for him to sing, for the lines of the ballads slipped from his tongue like his own spoken language. What is poetry to us was his natural expression, and words which seem to us archaic, or illiterate, or poetic, were his daily speech. As his tunes belonged to the usage of a bygone day, rejected by the literate, so did his daily speech. It is of course not a new discovery that dialect was once polite speech. "Those words that are no more in use in town do still continue among the men of the countrie, and are refused of the gentlemen for words corrupt and decayed by antiquitie." [7]

So we find that a doll is a poppet, that maidenhair fern is neverstill, that a safety pin is a latch-pin and an orange is an orange-apple. A young girl is "in the rise of her bloom," the white heads of old people are "a-bloomin' for the grave." Good health makes you feel "gaily as a buck," a phrase which echoes the old song, "as merry as

[4] See *Favorite Songs and Play Party Games from the Ritchie Family*, Cooperative Recreation Service Pamphlet, Delaware, Ohio.
[5] See page 122.   [6] See page 167.
[7] Castiglione, *The Courtier*, (Trans. Hoby. New York, Dutton, 1928), p. 54.

bucks in pale." The words of the child who refused ice cream on a trip to town because "hit friz her jowls" harked back to Chaucer. A little boy, homesick in the city and longing to be back in the hills in the spring, said, "Ploughin's just music to me." There is much condensed and pithy philosophy. "I'd druther not go, but a body don't allus git his druthers in this world." Or, in the same vein, "I don't aim to want what I haint a-goin' to git." There is an inspired use of the wrong word, just for the mere sound of it. A district nurse is "a diadem among them that follers carin' for the sick." A letter of application to a mountain school is addressed ("backed" is the word used, from the days when there were no envelopes) "To the Mistress of the Schule—goe in haste." The married woman is often saluted as mistress. The expression of pleasure in natural beauty is characteristic. The mountain is "October-colored"; a little boy dreams away a summer day "a-layin' on my back in the field, a-studyin' how blue them clouds is a-gittin'." Lindy, who arrived at school with her entire wardrobe of four dresses sewed one on top of the other, talks in homesick vein of home, where she could run outdoors "atter dark, and see the moonball a-glistenin' and a-gleamin' on Isaac's Run." Many a fotched-on visitor in a mountain home has been roused by her hostess with "Hit's peep-o'-day, time to be stirrin'." There are girls named Ellender like Lord Thomas' true-love, and Fair-Annie, out of a ballad; and Barbary Ellen is echoed in Cindy-Ellen and Stacy-Ellen. Dee's Branch is named after Jake's Dick's Dee, not Sol's Hi's Dee, information which calls from your memory "The Laird's Jock" and "The Laird's Wat" from a Border ballad. Becky Mae, checked by the teacher's anemic request not to throw stones, replies, "I hain't a-throwin' stones, I'm a-flingin' rocks!" Thus the ballad's diction, imagery, force and economy of words, and ability to meet expressive demands are all reflected in the mountain singer's daily speech.

The ballad's directness of action is as familiar to the singer as its diction. For the mountaineer a situation needs not comment, but doing. He kills his man as quickly as Lord Dannel, he acts without the law like the borderer, he steals his wife from an enemy clan as gallantly as the hero of "The Gay Goshawk." He is as satirical about human frailty as any past singer of "The Farmer's Curst Wife," and as fatalistic as Edward about those things "which will never be, be, be."

In this society, isolated from without by physical barriers of mountains and swollen streams, and within by lack of communication between every family and the next, each man fended for himself. The people thus cut off, though not the "pure Anglo-Saxons" once romantically written about, represented to a considerable degree a common inheritance and homogeneity of culture. In their manner of life and their necessary occupations lay the ground for their folk arts. Old and young alike shared the whole of life, from bornings to buryings. The days, filled with lonely manual tasks, afforded a chance to sing. Leisure time threw them back on their own resources, and illiteracy on their inherited tales and songs, while their creativeness turned the events of frontier life into new tales and songs made in the traditional idiom. Illiteracy, too, with its freedom from bookish conventions, lent poetic vigor to their daily speech. Their complete removal from the drive of competition and from commercially standardized values further individualized their cultural development. Independent, conservative, taciturn, shrewd readers of human nature, they found in the ballad a perfect vehicle for their experience and emotions.

Our two richest ballad fields, the Southern Appalachians and the Scottish Border, have much in common, though the borderer never left his own soil and the Southern mountaineer dug new roots for himself with cultural tools brought from far away. For both society was feudally organized, and the family or clan was the unit. For both the physical character of the country shut out the rest of the world, and the law was a faraway unreality.

THE PIONEER SOUTHWEST

We turn to the Southwest cattle country expecting to find some of the Border Raid ballads, and some kinship between the bad-man of the frontier and the Border reiver. But the theme of cattle-stealing is strangely absent from the cowboy songs, and while many heroes make their moan from within prison walls, they are seldom intrepidly rescued as in the Scottish ballads, though there must have been plenty of jail deliveries in actual life.

The folk song of the pioneer Southwest was conditioned not by homogeneity of background, as in the case of the Scottish Border and the Southern Appalachians, but by its miscellaneous cultural strains and the shifting quality of its life.[8] The cowboy—Mexican, mountaineer, Negro or Southern planter's son—brought to the plains all the current songs of his own culture. Many are frankly parodied from printed collections. One easily recognizes the forebears of "the little old sod shanty on the claim." "The Cowboy's Lament" is done over from a popular Irish song of the last century. "Bury me not on the lone prairie" is just a step from "Bury me not in the lonesome sea." In "Ripplin' Water" the nightingale of the English broadside still sings, but the lady's escort is a cowboy, not a soldier, and the one wife that is enough for any man is back on the ranch in Arizona, instead of in London. A final stanza is borrowed from the "betrayed girl" family of songs:

> Come all you young maidens, take warning from me;
> Never place your affections in a cowboy too free;
> He'll go away and leave you like mine did me;
> Leave you to rock cradles, sing "Bye-a-ba-bee." [9]

As long as the cattle country remained isolated, conditions bade fair to create a true folk song, but the cowboy period was too short, and the railroad, the small farm, and the discovery of oil prevented even the beginning of the winnowing process of oral tradition. Thus we still find subjectivity, pathos, and lack of originality. Or worse, in Owen Wister's phrase, "the ill-smelling saloon cleverness" [10] of the music hall song. There is continual harping on the orphan state of the poor lonesome cowboy, far from home ("Mother dear never did think I would wear a felon's chain"),[11] which is obvious and pathetic, rather than allusive and imaginative as in "The Four Maries." Jingling meter and inevitable rhyme are the rule:

> He was just a lonely cowboy, with a heart so brave and true,
> And he learned to love a maiden with eyes of heav'ns own blue.[12]

"True love" of the girl he left behind him often emasculates the picture of his life on the plains in a way unknown in the Scottish raid ballads. Indeed, one of the main reasons for the failure of the cowboy

---

[8] This is also true of the lumberjack's songs, which deal largely with life in the woods. See Barry, *The Maine Woods Songster*, and Gray, *Songs and Ballads of the Maine Lumberjacks*.

[9] Lomax, *Cowboy Songs*, p. 183.

[10] *Ibid.*, frontispiece facsimile of letter from Theodore Roosevelt.

[11] *Ibid.*, p. 90.   [12] *Ibid.*, p. 230.

song to become true folk song is the singer's lack of identification with his surroundings. Although he is charmed and absorbed by the trail and its adventures, he is continually looking back sentimentally to parents, home, women, friends, piously aware of the better life he has left. If his sins catch up with him, his reform before death is much like that of the earlier broadside "goodnight" of the English criminal on a seventeenth-century gallows.

And yet with all these limitations the cowboy has contributed to American song a freedom, gusto, and rhythm all its own. The curious adaptation of its themes and attitudes to the functional uses of a song which must stir up dull or weary beasts on the trail (Coma ti yi yippy yea) or soothe the herd at night (Lay down, little dogies, lay down) compensates somewhat for poverty of invention or inspiration. He sings to his horse like a lover, and shoots up the town on a drunken spree as if he had never heard a gospel hymn. "The Old Chisholm Trail" is a documentary record as circumstantial as "Chevy Chase." The spirit of the pioneer is idealized with economy and satiric humor in the newspaper ballad describing "Great Gran-dad," who barred the door with a wagon-tongue, wore the same suit all his life, and raised his twenty-one boys rough but well:

> He was a citizen tough and grim,
> Danger was duck-soup to him.
> He ate corn-pone and bacon fat.
> Great-grandson would starve on that.[13]

Of enormous popularity, judging from its wide circulation, was the Irish come-all-ye, "Brennan on the Moor." The tune was used for almost any highwayman story. The Somerset traditional version recovered by Cecil Sharp is included here for comparison with the Charlie Quantrell legend of the Southwest. Here is Robin Hood *redivivus*: he helps the poor widow and robs only the rich; he meets a peddler and finding him as good a man as himself, takes him on as a boon companion; his end comes through the law he despises, the mayor of Casmeyer having replaced the sheriff of Nottingham. The "bold and undaunted" Irishman has become debonairly "brave, gay and daring." The "tenpence," Revolutionary slang for musket, has been taken literally and inflated with western amplitude to "dollar"— with some loss of effect. But where the Somerset singer lets well

---

[13] Lomax, *op. cit.*, p. 302.

enough alone and with a fine sense of climax winds up with the judge's sentence, the taste of the Kansas plains demands a final stanza of pathetic farewell to the dear wife who handed him the blunderbuss, and also to several people not mentioned before, his children three, aged father, and dear old mother.

The story of another famous highwayman, Irish Jack Donahue of Australia, is also very generally known. Our version comes from Vermont, and uses a "Brennan on the Moor" tune, though without the effective refrain.

BRENNAN ON THE MOOR [14]

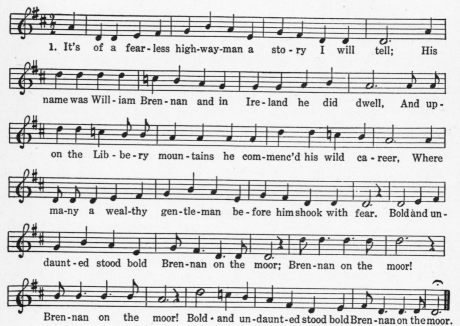

1. It's of a fearless highwayman a story I will tell;
   His name was William Brennan and in Ireland he did dwell,
   And upon the Libbery mountains he commenc'd his wild career,
   Where many a wealthy gentleman before him shook with fear.
       Bold and undaunted stood bold Brennan on the moor;
         Brennan on the moor! Brennan on the moor!
       Bold and undaunted stood bold Brennan on the moor.

[14] From *Novello's School Songs* (1908), No. 966. Reprinted by permission of Novello and Co., London, Publishers.

2. A brace of loaded pistols he did carry night and day,
   He never robbed a poor man all on the King's highway;
   But what he'd taken from the rich, like Turpin and Black Bess,
   He always did divide between the widows in distress.

3. One day he robbed a packman and his name was Pedlar Bawn;
   They travelled on together till the day began to dawn;
   The pedlar found his money gone, likewise his watch and chain,
   He at once encountered Brennan and he robbed him back again.

4. When Brennan saw the pedlar was as good a man as he,
   He took him on the highway his companion to be;
   The pedlar threw away his pack without any delay,
   And proved a faithful comrade bold unto his dying day.

5. One day upon the King's highway as Willie he sat down,
   He met the Mayor of Cashel just a mile outside the town;
   The Mayor he knew his feathers bold; O you're my man, said he,
   I think you're William Brennan, you must come along with me.

6. Now Willie's wife had been to town provisions for to buy,
   And when she saw her Willie she began to sob and cry;
   He said: Give me that ten-pence, And as quick as Willie spoke,
   She handed him a blunderbuss from underneath her cloak.

7. Now with this loaded blunderbuss, the truth I will unfold,
   He made the Mayor to tremble, and he robbed him of his gold;
   A hundred pounds was offered for his apprehension there,
   But he with horse and saddle to the mountains did repair.

8. He lay among the fern all day, 'twas thick upon the field,
   And many wounds he did receive before that he would yield;
   He was captured and found guilty, and the judge made this reply:
   For robbing on the King's highway you are condemned to die.

QUANTRELL [15]

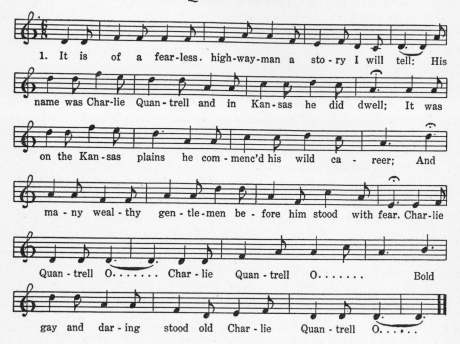

1. It is of a fear-less. high-way-man a sto-ry I will tell: His
name was Char-lie Quan-trell and in Kan-sas he did dwell; It was
on the Kan-sas plains he com-menc'd his wild ca - reer; And
ma - ny weal-thy gen - tle-men be - fore him stood with fear. Char-lie
Quan - trell O . . . . Char - lie Quan - trell O . . . . Bold
gay and dar - ing stood old Char - lie Quan - trell O . . . .

1. It is of a fearless highwayman a story I will tell;
   His name was Charlie Quantrell and in Kansas he did dwell;
   It was on the Kansas plains he commenc'd his wild career;
   And many wealthy gentlemen before him stood with fear.
      Charlie Quantrell O,
      Charlie Quantrell O,
   Bold and gay and daring stood Charlie Quantrell O.

2. With a brace of loaded pistols he carried both night and day,
   Though he never robbed a poor man while on the highway,
   But what he taken from the rich, like tops and like best,
   He always did divide it with the widow in distress.

3. One night he met a packman whose name was Tideo Brown,
   And they travelled on together till the day began to dawn;
   When the packman found his money gone, likewise his watch and chain,
   He at once encountered Quantrell and he robbed him back again.

[15] From Lomax, *Cowboy Songs* (1938), p. 144. Reprinted by permission of The Macmillan Co., New York, Publishers, and The Republic National Bank of Dallas, Texas, executors for the Estate of John A. Lomax.
   (Original one fourth lower.)

4. Now Charlie saw the packman as good a man as he;
   He asked him as a comrade on the highway for to be;
   The packman he consented without a word's delay,
   And he proved a loyal comrade until his dying day.

5. As Charles went out to walk one day, 'twas early on one morn,
   He met the mayor of Casmeyer just outside of town;
   Now the mayor knew his features, and "Your name," he said, "must be,
   Oh, your name is Charlie Quantrell, you must come along with me."

6. Now Charlie's wife to town had gone provisions for to buy;
   When she saw her Charlie taken, she began to weep and cry;
   "Oh, I wish I had a dollar," said he; No sooner had he spoke,
   Than she handed him a blunderbuss from underneath her coat.

7. Now with this loaded blunderbuss, the truth it must be told,
   It caused the mayor to tremble and it robbed him of his gold;
   Five thousand pounds were there laid down and then pre-empted there,
   And with his horse and saddle to the mountains did repair.

8. Now Charlie being an outlaw, upon the mountains high,
   With both infantry and cavalry to take him they did try,
   But he hid among the brush that grew thick upon the field,
   And he received nine wounds before he would yield.

9. It was a little prairie the place they call Lamar,
   Where Charlie and his comrade were forced to suffer sore;
   The jury found them guilty and the judge gave this reply,
   "For robbing on the highway you're both condemned to die."

   "Now farewell, dear wife and my little children three,
   And you, my aged father who sheds those tears for me,
   And likewise my dear old mother," who tore gray hair and cried,
   Saying, "It were better, Charlie, in your cradle you had died."
       Charlie Quantrell O, Charlie Quantrell O,
       Brave, gay, and daring stood old Charlie Quantrell, O.

BOLD JACK DONAHUE [16]

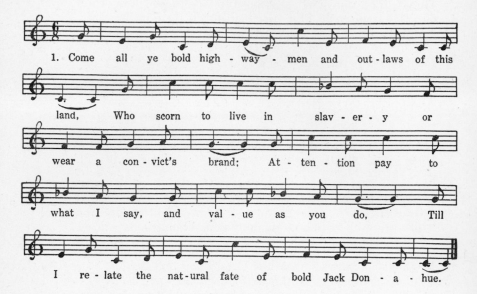

1. Come all ye bold high - way - men and out - laws of this
land, Who scorn to live in slav - er - y or
wear a con - vict's brand; At - ten - tion pay to
what I say, and val - ue as you do, Till
I re - late the nat - ural fate of bold Jack Don - a - hue.

1. Come all ye bold highwaymen and outlaws of this land,
   Who scorn to live in slavery or wear a convict's brand;
   Attention pay to what I say, and value as you do,
   Till I relate the natural fate of bold Jack Donahue.

2. He was a true-bred Irishman, as you shall plainly see,
   From Ireland deported, deprived of liberty,
   Of Dublin City of high renown, where he his first breath drew,
   . . . .   of honor entitled him to "Bold Jack Donahue."

3. He had not been . . . six months all on Australian shore,
   Before he took to robbery as he oft-times did before;
   There was Maclamore and Underwood, there was Weber and
           Winslow too,
   Those was the four associates of Bold Jack Donahue.

4. . . . .*
   Those tyrants was afraid of him to travel night or day,
   For every day the newspapers did print out something new,
   Concerning that bold highwayman they called Jack Donahue.

* In these stanzas the singer began with the 2nd phrase of the melody.
[16] As sung by Mr. Ed Dragon of Ripton, Vermont, to E. K. Wells, July 1941.

5. He happened to be taken again when he was in his prime,
   He was tried, convicted, sentenced to die, for a highway robber crime;
   But he left appealers that same day, he left them in the stew,
   And before that they reached Sydney jail they'd lost Jack Donahue.

6. As he and his companions walked out one afternoon,
   Not thinking of the pain of death that was to seal his doom,
   To his surprise the horse-police, well armed they came in view,
   And quickly they advanced to take that Bold Jack Donahue.

7. .   .   .   .*
   Oh now my boys, prove true to me, this day I'll call you fain,
   Be of good courage, stout and bold, be loyal and be true,
   This day we'll fight with all our might, says Bold Jack Donahue.

8. Up speaks the cowardly Winslow, To this we'll not agree;
   For there's ten or twelve of them, this time for us too few,
   And if we wait, we'll be too late, this battle we shall rue!
   Begone from me, you cowardly dogs, cries Bold Jack Donahue.

9. It never shall be said for me, that Donahue the brave
   Shall ever yield to government or die an English slave.
   I would rather roam this forest wild, like a wolf or a kangaroo
   Than to work one hour for government, says Bold Jack Donahue.

10. Oh Donahue, Oh Donahue, discharge your carabine,
    Or do you mean to fight us all, or will you not resign?
    To surrender to such cowardly dogs, it's a thing I shall never do;
    This day I'll fight with all my might, cries Bold Jack Donahue.

11. The corporal and the sergeant separated their men;
    Some fired from behind him, and some on every side,
    The corporal and the sergeant, they fired at him too,
    Till a rifle ball had pierced the heart of Bold Jack Donahue.

12. Nine rounds he fired at the police before the fatal ball,
    Which pierced the hearts of nine of them, and caused them for to fall;
    And when he closed his blood-shot eyes, he bid this world adieu,
    Saying, All good people pray for the soul of Bold Jack Donahue.

NOVA SCOTIA

Mrs. Carrie Grover, now nearly seventy and living in Gorham, Maine, reconstructs for us another society where folk song flourished. Until she was twelve, she lived in Nova Scotia, a part of the world now well known for its traditional song. Mrs. Grover embodies all the collector could desire, for she is a fine natural musician, with a large inherited repertoire from oral tradition, appreciating and loving her art, and able to recall and analyze the conditions which favored its survival. In her own words:

> I was born into a house where someone was singing most of the time, and when song was the only entertainment. The women made their labor sweeter by singing the old songs as they worked at spinning, weaving, knitting, piecing patchwork and hooking rugs. Father did some work as a cooper, and I remember he had a special song he always sang when he was finishing an axe handle. And every night he sang, excepting once a week when his newspaper came. That night he read the paper aloud to us,—every word of it.[17]

After the children's bedtime the grownups continued to sing, perhaps with less restraint than before, for the parents were properly particular about what songs their children learned. "But who's to prevent you learning a song by listening down the stovepipe?" "Playing grownup" included always the singing of grown-up songs, and Mrs. Grover recalls examining the mouth of a small playmate who couldn't carry a tune, to see if it was made differently from hers. "I was one of the lucky ones because my people could sing, as nature taught them. I can think of no heritage which I would rather have."

This picture is not unlike that of the Appalachians, where inherited song accompanied the family occupations and provided the family pleasures. But Nova Scotia in those days was a lively mart of song, and the situation was one not of isolation, but of communication. Mrs. Grover's father had added to a large inherited repertoire the songs he had learned in his young sailing days. Her reminiscences bring to life the docks and wharves, with the arrival of ships—and sailors with their songs—from distant ports; the gatherings at her uncle's public house, the coming and going from lumber camps in Maine and Michigan and the South. An older brother brought back from the West Virginia log woods Negro spirituals and Appalachian song-ballets, which she sings today with all their characteristic flavor, just as she heard them in her childhood. She used to hang about the smithy just to hear the blacksmith sing. She tells of a singing match, crowded with listeners, that went on till night turned into morning.

[17] Letter to the writer. Other quotations from Mrs. Grover are from correspondence or conversations.

As a result of all these early contacts Mrs. Grover now has a very large repertoire. On a single visit to her, one may hear perhaps a score of genuine Child ballads, many more of broadside origin, a choice collection of local ballads about sea-captains and wrecks, folk hymns, chanteys and nursery songs.[18] Although for forty years she has been writing down every song she could recall, there are still unplumbed depths in her memory which a chance question may stir.

Mrs. Grover is more than a folk singer. Her natural musicianship gives her an extraordinary appreciation of the beauty of the tune, and she usually comments on it before she begins to sing. She insists on exact notation, telling you that her songs are "modal, different from other music." But a song for her is a story too. Of the old-time singers she says, "With people who knew nothing of the rules of music all depended upon a natural ear for music and whether or not the singer *felt* the words he was singing." Mrs. Grover meets both qualifications. "When I sing these songs, it seems like I'm the feller it's all happening to." Fortunately, for with age she suffers increasingly from shortness of breath, she is not confined to one medium of expression. She will often emphasize the beauty of a tune by whistling it, or by playing it on the fiddle which is always by her. Her fiddling of dance tunes like "Soldier's Joy," "Flowers of Edinburgh," or "The Devil's Dream" puts new meaning into that jaded word "irresistible," and her stock includes all the Scotch reels and Irish jigs that circulated in her youth.

The vitality and rhythmic strength of her music cannot be put into words. Her singing, a natural expression bred from long handing down, makes any other kind seem pale and anemic. One can no more reproduce it from a system of notation than one can recall Irving's voice by looking at a page of Shakespeare, so impossible it is to catch the strong and elemental rhythm, the delicate nuances and embellishments and minute variations within the stable pattern. This is art, though artless—the technique and inheritance and individual response of the selfless enthusiast. It cannot successfully be set down, learned, or imitated.

[18] Thus I heard in one day "Robin Hood and the Pedlar" (132), "Geordie" (209), "The Cruel Mother" (20), "The Gypsy Laddie" (200), "Sweet William's Ghost" (77), "Little Musgrave" (81), "Captain Wedderburn's Courtship" (46), and "The Farmer's Curst Wife" (278). "Barbara Allen" (84) she would not bother with, for "everyone knew that." Her broadsides included "John Riley," "The Prentice Boy," "Pretty Caroline," "The High Barbaree," "Brennan on the Moor," "The Greenland Whale Fishery," "Little Mohee," "The Fair Maid on the Shore," and many others.

Mrs. Grover began writing down her songs for her children when she was made suddenly aware, by a chance remark of her mother, that "after you and I die our songs will be forgotten." Her local reputation as a singer took her to a meeting of the women's club, where to her surprise she heard herself being introduced as a singer of folk songs. "I'd heard of 'folk songs' all my life, but I never knew my songs were folk songs. So I just lilted up and sang 'em some of my ditties." A large scrapbook of clippings and letters shows the widening circle of her friends and horizon of her study. Before she acquired a copy of Child's collection for herself, she worked with the one in the town library, comparing her songs with his. "Since I became interested in the study of folk songs I have thought back over the years, and I understand some things better that I once took as a matter of course. What a fascinating study it is, to try to get more and more of the old songs and to compare them with others. It has helped me over many long hours of weakness when I could do little else to make life interesting." [19]

The story of Mrs. Grover is in a sense the story of American folk song. She represents the rich tradition, the fine folk art, the life that bred the practice of folk music, the devotion to songs which every good folk singer expresses in one way or another. Fortunately her songs are now preserved in about forty recordings in the Archive of National Music at the Library of Congress, as well as the privately recorded hundred-odd for her book. Transcription is at best inadequate, but something of her manner of singing may be caught by listening to the records themselves.

In one other respect Mrs. Grover embodies folk song. She is first of all herself—a person in her own right, with the innate dignity, the homely philosophy and wit, and the understanding of life which are so often the qualities of the folk singer. She reminds us of the comments of Addison and Sharp, that the soundness of the humanity behind the song accounts for the song itself.

[19] From Mrs. Grover's large repertoire she is now preparing for publication over a hundred of her best songs—no mean number to survive the process of selection.

Mrs. Betty Creech of Pine Mountain, Kentucky, and her granddaughter
(By permission of the Doris Ulmann Foundation, Berea, Kentucky)

Singing Willie Nolan of Incline, Kentucky, and his family

APPALACHIAN SINGERS

MR. AND MRS. BALUS RITCHIE OF VIPER, KENTUCKY

CECIL SHARP AND MAUD KARPELES NOTE A BALLAD FROM
AN APPALACHIAN SINGER

Chapter 16

THE LITERARY BALLAD

A LITERARY weekly recently reviewed or advertised in the same issue no fewer than four books titled from folk songs: *Hanging Johnny* (a sea-chantey), *The Running of the Deer* (from the refrain of "The Holly and the Ivy"), *Black Is My True-Love's Hair* (the first line of an Appalachian song), and *Such Counsels Ye Gave to Me* (the final line of the B-version of "Edward"). Ballad lines have infiltrated literature almost as frequently as tags from Shakespeare, to say nothing of themes and plots, while ballad technique, with its allusiveness, selection of concrete detail, and highlighting of parts of the story without regard for introductory or connective matter, has exercised a far-reaching literary influence.

Until the end of the sixteenth century story patterns were few, and there was no desire for originality, so plots were used over and over in different forms, and stories wandered back and forth between the courtly narrator and the popular singer. Chaucer's "Prioresse's Tale" and "Sir Hugh" (155), if they are not related, at least stem from a common source. Marie de France in the twelfth century used folk matter freely in her courtly *lais*, and her "La Fresne" is the story of "Fair Annie" (62). "Hind Horn" (17) and the King Horn romance are counterparts. Robin Hood plays in the sixteenth century were little more than dramatized ballads. As might have been expected, the revival of the ballad in the eighteenth century brought old themes to the notice of poets and dramatists. Percy's *Reliques* pointed out analogies between literary and popular poems. The ballad operas used ballad tunes of the day for their lyrics. Home's *Douglas* was founded on "Child Morrice" (83). A little later Wordsworth used the setting and plot of "The Rising of the North" (175) in "The White Doe of Rylstone." The nineteenth century poets responded generously to ballad influences, and one finds Matthew Arnold using the story of "The Queen of Elfan's Nourice" (40) in his "Forsaken Merman"; while Browning's "Flight of the Duchess" grew, as he says in a letter to Furnivall, "out of this one intelligible line of a song I heard a woman singing at a bon-fire Guy Faux [*sic*] night when I was a boy:—'Following the Queen of the Gypsies, O' " [1]—perhaps a version of "The Gypsy Laddie" (200). Many more examples could be cited to show direct borrowing from folk song by fiction and poetry. Minor echoes are endless too. "The Cruel Mother," who

> . . . pulled down her long yellow hair,
> All along in the ludeney,
> And she bound it around their little feet and hands,
> Down by the green-wood side

suggests Browning's "Porphyria's Lover," who

> found
> A thing to do, and all her hair
> In one long string [I] wound
> Three times her little throat around
> And strangled her.

But we must not, like Addison who saw in the ballads specific parallels to Vergil's morality, ride our hobbyhorse to death.

The present discussion is restricted, therefore, to the poems which deliberately imitate the ballad either in form, manner, or subject. "Imitation" is used in no derogatory sense: it implies no intent to deceive the reader into thinking this is a real folk ballad, nor criticism of the ballad imitation as a poem. "La Belle Dame sans Merci" for all its imaginative force may fail at some points as a ballad imitation; "The Last Rhyme of True Thomas," a highly successful literary ballad, contains much that is not poetry. Ballads and their imitations demand different criteria. But the prevalence of English and American narrative poetry in the period since 1765 bears witness to the truth of Words-worth's statement that "there is not an able writer of verse today who would not be proud to acknowledge his obligation to the *Reliques*."

The following notes on a few literary ballads [2] seek to answer certain questions: Is the ballad a good basis for "art" poetry? What ballad traits have the imitators most successfully appropriated? Is their use of the ballad form for their own ends poetically justified? Does the consideration of the ballad in the hands of modern poets cast new

---

[1] DeVane, *Browning Handbook*, pp. 155–57.
[2] For the texts of certain ballads here commented upon, see *Appendix*.

light on its own merits? Is its genuine simplicity, as has been claimed, wholly inimitable?

———

Of "William and Margaret" by David Mallet, written in 1724 and long antedating the *Reliques*, Saintsbury says, "No single copy of verse deserves so much credit for setting the eighteenth century back on the road of true romantic verse by an easy path, suited to its own tastes and powers." [3] The tastes of the eighteenth century are certainly reflected in this careful, explanatory, rational tale of horror. The supernatural is dwelt upon with fascination and fulness, rather than matter-of-fact economy as in true ballad verse. The tedious description and the long speeches are commonplace and diffuse, rather than direct and abbreviated. Balance and personification hold sway:

> Now let thy Pity hear the maid
> Thy Love refus'd to save.

The moralizing note was never in the folk rendering of this story. Yet in spite of the emphasis laid upon description and feeling, the story itself provides a true ballad theme, and it is a traditional cock that summons the revenant, even though the literary poet must comment on that call as "a long and late adieu."

Wordsworth writes in *The Prelude* of ballads heard in youth, as

> . . . low and wren-like warblings, made
> For cottagers and spinners at the wheel,
> And sunburnt travellers resting their tired limbs
> Stretched under wayside hedges, ballad tunes,
> Food for the hungry ears of little ones
> And of old men who have survived their joys . . .[4]

These sound very much like traditional ballads and traditional singers. Yet it is upon the broadside that he bases his poetic theory of simple language for simple themes, which was to reform English poetry. In the Preface to the *Lyrical Ballads* he compares Dr. Johnson's parody on ballad verse,

> I put my hat upon my head
> And walked into the Strand,
> And there I met another man
> Whose hat was in his hand

[3] *Cambridge History of English Literature*, IX, chap. vi, 208.
[4] Wordsworth, *Poetical Works*, III, Vol. VII, 108.

with a "justly admired" stanza from the jog-trotting "Babes in the Wood":

> Those pretty Babes with hand in hand
> Went wandering up and down;
> But never more they saw the man
> Approaching from the Town.[5]

Wordsworth says that Johnson's quatrain is bad poetry because it leads to nothing interesting, whereas the second quotation achieves a real effect by exciting the thought and feeling of the reader. He hopes, in his own verses, to arouse an excitement comparable to that induced by the artless meter and diction of the old ballads. He seeks to elevate the realistic, the commonplace, and the everyday in poetry, using the language of men in all its simplicity and contact with common life, sublimating it by the emotional stress of meter, trusting that in writing of plain people in their own language, which is free from "the foreign splendor of the Poet" (figures and elaborations) his own poems will become memorable. In humble and rustic life "the essential passions of the heart can find a better soil in which they can attain their maturity . . . and speak a plainer and more emphatic language." [5] "Lucy Gray" should be read in the light of this theory.

Like many a traditional ballad, "Lucy Gray" is based on a local incident. It is devoid of archaisms and poetic diction. The images are drawn from familiar nature—the fawn at play, the hare on the green, the mountain roe, the powdery snow. The suspense as to the child's fate and the hint that after death she revisits the scene are ballad motifs, handled with ballad restraint, and with confidence that the implications will speak for themselves.

The poem fails as a ballad because of its fulness of detail and its pedestrian monotony, particularly at the beginning. It is throughout as circumstantial as a broadside; its level of interest never shifts. There is a signal failure to follow the declared principle that a stanza should lead from the particular to the significant:

> That, father, will I gladly do;
> 'Tis scarcely afternoon,
> The minster clock has just struck two,
> And yonder is the moon.

Country folk, whose speech is often akin to poetry in its condensed

5 Wordsworth, *op. cit.*, II, Vol. V, 222 ff.   6 *Ibid.*, p. 193.

and suggestive phrases, have better ways of saying a thing. Tradition must winnow the pathetic passages if they are to be effective:

> They wept—and turning homeward, cried,
> 'In Heaven we all shall meet.'

Wordsworth's intent in *The Lyrical Ballads* was to infuse the commonplace with wonder; Coleridge's share was to make real the remote and the marvelous, calling for our "willing suspension of disbelief." His "Rime of the Ancient Mariner" has been called "a sublimation of ballad wonder," [7] telling a story which we accept with as much unquestioning naïveté as we do a ballad. Setting and time are vague, but the use of the present tense makes it seem here and now. The series of pictures is highlighted. In spite of the antique manner the archaisms are not forced. Strictly speaking, there is no refrain, but repeated phrases perform its function:

> The ice was here, the ice was there,
> The ice was all around.

> Water, water everywhere,
> And all the boards did shrink;
> Water, water everywhere,
> Nor any drop to drink.

> Alone, alone, all all alone,
> Alone on a wide, wide sea!

Many a ballad refrain, with more or less fitness, uses the magic of such syllables: "All alone, and a-lonelie oh!" "All alone in the ludeney," or "As he sailed upon the low and the lonesome low,/As he sailed upon the lonesome sea." By concrete allusion to the mariner's reckonings we learn of the ship's change of position: "The sun came up upon the left," and later, "The sun now rose upon the right." Two successive stanzas begin incrementally, "This seraph band, each waved his hand"; two others though separated are practically identical:

> And a good south wind sprung up behind;
> The Albatross did follow,
> And every day, for food or play,
> Came to the mariners' hollo!

> And the good south wind still blew behind,
> But no sweet bird did follow,
> Nor any day, for food or play,
> Came to the mariners' hollo!

[7] Hustvedt, *Ballad Criticism in Scandinavia and Great Britain during the Eighteenth Century*, pp. 294–95.

Description follows the ballad stereotype: there is the bride, red as a rose; the bright-eyed mariner, the brother's son. The siren's

> lips were red, her looks were free,
> Her locks were yellow as gold.

The lady whistles thrice; for seven days and seven nights the curse operates. In the unassigned speeches there is the ballad's dramatic force. The ballad stanza is so frequent as to give the impression of its use throughout the poem, and the occasional five- or six-line stanza is good ballad practice. The ear, however, catches the rather literary internal rhyme. Aspects of the voyage recall Thomas Rymer's journey to the otherworld, when

> For forty days and forty nights
> He wade in red blood to the knee,
> And he saw neither sun nor moon,
> But heard the roaring of the sea.

As in the ballad, the barrier between the real and the unreal is imperceptible. The bird with its strange powers, and the curse that comes from its slaying, belong to true folk beliefs.[8]

Coleridge, as he reworked the poem, increased his use of ballad methods. He omitted many connecting stanzas and some of the wedding guest's horrified comment. Descriptions of Death and the movements of the spectre-ship are more and more telescoped. Literary metaphor takes on a simpler air. "The mariners gave it biscuit worms" in the first draft becomes in the final form, "It ate the food it ne'er had eat"; "Like morning frost y-spread" is changed to "Like April hoar-frost spread";

> And she is far liker Death than he,
> Her flesh makes the still air cold

becomes

> The Nightmare Life-in-Death is she,
> Who thicks man's blood with cold.

But although the tale is important, the moral is more so. There is frequent delay for a sententious observation—"O sleep, it is a gentle thing . . ." The Christian background—prayers, allusions to the Godhead and invocations to Christ and Heaven's Mother, and the homely

---

[8] This is still a sailor's superstition. I have heard recently about a girl born at sea, and named for good luck, at the sailors' request, "Albatross," after the bird following the ship.

realism of "the kirk below the hill"—all prepare us for the lesson to be drawn:

> He prayeth best who loveth best
> All things both great and small,
> For the dear God who loveth us,
> He made and loveth all.

Of this moralizing Coleridge writes:

> Mrs. Barbauld once told me that she admired the Ancient Mariner very much, but that there were two faults in it—it was improbable, and it had no moral. As for the probability, I owned that I might admit some question; but as to the want of a moral, I told her that in my judgment it had too much; and that the only, or chief fault, if I might say so, was the obtrusion of the moral sentiment so openly on the reader as a principle or cause of action in a work of such pure imagination. It ought to have had no more moral than the Arabian Nights tale of the merchant's sitting down to eat dates by the side of a well, and throwing the shells aside, and Lo, a genie starts up and says he must kill the aforesaid merchant, because one of the shells, it seems, put out the eye of the genie's son.[9]

In a poem of this length, naturally the spectral elements are elaborated, but the poet does not obviously evoke horror; rather, he moves you by deft touches, like the ballad singer trusting to the story to do its work. There are few references to feeling as such. And yet, although like the ballad there is no palpable barrier between reality and unreality, the poem has not the ballad's matter-of-factness in dealing with the supernatural. Christian morality and philosophy underlie the idea of the otherworld, turning the story into a metaphysical rather than a physical experience. The important thing thus becomes not the killing of the bird and all that follows that act, but the revelation of a great truth to the human mind. A deeper depth than that of the ballad has thus been plumbed.

"The Inchcape Rock," for all Southey's friendship with Coleridge, shows little influence from the latter's work. Its dual theme of shipwreck and retribution would soon have been simplified by the folk to shipwreck alone, for retribution carries with it a moral comment. Such subtle villainy as Sir Ralph's is in a different key from the ballad's strong and elemental emotions.

Seven of the seventeen stanzas are introductory, and some of them are painstakingly anxious to set the atmosphere. Tradition would

[9] Raysor, *Coleridge's Miscellaneous Criticism*, p. 405.

soon have reduced if not wiped out this part, leaving you to guess the circumstances for yourself. The language, while simple and familiar, is often trivial. Such phrases as "still as she could be," "shining so gay," and "It made him whistle, it made him sing" (as in the nursery carol, "O one did whistle and one did sing") demean the verse at times to sing-song. The inconsistent use of the present tense (usually corrected by modern editors) shows the poet's inadequacy in handling this ballad device. There is often an echo of the "Mariner," as in the description of the becalmed ship, but where Southey is cumbersome and trite:

> No stir in the air, no stir in the sea,
> The ship was as still as she could be;
> Her sails from heaven received no motion;
> Her keel was steady in the ocean.   .

Coleridge is elliptical, suggestive, and hence exciting:

> Day after day, day after day
> We stuck, nor breath nor motion;
> As idle as a painted ship
> Upon a painted ocean.

Southey was much interested in traditional poetry, and made many translations from the Spanish and the German. Here, however, he has failed to catch its genius, and one is tempted to apply to his ballads the statement about his longer works, that "probably no man who wrote so much has contributed so little to the progress of poesy." [10]

Of Sir Walter Scott's prolific ballad imitations no more is attempted here than to point out one or two instances. His "Lochinvar" is an expansion of the traditional "Katherine Jaffray" (221). He has responded to the romance and drama of the story by individualizing the characters: the poor craven bridegroom is laggard in love, dastard in war, dangles his bonnet and plume speechless. The hero's reputation, debonair self-assurance, devotion and audacity, and his dramatic entrance at the critical moment, played up against the anxiety of the parents, all show an imaginative elaboration of the condensed and straightforward original. In a galloping rhythm and with growing intensity the story gathers speed:

[10] *The Concise Cambridge History of English Literature*, p. 586.

He stayed not for brake and he stopped not for stone,
He swam the Eske River where ford there was none.

With "one touch to her hand, and one word in her ear" they are off. In allusive folk idiom he cries, "They'll have fleet steeds that follow!" But the dance is too elegant, and the mocking speech of the lover too grandiloquent for the ballad's naïveté.

If "Lochinvar" is an expansion of ballad simplicity, "Proud Maisie" is a contraction. Like a well-worn fragment of traditional verse it recalls the bit of dialogue to which folk memory has reduced "The Bonny Earl of Murray" (181) or "Mary Hamilton" (173). But after the first stanza Scott loses the simplicity of folk question and answer; the riddling dialogue has taken on a hidden meaning and a sophisticated irony. The triple question formula is not exactly followed, and the speaking bird is a sort of oracle, not a participant in the story, as in "Young Hunting" (68) or "The Gay Goshawk" (96).

Keats's "La Belle Dame sans Merci" treats with inspired restraint the ballad story of a mortal captured by a fairy. In the ballad's best manner concrete terms indicate allusively the time of year, in the withered grass, the silent woods and the harvest; the knight's condition is read through his pallor and flush. Ballad-wise, we guess his doom as the fairy's child makes him garlands and gives him for his mortal kisses fairy food. In this dialogue-told story the poet highlights his disconnected scenes, making, as Gerould says, with a stroke of genius an artistic virtue out of folk-song necessity.[11] As in many folk songs, the first stanza is repeated at the end. The ballad stanza is the basis of the verse form, but the last line, cut to two beats, interrupts the rhythm like a catch in the breath, thus adding to the tension.

But where the ballad readily accepts the mermaid or fairy queen, La Belle Dame is touched with strangeness. The important thing for us is her extraordinary effect on the knight; the central interest, announced in ballad formula, "O what can ail thee?" is in his state of mind. And where the moaning of Fair Annie (62) or the mother in "The Queen of Elfan's Nourice" (40) elicits questions about meat or fee, the Knight's lily brow and fever dew give a picture of mysterious mental anguish. The poem is a subjective description of a condition, rather than the recounting of an incident.

[11] *The Ballad of Tradition*, p. 97.

In "The Wreck of the Hesperus" Longfellow, like Southey, treats in rather jingling rhyme a double theme, a shipwreck and its emotional connotations; and like Southey also, although he is impregnated with the spirit of the medieval ballads, he has failed to reproduce their simple charm.

Obviously "Sir Patrick Spens" (58) is in his mind. The framework is the same: a seasoned sailor gives warning of "a deidly storm" and the ship sails to its doom, but the skipper here is merely foolhardy, not ironically forced to act counter to his weather-wisdom. In twice the number of verses of "Sir Patrick Spens," with its cloud wrack lifting for a split second to show us the cabin boy snatching the helm from his master, or the hats of the haughty Scots bobbing on the water, the Hesperus tragedy plods its way as circumstantially as a novel. Nobody who learned in the nursery that "The moon is round as round can be, / Two eyes, a nose, and mouth we see," can take seriously the lines

> Last night the moon had a golden ring,
> Tonight no moon we see

—lines which cannot stand beside their prototype,

> Late, late yestreen I saw the new Moone
> With the old moon in her arm.

Longfellow's

> The skipper, he blew a whiff from his pipe,
> And a scornful laugh laughed he

echoes only faintly the ballad's corresponding lines. The ballad's triple question method breaks down here after the second question, interfering with pace and balance. An open stanza and half the next are needed to describe the dead skipper. Occasionally, to be sure, real poetic strength asserts itself in the usually pedestrian verse:

> The breakers were right beneath her bows,
> She drifted a weary wreck,
> And a whooping billow swept the crew
> Like icicles from her deck.

But in general, the facility, pathos, and mediocre diction of this poem reduce it far below the level of good poetry, not to mention good balladry, and explain why this awful tale, so popular in a sentimental period, has long since been relegated to the trite and the near-ridiculous.

The humorous story of the tongue-tied lover, told by Lowell in
"The Courtin'," may be compared with the Appalachian "Aunt Sal's
Song." In the old-fashioned mountain home privacy for young people
who are "talking" is gained only after the family has gone to bed in
various four-posters in the corners of the one-room cabin, turned its
backs on the couple by the fire and begun to snore. The two hickory-
split chairs are moved together for warmth as well as society; the still
night passes hour by hour and the early crowing of the cock sounds
the suitor's release from ordeal, for the family stirs at peep o' day. But
even without knowing all this one may understand the girl's amused
chagrin at the downfall of her hopes, her feminine coquetry in refus-
ing to help her lover out, his own despair and decision to abandon
courting, and his loss of reputation as a ladies' man. Lowell, enlarging
for readers beyond New Hampshire, develops all the nuances of the
lover's feelings, and overloads his descriptions, losing in the process the
dry and laconic flavor of New England humor. Yet there is an echo of
folk idiom sometimes in a consciously artful phrase:

> The side she breshed felt full o' sun
> Ez a south slope in Ap'il

is not far from a Newfoundland folk lyric,

> She's like the swallow that flies so high,
> She's like the river that never runs dry,
> She's like the sunshine on the lee shore . . .[12]

The mountaineer's "October-colored" is like Lowell's "Snow-hid,"
but Lowell's line is preceded by the subtlety of "Like streams that
keep a summer mind." Lowell, a strong supporter of the legitimacy
of dialect in poetry, uses it here to emphasize country atmosphere and
quaintness, but its abundance acts as a barrier between reader and
story, making us think, "How differently these people talk, and how
hard it is to understand them!" rather than "How true to life this
is!" A stanza or two from "Aunt Sal's Song," turned into dialect, will
show how the point immediately shifts from enjoyment of the human
comedy to ridicule of rustic speech:

> A gen'lemun come to air haouse, he would not tell 'is name,
> I know'd he come a-cyourtin', although he were asham'.

> He moved his cheer up to my side, his faincy please me well,
> I thought the sperrit moved him some hansom' tale to tell.

[12] Karpeles, *Folk Songs from Newfoundland*, II, 112.

True folk song transcends speech differences by its appeal to common experience and sympathy. In the Child ballads there is no assuming of an unnatural role by the folk poet; this is the way he talks. But Lowell is here aping a speech not naturally his—and with a hint of patronage.

Of "Skipper Ireson's Ride" the same criticism may be made. The refrain (turned by Whittier into dialect at Lowell's suggestion) is highly artificial, the more so from contrast with the stanza. This poem, too, develops sentiment at the expense of story.

Some Victorians found in the ballad's flexibility and lightness an excellent medium for humor. Peacock's outrageous parodies in the late Romantic period led the way. Thackeray's "Little Billee" derives its fun from ridicule, not of form but of situation, as do the comic ballads of tradition. The mock literary form is usually based on appreciation, rather than ridicule of that form. Child, writing to his friend Grundtvig of this ballad, says, "It is really more like the genuine popular ballads—corrupted by tradition—than any of the Jamieson or Scott imitations. . . . Thackeray used to sing it." [13] We too find ourselves fitting the tune of "Lord Bateman" or "Henry Martyn" around these verses. Here is the prototype in form, facile rhyme, diction, and farcical situation of the *Bab Ballads*.

William Morris and Dante Gabriel Rossetti in their pre-Raphaelite enthusiasm for the medieval, and their greater knowledge, through the Norse revival, of connections between Scandinavian and British ballads, have resorted with some success to ballad form and stories.

The couplet form of Morris' "Two Red Roses" carries us back to the earlier ballads. Like "The Fair Flower of Northumberland" (9) the refrain here acts as connective tissue and unifies the mood, becoming in turn the lady's song, the battle cry, and the lover's kiss. Morris, weaver and painter as well as poet, blends good ballad reds and blues and golds into his poem like a tapestry. But at times there is a sense of strain as he follows his pattern, and one misses, particularly in the battle stanzas, the strength of the ballad. The subtle suggestion of final festival and pageant brings the story to a fitting climax.

In a vaguely feudal setting Rossetti's "Sister Helen" plunges at once into a story told in dialogue like the best of ballads. From the

[13] Hustvedt, *Ballad Books and Ballad Men*, p. 295.

first question, suggesting recourse to magic for jealous revenge, the story of tragic love proceeds with unfaltering concentration, as brother, sister, and lover's kin appear in incremental order. The verse form is deceptively ballad-like with its internal and external refrains, but here are three rhyming lines instead of two or four. The refrain is built on the pattern of "Edward" (13 B), and there is other repetition, notably in the structure of the story, as rider after rider appears and is dealt with in practically identical words. Fire burns red as blood, hair is golden, plumes white; the broken coin and the lover's ring are familiar ballad tokens.

Outward similarities to the ballad are counteracted, however, by subtle differences. Though there are many good ballad lines, like "Flank to flank have the three steeds gone," little can be said for "Her clasped hands stretch from her bending head." The continual use of assonance shows the conscious artist playing upon sound for his effect: "In the shaken trees the chill stars shake." Rossetti's treatment of the supernatural is remarkably free from Gothic horrors; but he does succumb in the final stanza to a ghostly emanation and a spectral sigh, quite alien to the simple and credible folk ghost. But it is in the subtle irony of the child's innocence as he transmits his messages and asks his questions—"How like dead folk he has dropped away!"—all designed to tell us more than they say, that this becomes more than a ballad. Above all, the refrain is far more than a repeated choral element: it is a continued comment on the struggles of the girl's tortured soul. The outer trappings of the ballad are used with masterly ease, but, like "La Belle Dame," in order to tell a story of inner conflict rather than outward occurrence.

Two poems by Kipling and Noyes are ballad-allegories with the same message, that the poet lives in a world of imagination which others cannot enter, and that poetry is not to be measured by worldly standards.

In the Robin Hood atmosphere of Noyes's lyric from "A Coiner of Angels" the legend of Shakespeare's poaching on Sir Thomas Lucy's land is used to imply that the poet is a magician who can create miracles invisible to the literally minded. Ballad devices help at every turn—the dramatic division into scenes, satiric repetition ("If you would eat of elfin meat—elfin food"), the use of the perfect tense, unassigned dialogue and a minimum of connecting narrative.

In Kipling's "Last Rhyme of True Thomas," the complete assimilation of ballad idiom and atmosphere, the devices of iteration, ellipsis, and allusion, the speed and sweep of verse, story quality, and suggestion of the otherworld all convey the poet's mastery of the ballad—one might almost say, the ballad's mastery of the poet.

This story of True Thomas, already a ballad hero, might be a sequel to "Thomas Rymer" (37). Huntley Bank, we remember, was Thomas' favorite trysting place and "guards the gates of Faerie" on the actual property of Abbotsford. The first two stanzas, in their skilful inclusiveness conventional ballad to the last word, plunge at once into a dramatic situation, and our imagination leaps to consider the pageantry of the investiture the king has ordered, and the search for the hero, found at the very gates of the otherworld. There are many ballad phrases—"spur and blade," "priest and cup," "milkwhite thorn," "horse o' pride," "Earls three by three," "silver groat," "white monie," "the first least word—the next least word," etc. Thomas' magic harping is like that of the lady in "The Twa Brothers" (49) who "harped the small birds off the briers/And her true love out of the grave." The three structural divisions beginning "It was bent beneath and blue above" introduce the changes in the Rymer's singing and prepare us for the idea that this Thomas is symbolic—he is free and unfettered poesy, poetic craft living on other food than worldly recognition. His pay is not fame and glory, but the love of the human hearts of simple people. He is the power of poetry, which soars to heaven and dips to hell, greater than the power of the world. Thus Kipling uses the ballad medium for a second story, written at a deeper level, making a plea for art and inspiration, but in his weaving together of the two webs he has not lost the beauty of either one. The ballad is here the poet's means to a new end, his way of stating his own sense of values. There could be no better example of T. S. Eliot's comment that in Kipling's ballads "you cannot draw a line beyond which some of the verse becomes poetry." [14]

A critic of Housman finds in his use of his literary heritage his distinct and lasting quality. Housman is Shakespeare and Jonson and Wordsworth, and he is also the popular ballad.

This traditionalism, far from being a fault, is the best of Housman. That it is English traditional poetry is true, and I should think, con-

[14] Eliot, A Choice of Kipling's Verse, p. 12.

sidering English poetry, that is in its favor; but I do not believe its origins have been sufficiently realized. The old Scottish ballad, the most simple and direct expression of experience ever known, is a sure test of Housman's excellence, and should be compared with his "The Culprit." [15]

He then quotes, as we do when we read the poem, two stanzas of "Mary Hamilton." The mordant fifth line added by Housman to the folk formula is his ironic comment on society, the artistic opposite of the mawkish clichés of "Charles Guiteau," emanating from the same model and found throughout this country:

> My name is Charles Guiteau,
>   My name I'll never deny,
> To leave my aged parents
>   In sorrow for to die.
>
> But little did I think
>   While in my youthful bloom
> I'd be taken to the scaffold
>   To meet my fatal doom.
>
> Black cap's over my face
>   And tomorrow I must die
> For the murder of James Garfield
>   Upon the scaffold high.[16]

Stephen Benét's "Jack of the Feather" has the theme, pace, and atmosphere of the Border ballad, and makes no attempt to do more than tell a story. The plunge into immediate crisis—"Jack of the Feather's out again"—is the alarm bell. The narrative stride, with its variations in tense, gives one the feeling of something that has just happened—this is the newsbearer, like its broadside progenitor. Occasional unassigned dialogue brings the action into the present again—"The savage wears our master's cap"; and at the end, the vow of the men to revenge themselves leaves us with the feeling of immediacy. The fallen are counted, as they are in "Chevy Chase" (162), and the good English names—Martin, Powell, Baldwin, Morgan—bring before us that huddle of houses in its pathetic insecurity, surrounded by dark woods and watercourses. Revenge and savage cruelty are the underlying theme, pathos and sympathy are implicit and never directly

[15] Peter Munro Jack, in *The New York Times Book Review* for March 17, 1940, reviewing a definitive edition of Housman's poems.

[16] Chappell, *Folk-Songs of Roanoke and the Albemarle*, p. 188.

induced. The heroism of Mistress Proctor is not named, but is the more effective for the picture of her essentially feminine nature. There is a spontaneous variation in the meter:

> Alas for Martin's Hundred
> Where seventy-three lie slain,
> Alas for the six counselors
> We shall not see again!

Time is specific, as in the Border ballad. So is place: "He passed, he passed by Morgan's house." The Indian marauder is a far cry from King Jamie, but a line from "Flodden Field" (168) must have prompted his naming:

> And Jack with a feather
> Was dressed all in leather

There is a sense of incremental repetition, though not a literal use of it. There is ballad irony in the metaphor of the final stanzas, like that of "The Clerk's Twa Sons of Owsenford" (72):

> It's I've putten them to a deeper lair
> And to a higher schule;
> Yer ain twa sons 'll no' be here
> Till the hallow days of Yule.

The concrete item stands for much: "our master's cap" and the "heathen fields" are simple enough to have literal weight, yet remain highly allusive.

Benét is unusually sensitive to the power of the ballad.[17] He uses its devices with judgment rather than slavishly, respecting its form and style as worthy of straight narrative, and working freely in its medium.

———

The ballad has thus shown itself, even in the few examples here commented upon, as a proving ground for poets. Its stanza and occasional refrain enclose actual ballad stories reworked with new stresses, or popular legends balladed for the first time. From the more pedes-

[17] See "The Captives," *Atlantic Monthly*, February, 1941, for Benét's story of the power of a ballad known in youth to restore the memory and identity of a girl stolen and raised by the Indians.

trian broadsides unfortunately many early imitations arose, as can be detected by their jog-trot verse. During the Romantic period the medieval ballad, often concerned with the supernatural, held sway, and the "antique patina" was cultivated. The modern poets are happier than the older ones in the judicious use of commonplace and concrete detail, the challenging "fifth act" beginning, vagueness of time and place, effective dialogue, and approach to climax through incremental repetition. No doubt increasing acquaintance with the ballad of tradition has helped them here; certainly recent imitations approximate the traditional ballad more nearly than the early ones.

The secret powers of ellipsis and allusion are hard to acquire. Rhyme and meter are apt to be unnaturally fluid; but some compensation must be found for that aid to smoothness in traditional verse, the ballad tune, and deliberate roughness would be more regrettable. The ballad's simplicity of language has led to some confusion between the trivial and the effective in everyday expression; and in the aping of a dialect unnatural to him the poet becomes, by an ironic turn of the tables, more instead of less literary. But in general, ballad imitation has disciplined the poet in discrimination, imagination, and economy of expression.

It is in objectivity, that veil behind which generations of folk poets have hidden themselves, that the modern imitator fails. He finds it hard to avoid interpretation; a moral, a personal reaction, or a reflection from his own experience slips out. Interest in the emotional and the pathetic lacks control, particularly when it is a motivating cause for the action; the story is not allowed to speak for itself. The supernatural becomes a source of subjective wonder and marvel, made deliberately eerie to evoke horror. The bounds of the simple ballad are thus broken down by the dual interest in action and emotion.

These tendencies are hard to suppress, even if the poet wished to do so. In many cases he does not. The ballad supplies him with an opportunity to speak symbolically in a texture of apparent simplicity. Beneath the spareness, the ellipsis, the paucity of detail, and the plain yet suggestive speech, he may imply his contrasts, comment in parables, harp us up to the throne of God or down to the hinges of Hell. From Wordsworth to Benét the study of the influence of the ballad upon conscious poetry is a chapter in the history of English verse, working in the direction of simplicity, sincerity, and art.

I kan namoore expounde of this mateere;
I lerne song, I kan but smal grameere.

Appendix

EXAMPLES OF LITERARY BALLADS

WILLIAM AND MARGARET [1]

By David Mallet, 1724

'Twas at the silent, solemn hour,
  When night and morning meet;
In glided Margaret's grimly ghost,
  And stood at William's feet.

Her face was like an April morn,
  Clad in a wintry cloud:
And clay-cold was her lilly hand,
  That held her sable shroud.

So shall the fairest face appear,
  When youth and years are flown;
Such is the robe that kings must wear,
  When death has reft their crown.

Her bloom was like the springing flower,
  That sips the silver dew;
The rose was budded in her cheek,
  Just opening to the view.

But love had, like the canker-worm,
  Consumed her early prime:
The rose grew pale, and left her cheek;
  She dy'd before her time.

Awake! she cry'd, thy True Love calls,
  Come from her midnight grave;
Now let thy Pity hear the maid,
  Thy Love refus'd to save.

This is the dumb and dreary hour,
  When injur'd ghosts complain;
When yauning graves give up their dead
  To haunt the faithless swain.

[1] From *Works of British Poets*, Vol. 20 (London: Stanhope Press, 1813), p. 56.

Bethink thee, William, of thy fault,
 Thy pledge, and broken oath:
And give me back my maiden vow,
 And give me back my troth.

Why did you promise love to me,
 And not that promise keep?
Why did you swear my eyes were bright,
 Yet leave those eyes to weep?

How could you say my face was fair,
 And yet that face forsake?
How could you win my virgin heart,
 Yet leave that heart to break?

Why did you say, my lip was sweet,
 And made the scarlet pale?
And why did I, young witless maid!
 Believe the flattering tale?

That face, alas! no more is fair;
 Those lips no longer red:
Dark are my eyes, now clos'd in death,
 And every charm is fled.

The hungry worm my sister is;
 This winding-sheet I wear:
And cold and weary lasts our night,
 Till that last morn appear.

But hark!—the cock has warn'd me hence;
 A long and late adieu!
Come, see, false man, how low she lies,
 Who dy'd for love of you.

The lark sung loud; the morning smil'd,
 With beams of rosy red:
Pale William quak'd in every limb,
 And raving left his bed.

He hy'd him to the fatal place
 Where Margaret's body lay:
And stretch'd him on the grass-green turf,
 That wrap'd her breathless clay.

And thrice he call'd on Margaret's name,
 And thrice he wept full sore:
Then laid his cheek to her cold grave,
 And word spake never more!

LOCHINVAR [2]

By Sir Walter Scott
1771–1832

expansion of Katherine Jaffray

O young Lochinvar is come out of the west,
Through all the wide Border his steed was the best;
And save his good broadsword, he weapon had none,
He rode all unarmed, and he rode all alone.
So faithful in love, and so dauntless in war,
There never was knight like the young Lochinvar.

He stayed not for brake, and he stopped not for stone,
He swam the Eske River where ford there was none,
But, ere he alighted at Netherby gate,
The bride had consented, the gallant came late;
For a laggard in love, and a dastard in war
Was to wed the fair Ellen of brave Lochinvar.

So boldly he entered the Netherby Hall,
Among bridesmen, and kinsmen, and brothers and all.
Then spoke the bride's father, his hand on his sword
(For the poor craven bridegroom said never a word,)
"O, come ye in peace here, or come ye in war,
Or to dance at our bridal, young Lord Lochinvar?"

"I long wooed your daughter, my suit you denied;—
Love swells like the Solway, but ebbs like its tide,—
And now I am come, with this lost love of mine,
To lead but one measure, drink one cup of wine,
There are maidens in Scotland more lovely by far,
That would gladly be bride to the young Lochinvar."

The bride kissed the goblet; the knight took it up,
He quaffed off the wine, and threw down the cup.
She looked down to blush, and she looked up to sigh,
With a smile on her lips, and a tear in her eye.
He took her soft hand ere her mother could bar,—
"Now tread we a measure," said young Lochinvar.

So stately his form, and so lovely her face,
That never a hall such a galliard did grace;
While her mother did fret, and her father did fume,
And the bridegroom stood dangling his bonnet and plume;
And the bridemaidens whispered, " 'Twere better by far
To have matched our fair cousin with young Lochinvar."

[2] From Scott, *Poetical Works* (Boston: Estes and Lauriat, 1873), p. 103.

One touch to her hand, and one word in her ear,
When they reached the hall-door, and the charger stood near;
So light to the croup the fair lady he swung,
So light to the saddle before her he sprung;
"She is won! we are gone! over bank, bush, and scaur;
They'll have fleet steeds that follow," quoth young Lochinvar.

There was mounting 'mong Graemes of the Netherby clan;
Forsters, Fenwicks and Musgraves, they rode and they ran;
There was racing and chasing on Cannobie Lee,
But the lost bride of Netherby ne'er did they see.
So daring in love, and so dauntless in war,
Have ye e'er heard of gallant like young Lochinvar?

PROUD MAISIE [3]
By Sir Walter Scott

Proud Maisie is in the wood
    Walking so early;
Sweet Robin sits on the bush,
    Singing so rarely.

"Tell me, thou bonny bird,
    When shall I marry me?"
"When six braw gentlemen
    Kirkward shall carry ye."

"Who makes the bridal bed,
    Birdie, say truly?"
"The grey-headed sexton
    That delves the grave duly.

"The glow-worm o'er grave and stone
    Shall light thee steady;
The owl from the steeple sing
    'Welcome, proud lady!' "

THE INCHCAPE ROCK [4]
By Robert Southey
1774–1843

1. No stir in the air, no stir in the sea,
    The ship was still as she could be;
    Her sails from heaven received no motion;
    Her keel was steady in the ocean.

[3] From Scott, *Poetical Works* (Boston: Estes and Lauriat, 1873), p. 457.
[4] From Southey, *Poetical Works*, VI (London: Longmans, 1838), p. 135.

2. Without either sign or sound of their shock
   The waves flowed over the Inchcape Rock;
   So little they rose, so little they fell,
   They did not move the Inchcape Bell.

3. The Abbot of Aberbrothok
   Had placed that bell on the Inchcape Rock;
   On a buoy in the storm it floated and swung,
   And over the waves its warning rung.

4. When the Rock was hid by the surge's swell,
   The mariners heard the warning bell;
   And then they knew the perilous Rock
   And blest the Abbot of Aberbrothok.

5. The Sun in heaven was shining gay.
   All things were joyful on that day;
   The sea-birds screamed as they wheel'd round,
   And there was joyaunce in their sound.

6. The buoy of the Inchcape Bell was seen
   A darker speck on the ocean green;
   Sir Ralph the Rover walked his deck,
   And he fixed his eye on the darker speck.

7. He felt the cheering power of spring,
   It made him whistle, it made him sing;
   His heart was mirthful to excess,
   But the Rover's mirth was wickedness.

8. His eye was on the Inchcape float:
   Quoth he, "My men, put out the boat,
   And row me to the Inchcape Rock,
   And I'll plague the Abbot of Aberbrothok."

9. The boat is lower'd, the boatmen row,
   And to the Inchcape Rock they go;
   Sir Ralph bent over from the boat,
   And he cut the Bell from the Inchcape float.

10. Down sunk the Bell with a gurgling sound,
    The bubbles rose, and burst around;
    Quoth Sir Ralph, "The next who comes to the Rock
    Won't bless the Abbot of Aberbrothok."

11. Sir Ralph the Rover sailed away,
    He scour'd the seas for many a day;
    And now grown rich with plunder'd store,
    He steers his course to Scotland's shore.

12. So thick a haze o'erspreads the sky
    They cannot see the Sun on high;
    The wind hath blown a gale all day,
    At evening it hath died away.

13. On the deck the Rover takes his stand,
    So dark it is they see no land.
    Quoth Sir Ralph, "It will be lighter soon,
    For there is the dawn of the rising Moon."

14. "Canst hear," said one, "the breakers roar?
    For methinks we should be near the shore."
    "Now where we are I cannot tell,
    But I wish we could hear the Inchcape Bell."

15. They hear no sound, the swell is strong;
    Though the wind hath fallen they drift along,
    Till the vessel strikes with a shivering shock:
    "O Christ! it is the Inchcape Rock!"

16. Sir Ralph the Rover tore his hair;
    He curst himself in his despair:
    The waves rush in on every side,
    The ship is sinking beneath the tide.

17. But ever in his dying fear
    One dreadful sound could the Rover hear,
    A sound as if with the Inchcape Bell
    The Devil below was ringing his knell.

THE COURTIN' [5]

By James Russell Lowell
1819–1891

God makes sech nights, all white an' still
    Fur'z you can look or listen,
Moonshine and snow on field an' hill,
    All silence an' all glisten.

Zekle crep' up quite unbeknown
    An' peeked in thru' the winder,
An' there sot Huldy all alone,
    'ith no one night to hender.

[5] From Lowell, *Poetical Works* (Boston: Houghton Mifflin, c. 1885, pub. 1887),
p. 220.

A fireplace filled the room's one side
　　With half a cord o' wood in—
There warn't no stoves (tell comfort died)
　　To bake ye to a puddin'.

The wa'nut logs shot sparkles out
　　Towards the pootiest, bless her,
An' leetle flames danced all about
　　The chiny on the dresser.

Agin the chimbley crook-necks hung,
　　An' in amongst 'em rusted
The old queen's-arm thet gran'ther Young
　　Fetched back from Concord busted.

The very room, coz she was in,
　　Seemed warm from floor to ceilin',
An' she looked ful ez rosy agin
　　Ez the apples she was peelin'.

'T was kin' o' kingdom-come to look
　　On sech a blessed cretur,
A dogrose blushin' to a brook
　　Ain't modester nor sweeter.

He was six foot o' man, A-1,
　　Clean grit an' human natur';
None could n't quicker pitch a ton
　　Nor dror a furrer straighter.

He'd sparked it with full twenty gals,
　　He'd squired 'em, danced 'em, druv 'em,
Fust this one, an' then thet, by spells—
　　All is, he couldn't love 'em.

But long o' her his veins 'ould run,
　　All crinkly like curled maple,
The side she breshed felt full o' sun
　　Ez a south slope in Ap'il.

She thought no v'ice hed sech a swing
　　Es hisn in the choir;
My! when he made Ole Hunderd ring,
　　She *knowed* the Lord was nigher.

An' she'd blush scarlit, right in prayer,
　　When her new meetin'-bunnet
Felt somehow thru' its crown a pair
　　O' blue eyes sot upon it.

Thet night, I tell ye, she looked *some!*
　　She seemed to've gut a new soul,
For she felt sartin-sure he'd come,
　　Down to her very shoe-sole.

She heered a foot, an' knowed it tu,
　　A-raspin' on the scraper,—
All ways to once her feelins flew
　　Like sparks in burnt-up paper.

He kin' o' l'itered on the mat,
　　Some doubtfle o' the sekle,
His heart kep' goin' pity-pat,
　　But hern went pity Zekle.

An' yit she gin her cheer a jerk
　　Ez though she wished him furder
An' on her apples kep' to work,
　　Parin' away like murder.

"You want to see my Pa, I s'pose?"
　　"Wall . . . no . . . I come dasignin'—"
"To see my Ma? She's sprinklin' clo'es
　　Again to-morrer's i'nin'."

To say why gals acts so or so,
　　Or don't, 'ould be presumin';
Mebbe to mean *yes* an' say *no*
　　Comes nateral to women.

He stood a spell on one foot fust,
　　Then stood a spell on t'other,
An' on which one he felt the wust
　　He couldn't ha' told ye nuther.

Says he, "I'd better call agin";
　　Says she, "Think likely, Mister";
Thet last word pricked him like a pin,
　　An' . . . Wal, he up an' kist her.

When Ma bimeby upon 'em slips,
　　Huldy sot pale as ashes,
All kin' o' smily roun' the lips,
　　An' teary roun' the lashes.

For she was jes' the quiet kind
　　Whose naturs never vary,
Like streams that keep a summer mind
　　Snowhid in Jenooary.

The blood clost roun' her heart felt glued
Too tight for all expressin',
Tell mother see how metters stood,
An' gin 'em both her blessin'.

Then her red come back like the tide
Down to the Bay o' Fundy,
An' all I know is they was cried
In meetin' come nex' Sunday.

SISTER HELEN [6]

By Dante Gabriel Rossetti
1828–1882

'Why did you melt your waxen man,
Sister Helen?'
Today is the third since you began.'
'The time was long, yet the time ran,
Little brother.'
(O Mother, Mary Mother,
Three days today, between Hell and Heaven!)

'But if you have done your work aright,
Sister Helen,
You'll let me play, for you said I might.'
'Be very still in your play tonight,
Little brother,'
(O Mother, Mary Mother,
Third night, tonight, between Hell and Heaven!)

'You said it must melt ere vesper-bell,
Sister Helen;
If now it be molten, all is well.'
'Even so,—nay, peace! you cannot tell,
Little brother,'
(O Mother, Mary Mother,
What is this, between Hell and Heaven?)

'Oh the waxen knave was plump today,
Sister Helen;
How like dead folk he has dropped away!'
'Nay, now, of the dead, what can you say,
Little brother?'
(O Mother, Mary Mother,
What of the dead, between Hell and Heaven?)

[6] From Rossetti, *Poems* (New York: American Publishing Corp., n.d.), p. 83.

'See, see, the sunken pile of wood,
                    Sister Helen,
Shines through the thinned wax red as blood!'
'Nay now, when looked you yet on blood,
                    Little brother?'
          (O Mother, Mary Mother,
How pale she is, between Hell and Heaven!)

'Now close your eyes, for they're sick and sore,
                    Sister Helen,
And I'll play without the gallery door.'
'Aye, let me rest,—I'll lie on the floor,
                    Little brother.'
          (O Mother, Mary Mother,
What rest tonight between Hell and Heaven?)

'Here high up in the balcony,
                    Sister Helen,
The moon flies face to face with me.'
'Aye, look and say whatever you see,
                    Little brother.'
          (O Mother, Mary Mother,
What sight tonight, between Hell and Heaven?)

'Outside it's merry in the wind's wake,
                    Sister Helen;
In the shaken trees the chill stars shake.'
'Hush, heard you a horse-tread as you spake,
                    Little brother?'
          (O Mother, Mary Mother,
What sound tonight, between Hell and Heaven?)

'I hear a horse-tread, and I see,
                    Sister Helen,
Three horsemen that ride terribly.'
'Little brother, whence come the three,
                    Little brother?'
          (O Mother, Mary Mother,
Whence should they come, between Hell and Heaven?)

'They come by the hill-verge from Boyne Bar,
                    Sister Helen,
And one draws nigh, but two are afar.'
'Look, look, do you know them who they are,
                    Little brother?'
          (O Mother, Mary Mother,
Who should they be, between Hell and Heaven?)

'O, it's Keith of Eastholm rides so fast,
   Sister Helen,
For I know the white mane on the blast.'
'The hour has come, has come at last,
   Little brother!'
  (O Mother, Mary Mother,
Her hour at last, between Hell and Heaven!)

'He has made a sign and called Halloo!
   Sister Helen,
And he says that he would speak with you.'
'O tell him I fear the frozen dew,
   Little brother.'
  (O Mother, Mary Mother,
Why laughs she thus, between Hell and Heaven?)

'The wind is loud, but I hear him cry,
   Sister Helen,
That Keith of Ewern's like to die.'
'And he, and thou, and thou and I,
   Little brother.'
  (O Mother, Mary Mother,
And they and we, between Hell and Heaven!)

'Three days ago, on his marriage-morn,
   Sister Helen,
He sickened, and lies since then forlorn.'
'For bridegroom's side is the bride a thorn,
   Little brother?'
  (O Mother, Mary Mother,
Cold bridal cheer, between Hell and Heaven!)

'Three days and nights he has lain abed,
   Sister Helen,
And he prays in torment to be dead.'
'The thing may chance, if he have prayed,
   Little brother!
  (Oh Mother, Mary Mother,
If he have prayed, between Hell and Heaven!)

'But he has not ceased to cry today,
   Sister Helen,
That you should take your curse away.'
'*My* prayer was heard,—he need but pray,
   Little brother!'
  (O Mother, Mary Mother,
Shall God not hear, between Hell and Heaven?)

'But he says, till you take back your ban,
　　　　　Sister Helen,
His soul would pass, yet never can.'
'Nay, then, shall I slay a living man,
　　　　　Little brother?'
　　　(O Mother, Mary Mother,
A living soul, between Hell and Heaven!)

'But he calls forever on your name,
　　　　　Sister Helen,
And says that he melts before a flame.'
'My heart for his pleasure fared the same,
　　　　　Little brother.'
　　　(O Mother, Mary Mother,
Fire at the heart, between Hell and Heaven!)

'Here's Keith of Westholm riding fast,
　　　　　Sister Helen,
For I know the white plume on the blast.'
'The hour, the sweet hour I forecast,
　　　　　Little brother!'
　　　(O Mother, Mary Mother,
Is the hour sweet, between Hell and Heaven?)

'He stops to speak, and he stills his horse,
　　　　　Sister Helen;
But his words are drowned in the wind's course.'
'Nay hear, nay hear, you must hear perforce,
　　　　　Little brother!'
　　　(O Mother, Mary Mother,
What word now heard, between Hell and Heaven?)

'O he says that Keith of Ewern's cry,
　　　　　Sister Helen,
Is ever to see you ere he die.'
'In all that his soul sees, there am I,
　　　　　Little brother!'
　　　(O Mother, Mary Mother,
The soul's one sight, between Hell and Heaven!)

'He sends a ring and a broken coin,
　　　　　Sister Helen,
And bids you mind the banks of Boyne.'
'What else he broke will he ever join,
　　　　　Little brother?'
　　　(O Mother, Mary Mother,
No, never joined, between Hell and Heaven!)

'He yields you these and craves full fain,
    Sister Helen,
You pardon him in his mortal pain.'
'What else he took will he give again,
    Little brother?'
   (O Mother, Mary Mother,
Not twice to give, between Hell and Heaven!)

'He calls your name in an agony,
    Sister Helen,
That even dead Love must weep to see.'
'Hate, born of Love, is blind as he,
    Little brother!'
   (O Mother, Mary Mother,
Love turned to hate, between Hell and Heaven!)

'O it's Keith of Keith now that rides fast,
    Sister Helen,
For I know the white hair on the blast.'
'The short, short hour will soon be past,
    Little brother!'
   (O Mother, Mary Mother,
Will soon be past, between Hell and Heaven!)

'He looks at me and he tries to speak,
    Sister Helen,
But oh! his voice is sad and weak!'
'What here should the mighty Baron seek,
    Little brother?'
   (O Mother, Mary Mother,
Is this the end, between Hell and Heaven?)

'O his son still cries, if you forgive,
    Sister Helen,
The body dies, but the soul shall live.'
'Fire shall forgive me as I forgive,
    Little brother!'
   (O Mother, Mary Mother,
As she forgives, between Hell and Heaven!)

'O he prays you, as his heart would rive,
    Sister Helen,
To save his dear son's soul alive.'
'Fire cannot slay it, it shall thrive,
    Little brother!'
   (O Mother, Mary Mother,
Alas, alas, between Hell and Heaven!)

'He cries to you, kneeling in the road,
    Sister Helen,
To go with him for the love of God!'
'The way is long to his son's abode,
    Little brother.'
   (O Mother, Mary Mother,
The way is long, between Hell and Heaven!)

'A lady's here, by a dark steed brought,
    Sister Helen,
So darkly clad, I saw her not.'
'See her now or never see aught,
    Little brother!'
   (O Mother, Mary Mother,
What more to see, between Hell and Heaven!)

'Her hood falls back, and the moon shines fair,
    Sister Helen,
On the Lady of Ewern's golden hair.'
'Blest hour of my power and her despair,
    Little brother!'
   (O Mother, Mary Mother,
Hour blest and bann'd, between Hell and Heaven!)

'Pale, pale her cheeks that in pride did glow,
    Sister Helen,
'Neath the bridal-wreath three days ago.'
'One morn for pride and three days for woe,
    Little brother!'
   (O Mother, Mary Mother,
Three days, three nights, between Hell and Heaven!)

'Her clasped hands stretch from her bending head,
    Sister Helen;
With the loud wind's wail her sobs are wed.'
'What wedding-strains hath her bridal-bed,
    Little brother?'
   (O Mother, Mary Mother,
What strain but death's between Hell and Heaven?)

'She may not speak, she sinks in a swoon,
    Sister Helen,—
She lifts her lips and gasps on the moon,'
'O, might I but hear her soul's blithe tune,
    Little brother!'
   (O Mother, Mary Mother,
Her woe's dumb cry, between Hell and Heaven!)

'They've caught her to Westholm's saddle-bow,
         Sister Helen,
And her moonlit hair gleams white in its flow.'
'Let it turn whiter than winter snow,
         Little brother!'
      (O Mother, Mary Mother,
Woe-withered gold, between Hell and Heaven!)

'O Sister Helen, you heard the bell,
         Sister Helen!
More loud than the vesper-chime it fell.'
'No vesper-chime, but a dying knell,
         Little brother!'
      (O Mother, Mary Mother,
His dying knell, between Hell and Heaven!)

'Alas! but I fear the heavy sound,
         Sister Helen;
Is it in the sky or in the ground?'
'Say, have they turned their horses round,
         Little brother?'
      (O Mother, Mary Mother,
What would she more, between Hell and Heaven?)

'They have raised the old man from his knee,
         Sister Helen,
And they ride in silence hastily.'
'More fast the naked soul doth flee,
         Little brother!'
      (O Mother, Mary Mother,
The naked soul, between Hell and Heaven!)

'Flank to flank are the three steeds gone,
         Sister Helen,
But the lady's dark steed goes alone.'
'And lonely her bridegroom's soul hath flown,
         Little brother.'
      (O Mother, Mary Mother,
The lonely ghost, between Hell and Heaven!)

'Oh the wind is sad in the iron chill,
         Sister Helen,
And weary sad they look by the hill.'
'But he and I are sadder still,
         Little brother!'
      (O Mother, Mary Mother,
Most sad of all, between Hell and Heaven!)

'See, see, the wax has dropped from its place,
    Sister Helen,
And the flames are winning up apace!'
'Yet here they burn but for a space,
    Little brother!'
  (O Mother, Mary Mother,
Here for a space, between Hell and Heaven!)

'Ah! what white thing at the door has cross'd,
    Sister Helen,
Ah! what is this that sighs in the frost?'
'A soul that's lost as mine is lost,
    Little brother!'
  (O Mother, Mary Mother,
Lost, lost, all lost, between Hell and Heaven!)

THE LAST RHYME OF TRUE THOMAS [7]

By Rudyard Kipling
1865–1936

The King has called for priest and cup,
 The King has taken spur and blade
To dub True Thomas a belted knight,
 And all for the sake o' the songs he made.

They have sought him high, they have sought him low,
 They have sought him over down and lea;
They have found him by the milk-white thorn
 That guards the gates o' Faerie.

'Twas bent beneath and blue above,
 Their eyes were held that they might not see
The kine that grazed beneath the knowes,
 Oh, they were the Queen o' Faerie!

"Now cease your song," the King he said,
 "Oh, cease your song and get you dight
To vow your vow and watch your arms,
 For I will dub you a belted knight.

"For I will give you a horse o' pride,
 Wi' blazon and spur and page and squire,
Wi' keep and tail and seizin and law,
 And land to hold at your desire."

[7] From Kipling, *The Seven Seas* (London, Methuen; New York, Appleton, 1897), p. 433. Copyright, 1893, by Rudyard Kipling. Reprinted by kind permission of Mrs. George Bambridge and Doubleday and Co., Inc.

True Thomas smiled above his harp,
  And turned his face to the naked sky,
Where, blown before the wastrel wind,
  The thistle-down she floated by.

"I ha' vowed my vow in another place,
  And bitter oath it was on me,
I ha' watched my arms the lee-long night,
  Where five-score fighting men would flee.

"My lance is tipped o' the hammered flame,
  My shield is beat o' the moonlight cold;
And I won my spurs in the Middle World,
  A thousand fathom beneath the mould.

"And what should I make wi' a horse o' pride,
  And what should I make wi' a sword so brown,
But spill the rights o' the Gentle Folk
  And flyte my kin in the Fairy Town?

"And what should I make wi' blazon and belt,
  Wi' keep and tail and seizin and fee,
And what should I do wi' page and squire
  That am a king in my own countrie?

"For I send east and I send west,
  And I send far as my will may flee,
By dawn and dusk and the drinking rain,
  And syne my Sendings return to me.

"They come wi' news of the groanin' earth,
  They come wi' news o' the roarin' sea,
Wi' word of Spirit and Ghost and Flesh,
  And man, that's mazed among the three."

The King he bit his nether lip
  And smote his hand upon his knee:
"By the faith o' my soul, True Thomas," he said,
  "Ye waste no wit in courtesie!

"As I desire, unto my pride,
  Can I make Earls by three and three,
To run before and ride behind
  And serve the sons o' my body."

"And what care I for your row-foot earls,
  Or all the sons o' your body?
Before they win to the Pride o' Name,
  I trow they all ask leave o' me.

"For I make Honour wi' muckle mouth,
    As I make Shame wi' mincin' feet,
To sing wi' the preests at the market-cross,
    Or run wi' the dogs in the naked street.

"And some they give me the good red gold,
    And some they give me the white monie,
And some they give me a clout o' meal,
    For they be people o' low degree.

"And the song I sing for the counted gold
    The same I sing for the white monie,
But best I sing for the clout o' meal
    That simple people given me."

The King cast down a silver groat,
    A silver groat o' Scots monie,
"If I come wi' a poor man's dole," he said,
    "True Thomas, will ye harp to me?"

"Whenas I harp to the children small,
    They press me close on either hand.
And who are you," True Thomas said,
    "That you should ride while they must stand?

"Light down, light down from your horse o' pride,
    I trow ye talk too loud and hie,
And I will make you a triple word,
    And syne, if ye dare, ye shall 'noble me."

He has lighted down from his horse o' pride,
    And set his back against the stone.
"Now guard you well," True Thomas said,
    "Ere I rax your heart from your breast-bone!"

True Thomas played upon his harp,
    The fairy harp that couldna lee,
And the first least word the proud King heard,
    It harpit the salt tear out o' his ee.

"Oh, I see the love that I lost long syne,
    I touch the hope that I may not see,
And all that I did o' hidden shame,
    Like little snakes they hiss at me.

"The sun is lost at noon—at noon!
    The dread o' doom has grippit me.
True Thomas, hide me under your cloak,
    God wot, I'm little fit to dee!"

'Twas bent beneath and blue above—
  'Twas open field and running flood—
Where, hot on heath and dike and wall,
  The high sun warmed the adder's brood.

"Lie down, lie down," True Thomas said.
  "The God shall judge when all is done.
But I will bring you a better word
  And lift the cloud that I laid on."

True Thomas played upon his harp,
  That birled and brattled to his hand,
And the next least word True Thomas made,
  It garred the King take horse and brand.

"Oh, I hear the tread o' the fighting men,
  I see the sun on splent and spear.
I mark the arrow outen the fern
  That flies so low and sings so clear!

"Advance my standards to that war,
  And bid my good knights prick and ride;
The gled shall watch as fierce a fight
  As e'er was fought on the Border side!"

'Twas bent beneath and blue above,
  'Twas nodding grass and naked sky,
Where ringing up the wastrel wind,
  The eyas stooped upon the pie.

True Thomas sighed above his harp,
  And turned the song on the midmost string;
And the last least word True Thomas made,
  He harpit his dead youth back to the King.

"Now I am prince, and I do well
  To love my love withouten fear;
To walk wi' man in fellowship,
  And breathe my horse behind the deer.

"My hounds they bay unto the death,
  The buck has couched beyond the burn,
My love she waits at her window
  To wash my hands when I return.

"For that I live am I content
  (Oh! I have seen my true love's eyes)
To stand wi' Adam in Eden-glade,
  And run in the woods o' Paradise!"

'Twas naked sky and nodding grass,
    'Twas running flood and wastrel wind,
Where, checked against the open pass,
    The red deer belled to call the hind.

True Thomas laid his harp away,
    And louted low at the saddle-side;
He has taken stirrup and hauden rein,
    And set the King on his horse o' pride.

"Sleep ye or wake," True Thomas said,
    "That sit so still, that muse so long;
Sleep ye or wake?—till the latter sleep
    I trow ye'll not forget my song.

"I ha' harpit a shadow out o' the sun
    To stand before your face and cry;
I ha' armed the earth beneath your heel,
    And over your head I ha' dusked the sky.

"I ha' harpit ye up to the throne o' God,
    I ha' harpit your midmost soul in three;
I ha' harpit ye down to the Hinges o' Hell,
    And—ye—would—make—a Knight o' me!"

FROM "A COINER OF ANGELS" [8]

By Alfred Noyes

1880——

1. Will Shakespeare's out like Robin Hood
        With his merry men all in green,
    To steal a deer in Charlecote wood
        Where never a deer was seen.

2. He's hunted all a night of June
        He's followed a phantom horn,
    He's killed a buck by the light of the moon,
        Under a fairy thorn.

3. He's carried it home with his merry merry band,
        There was never a haunch so fine;
    For this buck was born in Elfinland,
        And fed upon sops-in-wine.

[8] From Noyes, *Tales of the Mermaid Tavern* (London, William Blackwood & Sons, Ltd.; Philadelphia, J. B. Lippincott, 1913), p. 19. Reprinted by kind permission of Mr. Alfred Noyes and of the publishers.

4. This buck had browsed on elfin boughs
    Of rose-marie and bay,
   And he's carried it home to the little white house
    Of sweet Anne Hathaway.

5. 'The dawn above your thatch is red!
    Slip out of your bed, sweet Anne!
   I have stolen a fairy buck,' he said,
    'The first since the world began.

6. 'Roast it on a golden spit,
    And see that it do not burn;
   For we never shall feather the like of it
    Out of the fairy fern.'

7. She scarce had donned her long white gown
    And given him kisses four
   When the surly Sheriff of Stratford-town
    Knocked at the little green door.

8. They have gaoled sweet Will for a poacher,
    But squarely he fronts the squire,
   With 'When did you hear in your woods of a deer?
    Was it under a fairy briar?'

9. Sir Thomas he puffs,—'If God thought good
    My water-butt ran with wine,
   If He dropt me a buck in Charlecote wood,
    I wot it is mine, not thine!'

10. 'If you would eat of elfin meat,'
     Says Will, 'You must blow up your horn!
    Take your bow, and feather the doe
     That's under the fairy thorn!

11. 'If you would feast on elfin food,
     You've only the way to learn!
    Take your bow, and feather the doe
     That's under the fairy fern!'

12. They're hunting high, they're hunting low,
     They're all away, away,
    With horse and hound to feather the doe
     That's under the fairy spray!

13. Sir Thomas he raged! Sir Thomas he swore!
     But all and all in vain;
    For there never was deer in his wood before,
     And there never would be again!

THE CULPRIT[9]

By A. E. Housman
1859–1936

The night my father got me
His mind was not on me;
He did not plague his fancy
To muse if I should be
The son you see.

The day my mother bore me
She was a fool and glad,
For all the pain I cost her,
That she had borne the lad
That borne she had.

My father and my mother
Out of the light they lie;
The warrant would not find them,
And here 'tis only I
Shall hang so high.

O let not man remember
The soul that man forgot,
But fetch the county kerchief
And noose me in the knot,
And I will rot.

For so the game is ended
That should not have begun.
My father and my mother,
They had a likely son
And I have none.

JACK OF THE FEATHER[10]

By Stephen Vincent Benét
1898–1943

1. Jack of the Feather's out again,
   That savage, bold and sly,
   He passed, he passed by Morgan's house
   And so did Morgan die.

[9] From Housman, *Collected Poems* (London, Jonathan Cape; New York, Henry Holt, 1940), p. 114. Reprinted by kind permission of the Author's Trustees (The Society of Authors) and the publishers.

[10] From Benét, *Western Star* (London, Oxford University Press; New York, Farrar & Rinehart, 1943), p. 152. Copyright, 1943, by Rosemary Carr Benét. Reprinted by kind permission of Rosemary Carr Benét and the publishers.

2. He took poor Morgan into the wood
   And there he made him bleed.
   Then he came back to Morgan's house
   Not three days after the deed.

3. The boys who dwelt at Morgan's house
   Beheld him in his pride,
   "The savage wears our master's cap,
   But where does Master bide?

4. "The villain wears our master's cap
   And it is stained with red.
   Now Jack of the Feather shall not live
   With that cap upon his head."

5. They primed their pieces handily,
   They talked with him awhile
   And they shot Jack of the Feather down
   Ere he had gone a mile.

6. Yet, ere he died, he said a word
   And it was grimly said,
   "My chieftain loved me while I lived.
   He'll prize me when I'm dead.

7. "He is not sleepy Powhatan,
   To bluster and forget.
   My chieftain, Ophechancanough,
   Who will avenge me yet."

8. It was only a few days afterwards,
   It was on Good Friday morn,
   That the savages to our houses came
   With fish and fruit and corn.

9. The savages to our houses came
   As friend goes in to friend.
   We thought they came in peace and trade
   But that was not their end.

10. For, hardly had they entered in
    (And some of us still at meat)
    When they began the bloody work
    That is not yet complete.

11. They sat and broke their fast with us
    And then they rose with a shout
    —And then you could hear the women scream
    As the English blood ran out.

12. They fell upon us in the field
   And by the cradle-head,
   And they were lucky who died the first,
   For they were quickly dead.

13. They fired Lieutenant Basse's house.
   They burned at Flowerdieu.
   And Captain Berkeley and all his folk
   They barbarously slew.

14. At Master Macock's Divident
   They slew but only four,
   But at the college we'd begun,
   They slew almost a score.

15. Alas for Martin's Hundred
   Where seventy-three lie slain,
   Alas for the six counselors
   We shall not see again!

16. Alas, alas, for Powell's Brook,
   'Tis bloody water there,
   And, where the kindly houses stood
   The haggled corpses stare.

17. Yet Master Baldwin beat them off.
   And Captain Hamer, too,
   And Mistress Proctor would not flee
   For all that they might do.

18. A civil and modest dame she was
   As ever squeaked at a mouse,
   But she kept her house like a musketeer
   Till the rescue came to her house.

19. A modest and gentle dame she was
   As ever sewed on a clout,
   But she would not leave her lovesome house
   Till the soldiers forced her out.

20. God's blessing on the providence
   That made one heathen hark
   And so betrayed the deadly plot
   Ere all of us lay stark.

21. God's blessing on the providence
   That moved that heart of brass,
   God's curse on Ophechancanough
   That brought the thing to pass.

22. And now we plant the corn again
And reckon up the score.
Three hundred forty-seven dead
From the forest to the shore.

23. And now we plant the corn again
But, when the harvest's due
We'll see that Ophechancanough
Shall have a harvest too.

24. We'll reap among his heathen fields
With musket and with gun,
And there'll be little left to glean
When that red reaping's done.

25. Three hundred forty-seven dead.
They shall not lie alone
When we meet with Ophechancanough
And reap what he has sown.

BIBLIOGRAPHY

* Collections—words only.   ** Collections with tunes.

ALFORD, VIOLET, and GALLOP, RODNEY. *The Traditional Dance.* London, Methuen, 1935.

AUBREY, JOHN. *Anecdotes and Traditions of Early English History and Literature.* London, Camden Society, 1839.

———. *Remains of Gentilisme and Judaisme.* London, Folklore Society, 1881.

*Bagford Ballads, ed. J. W. Ebsworth. Hertford, Ballad Society, 1878.

BALDWIN, CHARLES S. *An Introduction to English Medieval Literature.* New York, Longmans Green, 1914.

BARBER, JOHN. *The Bruce*, ed. W. W. Skeat. 2 vols. London, Early English Text Society, 1889.

**BARING-GOULD, S., SHEPPARD, H. F., and BUSSELL, F. W. *Songs of the West.* London, Methuen, 1905.

BARRY, PHILLIPS. "The Bridge of Sunbeams," *Journal of American Folklore,* XXVII (1914), 79–89.

*———. *The Maine Woods Songster.* Cambridge, Powell, 1939.

**———, ECKSTORM, F. H., and SMYTH, M. W. *British Ballads from Maine.* New Haven, Yale University Press, 1929.

BAUM, PAULL F. "The English Ballad of Judas Iscariot," *Publications of the Modern Language Association,* XXXI (1916), 181–89.

BEATTY, ARTHUR. "Some New Ballad Variants," *Journal of Folklore,* XX (1907), 154–56.

BELDEN, H. M. "The Relation of Balladry to Folklore," *Journal of American Folklore,* XXV (1912), 1–13.

BOSWELL, JAMES. *Journal of a Tour of the Hebrides.* London, Oxford University Press, 1930.

**BREWSTER, PAUL G. *Ballads and Songs of Indiana.* Bloomington, University of Indiana Press, 1942.

**BROADWOOD, LUCY E. *English Traditional Songs and Carols.* London, Boosey, 1908.

**———, and FULLER-MAITLAND, J. *English County Songs.* London, Cramer, n.d.

BROCKINGTON, ALLEN. "Cecil J. Sharp," *London Mercury,* XVII (1928), 668–72.

BRONSON, BERTRAND H. *Joseph Ritson, Scholar-at-Arms.* Berkeley, University of California Press, 1938.

BROWN, JOSEPH EPES. *The Critical Opinions of Samuel Johnson.* Princeton, Princeton University Press, 1926.

BRYANT, FRANK. *A History of English Balladry.* Boston, Badger, 1913.

BUCHAN, JOHN (Lord Tweedsmuir). *A History of English Literature.* New York, Nelson, 1927.

———. *Pilgrim's Way.* Boston, Houghton Mifflin, 1940.

———. *Sir Walter Scott.* London, Cassell, 1932.

**BUCHANAN, ANNABEL M. *Folk Hymns of America.* New York, J. Fischer, 1938.

The Cambridge History of English Literature, ed. A. W. Ward and A. R. Waller. 14 vols. New York, Putnam, 1913.

CAMPBELL, JOHN C. *The Southern Highlander and His Homeland.* New York. Russell Sage Foundation, 1921.

**CAREY, CLIVE. *Ten English Folk-Songs.* London, Curwen, 1915.

CHAMBERS, E. K. *The English Folk Play.* Oxford, Clarendon Press, 1933.

————. *The Medieval Stage.* 2 vols. Oxford, Clarendon Press, 1903.

CHAPPELL, LOUIS W. *Folk-Songs of Roanoke and the Albemarle.* Morgantown, The Ballad Press, 1939.

**CHAPPELL, WILLIAM. *Old English Popular Music,* ed. H. E. Wooldridge. 2 vols. London, Chappell, 1893. (New edition of *Popular Music of the Olden Time*)

**————. *Popular Music of the Olden Time.* 2 vols. London, Cramer, Beall and Chappell [1855–59].

CHASE, RICHARD. *The Jack Tales.* Boston, Houghton Mifflin, 1943.

Check-List of Folk Songs. Archive of American Folk Song, Music Division, U. S. Library of Congress, Washington, 1940.

CHILD, FRANCIS JAMES. "Ballads," *The Universal Cyclopedia.* 12 vols. New York, Appleton, 1902.

*————. *The English and Scottish Popular Ballads.* 5 vols. Boston, Houghton Mifflin, 1882–1898. (See also Sargent)

CLARK, ELEANOR G. *Elizabethan Fustian.* New York, Oxford Press, 1937.

*COMBS, JOSIAH. *Folk-Songs du Midi des Etats-Unis.* Paris, Les Presses Universitaires de France, 1925.

The Complaynt of Scotland, ed. J. A. H. Murray. London, Early English Text Society, 1872–1873.

The Concise Cambridge History of English Literature, ed. George Sampson. 1 vol. New York, Macmillan, 1941.

COWPER, WILLIAM. *Correspondence of,* ed. Wright. 4 vols. London, Hodder and Stoughton, 1904.

**COX, JOHN HARRINGTON. *Folk-Songs from the South.* Cambridge, Harvard University Press, 1925.

**CREIGHTON, HELEN. *Songs and Ballads from Nova Scotia.* Toronto, Dent, 1932.

DAVIS, ARTHUR K. *Folk-Songs of Virginia, a Descriptive Index and Classification.* Durham, Duke University Press, 1949.

**————. *Traditional Ballads of Virginia.* Cambridge, Harvard University Press, 1929.

DELONEY, THOMAS. *Jack of Newburie,* ed. Francis O. Mann. Oxford, Clarendon Press, 1912.

DEVANE, WILLIAM. *A Browning Handbook.* New York, Crofts, 1935.

DICKENS, BRUCE. "Yorkshire Hobs," *Transactions of the Yorkshire Dialect Society,* XLIII, Vol. VII (1942), 9–22.

DRYDEN, JOHN. *Miscellany Poems.* 3 vols. London, Tonson, 1927.

ECKENSTEIN, LINA. *Comparative Studies in Nursery Rhymes.* London, Duckworth, 1906.

————. "Personal Amulets in Europe," *Transactions of the Third International Congress for the History of Religions,* I, 79–83. Oxford, Clarendon Press, 1908.

**EDDY, MARY O. *Ballads and Songs from Ohio.* New York, Augustin, 1939.

ELIOT, T. S. *A Choice of Kipling's Verse.* New York, Scribner's, 1943.

ENTWISTLE, WILLIAM. *European Balladry.* Oxford, Clarendon Press, 1939.

FABYAN, ROBERT. *The New Chronicles of England and France,* ed. H. Ellis. London, Rivington, 1811.

**FLANDERS, HELEN HARKNESS, BROWN, GEORGE, and BARRY, PHILLIPS. *The New Green Mountain Songster.* New Haven, Yale University Press, 1939.

**————, and BROWN, GEORGE. *Vermont Folk-Songs and Ballads.* Brattleboro, Stephen Daye Press, 1931.

*FIRTH, C. H. *Ballads Relating to America.* Oxford, Blackwell, 1915.

FOX STRANGWAYS, A. H., and KARPELES, MAUD. *Cecil Sharp.* London, Oxford University Press, 1933.

FRANKLIN, BENJAMIN. *Writings of,* ed. Smyth. Vol. II. New York, Macmillan, 1905.

FRAZER, SIR JAMES G. *The Golden Bough.* (1) 12 vols. London, Macmillan, 1914–1920. (2) 1 vol. New York, Macmillan, 1940.

**GARDNER, EMELYN ELIZABETH, and CHICKERING, G. J. *Ballads and Songs of Southern Michigan.* Ann Arbor, University of Michigan Press, 1939.

——. *Folklore from the Schoharie Hills of New York*. Ann Arbor, University of Michigan Press, 1937.

GAY, JOHN. *The Beggars' Opera*. London, Longmans, Hurst, n.d.

——. *Poetical Works*, ed. G. C. Faber. London, Oxford University Press, 1926.

GEOFFREY OF MONMOUTH. *History of the Kings of Britain*. London, Dent, 1912.

——. *Historia Regum Britanniae*, ed. R. E. Jones. London, Longmans, Green, 1929.

GEROULD, GORDON H. "The Ballad of the Bitter Withy," *Publications of the Modern Language Association*, XXIII (1908), 141–67.

——. *The Ballad of Tradition*. Oxford, Clarendon Press, 1932.

**GILCHRIST, ANNE G. "Ten Songs from Scotland and the Scottish Border," *Journal of the English Folk Dance and Song Society*, III (1936), 53–71.

**——. "The Croodin' Doo," *Journal of the Folk-Song Society*, V, No. 19 (1915), 117–19.

GOLDSMITH, OLIVER. *Collected Letters*, ed. K. C. Balderston. Cambridge, Cambridge University Press, 1928.

——. *Works*, ed. J. W. M. Gibbs. London, Ball, 1892.

GORMAN, HERBERT. *The Scottish Queen*. New York, Farrar & Rinehart, 1932.

**GOSS, JOHN. *Ballads of Britain*. London, John Lane, 1937.

*GRAVES, ROBERT. *The English Ballad*. London, Benn, 1927.

*GRAY, ROLAND P. *Songs and Ballads of the Maine Lumberjacks*. Cambridge, Harvard University Press, 1924.

GRAY, THOMAS. *Poetical Works*, ed. Gosse. New York, Stokes, 1885.

GREEN, JOHN RICHARD. *A Short History of the English People*. New York, American Book Co., 1916.

*GREENE, RICHARD L. *The Early English Carols*. Oxford, Clarendon Press, 1935.

GREENE, ROBERT. *A Pleasant Conceited Comedy of George a Green, The Pinner of Wakefield*. Malone Reprints, n.d.

GREENLAW, EDWIN. "Spenser and the Earl of Leicester," *Publications of the Modern Language Association*, XVIII (1910), 535–61.

**GREENLEAF, ELIZABETH B., and MANSFIELD, GRACE Y. *Ballads and Sea Songs of Newfoundland*. Cambridge, Harvard University Press, 1933.

**GREIG, GAVIN. *Last Leaves of Traditional Ballads and Ballad Airs Collected in Aberdeenshire*. Aberdeen, The Buchan Club, 1925.

GUMMERE, FRANCIS B. *The Popular Ballad*. Boston, Houghton Mifflin, 1907.

GWYNN, STEPHEN L. *The Life of Sir Walter Scott*. London, Butterworth, 1930.

*HALLIWELL, JAMES ORCHARD (ed.). *The Nursery Rhymes of England*. London, The Percy Society, Vol. IV, 1842.

The Harleian Miscellany, ed. Wm. Oldys. 12 vols. London, printed for T. Osborne, 1744–1746.

HARRISON, JANE ELLEN. *Ancient Art and Ritual*. New York, Henry Holt, 1913.

——. *Themis*. Cambridge, Cambridge University Press, 1912.

HART, WALTER M. *Ballad and Epic*. (Studies and Notes in Philology and Literature, XI) Boston, Ginn, 1907.

——. "Professor Child and the Ballad," *Publications of the Modern Language Association*, XXI (1906), 755–807.

HARTLAND, EDWIN S. *The Science of Fairy Tales*. London, Scott, 1891.

HAZEN, A. T. *Johnson's Prefaces and Dedications*. New Haven, Yale University Press, 1937.

HECHT, HANS (ed.). "Thomas Percy und William Shenstone," *Quellen und Forschungen*, CIII. Strassburg, Trübner, 1909.

HEMINGWAY, SAMUEL (ed.). *English Nativity Plays*. (Yale Studies in English, XXXVIII.) New York, Henry Holt, 1909.

HENDERSON, THOMAS F. *The Ballad in Literature*. Cambridge, Cambridge University Press, 1912.

HENDREN, J. W. *A Study in Ballad Rhythm*. (Princeton Studies in English.) Princeton, Princeton University Press, 1936.

HENRY, MELLINGER E. *A Bibliography of American Folk-Songs.* Privately printed, n.d.
**———. *Folk-Songs from the Southern Highlands.* New York, Augustin, 1938.
HERD, DAVID. *Ancient and Modern Scottish Songs.* 2 vols. Glasgow, Kerr and Richardson, 1869.
HOGG, JAMES. *The Domestic Manners and Private Life of Sir Walter Scott.* Glasgow, 1834.
HOLINSHED, RAPHAEL. *Chronicles.* 6 vols. London, Johnson, 1803.
HOME, JOHN. *Douglas, A Tragedy.* London, John Bell, 1791.
*HUDSON, ARTHUR P. *Folksongs of Mississippi.* Chapel Hill, University of North Carolina Press, 1936.
HUNTER, JOSEPH. *The Great Hero of the Ancient Minstrelsy of England, Robin Hood.* London, John Russell Smith, 1852.
HUSTVEDT, SIGURD B. *Ballad Books and Ballad Men.* Cambridge, Harvard University Press, 1930.
———. *Ballad Criticism in Scandinavia and Great Britain during the Eighteenth Century.* London, Oxford University Press, 1916.
———. "A Melodic Index of Child's Ballad Tunes," *Publications of the University of California,* I (1936), 2.
**JACKSON, GEORGE PULLEN. *Down-East Spirituals and Others.* New York, Augustin, n.d.
**———. *Spiritual Folk-Songs of Early America.* New York, Augustin, 1937.
**———. *White and Negro Spirituals.* New York, Augustin, 1943.
**———. *White Spirituals of the Southern Uplands.* Chapel Hill, University of North Carolina Press, 1933.
*JAMIESON, ROBERT. *Popular Ballads and Songs from Tradition.* 2 vols. Edinburgh, Archibald Constable, 1806.
*JEWETT, SOPHIE. *Folk Ballads of Southern Europe.* New York, Putnam, 1913.
JOHNSON, SAMUEL. *Lives of the Poets.* "Life of Gray," ed. Hill. Oxford, Clarendon Press, 1905.
JONES, A. WATKINS. "Bishop Percy and the Scottish Ballads," *Essays and Studies,* XVIII (1932), 110–21.
Journal of American Folklore (Organ of the American Folklore Society). Boston, 1888——.
**Journal of the English Folk Dance and Song Society.* London, 1931——.
**Journal of the Folk-Song Society.* Vols. I–VIII. London, 1889–1931.
**KARPELES, MAUD. *Folk Songs from Newfoundland.* London, Oxford University Press, 1934.
KEPHART, HORACE. *Our Southern Highlanders.* New York, Outing, 1913.
KER, W. P. *On the History of Ballads, 1100–1500.* (Proceedings of the British Academy, Vol. 4) London, Frowde, 1910.
**KIDSON, FRANK. *Traditional Tunes.* Oxford, Taphouse, 1891.
———, and NEAL, MARY. *English Folk Song and Dance.* Cambridge, Cambridge University Press, 1915.
*KINLOCH, G. R. *Ancient Scottish Ballads.* London, Longmans, 1827.
des Knaben Wunderhorn, ed. Ludwig A. von Arnim and C. M. Brentano. Munich, Müller, 1905.
KNOX, JOHN. *History of the Reformation,* ed. Laing. 6 vols. Edinburgh, Wodrow Society, 1846.
Robert Laneham's Letter, ed. F. W. Furnivall. New York, Duffield, 1907.
LANG, A. and J. *Highways and Byways in the Border.* London, Macmillan, 1933.
LANG, ANDREW. "The Mystery of The Queen's Marie," *Blackwood's Magazine,* CLVIII (September, 1895), 381–90.
LANGLAND, WILLIAM. *Piers Plowman.* London, Dent, 1916.
LATHAM, MINOR WHITE. *The Elizabethan Fairies.* New York, Columbia University Press, 1930.
LELAND, JOHN. *Itinerary,* ed. T. Hearne. 9 vols. Printed at the theater for J. Fletcher and J. Pote. Oxford, 1745.

LOCKHART, JOHN GIBSON. *Memoirs of the Life of Sir Walter Scott.* 10 vols. Edinburgh, Black, 1852–1853.

LOMAX, ALAN, and COWELL, SIDNEY R. *A Regional Bibliography of American Folk Song and Folk Lore.* New York, Progressive Education Association, 1942.

**LOMAX, JOHN and ALAN. *American Ballads and Folk-Songs.* New York, Macmillan, 1934.

**———. *Cowboy Songs.* New York, Macmillan, 1938.

**MACKENZIE, WILLIAM R. *Ballads and Sea Songs from Nova Scotia.* Cambridge, Harvard University Press, 1928.

———. *The Quest of the Ballad.* Princeton, Princeton University Press, 1919.

*MAIDMENT, JAMES. *Scottish Ballads and Songs.* Edinburgh, W. Paterson, 1868.

MANNYNG, ROBERT, OF BRUNNE. *Handlyng Synne,* ed. F. W. Furnivall. London, Early English Text Society, 1901.

Massachusetts Historical Society Collections. 7th Series, Vol. VII, *Diary of Cotton Mather,* 1709–1724. Boston, Massachusetts Historical Society, 1912.

MILES, CLEMENT A. *Christmas in Ritual and Tradition.* London, Unwin, 1912.

MILLER, G. M. "The Dramatic Element in the Popular Ballads," *University of Cincinnati Studies,* Bulletin 19, University of Cincinnati, n.d.

**MOFFAT, ALFRED. *The Minstrelsy of the Scottish Highlands.* London, Bayley and Ferguson, n.d.

MOORE, JOHN ROBERT. "The Influence of Transmission on the English Ballads," *Modern Language Review,* XI (1916), 385–408.

MOTHERWELL, WILLIAM. Manuscripts and Notebooks. Harvard College Library.

———. *Minstrelsy, Ancient and Modern.* 2 vols. Glasgow, Wylie, 1827.

MURRAY, MARGARET A. *The Witch Cult in Western Europe.* Oxford, Clarendon Press, 1921.

NASHE, THOMAS. *Works,* ed. McKerrow. 5 vols. "The Anatomie of Absurditie." London, Sidgwick and Jackson, 1910.

NELLES, WALTER R. "The Ballad of Hind Horn," *Journal of American Folklore,* XXII (1901), 42–62.

Notes from the Pine Mountain Settlement School, 1919–1949. Pine Mountain, Harlan Co., Kentucky.

**Novello's School Songs.* Nos. 950–1288. London, Novello, n.d.

NUTT, ALFRED. *The Fairy Mythology of Shakespeare.* (Popular Studies in Mythology, Romance, and Folklore, No. 6.) London, David Nutt, 1900.

OGBURN, VINCENT H. "Further Notes on Thomas Percy," *Publications of the Modern Language Association,* LI, Pt. I (1936), 449–58.

———. "Thomas Percy's Unfinished Collection, 'Ancient English and Scottish Poems,'" *English Literary History,* III, Pt. 3 (1936), 183–89.

*OLRIK, AXEL. *A Book of Danish Ballads,* trans. E. M. Smith-Dampier. Princeton, Princeton University Press, 1939.

Osterley Park Ballads, ed. F. B. Fawcett. London, John Lane, 1930.

OVERBURY, SIR THOMAS. *Miscellaneous Works in Prose and Verse,* ed. Rimbault, "A Faire and Happy Milkemayd," p. 118. London, John Russell Smith, 1856.

Oxford Book of Carols, ed. Shaw, Dearmer and Vaughan Williams. London, Oxford University Press, 1928.

PEATTIE, RODERICK, and others. *The Great Smokies and the Blue Ridge.* New York, Vanguard, 1943.

PEPYS, SAMUEL. *Diary and Correspondence,* ed. Mynors Bright. 5 vols. New York, Dodd Mead, 1887.

*PERCY, THOMAS. *Bishop Percy's Folio Manuscript,* ed. Hales. 3 vols. London, Trübner, 1867.

*———. *Reliques of Ancient English Poetry,* ed. Wheatley. 3 vols. London, Swan Sonnenschein, 1886.

*PHILLIPS, AMBROSE (?). *A Collection of Old Ballads.* 3 vols. London, J. Roberts, 1723–1725.

PLAYFORD, JOHN. *The English Dancing Master*, 1650, ed. Bridgewater and Mellor. London, Mellor, 1934.

POTTS, WILLIAM. *Banbury Cross and the Rhyme*. Banbury, 1930.

POUND, LOUISE. *Poetic Origins and the Ballad*. New York, Macmillan, 1921.

RAGLAN, LORD. *The Hero*. London, Oxford University Press, 1937.

*RAMSAY, ALLAN. *The Ever Green*. 2 vols. Edinburgh, printed by Thomas Ruddiman for the publisher, 1724.

**RANDOLPH, VANCE. *Ozark Folksongs*, ed. Shoemaker and Emberson. Vols. I–III. Columbia, State Historical Society, 1947–1949.

**RAVENSCROFT, THOMAS. *Deuteromelia, Pammelia, Melismata*. London, W. Stansby for T. Adams, 1611.

RAYSOR, THOMAS M. *Coleridge's Miscellaneous Criticism*. Cambridge, Harvard University Press, 1936.

*REED, EDWARD BLISS. *Christmas Carols Printed in the XVI Century*. Cambridge, Harvard University Press, 1932.

**RICKABY, FRANZ. *Ballads and Songs of the Shanty Boy*. Cambridge, Harvard University Press, 1926.

RITSON, JOSEPH. *Ancient Songs*. London, Payne and Foss, 1829.

ROLLINS, HYDER E. "An Analytical Index to the Ballad Entries of the Register of the Company of Stationers," *Studies in Philology*, XXI (1924), 8–324.

———. "The Blackletter Broadside Ballad," *Publications of the Modern Language Association*, XXXIV (1919), 258–339.

*———. *Cavalier and Puritan*. New York, New York University Press, 1923.

*———. *The Pepys Ballads*. 9 vols. Cambridge, Harvard University Press, 1929–1932.

*———. *The Phoenix Nest*. Cambridge, Harvard University Press, 1931.

———. "William Elderton," *Studies in Philology*, XVII (1920), 199–245.

ROWE, NICHOLAS. *Jane Shore*. Boston, Heath, 1907.

Roxburghe Ballads, ed. William Chappell and Joseph W. Ebsworth. 9 vols. Hertford, The Ballad Society, 1871–1899.

SABATIER, PAUL. *The Life of St. Francis of Assisi*, trans. Louise S. Houghton. New York, Scribner's, 1894.

SACHS, CURT. *A World History of the Dance*, trans. Bessie Schönberg. New York, Norton, 1937.

**SANDBURG, CARL. *The American Songbag*. New York, Harcourt Brace, 1927.

**SANDYS, WILLIAM. *Christmas Carols Ancient and Modern*. London, Beckley, 1833.

*SARGENT, HELEN C., and KITTREDGE, G. L. *The English and Scottish Popular Ballads* (1 vol. selection from Child's full work). Boston, Houghton Mifflin, 1904.

SCOTT, SIR WALTER. *The Antiquary*. 2 vols. Boston, Dana Estes, 1900.

*———. *Minstrelsy of the Scottish Border*, ed. Henderson. (1) 4 vols. New York, Scribner's, 1902. (2) 1 vol. New York, Crowell, n.d.

———. *Poetical Works*. New York, Knox, n.d.

SHARP, CECIL J. *The Country Dance Book*. Pts. I-VI. London, Novello, 1909–[1922].

**———. *English Folk Carols*. London, Novello, 1911.

———. *English Folk-Song, Some Conclusions*. London, Novello, 1907.

———. *The Morris Book*. Pts. I–V. London, Novello, 1912–1913.

**———. *One Hundred English Folksongs*. Boston, Oliver Ditson, 1916.

———. *The Sword Dances of Northern England*. Pts. I–III. London, Novello, n.d.

**———. *English Folk Songs from the Southern Appalachians*, ed. Maud Karpeles. 2 vols. London, Oxford University Press, 1932.

SHARP, EVELYN. *Here We Go Round*. London, Howe, 1928.

*SHARPE, CHARLES KIRKPATRICK. *A Ballad Book*. Edinburgh, Blackwood, 1823.

SHEARIN, HUBERT G., and COMBS, JOSIAH. "A Syllabus of Kentucky Folk-Songs," *Transylvania Studies in English*, II. Lexington, 1911.

The Shirburn Ballads, ed. Andrew Clark. Oxford, Clarendon Press, 1907.

SHULDHAM SHAW, WINIFRED. *Cecil Sharp and English Folk Dances*. Oxford, Hall, n.d.

SIDGWICK, FRANK. *The Ballad*. New York, George Doran, n.d.

SIDNEY, PHILIP. A *Defence of Poesie*, ed. Feuillerat. Cambridge, Cambridge University Press, 1923.

SKEAT, W. W. *The Tale of Gamelyn*. Oxford, Clarendon Press, 1884.

**SMITH, REED. *South Carolina Ballads*. Cambridge, Harvard University Press, 1928.

**———, and RUFTY, HILTON. *American Anthology of Old World Ballads*. New York, J. Fischer, 1937.

SMITH, WINIFRED. "Elements of Comedy in the English and Scottish Ballads," *Vassar Medieval Studies*. New Haven, Yale University Press, 1928.

The Spectator, ed. Henry Morley. London, Routledge, 1868.

STEEHOLM, CLARA and HARDY. *James I of England*. New York, Covici Friede, 1938.

STEENSTRUP, J. O. H. R. *The Medieval Popular Ballad*, trans. Cox. Boston, Ginn, 1914.

STORK, CHARLES W. "The Influence of the Popular Ballad on Wordsworth and Coleridge," *Publications of the Modern Language Association*, XXIX (1914), 299–326.

STRICKLAND, AGNES. *Life of Queen Elizabeth*. London, Dent, 1906.

**STURGIS, EDITH, and HUGHES, ROBERT. *Songs from the Hills of Vermont*. New York, G. Schirmer, 1919.

TAYLOR, ARCHER. *"Edward" and "Sven I Rosengard."* Chicago, University of Chicago Press, 1931.

TAYLOR, W. *A Historical Survey of German Poetry*. 3 vols. London, Treutel and Würtz, 1830.

THOMAS, KATHERINE ELWES. *The Real Personages of Mother Goose*. Boston, Lothrop, Lee & Shepard, 1930.

THOMPSON, STITH. *The Folk Tale*. New York, Dryden, 1946.

TOLMAN, ALBERT H. " 'Mary Hamilton'; the Group Authorship of Ballads," *Publications of the Modern Language Association*, XLII (1927), 422–32.

A Transcript of the Registers of the Company of Stationers of London, ed. E. Arber. London, privately printed, 1875–1895.

VAUGHAN WILLIAMS, RALPH. *National Music*. London, Oxford University Press, 1934.

VEITCH, JOHN. *The History and Poetry of the Scottish Border*. 2 vols. Edinburgh, Blackwood, 1893.

WAGER, W. *The Longer Thou Livest, the More Fool Thou Art*, ed. John S. Farmer. Tudor Facsimile Texts.

WALKER, J. W. "Robin Hood Identified," *Yorkshire Archaeological Journal*, May 1944, 4–47.

WALTON, IZAAK. *The Compleat Angler*. Boston, Little Brown, 1889.

WEBBE, WILLIAM. *A Discourse of English Poetrie*, ed. E. Arber. Englis Reprints, London, 1870.

WELLS, EVELYN K. "Playford Tunes and Broadside Ballads," *Journal of English Folk Song and Dance Society*, III, Nos. 2, 3, 4, (1937–1939).

WESTON, JESSIE. *From Ritual to Romance*. Cambridge, Cambridge University Press, 1920.

WILLIAM OF MALMESBURY (Willelmi Malmesbiriensis monachi). *Gesta regum Anglorum, atque Historia novella*, rec. Hardy. Londini, sumptibus Societatis, 1840. (Historical Society.)

WIMBERLY, LOWRY C. *Folklore in the English and Scottish Ballads*. Chicago, University of Chicago Press, 1928.

WINGFIELD-STRATFORD, ESMÉ. *The History of British Civilization*. 2 vols. New York, Harcourt, Brace, 1928.

WORDSWORTH, WILLIAM. *Poetical Works*. 3 vols. Boston, Houghton Mifflin, 1854.

WRIGHT, ELIZABETH MARY. *Rustic Speech and Folklore*. London, Humphrey Milford, 1913.

WRIGHT, LOUIS B. *Middle Class Culture in Elizabethan England*. Chapel Hill, University of North Carolina Press, 1935.

**WYMAN, LORRAINE, and BROCKWAY, HOWARD. *Lonesome Tunes*. New York, H. W. Gray, 1916.

**————. *Twenty Kentucky Mountain Songs*. Boston, Oliver Ditson, 1920.

Note: Phonograph recordings of ballads by traditional singers are best secured from the ever-growing publications of the Archive of Folk Music of the U. S. Library of Congress, Washington, D. C., whose catalogue is available upon request.

Richard Dyer-Bennet, John Jacob Niles, Susan Reed, Burl Ives, and other popular concert and radio singers have also recorded many traditional ballads and folk songs. This list is constantly changing.

INDEX OF BALLAD AND SONG TITLES

(Boldface type indicates full text)

INDEX OF FIRST LINES

INDEX OF NAMES AND SUBJECTS

Adam de la Hâle, *Le Jeu de Robin et Marion,* 20
Addison, 217, 225 ff., 235, 267
Animal satires, 159
Arnold, "The Forsaken Merman," 309
Arthur, *see* King Arthur
Aubrey, John, 213, 217, 224

Ball, John, 15
Ballad: ARCHIVES, 7, 308. CENSORSHIP OF, 177, 179, 212, 213, 214, 224, 226. CHARACTERISTICS, GENERAL, 5–6. CHARACTERISTICS, LITERARY: action in, 22, 68, 296; alliteration, 21, 209; allusion, 85, 142, 214, 325; audience, sense of, 209, 214; characterization, 23; Christian touches, 23, 146, 176, 178, 179; commonplace, 45, 83, 325; concrete for abstract, 84–85, 325; dating of, 99, 140, 180; derivation of word, 4, 205; descriptive detail, 22, 65, 83, 209, 214, 325; dialogue, 24, 64, 90, 180; dramatic quality, 88, 89, 214, 325; fatalism, 65, 162, 296; humor, 24, 67, 78, 100; hyperbole, 83–84; introductions, 67, 88, 99, 228, 229; irony, 22, 66, 67, 86; moral comment in, 178; motivation, 21, 42, 215; number of actors, 22, 64, 79; objectivity, 81, 91, 97, 298, 325; realism, 63, 87, 98, 183, 184; refrain, 92–97, 196, 204, 214; repetition, 90; incremental repetition, 91, 180, 282, 284; setting, 82; single incident, 90; social status of actors, 82; stanza, 21, 92 ff., 194, 204, 215, 281; tags, 164; themes, 12, 21, 299; tempo, 22, 68, 96–97, 214; time of action, 63, 82, 90, 214; transitions, 21, 180; variants, 98–100, 161, 299; veracity, claim to, 210. CHARACTERISTICS, MUSICAL: attitudes toward tunes, 263, 268, 269; circular tunes, 278–79; color, 283; intervals, 279; modes, 271, 275; notation, 46, 269, 270; phrases, 282; relation to stanza, 281; relation to words, 140, 203, 219, 280, 281; repetition, 282, 284; rhythm, 280; scales, gapped, 278; solo, 283; variants, 284; variety, 284. DANCE AND, 4, 193, 195, 197, 203, 204. DEFINED, 5. FORGERIES, 231. HISTORY AND,

41 ff., 206, 217. LITERARY ATTITUDES TOWARD, 212, 225 ff., 232, 235, 237, 247, 260, 267, 309 ff. OPERAS (BALLAD), 227, 309. ORIGIN AND AUTHORSHIP: broadsides, 41, 211 ff., 225; carole and, 196 ff.; communal, 91, 193, 194; historical incident, 41; individual poet, 193, 194, 213; minstrels, 193, 194–95, 207 ff.; monks, 177, 193, 194; ROMANCES AND, 250 n.; ROMANTIC MOVEMENT AND, 238, 251; SATIRES ON, 251; SOCIETIES, 251; SURVIVAL OF, conditions favoring, 77, 100, 164, 213, 223, 236, 260, 285 ff., 297, 306; TRADITIONAL CHANGES, 42, 48, 52, 54, 68, 77–78, 96, 98, 100, 146, 161–63, 181, 186, 215, 217, 223, 271. TYPES OF: Border Raid, 62 ff.; broadsides, 79, 211 ff., 311; cowboy, 298; Danish, relation to, 255; historical, 217; minstrel, 207 ff.; riddle, 78, 162 ff.; romantic, 77 ff.; Robin Hood, 3, 11–41, 77, 138, 177 n., 209, 214, 223–25, 267
Barbauld, Mrs. L., 315
Barbour, *The Bruce,* 204
Barry, Phillips, 99, 100, 281
Beauty and the Beast, 134
Bell, Dr. John, 247
Benét, Stephen, "The Captives," 324 n., "Jack of the Feather," 323, 348
Bible stories, popular knowledge of, 177, 184
Boggs, Abner, *see* Folk singers
Border: ballads, 62; compared with Southern Appalachians, 297; compared with Southwest, 68, 297; geography, 55; history, 57; life, 59 ff., 66; poetic tradition of, 73 ff.
Broadwood, Lucy, 262
Browning, "Flight of the Duchess," 309, "Porphyria's Lover," 310
Buchan, John (Lord Tweedsmuir), 57, 59
Buchan, Peter, 250, 256
Bürger, G. A., "Lenore," 238 ff.
Burns, 119 n.

Călușari, *see* Folk dance
Campbell, Olive D., 262
Carol, 179, 195 ff.
Carole, *see* Folk dance